Key Accounting Principles Volume II
An Introductory Financial Accounting Course

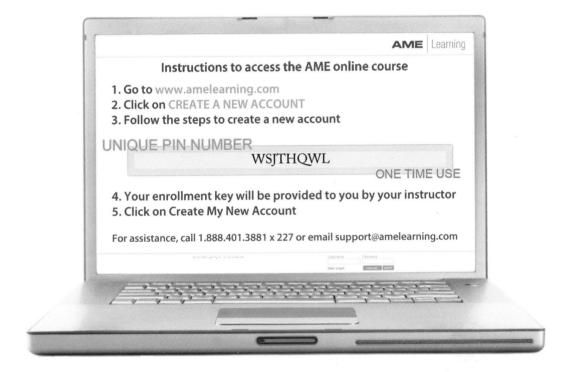

AME | Learning

Instructions to access the AME online course

1. Go to www.amelearning.com
2. Click on CREATE A NEW ACCOUNT
3. Follow the steps to create a new account

UNIQUE PIN NUMBER

WSJTHQWL

ONE TIME USE

4. Your enrollment key will be provided to you by your instructor
5. Click on Create My New Account

For assistance, call 1.888.401.3881 x 227 or email support@amelearning.com

Neville Joffe

AME | Learning

ISBN: 978-1-926751-11-5

Key Accounting Principles Volume II
Author: Neville Joffe
Publisher: AME Learning
Content Contributor: Penny Parker
Content Contributor: Graeme Gomes
Editor: Miresh Puradchithasan
Typesetter: Paragon Prepress Inc.
Project Manager: Linda Zhang
Cover Design: Edward Phung
Online Course Design & Production: AME Multimedia Team

This book is written to provide accurate information on the covered topics. It is not meant to take place of professional advice.

For more information contact:

AME Learning Inc.
303-1200 Sheppard Avenue East
Toronto, ON, Canada M2K 2S5
Phone: 416.848.4399
Toll-free: 1.888.401.3881
E-mail: info@amelearning.com
Visit our website at: www.amelearning.com

About the Author

Neville Joffe is the founder and CEO of AME Learning Inc. Prior to AME Learning, Neville spent over 20 years as owner, President, and manager of small and large manufacturing companies internationally. Neville is a member of the Worldwide Presidents Organization and former member of the Young Presidents Organization. He holds a patent related to the unique methodology he developed to teach accounting concepts. Neville is the author of 5 leading college textbooks. He has been featured in newspapers and magazines, and is a frequent speaker at national conferences where he presents as a thought leader in introductory accounting curriculum. The AME system has been used to train tens of thousands of employees at leading Fortune 1000 firms and students at premier colleges and universities across North America. Students have commented that they find the course remarkably easy to follow, using the numerous interactive tools that supplement the textbook and workbook. Students using AME materials consistently achieve higher grades compared to those who use traditional materials, and student engagement and retention rates have improved significantly. Professors have described the AME methodology as "refreshing", "intriguing", "amazing", "never thought it could be this simple", "inspiring to see that someone has changed the rules of teaching accounting" and "you have broken the mold of the way this subject has been taught".

Preface by Neville Joffe

Fourteen years ago, I founded AME Learning with a mission to change the perception of accounting from dry and boring to intuitive, engaging, and an essential life skill. Today, the AME system is used by some of the most prestigious corporations and academic institutions in the world with outstanding results, and the company has been recognized with top training and education awards including the 2009 CODiE Finalist for the Best Postsecondary Instructional Solution.

The AME System was initially conceived after I experienced the power of financial education as part of a turnaround I managed at a mid-size manufacturing company. As part of the turnaround process I adopted an assortment of initiatives including Just In Time Inventory (JIT), Lean Manufacturing, The Theory Of Constraints (TOC), and Total Quality Management (TQM). The most powerful enabler of the turnaround was the creation of an open book environment and profit-sharing program with 400 unionized workers. The initiative required non-finance employees to understand and interpret financial statements and the financial implications of their actions.

I began educating the employees about income statements and balance sheets using traditional materials, including some content from college accounting curriculum. The materials over-complicated simple concepts and ineffectively connected the lessons to the practical implications of personal and business financial management. I then tried a very non-traditional approach to teaching these concepts. I cashed $2,000 in small bills and crumpled them into a plastic garbage bag. I assembled all the staff in a room and then poured the crumpled bills onto a table. "This is called revenue" I said. I placed a handful of cash in a bucket and labelled it "wages". I continued the exercise with different buckets labelled "material", "rent", "maintenance", "insurance" and then started tearing up $20 bills and throwing them into a bucket called "waste". The employees were silently shocked when I tore up the bills. "Why are you so surprised?" I asked, "you do this every day but just don't see it".

At the end of the demonstration, some cash remained on the table and I said "what is left and lying on the table is called profit." I shifted some of the remaining cash toward the crowd and said "this is for all of you for your special hard work performed this year. The remainder is for the owners in return for all the financial risk they take to support this business." The group was stunned, and they finally understood the message I was trying to deliver. As a result of successfully implementing this initiative, key financial metrics dramatically improved; inventory levels decreased, accounts receivable were collected faster, low margin products were eliminated, unprofitable customers were turned away.

So how did the crumpled-money exercise have such a profound impact on the company? It was not the employees' fault they didn't understand the traditional materials, it was the fault of the materials that taught the concepts from the teacher's point of view.

Elizabeth Newton summed it up:

> *In 1990, Elizabeth Newton earned a Ph.D. in psychology at Stanford by studying a simple game in which she assigned people to one of two roles: "tappers" or "listeners." Tappers received a list of twenty-five well-known songs, such as "Happy Birthday to You" and "The Star Spangled Banner." Each tapper was asked to pick a song and tap out the rhythm to a listener (by knocking on a table). The listener's job was to guess the song, based on the rhythm being tapped.*
>
> *The listener's job in this game is quite difficult. Over the course of Newton's experiment, 120 songs were tapped out. Listeners guessed only 2.5 percent of the songs: 3 out of 120. But here's what made the result worthy of a dissertation in psychology. Before the listeners guessed the name of the song, Newton asked the tappers to predict the odds that the listeners would guess correctly. They predicted that the odds were 50 percent. The tappers got their message across 1 time in 40, but they thought they were getting their message across 1 time in 2. Why?*
>
> *When a tapper taps, she is hearing the song in her head and it's impossible to avoid hearing the tune in your head. Meanwhile, the listeners can't hear that tune — all they can hear is a bunch of disconnected taps, like a kind of bizarre Morse Code.*
>
> *It's hard to be a tapper. The problem is that tappers (teachers) have been given knowledge (the song title) that makes it impossible for them to imagine what it's like to lack that knowledge. When they're tapping, they can't imagine what it's like for the listeners (the student) to hear isolated taps rather than a song. This has been referred to as the Curse of Knowledge. Once we know something, we find it hard to imagine what it was like not to know it. And it becomes difficult for us to share our knowledge with others, because we can't readily re-create our listeners' state of mind.*

After successfully turning around the company and selling my ownership, I founded AME Learning and spent years refining a teaching tool that would help teach non-financial people financial accounting principles. The AME system has been used to train over 30,000 people ranging from front line employees to Directors of publicly traded companies. I am still surprised at the lack of financial literacy of managers and executives. Why is it then, that so many adults in the business world lack basic financial acumen when they have studied one or more accounting courses at college or university? It would appear that many people underestimate the importance and usefulness of basic accounting skills and learn by rote memory rather than practical lessons that have long term retention and applicability. Perhaps our economic world would be better off if more people were financially literate.

Over the years I have learned to appreciate the concept of "tappers and listeners" every time I deliver a management training program or when writing textbooks for college and university students. My years of research and experiments both on the factory floor and in the boardroom was the start of the development of AME, which has become an award winning patented system of teaching accounting as it is used today.

I strongly believe in "getting the basics right and the rest will follow". I believe that basic financial literacy is a crucial life skill that is required of everyone, not only accountants. I have written this material from the students' point of view while still meeting curriculum requirements. You will notice that I have eliminated unnecessary jargon wherever possible.

I have a wonderful dedicated team that produces world class material with one thought in mind: to educate the student so they can transfer basic accounting skills either to their professional lives or be better prepared for a higher level of accounting. Like all good science, AME is a solid base that prepares students for either an accounting or business career.

I am a true advocate of student-centric teaching and believe that I have successfully offered the opportunity to bring together the minds of both the "tappers" and the "listeners".

So my message to you the student is this: whether you choose to continue your accounting studies or not, take this subject seriously since it will stand you in good stead when you enter your professional life regardless of the career you choose.

Neville Joffe
Author

Brief Table of Contents

Detailed Table of Contents

Chapter 3: Accounts and Notes Receivable

Chapter 4: Inventory

Chapter 8: Non-Current Liabilities

Chapter 9: Partnerships

Chapter 10: Corporations: Share Capital and Dividends

Chapter 11: Corporations: The Financial Statements

Chapter 12: The Statement of Cash Flow

Chapter 13: Financial Statement Analysis

The AME Method of Learning Accounting

AME utilizes a unique and patented method that has simplified accounting principles, using step-by-step logic to ensure that the subject is extremely easy to understand. Accounting concepts are communicated using straightforward language and AME Accounting Maps™ that make potentially complex transactions simpler and easier to follow.

This textbook is part of a larger and blended program that is being used to teach the course. The steps of the program are as follows:

1. A highly interactive online section must be completed before attending each class.
2. At the start of the class, a quiz will be given to test your knowledge and comprehension of the online section that you would have completed before class.
3. Building on the online segment and the quiz, the class will then reinforce and improve your understanding of the concepts that have already been introduced and studied.
4. Once the basic learning is done, it will be time to take the next step and apply the lessons learned by completing the exercises provided in the workbook.

The *name*, *value*, and *timing* of each transaction

As you embark on this unique way of learning accounting you should be aware of the importance of financial statements to both internal and external stakeholders. You should also be familiar with the balance sheet, income statement and cash flow statement — and how they link together. Students familiar with our approach will know that the technical process of double entry accounting isn't really that complicated and that there are very few debit and credit combinations.

Additionally, there are three basic components to every accounting transaction that must be remembered each time entries are made or accounts are adjusted. These three components are:

1. *Name:* What are the names of the accounts involved?
2. *Value:* What value is involved?
3. *Timing:* When is it occurring?

These three components need to be considered in any adjustment made on the company's records to ensure accuracy and thoroughness.

Here is a brief example to illustrate the importance of these three components.

Assume that you are an accountant for a company whose fiscal year ends on December 31. On December 20, an upfront payment of $60,000 (related services to be rendered in the following year) is deposited in the company's bank account. The project is expected to be completed in about six months (i.e. by June of the next year).

What are the names of the accounts that should be used for the transaction? As any introductory accounting course indicates, Cash is debited for the amount deposited. However, which account receives the corresponding credit? If you guessed Revenue, your guess is incorrect. Since the money isn't earned until the service is performed, it is the Unearned Revenue account that is used. This makes a big difference when the company reports its financial position.

What is the value of the transaction? Your first thought may be that the value of this transaction is $60,000. However, the transaction may need to be sliced into smaller sections to reflect work performed in due course. This may be done on a monthly basis, using a measure such as materials delivered. Depending on the kind of transaction involved, the amount to be recorded isn't as obvious as it might appear.

What is the timing of the transaction? The first two questions have touched upon the third. Revenue should only be recognized in the period in which it is earned. In our present example, this cannot be done in the current fiscal period. It has to be done in the next fiscal period (when the work is finally started) and in a way that reflects the gradual completion of the work done. In other words, the revenue cannot be recognized as earned right away. It will take six months to complete this project, and the same amount of time to transfer the entire $60,000 into the Revenue account.

We will explore these principles throughout the remainder of the course.

The AME Approach

The AME approach has always emphasized the importance of accounting in our everyday lives and how these principles can be applied to professional accounting in general. This approach will be expanded upon in this course. We will examine various aspects of the balance sheet and income statement and how the information contained therein impacts both internal and external stakeholders.

The design and structure of the course covers this text (Key Accounting Principles Volume 1) and a second text (Key Accounting Principles Volume 2). This textbook covers an introduction to the accounting cycle and related topics such as managing inventory, cash controls and analyzing business performance. Key Accounting Principles Volume2 then focuses on the balance sheet accounts in the order they are presented.

This course begins with an application of accounting principles and transactions in our personal life before making the transition to applying accounting principles in a business environment. By the time debit and credit terminology are introduced, students will be comfortable increasing and decreasing accounts. Making the switch to debit and credit rules will relatively straight-forward.

The second part of this course will cover concepts such as merchandising and inventory, cash control, payroll, the cash flow statement and analyzing business performance. By the end of this course, students should be comfortable in accounting for typical, day-to-day business operations.

Key Accounting Principles Volume 2 examines the balance sheet in order of the balance sheet items. Each asset and liability is discussed in detail regarding how related activities are accounted for in the financial statements. The chapters also discuss how a company will collect and organize information to generate reports, and ethical considerations surrounding each account. The latter part of Key Accounting Principles Volume 2 will involve an in-depth examination of equity and how it is structured in entities such as corporations and partnerships.

Navigating the Accounting Map™

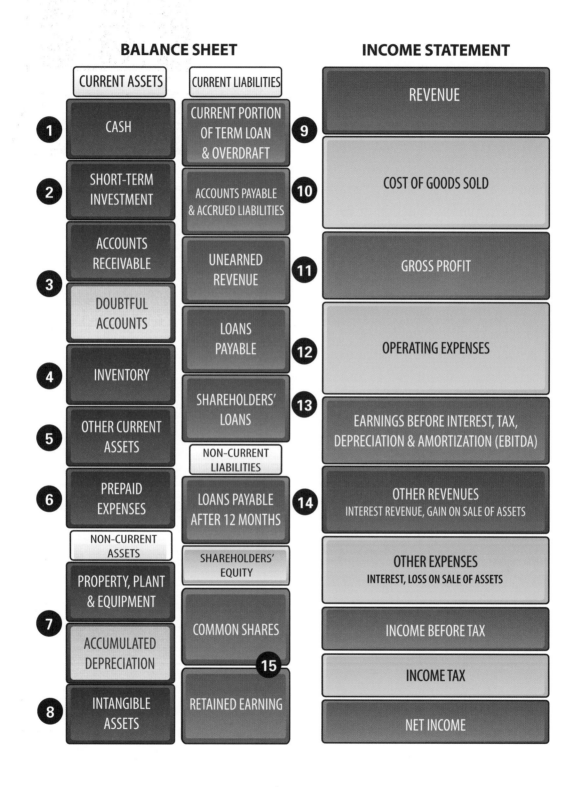

BALANCE SHEET

INCOME STATEMENT

CURRENT ASSETS	CURRENT LIABILITIES
1 CASH	**9** CURRENT PORTION OF TERM LOAN & OVERDRAFT
2 SHORT-TERM INVESTMENT	**10** ACCOUNTS PAYABLE & ACCRUED LIABILITIES
3 ACCOUNTS RECEIVABLE / DOUBTFUL ACCOUNTS	**11** UNEARNED REVENUE
4 INVENTORY	**12** LOANS PAYABLE
5 OTHER CURRENT ASSETS	**13** SHAREHOLDERS' LOANS
6 PREPAID EXPENSES	NON-CURRENT LIABILITIES
NON-CURRENT ASSETS	**14** LOANS PAYABLE AFTER 12 MONTHS
7 PROPERTY, PLANT & EQUIPMENT / ACCUMULATED DEPRECIATION	SHAREHOLDERS' EQUITY
8 INTANGIBLE ASSETS	COMMON SHARES
	15 RETAINED EARNING

INCOME STATEMENT:

- REVENUE
- COST OF GOODS SOLD
- GROSS PROFIT
- OPERATING EXPENSES
- EARNINGS BEFORE INTEREST, TAX, DEPRECIATION & AMORTIZATION (EBITDA)
- OTHER REVENUES — INTEREST REVENUE, GAIN ON SALE OF ASSETS
- OTHER EXPENSES — INTEREST, LOSS ON SALE OF ASSETS
- INCOME BEFORE TAX
- INCOME TAX
- NET INCOME

Why learn this material?

Many of you may be taking this course as a step towards becoming an accountant. Learning this material will help you understand the importance and logic underlying most business decisions. For example, a manager of a medium-sized business needs to operate the company in a responsible fashion, while at the same time providing financial statements to the board of directors every month. This course will help a student do just that, as well as calculate net income, award bonuses based on those profits, and do a number of other things that are crucial for any size of business.

In other words, a thorough knowledge of a company's accounts, and the procedures involved in recording and analyzing related transactions, is vital for most important decision-makers within a company.

How this material is organized

The following is a description of the financial statement items that will be examined in Key Accounting Principles Volume 1 and 2.

1. **Cash** — This account includes petty cash, bank reconciliations and the controls necessary to protect cash. The Cash account is at the centre of almost every transaction. For example, businesses often find themselves with a surplus of cash that needs to be invested for short periods of time.

2. **Investments** — Organizations often invest surplus cash in investments outside the company. These investments can include short-term and long-term debt and equity. We will look at each of these types of investments in Key Accounting Principles Volume 2.

   ### Issues to keep in mind:
   - Where is the cash to be invested?
   - What is the risk of losing the money being invested?
   - Is the return worth the investment?
   - What happens if the business needs to cash the investment urgently? Does the investment chosen allow for such cashing out (i.e. is it liquid)?
   - How is the interest or return on the investment recorded? If it is recorded as a regular form of revenue, it may give the impression that the business is operating with a larger net income than is actually the case.

3. **Accounts receivable and doubtful debts** — One of a company's most important assets is its accounts receivable, which constitutes debt owed by customers who have bought goods or services using payment terms. This course will examine how transactions involving accounts receivable are input. Key Accounting Principles Volume 2 will also examine how to deal with non-paying customers, and allowing for bad or doubtful debts. Various controls, as well as reports used to manage accounts receivable and related information will also be examined.

Issues to keep in mind:

- Are there adequate controls to ensure that customers pay on time?
- How certain is it that the company will actually get paid? Some methods to predict frequency of payment will be examined.
- How do we know that customers are being billed correctly?
- Are there adequate controls to ensure that no unauthorized refunds are being issued?
- How are potential losses being assessed? If these losses are underestimated, then it will appear as though the company is making more net income than it actually is.
- Conversely, an overestimation of losses will understate net income. Among other things, this could have an impact on taxes and payment of bonuses.
- Higher or lower earnings may also influence the manner in which pricing policies are established for the upcoming year.

4. **Inventory** — The basic concepts associated with inventory, including cost of goods sold (COGS) and the perpetual inventory system are covered in this course. In addition, we will also examine the different methods of valuing inventory, as well as issues related to inventory controls and ethics.

Issues to keep in mind:

- Is the inventory system being used appropriate for the industry?
- How is the inventory valued? Overstated values will affect figures related to gross and net income. Conversely, if the value of inventory is too low, it will appear that gross profit margins have been compromised, reflecting badly on management.
- The value of inventory impacts net income and bonuses.
- Lack of proper controls for inventory could lead to theft and lower than expected inventory levels.

5. **Other current assets** — This section comprises items that are not used on a regular basis and do not warrant the assignment of a special account code. Some examples of other current assets include tax refunds owing, interest owing and employee loans.

Issues to keep in mind:

- Are certain entries made in the hope they will be overlooked and scrutinized less?
- Are adequate controls in place to ensure that all refunds (including tax refunds) are collected on a timely basis?

6. **Prepaid expenses** — This type of asset addresses prepayments that are not considered expenses at the time they are paid. We will examine prepaid expenses in connection with other parts of a company's financial statements.

Issues to keep in mind:

- Are staff members informing the accounting department that travel expenses, for example, are related to a future event? Is the staff aware of the implications of not reporting these expenses properly?
- Not accruing prepaid expenses can skew the operating results of the company.
- Is the value of prepaid services being monitored as to when the services are actually provided? How much of the prepaid expense should be recognized? When?
- What happens to refunds? Are proper controls in place to ensure that these refunds are made to the company, and not specific to individuals?

7. **Property, Plant & Equipment and depreciation** — Property, plant and equipment are long-term assets. They usually consist of the company's most highly valued assets and often consume most of the available cash resources. We will examine different methods of depreciating long-term assets and their impact on company profits.

Issues to keep in mind:

- Who in the company is authorized to purchase long-term assets?
- Are some expenses considered assets, which will falsely increase net income?
- Are assets properly depreciated over their expected useful life?
- Are the company's long-term assets financed using long-term debt or operating capital?
- Does the business generate sufficient profits and cash flow to finance debt?
- Does the business have an asset register to keep track of its long-term assets, such as laptops, that may disappear?

8. **Intangible assets** — The word intangible literally describes something that cannot be touched or felt. It is therefore understood that intangible assets comprise things that aren't physical in nature but that, nevertheless, the company owns — such as goodwill, copyright, trademarks and patents. We will examine these kinds of assets in Key Accounting Principles Volume 2.

Issues to keep in mind:

- The decision to capitalize or expense an item is one of the most important on the company's balance sheet. It affects the bottom line, as well as bonuses awarded to employees.
- What is the company's policy when capitalizing intangible assets related to the creation of material such as software?
- If an item is to be capitalized, over what period should its total cost be amortized?
- The method of amortization chosen could impact other aspects of the business, such as pricing policy.

9.-13. **Debt** — Items 9 to 13 on our Accounting Map™ represent the company's current liabilities, or debt owing, ranging from bank loans to shareholder loans. We will examine the various ways in which these items should be categorized, as well as the transactions associated with each.

Issues to keep in mind:

- Can the business actually pay its debts? Are there sufficient current assets to pay for current liabilities?
- Are discount opportunities taken advantage of?
- How are unearned revenues accounted for? Falsely classifying them as earned when deposited will significantly overstate net income for the period.
- Are unearned revenues properly matched to related expenses?
- Are unearned revenues recognized as earned by sales staff, simply to collect a commission?

14. **Long term debt** — This category of liabilities represents amounts owing after 12 months.

Issues to keep in mind:

- Can the business finance its debt?
- Are the lenders taking more risk than the owners? If so, it may be difficult to secure additional loans.
- If the business is running out of operating capital to finance inventory and accounts receivable, should some of the current debt be converted to long-term debt?
- Is the business generating sufficient profits and cash flow to support any additional debt?

15. **Equity** — Equity represents a company's net worth and is structured according to entity type. Key Accounting Principles Volume 1 will focus on proprietorships and introduce corporations. Key Accounting Principles Volume 2 will examine how to account for partnerships and corporations in detail.

Issues to keep in mind:

- Should profits be distributed to owners for personal use, or should some of the profits be retained in the business?
- If the business needs more cash but cannot secure more financing from the bank, should shares be issued? At what price? Will control of the business change as a result?

Beyond the company's balance sheet, other aspects of financial statements examined in this course, will include:

The income statement - Although every company has an income statement on its books, they don't all look the same. We will examine the various types of income statements that companies use, their layouts and which are most common or appropriate for certain industries.

Cash flow - Once the balance sheet and income statement are fully understood, we will address the cash flow statements that provide information related to the sources and uses of cash.

Financial analysis - Sometimes it is the simple numbers that can tell the story of a business. We will examine various financial ratios and key performance indicators that provide a telling glimpse into the health of a company.

IFRS - We will examine International Financial Reporting Standards, which is a modified form of GAAP.

In summary, this course should not only serve as preparation for the accounting profession, it should also serve as preparation for business decision-making in general. By knowing the name, value and timing associated with any transaction of interest, the business professional has at their disposal the tools to make informed and strategic decisions. This is the basic foundation of the course, one which you can take with you in all your future endeavors.

Some additional segments

This textbook was designed to make your learning experience productive and engaging. To that end, we have added some segments to each chapter that highlight learning objectives. They include:

A CLOSER LOOK

The *Closer Look* segments in each chapter are meant to more closely examine a part of the chapter that might need to be expanded in order to broaden your understanding of an underlying concept or principle. Or they might include an example that applies the concepts being learned, in a way that is easy to understand and follow.

WORTH REPEATING...

The *Worth Repeating* segments in each chapter are meant to remind students of concepts in accounting already learned, and to highlight current concepts being taught that are "worth repeating."

IN THE REAL WORLD

The *In The Real World* segments in each chapter are meant to provide applied examples of elements being learned in a particular chapter. They are meant to put some of the concepts being learned in context and to drive home the point that eventually, accounting has to be done outside the classroom. We hope that these segments give you a sense of what "the real world" can be like for the accountant or business professional.

Notes

Chapter 1
ACCOUNTING INFORMATION SYSTEMS

LEARNING OUTCOMES:

❶ Review GAAP and IFRS

❷ Understand the flow of accounting information and the use of modern accounting systems

❸ Describe and record in special journals

❹ Describe and post in subsidiary ledgers

❺ Apply controls and ethics related to the accounting information system

An Integrated Approach to Learning Accounting

The accounting information system refers to the system companies use to collect and process financial transactions as well as provide financial information. The challenge in teaching a modern course in accounting involves the need to integrate traditional concepts and methods with modern technology. This can easily become a formidable task considering that modern accounting information systems have been incorporated so quickly into business that many of the education materials available to accounting students have become outdated.

The reality is that with current "point-and-click" software, accounting students may never see or get to use a set of paper journals and ledgers. This means that the traditional methods used to develop modern accounting systems are being used less and less.

Due to their affordability and usefulness, computerized systems are now a common occurrence in the workplace. They make gathering and analyzing information easier for the accountants and are capable of providing a high level of internal control. Understanding the flow of information in a manual accounting system (journal to ledger to financial statements) will make it easier to understand the flow of information in a computerized accounting system.

Before reviewing the flow of accounting information, it would be best to refresh our minds on the accounting environment we operate in.

GAAP and IFRS Review

In prior accounting courses, Generally Accepted Accounting Principles (GAAP) and International Financial Reporting Standards (IFRS) may have been introduced. Both are sets of accounting standards and acceptable ways of reporting accounting activities. These guidelines for financial reporting must be interpreted and applied by accountants based on the circumstances that they face. GAAP and IFRS have a variety of principles that apply to all businesses, such as the revenue recognition principle and the matching principle.

In January 2011, Canada adopted the International Financial Reporting Standards (IFRS) as the accounting standards guideline for publicly traded corporations. This adoption required public corporations to change the way they prepared their accounting records and how they presented their financial information.

There are two important points regarding the relationship between GAAP and IFRS in Canada:

1. GAAP and IFRS are very similar. The basic principles from GAAP are embedded in IFRS. IFRS requires certain details for financial reporting that GAAP does not, which is where the bulk of the changes occurred. Aside from these details, the bookkeeping function has not changed.

2. Public corporations are required to report using IFRS. Private corporations on the other hand, have a choice of following IFRS or the new GAAP specifically updated for private companies.

As part of the change between GAAP and IFRS, some terms have been renamed. The following chart lists some terms that can be used interchangeably.

GAAP Term	IFRS Term
Fixed Assets / Capital Assets	Property, Plant and Equipment / Non-Current Assets
Long-Term Liabilities	Non-Current Liabilities
Income Statement	Statement of Comprehensive Income
Balance Sheet	Statement of Financial Position
Statement of Owner's Equity	Statement of Changes in Equity
Cash Flow Statement	Statement of Cash Flows

FIGURE 1.1

Each chapter in this text will include a discussion of how IFRS might apply to the topic. The application of IFRS to public corporations will be discussed in more detail later in this text when accounting for corporations is covered.

The Accounting Paper Trail

After reviewing GAAP and IFRS, it would also be good to review the flow of accounting information. Basic elements of a manual/paper-based accounting system include source documents, journals, subsidiary ledgers, ledgers, worksheets, trial balances and financial statements. Subsidiary ledgers provide more details regarding the balance of an account in the general ledger and will be expanded upon in the next section.

Source Documents, which provide evidence that a business transaction has occurred, come in many different forms. The most common examples of source documentation are usually associated with accounts payable and accounts receivable. Source documentation includes purchase orders, sales invoices, cash receipts and contracts.

Accountants use source documentation (in addition to other sources of information) to update the accounting records of an organization. For example, when the accounting department issues a sales invoice, the corresponding journal entry regarding the sale should be made. Note that the procedures surrounding this entry will differ slightly between manual and computerized accounting systems (e.g. in a computerized accounting system, the revenue and accounts receivable accounts are automatically updated while the sales invoice is generated). Our focus in this section, however, will be on manual accounting systems.

Figure 1.2 below outlines the traditional accounting paper trail. Once source documentation is received, the accountant updates the journal. At specified points, this information is transferred to the general ledger (either directly or through a subsidiary ledger). At the end of the accounting period, a trial balance is produced. A trial balance lists all the company's accounts and their corresponding balances. The main purpose of a trial balance is to ensure that all debits equal all credits. The trial balance may need to be adjusted (e.g. to take into account recognition of prepaid expenses, depreciation of assets etc.) before the financial statements are produced. The financial statements are then organized into a financial report for management to review.

The Traditional Accounting Paper Trail

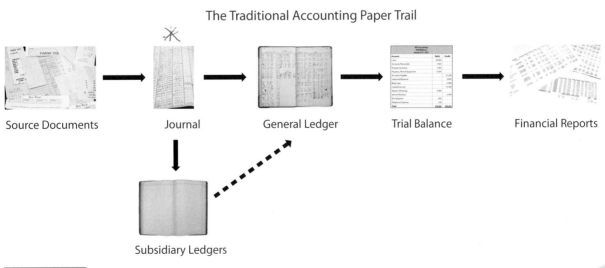

Source Documents   Journal   General Ledger   Trial Balance   Financial Reports

Subsidiary Ledgers

FIGURE 1.2

Regardless of whether one is dealing with a manual or a computerized system, an effective accounting system should ensure:

- Adequate internal controls to prevent misuse of assets
- Accurate information is provided on a timely basis
- Effective communication across the various components of the system
- Flexibility to allow for changes as the organization grows and evolves
- Maximum benefits at a reasonable cost

In this section, we will focus on two components of the traditional accounting information system. They are *special journals* and *subsidiary ledgers*.

Special Journals

Following our manual accounting paper trail, after the source documentation has been received, the next step for the accountant is to record the transaction in **journal** format.

In a traditional accounting system, recording all business transactions in one journal could be very time consuming – especially when there are lots of activities concerning specific transactions. For transactions that occur regularly, it is wise to maintain a separate book called a **special journal**. Examples of regular transactions include sales, purchases, cash payments, cash receipts and payroll. Maintaining these events in a separate set of books will allow one to easily access information pertaining to these activities. For example, if a sales manager wants to see the amount of credit sales generated in May, she could examine the sales journal and add up all the sales for that month. In other words, accounting information is organized into a specific category so that people can look back later and easily extract information. Examples of special journals are listed below.

Sales Journal: This journal is used to record all sales made on account.

Purchases Journal: This is similar to the sales journal, but is used to record all purchases (products or services) made on account.

Cash Payments Journal: This journal is used to record all cash payments made by the business (e.g. rent and wages expense) including payments made to suppliers.

Cash Receipts Journal: This journal is used to record all cash deposits (e.g. cash sales) and collections from outstanding accounts receivable.

When transactions are not recorded in sufficient volume to justify a special journal or they don't 'fit' into one of the special journals, they are recorded directly in the **general journal**. The general journal is simply another name for the journal that has been used in previous accounting courses. The term *general* simply separates it from the other special journals. Some typical entries that would be recorded in the general journal may include:

- Purchase and Sales Returns
- Depreciation
- Recognition of a Prepaid Expense as an expense
- Correction of a mistake

Subsidiary Ledgers

Subsidiary ledgers (also called *subledgers*) are used to provide details that are not kept in the general ledger because there is so much information that it will clutter up the general ledger accounts. For example, a company usually deals with many suppliers and customers at the same time and certain information about each supplier and customer is important to the accounting function. This information would include invoice numbers and amounts, dates of purchases or sales and terms of the purchase or sale. Thus, the accounts receivable account in the general ledger would have a subledger for each individual customer, and the accounts payable account in the general ledger would have a subledger of each individual supplier.

Transactions are initially recorded in the general journal or the special journals and are then posted to the general ledger or the subledgers as needed. The subledgers are usually updated after each transaction, while the general ledger is updated after a specified period, such as a month. The general ledger has one summary amount representing the total of all the activity. Since subledger accounts only contain details about general ledger accounts and are not used in preparing financial statements or for posting to the general ledger, they are not assigned account numbers.

The accounts receivable account in the general ledger is a *control* account for the individual accounts in the accounts receivable subledger. A control account keeps track of the grand total of the amounts in the subledger. For example, suppose a company had the following list of customers that each owed a certain amount:

- Customer A owes $400
- Customer B owes $500
- Customer C owes $600

The subsidiary ledger tracks each customer and the amount owing, while the accounts receivable control account would simply show the total amount, $1,500. It is important to note that we do not post amounts from the subledger to the general ledger. Subledgers simply keep a record of detailed information about specific general ledger accounts. All amounts in the general ledger are posted from either the special journal or the general journal.

At the end of a period, the total of the subledger accounts is compared with their respective control account balance. If the sum of the individual ledger accounts is not equal to the control account, an error has occurred and must be corrected. The comparison between the subsidiary and control account acts as a detective control because it is designed to find errors or irregularities after they have occurred.

Subsidiary ledgers protect assets by confirming that accounts receivable are properly accounted for and can, similarly, be used to confirm that accounts payable (liabilities) are correctly recorded. For example, a manager may want to know how much product was purchased from a particular supplier, over what time period, when it was paid for, what discounts were allowed for early payment, etc. To have easy access to this information, an individual ledger should be maintained for each supplier. The ledger, which records the activities for each individual supplier, is called the **accounts payable subsidiary ledger**. The total of all the closing balances for each account in the accounts payable subsidiary ledger would be equal to the accounts payable general ledger balance.

The relationship between the general ledger and the subledger is demonstrated in figure 1.3 and figure 1.4.

Subsidiary Ledger

Accounts Payable Subsidiary Ledger					
Sellmore Advertising Agency					
DATE	PR	DR	CR	BALANCE (DR or CR)	
O/B				4,600	CR
Apr 1		4,600		0	
Apr 12			4,600	4,600	CR

ABC Prize Supply Store					
DATE	PR	DR	CR	BALANCE (DR or CR)	
Apr 12			500	500	CR

Sparkies Computer Repairs					
DATE	PR	DR	CR	BALANCE (DR or CR)	
Apr 8			400	400	CR
Apr 12		100		300	CR

FIGURE 1.3

Control Account

General Ledger				
Accounts Payable				
DATE	PR	DR	CR	BALANCE
Apr 12			5,400	5,400

Sellmore	$4,600
ABC Prize	$500
Sparkies	$300
Accounts Payable	$5,400

A **subsidiary ledger** is a group of accounts.

The total of the subsidiary ledger accounts is equal to the **control account**

There are different subsidiary ledgers to control various activities (e.g. inventory, cash and sales). Figure 1.4 shows how the accounts payable, accounts receivable and inventory subsidiary ledgers are totaled and reconciled to their corresponding control account in the general ledger.

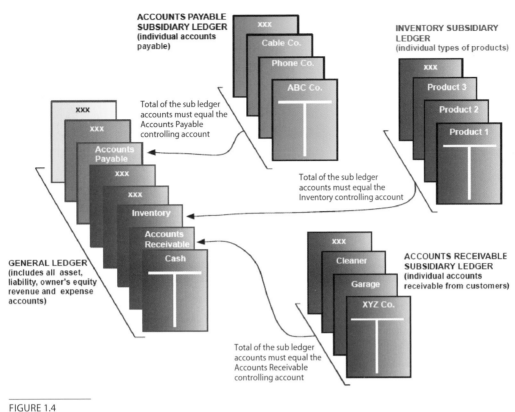

FIGURE 1.4

Once the subledgers have been reconciled to the control accounts in the general ledger, a trial balance can be created with the general ledger accounts and balances. The rest of the accounting cycle continues as you have already learned.

Using Special Journals and Subsidiary Ledgers

It is important to repeat that the special journals are used to group similar transactions that would normally appear in the general journal. Transactions are entered into the appropriate journal when they occur. For the most part, the subledgers are updated from the special journals immediately, while the general ledger is updated at the end of the accounting period. The details of posting from the special journals to the ledgers will be discussed with each journal.

The Sales Journal

The sales journal records all the details of sales on account. Cash sales are not included in this journal. They will appear in the cash receipts journal, since that is where all cash received is recorded. The sales journal includes 1) the date of the sale, 2) the name of the customer, 3) the invoice number and 4) the value of the sale and inventory. These items are shown in figure 1.5.

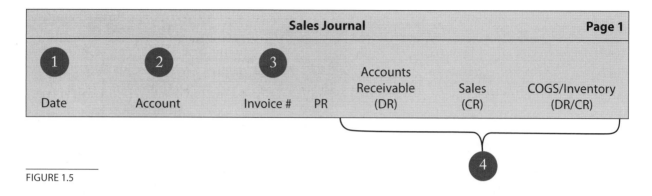

FIGURE 1.5

FIGURE 1.5

When a sale is made, as shown on January 5 in figure 1.6, the customer subledger account must be updated immediately. The date and the amount of accounts receivable is transferred from the journal to the subledger. The PR in the subledger is the page number of the sales journal. The subledger account does not have a number like the general ledger does, so the post reference in the sales journal will show a checkmark to indicate the amount was properly posted to the subledger account. Every sales transaction made on account will be recorded the same way.

Some companies will offer sales terms to their customers. If a customer pays the amount owing within a certain number of days, they would receive a discount. The terms of a sale can be written as 2/10, n 30. This means that customers will receive a 2% discount if they pay the amount owing within 10 days, otherwise the total or net amount is due within 30 days. If a company provides the same sales terms to all its customers, there is no need to record the terms in the sales journal.

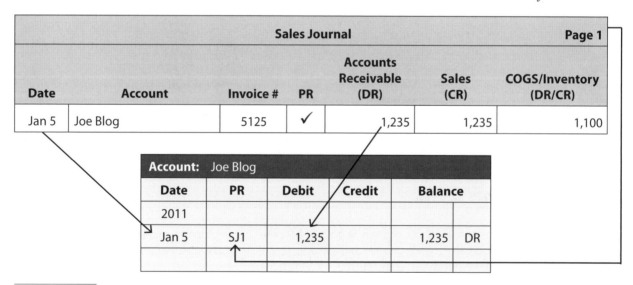

FIGURE 1.6

At the end of the month, the totals of all the columns will be posted to the appropriate ledger accounts. The numbers in brackets under the totals represent the ledger numbers of the accounts being used. In this example, we are focusing on accounts receivable, which is account number 110. Assume accounts receivable totals to $2,191.

Sales Journal						Page 1
Date	Account	Invoice #	PR	Accounts Receivable (DR)	Sales (CR)	COGS/Inventory (DR/CR)
Jan 5	Joe Blog	5125	✓	1,235	1,235	1,100
Jan 16	Furniture Retailers	5126	✓	956	956	850
Jan 31	Total			$2,191	$2,191	$1,950
				(110)	(400)	(500/120)

Account:	Accounts Receivable				GL. No.	110
Date	Description	PR	Debit	Credit	Balance	
2011						
Jan 31		SJ1	2,191		2,191	DR

Account: Joe Blog				
Date	PR	Debit	Credit	Balance
2011				
Jan 5	SJ1	1,235		1,235	DR

Account: Furniture Retailers				
Date	PR	Debit	Credit	Balance
2011				
Jan 16	SJ1	956		956	DR

FIGURE 1.7

The total of accounts receivable in the sales journal, $2,191, is posted to accounts receivable in the general ledger as a debit. The total of the two customer accounts ($1,235 and $956) is equal to the balance of the accounts receivable control account.

The Cash Receipts Journal

The cash receipts journal will record all receipts of cash for whatever reason. A list of common reasons for the receipt of cash is listed in the columns (Accounts Receivable, Sales and Bank Loan) which will vary depending on the company. A column titled *Other* is used to record cash receipts that do not fall under one of the common reasons. The Sales Discount column will be used if customers make a payment within the discount days specified by the company.

Cash (DR)	Sales Discount (DR)	Accounts Receivable (CR)	Sales (CR)	Bank Loan (CR)	Other (CR)	COGS/Inventory (DR/CR)

FIGURE 1.8

A cash sale would be recorded in the cash receipts journal, as shown in figure 1.9. Since accounts receivable is not affected, nothing must be posted to the subledger accounts. Also, since the Other column was not used, no entry is posted to the general ledger at this time. Only at the end of the month when the columns are totaled will the general ledger be updated.

				Cash Receipts Journal						Page 3
				Sales	Accounts					
			Cash	Discount	Receivable	Sales	Bank Loan	Other	COGS/Inventory
Date	Account	PR	(DR)	(DR)	(CR)	(CR)	(CR)	(CR)	(DR/CR)
Jan 2	Cash Sale		350			350			280

FIGURE 1.9

The transaction on January 4 in figure 1.10 is an investment into the company by the owner. Since there is no column with Capital Account as a heading, the amount will be recorded in the Other column. The post reference (300) indicates that the amount of the investment shown is immediately updated to the capital account in the general ledger. At the end of the month, the total of the Other column will not be posted since any amount in this column is posted immediately to the appropriate ledger account.

				Cash Receipts Journal						Page 3
				Sales	Accounts					
			Cash	Discount	Receivable	Sales	Bank Loan	Other	COGS/Inventory
Date	Account	PR	(DR)	(DR)	(CR)	(CR)	(CR)	(CR)	(DR/CR)
Jan 2	Cash Sale		350			350			280
Jan 4	Capital Account	300	4,000					4,000	

FIGURE 1.10

The partial payment from a customer on January 10 will immediately update the subledger account because it impacts the accounts receivable account. Since the payment is made within 10 days of the original sale, the customer will receive a 2% discount on the amount that is being paid. The discount therefore reduces the amount of cash received, but does not reduce the amount of accounts receivable that is being paid off. Similar to the sales journal, the posting to the subledger is shown in the cash receipts journal with a checkmark.

Cash Receipts Journal								Page 3
Date	Account	PR	Cash (DR)	Sales Discount (DR)	Accounts Receivable (CR)	Sales (CR)	Bank Loan (CR)	Other (CR)	COGS/Inventory (DR/CR)
Jan 2	Cash Sale		350			350			280
Jan 4	Capital Account	300	4,000					4,000	
Jan 10	Joe Blog	✓	588	12	600				

Account:	Joe Blog					
Date	PR	Debit	Credit	Balance	
2011					
Jan 5	SJ1	1,235		1,235	DR
Jan 10	CR3		600	635	DR

FIGURE 1.11

At the end of the month, all columns will be totaled and the amounts posted to the appropriate general ledger accounts. In figure 1.12, this means that $600 is posted as a credit to accounts receivable. The Other column total is not posted, thus an X is used to indicate that no posting is required.

Cash Receipts Journal								Page 3
Date	Account	PR	Cash (DR)	Sales Discount (DR)	Accounts Receivable (CR)	Sales (CR)	Bank Loan (CR)	Other (CR)	COGS/Inventory (DR/CR)
Jan 2	Cash Sale		350			350			280
Jan 4	Capital Account	300	4,000					4,000	
Jan 10	Joe Blog	✓	588	12	600				
Jan 22	Bank Loan		2,000				2,000		
Jan 31	Total		$6,938	$12	$600	$350	$2,000	$4,000	$280
			(101)	(405)	(110)	(400)	(220)	(X)	(500/120)

Account:	Accounts Receivable				GL. No.	110
Date	Description	PR	Debit	Credit	Balance	
2011						
Jan 31		SJ1	2,191		2,191	DR
Jan 31		CR3		600	1,591	DR

Account:	Joe Blog					
Date	PR	Debit	Credit	Balance	
2011					
Jan 5	SJ1	1,235		1,235	DR
Jan 10	CR3		600	635	DR

Account:	Furniture Retailers				
Date	PR	Debit	Credit	Balance	
2011					
Jan 16	SJ1	956		956	DR

FIGURE 1.12

The Purchases Journal

The purchases journal records all purchases on account. Several columns are provided to account for the more common items that the company purchases on account (inventory and office supplies in our example). If anything else is purchased, it would be recorded in the Other column.

Inventory (DR)	Office Supplies (DR)	Other (DR)	Account Payable (CR)

FIGURE 1.13

When a purchase is made, as shown on January 3 in figure 1.14, the supplier subledger account must be updated immediately. The date and the amount of accounts payable is transferred from the journal to the subledger. As with the other journals, a checkmark is used to indicate the amount was properly posted to the subledger account. Every purchase transaction made on account will be recorded the same way. Notice that the purchases journal has a column for terms. Some suppliers will provide payment terms. Since terms differ from supplier to supplier, the terms column is provided to keep track of them.

	Purchases Journal								Page 6
Date	Account	Invoice #	Terms	PR	Inventory (DR)	Office Supplies (DR)	Other (DR)	Account Payable (CR)
Jan 3	Antonio's Electric	2089	3/15, n 30	✓	4,200			4,200

Account:	Antonio's Electric				
Date	PR	Debit	Credit	Balance	
2011					
Jan 3	PJ6		4,200	4,200	CR

FIGURE 1.14

At the end of the month, the total of the columns are posted to the general ledger accounts. Assume the company also purchased $80 worth of office supplies from Young Office Supplies this month and total amounts to $4,280. The posting of the accounts payable is shown in figure 1.15. The totals of the individual subledger accounts must equal the balance of accounts payable.

Purchases Journal								Page 6
Date	Account	Invoice #	Terms	PR	Inventory (DR)	Office Supplies (DR)	Other (DR)	Account Payable (CR)
Jan 3	Antonio's Electric	2089	3/15, n 30	✓	4,200			4,200
Jan 19	Young Office Supplies	6091		✓		80		80
Jan 31	Total				$4,200	$80		$4,280
					(120)	(115)		(200)

Account:	Accounts Payable				GL. No.	200
Date	Description	PR	Debit	Credit	Balance	
2011						
Jan 31		PJ6		4,280	4,280	CR

Account:	Antonio's Electric				
Date	PR	Debit	Credit	Balance	
2011					
Jan 3	PJ6		4,200	4,200	CR

Account:	Young Office Supplies				
Date	PR	Debit	Credit	Balance	
2011					
Jan 19	PJ6		80	80	CR

FIGURE 1.15

The Cash Payments Journal

The cash payments journal records all cash payments made by the company. There is a column to record the cheque number, since a good control is to have all payments made by a cheque. Various columns are provided for the most common reasons for paying with cash, and an Other column is used to record cash payments for items that do fall under one of the given columns. Notice that Inventory appears with both a debit and credit column. The debit side will be used if inventory is purchased with cash (cheque) and the credit side will be used if the company pays a supplier of inventory early and receives a discount.

Chq #	PR	Accounts Payable (DR)	Other (DR)	Inventory (DR)	Inventory (CR)	Cash (CR)

FIGURE 1.16

A cash purchase would be recorded in the cash payments journal, as shown in figure 1.17. Since accounts payable is not affected, no entry should be posted to the subledger accounts. Also, since the Other column was not used, no entry should be posted to the general ledger at this time. Only at the end of the month when the columns are totaled will the general ledger be updated.

Cash Payments Journal								Page 4
Date	Account	Chq #	PR	Accounts Payable (DR)	Other (DR)	Inventory (DR)	(CR)	Cash (CR)
Jan 6	Inventory	748				1,500		1,500

FIGURE 1.17

The transaction on January 15 in figure 1.18 is a withdrawal from the company by the owner. Since there is no column with Owner's Drawings as a heading, the amount will be recorded in the Other column. The post reference (310) indicates that the amount of the withdrawal shown is immediately updated to the owner's drawings in the general ledger. At the end of the month, the total of the Other column will not posted since any amount in this column is posted immediately to the appropriate ledger account.

Cash Payments Journal								Page 4
Date	Account	Chq #	PR	Accounts Payable (DR)	Other (DR)	Inventory (DR)	(CR)	Cash (CR)
Jan 6	Inventory	748				1,500		1,500
Jan 15	Owner's Drawings	749	310		500			500

FIGURE 1.18

The payment to a supplier on January 18 will immediately update the subledger account since it impacts the accounts payable account. Similar to the other journals, the posting to the subledger is shown in the cash payments journal with a checkmark. Since the terms of the purchase were 3/15, n 30, the company can take a 3% discount on the payment (the original purchase was on January 3). The discount amount will be a credit to inventory and reduces the amount of cash that must be paid to the supplier.

Cash Payments Journal								Page 4
Date	Account	Chq #	PR	Accounts Payable (DR)	Other (DR)	Inventory (DR)	(CR)	Cash (CR)
Jan 6	Inventory	748				1,500		1,500
Jan 15	Owner's Drawings	749	310		500			500
Jan 18	Antonio's Electric	750	✓	4,200			126	4,074

Account:	Antonio's Electric			
Date	PR	Debit	Credit	Balance
2011				
Jan 3	PJ6		4,200	4,200 CR
Jan 18	CP4	4,200		0 CR

FIGURE 1.19

At the end of the month, all columns will be totaled and the amounts posted to the appropriate general ledger accounts. In figure 1.20, this means that $4,200 is posted as a debit to accounts payable. The Other column total is not posted, thus an X is used to indicate that no posting is required.

Cash Payments Journal								Page 4
Date	Account	Chq #	PR	Accounts Payable (DR)	Other (DR)	Inventory (DR)	(CR)	Cash (CR)
Jan 6	Inventory	748				1,500		1,500
Jan 15	Owner's Drawings	749	310		500			500
Jan 18	Antonio's Electric	750	✓	4,200			126	4,074
Jan 31	Total			$4,200	$500	$1,500	$126	$6,074
				(200)	(X)	(120)	(120)	(101)

Account:	Accounts Payable				GL. No.	200
Date	Description	PR	Debit	Credit	Balance	
2011						
Jan 31		PJ6		4,280	4,280	CR
Jan 31		CP4	4,200		80	CR

Account:	Antonio's Electric				
Date	**PR**	**Debit**	**Credit**	**Balance**	
2011					
Jan 3	PJ6		4,200	4,200	CR
Jan 18	CP4	4,200		0	CR

Account:	Young Office Supplies				
Date	**PR**	**Debit**	**Credit**	**Balance**	
2011					
Jan 19	PJ6		80	80	CR

FIGURE 1.20

Remember that at the end of the month, when the general ledger is updated by the journals, the total of all the subledger accounts must equal the balance of the appropriate control account (accounts receivable or accounts payable).

To prove that the total of the individual subledger accounts is equal to the respective control account balance in the general ledger, a reconciliation is prepared. From figure 1.12, the balance of accounts receivable was $1,591. By finding the total of the accounts receivable subledger account, we can prove that the control account and subledger are in balance.

Company Name	
Schedule of Accounts Receivable	
January 31, 2011	
General Ledger	
Accounts Receivable	$1,591

Control account in the general ledger

Company Name	
Schedule of Accounts Receivable	
January 31, 2011	
Joe Blog	$635
Furniture Retailers	956
Total Accounts Receivable	$1,591

The total of all subledger accounts

FIGURE 1.21

A similar listing can be done for the accounts payable subledger. From figure 1.20, the balance of accounts payable was $80. The total of the accounts payable subledger is shown below.

Company Name	
Schedule of Accounts Payable	
January 31, 2011	
General Ledger	
Accounts Payable	$80

Control account in the general ledger

Company Name	
Schedule of Accounts Payable	
January 31, 2011	
Antonio's Electric	$0
Young Office Supplies	80
Total Accounts Payable	$80

The total of all subledger accounts

FIGURE 1.22

If the comparison of the general ledger control account and the total of the subledger accounts shows that they do not balance, the difference must be investigated. The difference must be resolved before the trial balance can be completed.

Returns

The special journals are designed to record specific types of transactions, but some transactions that must be recorded do not fit into these special journals. As mentioned earlier, if a transaction does not 'fit' into one of the special journals, it must be recorded in the general journal. As an example, sales and purchase returns do not fit into the special journals and must be recorded in the general journal. The only change to the way these transactions are recorded is how the posting is processed for accounts receivable or accounts payable.

Suppose Furniture Retailers, a customer from figure 1.7, returned some items worth $300 that had a cost of $170 on January 18. The journal entry would be entered as shown below. The PR for accounts receivable will update the general ledger (as shown by the account number 110) and the subsidiary ledger for the customer (as shown by the check mark).

JOURNAL				Page 1
Date	Account Title and Explanation	PR	Debit	Credit
Jan 18	Sales Returns & Allowances	410	300	
	Accounts Receivable	110/✔		300
	Customer returned items			
	Inventory	120	170	
	Cost of Goods Sold	500		170
	Returned Items to supplier			

FIGURE 1.23

Also, suppose the company returned $500 of the inventory it purchased from Antonio's Electric on January 10 (from figure 1.15). This purchase return would be completed in the general journal, as shown below. The PR for accounts payable will update the general ledger (as shown by the account number 200) and the subsidiary ledger for the supplier (as shown by the check mark).

JOURNAL				Page 1
Date	Account Title and Explanation	PR	Debit	Credit
Jan 10	Accounts Payable	200/✔	500	
	Inventory	120		500
	Returned Items to supplier			

FIGURE 1.24

Shown below is an example of how reports generated from the accounts receivable subledger and sales journal can be used to examine amounts owing from individual customers. Figure 1.25 shows amounts owing from four different customers and is otherwise known as an aging analysis of accounts receivable. It shows how long it has been since customers have been invoiced (e.g. Better Late Ltd. was invoiced 60-90 days ago and have still not paid their bill(s) which amounts to $1,720). In this particular figure we are also drawn to Slo-Pay Joe because the amount owing ($5,950) makes up over 70% of the total accounts receivable balance of $8,290.

ANALYZE RECEIVABLES

Customer Report - all customers

	Customer	Total	0-30	31-60	60-90	90+
⇨	Slo-Pay Joe	5,950.00	580.00	900.00	3,900.00	570.00
⇨	On The Ball Inc.	50.00		50.00		
⇨	Better Late Ltd.	1,720.00			1,720.00	
⇨	Way Past Due Corp.	5,70.00				570.00
	Total	8,290.00	580.00	950.00	5,620.00	1,140.00
	Aging percent	100%	65%	8%	21%	7%

This drills down to detailed analysis per customer below.

FIGURE 1.25

The accounts receivable subsidiary ledger and the sales journal are used to generate a detailed customer report for Slo-Pay Joe (see figure 1.26). This report gives us the breakdown of each invoice billed to Slo-Pay Joe and how long it has been since the outstanding invoice was billed. When we contact Slo-Pay Joe regarding the billable amounts, we can use this report to focus on Invoice #122222 which has an amount of $3,900 that has not been paid in at least two months to determine the cause of the late payment. This is one way in which special journals and subledgers can be used in the course of regular business operations.

Detailed Customer Report - by customer:		**Slo-Pay Joe**				
	Invoice #	Amount	0-30	31-60	60-90	90+
⇨	122222	4,470.00			3,900.00	570.00
⇨	122255	900.00		900.00		
⇨	122280	300.00	300.00			
⇨	122262	280.00	280.00			
	Total	5,950.00	580.00	900.00	3,900.00	570.00
	Aging percent	100%	10%	15%	66%	10%

This drills down to each invoice

FIGURE 1.26

Modern Accounting Information Systems

In the traditional systems, all financial records need to be examined manually. For example, if the accountant needs to analyze accounts receivable, then all related journals and ledgers are pulled and looked at for reference. If inventory needs to be examined, then the paper trail from receipt to shipping must be tracked accordingly.

With most modern computerized systems, however, the logic of accounting is already built into the software. There is no need to keep a separate set of books and documents for specific types of transactions. Instead, just about every transaction is entered as an input to the system to produce one central database (general ledger). The software, or various different types of software, will then process the information and transfer it when and where it is needed; the software will produce the view that the accountant wants at any given time.

The data in a modern, computerized accounting system flows through three stages:

1. The first stage is user *input*. These can come from source documents such as sales receipts and purchase orders. A user with access to the accounting system would enter the necessary information on the source document into the computer.

2. The second stage is *data processing*. In this stage, after user input is complete, the computer automatically creates a journal entry in the system and posts the data to the ledger, which eventually flows through to the financial statements. In other words, the computer is processing the information input by the user.

3. The third stage is *output*. Output is the set of reports and financial statements that are created after all necessary information has been processed. They are used internally for decision making purposes and may also be communicated to external users such as creditors and investors.

Depending on how comprehensive the data is regarding recorded transactions, the accounting software will be able to produce a variety of useful reports to aid in the management of the business. Note that with computerized accounting systems, information in the special journal and subledger can be accessed as an output report with relative ease.

As an example, the recording of a payment from a customer can contain ten fields of information as follows:

Transaction Type	Date	Debit Account	Debit Amount	Credit Account	Credit Amount	Payee Name	Payee a/c #	Invoice Date	Due Date

FIGURE 1.27

These fields are not only used for accounts receivable, but for any purpose at any point in the traditional document trail — from initial sale to financial reporting. Countless transactions can be entered as an input into a system, which can then be sorted to produce the following reports:

- Financial statements
- Accounts receivable and accounts payable aging reports
- Detailed product inventory listings
- Detailed fixed asset reports containing asset costs and depreciation schedules
- Breakdown of sales per product, department, division etc...
- Breakdown of expense accounts
- Loan amortization schedules

Although some computerized systems require an initial manual entry of source documentation into the system, other systems do not require any paper documentation. For example, electronic data interchange, or EDI, is a computerized system that allows companies to transfer electronic information to one another. Sending a bill electronically to a customer is one potential use of such a system.

With the heavy reliance on electronic data in modern accounting systems, you may be concerned about how this information is stored. Many companies store financial data in-house (on the premises) and/or at off-site locations. Storing the information in-house under the eye of internal employees can increase privacy controls and allow for quicker service when required. On the other hand, many smaller companies may not have the resources to hire an IT expert and have to outsource the data storage function. Note that even though an accountant does not have to be an expert in these systems, he should have a clear idea of what IT services are available and what issues can come up so that he can protect the integrity of the company's accounting information.

Ultimately, it is up to the management and the accounting department to work with information technology personnel to buy and design a system that meets organizational objectives. Manual systems help accountants learn the ABC's of their profession. However, in today's business world, a properly designed computer system, tailored to the needs of a specific company, can make accounting more efficient.

IN THE REAL WORLD

Although the information age has been forging full speed ahead for more than a decade, efficiencies and innovations are still sought after in almost every sector of technology. This is particularly true regarding how financial entities communicate electronically with one another. A recent development in the field might constitute a great leap forward.

Extensible Business Reporting Language, or XBRL, is a new computer language that will facilitate the exchange of financial information in all sectors of the economy – and it is coming very soon.

What XBRL does is essentially package bits of financial information, standardize this information and make it easier to use and manipulate. The ramifications for this kind of development are almost limitless.

XBRL can be used by companies to publish financial reports for the public. Governments and regulators can use XBRL to receive this information and transmit their own. Stock exchanges can serve as a conduit between business and government in exchanging financial information quickly and easily. Even software companies can get in on the action to create various IT solutions for specific sectors.

In a sense, what XBRL will do for the communicating of financial information is similar to what highways did for the transport of people in vehicles. One system can be used more quickly and efficiently by everyone.

Controls and Ethics

By having a detailed subledger for both accounts receivable and accounts payable, a business is able to properly monitor and control these accounts.

The accounts receivable subledger will provide information on amounts due, and when they are due. Customers who are struggling to make payments can be identified in order to properly collect funds from them. It is also easy to view the history of sales and payments related to a particular customer.

Accounts payable controls will ensure that suppliers are paid on time. If discounts are available for early payment, the subledger will identify when payments should be made to take advantage of these discounts.

Both the customer list and the list of suppliers can be valuable information. For example, the list of clients of an insurance company should be considered private information since it can be valuable to competing insurance companies. Thus, access to the client list should be limited only to those that need client information. Publishing or making the client list widely available may be breaking confidentiality agreements. In Canada, personal information is protected by the Personal Information Protection and Electronic Documents Act (PIPEDA).

From another perspective, employees that do have access to client lists while employed at one company may be tempted to take that client list with them if they decide to change jobs and work for a competing company. This type of behaviour is actually considered as theft. The client list is private information belonging to the first employer. Depending on the type of employment contract that the employee signed, the employee could be sued for their theft of information.

The IFRS Perspective

The integrity of the accounting information system relies on rules such as the generally accepted accounting principles (GAAP). As the world changes, so does the accounting profession. Specifically, instead of following GAAP guidelines, most of the world will be soon adhering to International Financial Reporting Standards (IFRS). Canada became IFRS compliant in 2011.

In Summary

The challenge for today's accountant is to use principles established with traditional methods and apply them using today's technology. This involves knowledge and familiarity with the traditional paper trail. It also involves an understanding of how these traditional methods are handled today using computer software. This chapter essentially provides a basic framework, which is to use traditional techniques to understand how modern accounting is done.

Here is a summary of some of the specific concepts and principles you have learned in this chapter:

- Modern accounting involves a need to understand traditional accounting procedures and apply them to current technological realities.

- The basic elements of the traditional accounting paper trail include: *source documents, journals, subsidiary ledgers, general ledgers, worksheets, trial balances* and *financial statements.*

- Special journals are special books used to record events of a regular nature such as sales, purchases, cash receipts/payments, payroll, etc.

- Subsidiary ledgers provide supporting details on individual balances.

- Accountants used to categorize transactions and track them accordingly. Today, computer software simply gathers all the information in one database and distributes it as instructed.

Review Exercise

Lin-Z Inc. is an owner-operated office furniture retailer. The following is a list of transactions for the month of June.

Jun 4	Received $4,000 from a cash sale to Gus Van Sand (sold office furniture costing $2,015)
Jun 5	Lin-Z received a bill (Invoice #4053) for $100 worth of supplies from Stapl-EZ Inc.
Jun 6	Received $480 from Bo Didley regarding outstanding accounts receivable
Jun 9	Received $2,160 for the cash sale of a lounge suite (costing $1,050) to ReetaPetita
Jun 9	Lin-Z received a bill from Building Services Inc. (Invoice #124) for $350 for repairs and maintenance of office building
Jun 10	Received $25 in interest from loan to Kurt Domino
Jun 12	Paid amount owing (Invoice #4053) to Stapl-EZ Inc. (Cheque #465)
Jun 15	Jo Jo Inc. paid back loan of $2,400
Jun 18	Made a sale on account (Invoice #10022) to Richard Starkey Jr., for office furniture for $3,000 (and costing $2,000).
Jun 21	Handed over cheque #466 to Noel's Inc for $4,000 worth of inventory
Jun 22	Paid amount owing (Invoice #124) to Building Services Inc. for repairs (Cheque #467)
Jun 25	Paid $175 to SKG Inc., for general expenses (Cheque #468)
Jun 26	Received bill from The Brick & Mortar Inc. (Invoice #404241) for $3,500 worth of inventory
Jun 28	Made a sale, on account (Invoice #10023), to Pete Best for $5,000 worth of desks and tables (costing $3,700)

Required

Record these transactions in the Cash Receipts, Sales, Purchases and Cash Payments Journal.

Use the following headings:

Cash Receipts Journal								Page 1
Date	Account	PR	Cash (DR)	Sales (CR)	Accounts Receivable (CR)	Interest Revenue (CR)	Loans Payable (CR)	Other (CR)	COGS/ Inventory (DR/CR)

Sales Journal						Page 1
Date	Account	Invoice #	PR	Sales (CR)	Accounts Receivable (DR)	COGS/Inventory (DR/CR)

Purchases Journal							Page 1
Date	Account	Invoice #	PR	Repairs Expense (DR)	Office Supplies (DR)	Inventory (DR)	Accounts Payable (CR)

Note: *the column titled "Terms" in the purchase journal is not included for the purpose of this exercise. This "Terms" column will be presented in the workbook questions wherever necessary.*

Cash Payments Journal							Page 1
Date	Account	Cheque #	PR	Other (DR)	Inventory (DR)	Accounts Payable (DR)	Cash (CR)

Post from the special journals to the accounts receivable subledger. At the end of the month, post from the special journals to the general ledger control account. Assume opening subledger balances of:

- Bo Didley : $2,000 (DR)
- Richard Starkey Jr. : $1,000 (DR)
- Pete Best : $1,500 (DR)

Note that Lin-Z's accounts receivable records consist of only these three subledgers. Assume no entries were made directly to accounts receivable through the general journal. Reconcile the subledger to the control account at the end of the month.

Use the following ledgers:

Accounts Receivable Subsidiary Ledger Bo Didley				
Date	PR	Debit	Credit	Balance

Accounts Receivable Subsidiary Ledger Richard Starkey Jr.				
Date	PR	Debit	Credit	Balance

Accounts Receivable Subsidiary Ledger Pete Best				
Date	PR	Debit	Credit	Balance

General Ledger Accounts Receivable				
Date	PR	Debit	Credit	Balance

Post from the special journals to the accounts payable subledger and then to the general ledger control account at the end of the month. Assume opening subledger balances of:

- Staple-EZ : $500 (CR)
- Building Services Inc.: $750 (CR)
- Brick & Mortar Inc: $2500 (CR)

Note that Lin-Z's accounts payable records consist of only these three subledgers. Assume no entries were made directly to accounts payable through the general journal. Reconcile the subledger to the control account at the end of the month.

Use the following ledgers:

Accounts Payable Subsidiary Ledger Stapl-EZ Inc.				
Date	PR	Debit	Credit	Balance

Accounts Payable Subsidiary Ledger Building Services Inc.				
Date	PR	Debit	Credit	Balance

Accounts Payable Subsidiary Ledger Brick & Mortar Inc.				
Date	PR	Debit	Credit	Balance

General Ledger Accounts Payable				
Date	PR	Debit	Credit	Balance

Review Exercise - Answer

Cash Receipts Journal									Page 1
Date	Account	PR	Cash (DR)	Sales (CR)	Accounts Receivable (CR)	Interest Revenue (CR)	Loans Payable (CR)	Other (CR)	COGS/ Inventory (DR/CR)
Jun 4	G.V.Sand sale		4,000	4,000					2,015
Jun 6	B. Didley paid account	✓	480		480				
Jun 9	R.Petita sale		2,160	2,160					1,050
Jun 10	Interest from K. Domino		25			25			
Jun 15	Jo Jo Inc. returned principal		2,400				2,400		
	TOTAL		9,065	6,160	480	25	2,400		3,065

Sales Journal						Page 1
Date	Account	Invoice #	PR	Sales (CR)	Accounts Receivable (DR)	COGS/ Inventory (DR/CR)
Jun 18	Richard Starkey Jr.	10022	✓	3,000	3,000	2,000
Jun 28	Pete Best	10023	✓	5,000	5,000	3,700
	TOTAL			8,000	8,000	5,700

Purchases Journal							Page 1
Date	Account	Invoice #	PR	Repairs Expense (DR)	Office Supplies (DR)	Inventory (DR)	Accounts Payable (CR)
Jun 5	Stapl-EZ	4053	✓		100		100
Jun 9	Building Services Inc.	124	✓	350			350
Jun 26	Brick & Mortar	404241	✓			3,500	3,500
	TOTAL			350	100	3,500	3,950

Cash Payments Journal							Page 1
Date	Account	Chq #	PR	Other (DR)	Inventory (DR)	Accounts Payable (DR)	Cash (CR)
Jun 12	Stapl-EZ Inc.	465	✓			100	100
Jun 21	Noel's Inc	466			4,000		4,000
Jun 22	Building Services Inc.	467	✓			350	350
Jun 25	SKG Inc.	468		175			175
	TOTAL			175	4,000	450	4,625

Accounts Receivable Subsidiary Ledger Bo Didley				
Date	PR	Debit	Credit	Balance
Opening Bal				2,000 DR
Jun 6	CR1		480	1,520 DR

Accounts Receivable Subsidiary Ledger Richard Starkey Jr.				
Date	PR	Debit	Credit	Balance
Opening Bal				1,000 DR
Jun 18	SJ1	3,000		4,000 DR

Accounts Receivable Subsidiary Ledger Pete Best				
Date	PR	Debit	Credit	Balance
Opening Bal				1,500 DR
Jun 28	SJ1	5,000		6,500 DR

Post to general ledger.

General Ledger Accounts Receivable				
Date	PR	Debit	Credit	Balance
Opening Bal.				4,500 DR
Jun 30	CRI		480	4,020 DR
Jun 30	SJ1	8,000		12,020 DR

Lin-Z Inc. Schedule of Accounts Receivable June 30, 2011 General Ledger	
Accounts Receivable	$12,020

Lin-Z Inc. Schedule of Accounts Receivable June 30, 2011	
Bo Didley	$1,520
Richard Starkey Jr.	4,000
Pete Best	6,500
Total Accounts Receivable	$12,020

Accounts Payable Subsidiary Ledger Stapl-EZ Inc.				
Date	**PR**	**Debit**	**Credit**	**Balance**
Opening Bal.				500 CR
Jun 5	PJ1		100	600 CR
Jun 12	CP1	100		500 CR

Accounts Payable Subsidiary Ledger Building Services Inc.				
Date	**PR**	**Debit**	**Credit**	**Balance**
Opening Bal.				750 CR
Jun 9	PJ1		350	1,100 CR
Jun 22	CP1	350		750 CR

Accounts Payable Subsidiary Ledger Brick & Mortar Inc.				
Date	**PR**	**Debit**	**Credit**	**Balance**
Opening Bal.				2,500 CR
Jun 26	PJ1		3,500	6,000 CR

Post to general ledger.

General Ledger Accounts Payable				
Date	**PR**	**Debit**	**Credit**	**Balance**
Opening Bal.				3,750 CR
Jun 30	PJ1		3,950	7,700 CR
Jun 30	CP1	450		7,250 CR

Lin-Z Inc. Schedule of Accounts Payable June 30, 2011 General Ledger	
Accounts Receivable	$7,250

Lin-Z Inc. Schedule of Accounts Payable June 30, 2011	
Staple-EZ Inc.	$500
Building Services Inc.	750
Brick & Mortar Inc.	6,000
Total Accounts Payable	$7,250

Chapter 2
CASH AND SHORT-TERM INVESTMENTS

LEARNING OUTCOMES:

❶ Prepare a bank reconciliation and the related journal entries

❷ Establish a petty cash fund and record related transactions

❸ Apply cash controls

❹ Understand different types of short-term investments

❺ Prepare journal entries for loan investments

❻ Prepare journal entries for debt investments

❼ Prepare journal entries for equity investments

❽ Apply controls for short-term investments

Cash and Short-Term Investments: An Introduction

FIGURE 2.1

Our Accounting Map™ in figure 2.1 starts with cash because it is the most liquid asset and the first asset to appear on a balance sheet. A business receives cash from providing services or selling products to customers and uses that cash to purchase assets and pay for expenses. Without cash, a business will likely fail. Thus, it is important for a business to ensure that controls are in place to protect this valuable asset.

This chapter will focus on monitoring the movement of cash in and out of the business bank account and how to use a petty cash fund for small and incidental purchases. Lastly, some businesses may occasionally have more cash in their bank account than they currently need. We will explore options that businesses have in buying short-term investments to make a return on this excess cash.

Bank Reconciliations

Although banking institutions have high standards, it is still possible for them to make errors. At the end of each month, a bank provides its clients with records (bank statements) prepared by its computer system and employees. A company requires its bookkeeper to update the general ledger on a regular basis. Errors that may occur include recording incorrect amounts and charging amounts to the wrong account.

Moreover, even if both the bank and the company record their transactions correctly, differences between the bank statement and the company's general ledger cash account may still occur as a result of the time lag in recording transactions. A simple internal control involves comparing and reconciling the items in the company's cash records with the items shown on the bank statement. This is achieved by preparing a schedule called a ***bank reconciliation***.

In the process of comparing the items in your records with the items shown on the bank statement, you may notice that some items shown correctly on the bank statement may not appear in your records. Similarly, some items shown correctly in your records may not appear on the bank statement.

The following are some typical reasons for the bank making additional deductions from the company's cash account:

- loan interest charges
- repayment of a bank loan
- bank charges
- electronic fund transfers (EFTs): automatic cash payments to other accounts

The following are some typical reasons for the bank making additional deposits to the company's cash account:

- interest deposited directly into the account
- payment from a customer deposited directly into the account
- EFTs: automatic cash receipts from other accounts

Unrecorded Deposits from the Bank Statement

From time to time, the bank may automatically record a deposit, such as interest earned on the bank balance, in the company's bank account. The company would be unaware of the amount until it receives the bank statement. For example, let us compare the bank statement for HR Clothing Company to the company's cash ledger entries.

Company's Records:

GENERAL LEDGER					
Account: Cash				**GL. No.**	**101**
Date	**Description**	**Debit**	**Credit**	**Balance**	
2011					
Jun 1	Opening Balance			5,000	DR
Jun 2	Cheque #1		300	4,700	DR
Jun 3	Cheque #2		500	4,200	DR
Jun 10	Cheque #3		700	3,500	DR

Bank's Records:

Bank Statement			June 1 - June 30, 2011	
Date	**Description**	**Withdrawal**	**Deposit**	**Balance**
Jun 1	Opening Balance			5,000
Jun 2	Cheque #1	300		4,700
Jun 3	Cheque #2	500		4,200
Jun 10	Cheque #3	700		3,500
Jun 30	Interest		5	3,505

FIGURE 2.2

If the deposit is correct, you will have to record it in the ledger account. For example, in figure 2.2, the bank has recorded interest of $5 in the account of HR Clothing on June 30. All the other cheques have been recorded by the bank as well as by the company. Since the interest earned is correctly shown on the bank statement, it should also be recorded in the general ledger by debiting (increasing) cash and crediting (increasing) interest revenue.

Assume that HR Clothing's ledger balance is $3,500, and the bank statement for the month shows a balance of $3,505. The bank reconciliation for this item would look like this:

HR Clothing Bank Reconciliation June 30, 2011		
	Ledger	**Bank**
Balance as per records	$3,500	$3,505
Add: Unrecorded deposits		
Interest June 30	5	
Corrected balance	$3,505	$3,505

FIGURE 2.3

Notice that the adjusting amount is in the ledger column. This means that you must correct the general ledger balance with an adjusting journal entry. The entry is shown in figure 2.4.

JOURNAL			PAGE 1
Date	**Account Title and Explanation**	**Debit**	**Credit**
2011			
Jun 30	Cash	5	
	Interest Revenue		5
	Bank interest earned		

FIGURE 2.4

Unrecorded Charges From the Bank Statement

As with unrecorded deposits, there may be charges shown on the bank statement that are not yet recorded in the general ledger. Typical examples are the monthly bank charges or an annual fee for a safe deposit box. Such charges are legitimate and should be adjusted in the ledger.

Consider the following:

As reflected in figure 2.5, HR Clothing has a cash ledger balance of $3,500. The bank statement reflects a balance of $3,450. All cheques are recorded in both the bank statement and the general ledger. Upon comparison, the bookkeeper of the company notices that the bank recorded bank charges of $50 on the last day of the month. This change must be updated in the general ledger.

GENERAL LEDGER					
Account: Cash				**GL. No.**	**101**
Date	**Description**	**Debit**	**Credit**	**Balance**	
2011					
Jun 1	Opening Balance			5,000	DR
Jun 2	Cheque #1		300	4,700	DR
Jun 3	Cheque #2		500	4,200	DR
Jun 10	Cheque #3		700	3,500	DR

Bank Statement				June 1 - June 30, 2011
Date	**Description**	**Withdrawal**	**Deposit**	**Balance**
Jun 1	Opening Balance			5,000
Jun 2	Cheque #1	300		4,700
Jun 3	Cheque #2	500		4,200
Jun 10	Cheque #3	700		3,500
Jun 30	Bank Charges	50		3,450

FIGURE 2.5

The bank reconciliation for this item would look like this:

HR Clothing Bank Reconciliation June 30, 2011		
	Ledger	**Bank**
Balance as per records	$3,500	$3,450
Less: Unrecorded charges		
Bank Charges June 30	(50)	
Corrected balance	$3,450	$3,450

FIGURE 2.6

As with the unrecorded deposit shown previously, the adjustment is shown in the general ledger column, so it must be updated with a journal entry as shown in figure 2.7.

The journal entry is recorded by debiting (increasing) bank charge expense and crediting (decreasing) cash (an asset).

JOURNAL			PAGE 1
Date	**Account Title and Explanation**	**Debit**	**Credit**
2011			
Jun 30	Bank Charge Expense	50	
	Cash		50
	Bank service charges		

FIGURE 2.7

Another type of bank charge can occur as a result of **non-sufficient funds (NSF)** cheques. These are usually payments made to the company by a customer who does not have sufficient funds in their bank account to cover the amount of the cheque. For example, HR Clothing receives a $500 cheque from a customer and deposits the cheque into the company bank account on June 17. However, the bank cannot successfully collect the $500 from the customer's account because the customer does not have enough money in his account to support this withdrawal. The bank would return the cheque to the company and charge an additional service fee.

GENERAL LEDGER					
Account: Cash				GL. No.	101
Date	**Description**	**Debit**	**Credit**	**Balance**	
2011					
Jun 1	Opening Balance			5,000	DR
Jun 2	Cheque #1		300	4,700	DR
Jun 3	Cheque #2		500	4,200	DR
Jun 10	Cheque #3		700	3,500	DR
Jun 17	Deposit	500		4,000	DR

Bank Statement				June 1 - June 30, 2011	
Date	Description	Withdrawal	Deposit	Balance	
Jun 1	Opening Balance			5,000	
Jun 2	Cheque #1	300		4,700	
Jun 3	Cheque #2	500		4,200	
Jun 10	Cheque #3	700		3,500	
Jun 17	Deposit		500	4,000	
Jun 19	NSF Cheque	500		3,500	
Jun 19	NSF Charge	10		3,490	

FIGURE 2.8

The bank reconciliation would look like this:

HR Clothing Bank Reconciliation June 30, 2011		
	Ledger	Bank
Balance as per records	$4,000	$3,490
Less: **NSF cheque**	(500)	
Charges for NSF cheque	(10)	
Corrected balance	$3,490	$3,490

FIGURE 2.9

This adjustment should also be recorded in the journal and updated in the ledger. Since an NSF cheque represents the amount of cash receipts unsuccessfully collected, this amount should be added back to the company's accounts receivable account. In addition, the bank charge associated with the NSF cheque should also be recorded. The journal entries are shown in figure 2.10:

JOURNAL			PAGE 1
Date	Account Title and Explanation	Debit	Credit
2011			
Jun 30	Accounts Receivable	500	
	Cash		500
	NSF cheque returned by bank		
Jun 30	Bank Charge Expense	10	
	Cash		10
	Bank charge for NSF cheque		

FIGURE 2.10

IN THE REAL WORLD

Non-sufficient funds (NSF) cheques are commonly known as bad cheques or bounced cheques in the real world. In our example, it is assumed that non-sufficient funds (NSF) cheques occur because the issuer of the cheque does not have enough money in their own bank account to support the cheque. However, NSF cheques can result from a variety of reasons, including the following:

1. The issuer purposely cancels the cheque
2. The account is frozen
3. The account does not exist (i.e. the issuing party engaged in a fraudulent act)
4. The account is under investigation

Outstanding Deposits

An outstanding deposit is one that has been recorded in the company's general ledger but not shown on the bank statement. These are also referred to as **deposits in transit**. This can occur when the company makes a deposit in the bank (perhaps using the night deposit box) on the last day of the month, but the bank does not record the deposit until the following business day in the next month. The bank statement and the company's ledger account may appear as shown in figure 2.11.

GENERAL LEDGER

Account: Cash				GL. No.	101	
Date	Description	Debit	Credit	Balance		
2011						
Jun 1	Opening Balance			5,000	DR	
Jun 2	Cheque #1		300	4,700	DR	
Jun 3	Cheque #2		500	4,200	DR	
Jun 10	Cheque #3		700	3,500	DR	
Jun 30	Deposit	1,000		4,500	DR	

Bank Statement			June 1 - June 30, 2011		
Date	Description	Withdrawal	Deposit	Balance	
Jun 1	Opening Balance			5,000	
Jun 2	Cheque #1	300		4,700	
Jun 3	Cheque #2	500		4,200	
Jun 10	Cheque #3	700		3,500	

FIGURE 2.11

The balance on the bank statement is $3,500. The balance in the general ledger is $4,500. There was a deposit of $1,000 on June 30 that was not recorded by the bank. Since the balance is missing from the bank statement, it should be added to the bank balance as shown in figure 2.12.

HR Clothing Bank Reconciliation June 30, 2011		
	Ledger	**Bank**
Balance as per records	$4,500	$3,500
Add: **Outstanding deposit June 30**		**1,000**
Corrected balance	$4,500	$4,500

FIGURE 2.12

Notice that the corrected balances are the same for the bank and the ledger columns. As the entry is only in the bank account column of the bank reconciliation worksheet, there is no adjustment required in the ledger. The outstanding deposit is a timing difference; it should appear on the bank statement which includes the following business day (in July).

Outstanding Cheques

The next reconciling item to consider is *outstanding cheques*. An outstanding cheque (issued by the company) is one that has been recorded in the general ledger, but has not been recorded on the bank statement. This can happen because after the company records the cheque, it is mailed to the supplier. The supplier then records it in their books, prepares the deposit and takes it to the bank. The process can take several days, so the cheque mailed on June 29 may not appear on the bank statement until July 2 or 3.

Consider the following:

Three cheques have been recorded in the ledger between June 28 and 30, as reflected in figure 2.13. None of these cheques have been processed by the bank by June 30. The cheques are therefore outstanding.

To reconcile the ledger account with the bank statement, we must treat the cheques as if the transaction had been completed by the bank (i.e. deduct the amounts from the bank record).

GENERAL LEDGER

Account: Cash   GL. No. 101

Date	Description	Debit	Credit	Balance	
2011					
Jun 1	Opening Balance			5,000	DR
Jun 2	Cheque #1		300	4,700	DR
Jun 3	Cheque #2		500	4,200	DR
Jun 10	Cheque #3		700	3,500	DR
Jun 15	Deposit	1,000		4,500	DR
Jun 28	Cheque #4		400	4,100	DR
Jun 29	Cheque #5		800	3,300	DR
Jun 30	Cheque #6		700	2,600	DR

Bank Statement   **June 1 - June 30, 2011**

Date	Description	Withdrawal	Deposit	Balance
Jun 1	Opening Balance			5,000
Jun 2	Cheque #1	300		4,700
Jun 3	Cheque #2	500		4,200
Jun 10	Cheque #3	700		3,500
Jun 15	Deposit		1,000	4,500

FIGURE 2.13

The bank reconciliation for outstanding cheques would look as follows:

HR Clothing Bank Reconciliation June 30, 2011		
	Ledger	**Bank**
Balance as per records	$2,600	$4,500
Less: **Outstanding cheques**		
Cheque #4 June 28		(400)
Cheque #5 June 29		(800)
Cheque #6 June 30		(700)
Corrected balance	$2,600	$2,600

FIGURE 2.14

No adjustment is required in the ledger account because the cheques are correctly recorded in the general ledger but have not been cashed by the bank. The bank will eventually include them on the bank statement.

Bank Errors

Although rare, it is possible that banks will make errors, such as charging the company incorrectly with a cheque belonging to another company. In that case, the company's ledger balance is correct and the bank must correct the error.

Consider the following as shown in figure 2.15.

When the bookkeeper receives the bank statement and compares it with the company records, she notices that the bank processed a cheque for $800 on June 8, but the company has no knowledge of the cheque.

At that point, the bookkeeper calls the bank and discovers that the cheque belongs to another bank client.

GENERAL LEDGER						
Account: Cash					**GL. No.**	**101**
Date	**Description**		**Debit**	**Credit**	**Balance**	
2011						
Jun 1	Opening Balance				5,000	DR
Jun 2	Cheque #1			300	4,700	DR
Jun 3	Cheque #2			500	4,200	DR
Jun 10	Cheque #3			700	3,500	DR

Bank Statement		**June 1 - June 30, 2011**		
Date	**Description**	**Withdrawal**	**Deposit**	**Balance**
Jun 1	Opening Balance			5,000
Jun 2	Cheque #1	300		4,700
Jun 3	Cheque #2	500		4,200
Jun 8	Cheque #108	800		3,400
Jun 10	Cheque #3	700		2,700

FIGURE 2.15

The bank reconciliation for this item looks like this:

HR Clothing Bank Reconciliation June 30, 2011		
	Ledger	**Bank**
Balance as per records	$3,500	$2,700
Add: **Bank Error**, cheque incorrectly charged to account June 8		800
Corrected balance	$3,500	$3,500

FIGURE 2.16

Since the adjustment is in the bank column, it does not need to be adjusted in the company's books. The amount is an error, not a timing difference, and the bank must correct the error by depositing funds back into the company's account. The company needs to follow up to ensure that the bank corrects the error.

An incorrect deposit may also appear on the bank statement. In that case, the bank reconciliation would reflect a deduction from the bank balance because it is overstated as a result of the deposit. The company would follow up to ensure that the amount was deducted from its bank account.

Recording Errors

It is possible for bookkeepers to make errors. These errors would appear in the company's records.

Consider this situation as shown in figure 2.17:

Upon investigating the difference between the bank statement and the ledger, the bookkeeper discovers that a cheque recorded as $950 in the ledger should have been recorded as $590.

The bank cashed the correct amount of the cheque ($590). The bank reconciliation for this item looks like this:

GENERAL LEDGER						
Account: Cash					**GL. No.**	**101**
Date	**Description**	**Debit**	**Credit**	**Balance**		
2011						
Jun 1	Opening Balance			5,000	DR	
Jun 2	Cheque #1		300	4,700	DR	
Jun 3	Cheque #2		950	3,750	DR	
Jun 10	Cheque #3		700	3,050	DR	

Bank Statement				June 1 - June 30, 2011
Date	**Description**	**Withdrawal**	**Deposit**	**Balance**
Jun 1	Opening Balance			5,000
Jun 2	Cheque #1	300		4,700
Jun 3	Cheque #2	590		4,110
Jun 10	Cheque #3	700		3,410

FIGURE 2.17

In this situation, more was deducted from the general ledger than was on the cheque. To correct this error, the bookkeeper will have to add back to the general ledger the difference between what was recorded and the actual amount deducted by the bank. This amounts to $360 ($950 - $590). The bank reconciliation would appear as shown in figure 2.18.

HR Clothing Bank Reconciliation June 30, 2011		
	Ledger	**Bank**
Balance as per records	$3,050	$3,410
Recording error		
Add: **Error on cheque #2**	360	
Corrected balance	$3,410	$3,410

FIGURE 2.18

Because the correcting entry is in the ledger column, an adjusting entry must be recorded in the journal. Assuming the original cheque was written to purchase inventory, the journal entry to correct the ledger is shown in figure 2.19.

JOURNAL				PAGE 1
Date	**Account Title and Explanation**		**Debit**	**Credit**
2011				
Jun 30	Cash		360	
	Inventory			360
	Correct error in ledger			

FIGURE 2.19

For an error that is made by the bookkeeper, the bookkeeper must go back into the records to determine what the original entry was for. This will determine which account will be used to offset the cash account. In our example, the payment was for inventory. If the payment was to pay off an account, use accounts payable; payment for this month's rent, use rent expense; to pay a telephone bill, use telephone expense, etc.

As with the previous examples, any discrepancy between the bank statement and the ledger record should be examined and then corrected with the appropriate entries.

A CLOSER LOOK

In a computerized accounting systems, errors in the ledger, such as the one described in figure 2.19, are corrected using two entries instead of one. The first entry would be a $950 debit to cash and a $950 credit to inventory. This entry reverses the original incorrect entry. The second entry would be a $590 debit to inventory and a $590 credit to cash to record the correct amount of the June 3rd cheque. The net result is the same as the single entry in the amount of $360 shown above. Manual accounting systems will not use this method because it requires more entries and provides more room for error.

Incorrect amounts in the ledger can be more or less than the amounts shown on the bank statement. Each error must be analyzed carefully for appropriate adjustments.

Bank Reconciliation Summary

Once all the items on a bank statement and the ledger have been matched up, only a few items should remain that need to be reconciled. The table below summarizes how items will be treated on a bank reconciliation.

Add to Bank Balance	Subtract from Bank Balance
• Outstanding deposits • Bank error	• Outstanding cheques • Bank error
Add to Ledger Balance*	**Subtract from Ledger Balance***
• Interest earned • Direct deposit from customer • Receipts through EFT • Bookkeeper error	• Loan interest charges • Repayment of bank loan • Bank service charges • Payments through EFT • NSF cheques • Bookkeeper error

*Must also create a journal entry to update the ledger balance.

FIGURE 2.20

To illustrate a complete bank reconciliation with journal entries, examine the following bank statement, ledger and journal entries for HR Clothing for the month of October 2011.

Before comparing the new items, it is always important to consider the outstanding items from the last period. We need to ensure these items have been cleared.

From the September bank reconciliation, HR Clothing had the following outstanding items:

Outstanding Deposit	✓	$2,200
Outstanding Cheque #57	✓	$350
Outstanding Cheque #59	✓	$480

GENERAL LEDGER

Account: Cash   GL. No. 101

Date	Description	Debit	Credit	Balance	
2011					
Oct 1	Opening Balance			6,300	DR
Oct 2	Cheque #62		✓ 140	6,160	DR
Oct 4	Deposit M. Smith	✓ 200		6,360	DR
Oct 7	Cheque #63		570	5,790	DR
Oct 15	Cheque #64		820	4,970	DR
Oct 17	Deposit	✓ 1,200		6,170	DR
Oct 21	Cheque #65		✓ 540	5,630	DR
Oct 25	Cheque #66		320	5,310	DR
Oct 29	Cheque #67		410	4,900	DR
Oct 31	Deposit	900		5,800	DR

Bank Statement			October 1 - October 31, 2011	
Date	**Description**	**Withdrawal**	**Deposit**	**Balance**
Oct 1	Opening Balance			4,930
Oct 1	EFT Rent	1,300		3,630
Oct 2	Deposit		✓ 2,200	5,830
Oct 4	Cheque #57	✓ 350		5,480
Oct 5	Deposit		✓ 200	5,680
Oct 6	NSF Cheque	200		5,480
Oct 6	NFS Fee	15		5,465
Oct 8	Cheque #62	✓ 140		5,325
Oct 10	Cheque #59	✓ 480		4,845
Oct 15	EFT Deposit		300	5,145
Oct 18	Deposit		✓ 1,200	6,345
Oct 23	Cheque #63	750		5,595
Oct 25	Cheque #65	✓ 540		5,055
Oct 31	Service Charge	10		5,045

Cheque #63 was for advertising and was cashed for the correct amount by the bank
The NSF cheque was from a customer as payment of their account
The EFT deposit was a customer paying their account

FIGURE 2.21

The green check marks indicate that the item on the bank statement matches an item from the ledger or September's bank reconciliation. Only the items without a check mark will need to be included on the bank reconciliation for October.

HR Clothing Bank Reconciliation October 31, 2011		
	Ledger	**Bank**
Balance as per records	$5,800	$5,045
Add: Outstanding Deposit		900
Less: Outstanding Cheques		
Cheque #64		(820)
Cheque #66		(320)
Cheque #67		(410)
Add: EFT Deposit	300	
Less: EFT Rent	(1,300)	
NSF Cheque	(200)	
NSF Fee	(15)	
Service Charge	(10)	
Error on Cheque #63	(180)	
Corrected balance	$4,395	$4,395

FIGURE 2.22

Once the bank is reconciled to the ledger, all items that increase or decrease the ledger balance must be recorded in the journal.

JOURNAL			PAGE 1
Date	Account Title and Explanation	Debit	Credit
2011			
Oct 31	Cash	300	
	Accounts Receivable		300
	Collection from customer		
Oct 31	Rent Expense	1,300	
	Cash		1,300
	Payment for rent		
Oct 31	Accounts Receivable	200	
	Cash		200
	NSF cheque from customer		
Oct 31	Bank Charge Expense	25	
	Cash		25
	NFS fee and service charge		
Oct 31	Advertising Expense	180	
	Cash		180
	Correct error on cheque		

FIGURE 2.23

Petty Cash

At times, a business may require small amounts of cash to pay for petty (small) expenses such as parking, postage stamps and courier fees. Instead of issuing a cheque each time, the business will set up a petty cash fund to pay for these small amounts in cash.

Petty cash is usually operated on what is known as an *imprest system*. An imprest system for petty cash ensures that spending is limited to the amount available in petty cash fund. For example, if a petty cash fund starts with $100, that is the maximum amount that can be spent. When the amount spent approaches the $100 limit, the petty cash fund will be replenished up to $100.

Setting Up a Petty Cash Fund

1. **Designate one individual as the petty cash custodian.** There are many ways in which petty cash can be mishandled. Having one person responsible for the fund increases transparency and accountability. The petty cash custodian ensures that petty cash is properly safeguarded and disbursed for legitimate reasons and that an accurate record is maintained for all activities related to the fund.

2. **Establish the amount of the fund.** The petty cash custodian needs to determine the amount of the fund as well as the frequency with which it is replenished.

3. **Record the initial petty cash transaction.** The establishment of a petty cash fund requires one initial transaction. Here is the journal entry:

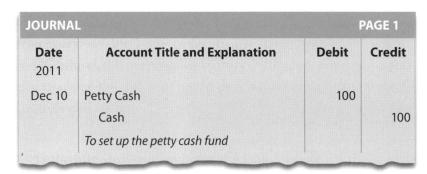

FIGURE 2.24

4. **Require users of petty cash to provide receipts.** Any employee who requires petty cash should provide a receipt from the supplier indicating the amount of money spent. The petty cash custodian will require the person to sign the receipt, indicating that the person has been reimbursed. Figure 2.25 shows a petty cash receipt.

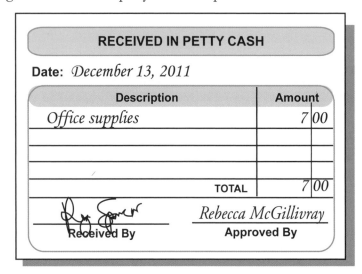

FIGURE 2.25

5. **Provide a summary of petty cash.** At the end of the period, which in this example is one week, the petty cash custodian prepares a summary that lists the details of the fund before it is reimbursed. The summary sheet is shown in figure 2.26.

The petty cash summary should include a list of all the items, in groups, paid with the petty cash fund.

Petty Cash Summary Sheet

Period: Dec. 10 - Dec. 17

Opening Balance		$100.00
Parking		
Dec. 10	$10.00	
Dec. 12	6.00	
Dec. 14	5.00	$21.00
Freight in		
Dec. 10	$18.00	
Dec. 11	6.00	$24.00
Office Supplies		
Dec. 13	$ 7.00	
Dec. 16	13.00	$20.00
Gasoline		
Dec. 14	$18.00	$18.00
Total Disbursements		**$83.00**
Cash over and short	$2.00	
Total to be reimbursed to Petty Cash		**$85.00**

Opening balance less disbursements

FIGURE 2.26

Both subtotals and a grand total should be calculated. In this example the grand total comes to $83. Subtracting $83 from the original balance of $100, which is also known as the float, gives us an amount of $17. This should be the remaining balance in the petty cash box.

6. **Reconcile any overage or shortage.** The petty cash custodian must take care of any amounts short or over in the petty cash box. This is done by making additions or subtractions to the account called *cash over and short*. In our current example, there was only $15 in the petty cash box, meaning there was a $2 shortage. Such discrepancies can result from a miscount of coins or an overpayment during the period. The total disbursements recorded, along with any cash short or over, constitute the total amount to be reimbursed to petty cash to restore it to its float level. In this case, the amount is $85.

7. **Summary slip is presented to a supervisor.** The petty cash custodian presents her supervisor with a summary slip, together with all supporting vouchers. After reviewing these documents, the supervisor provides the petty cash custodian with a cheque to reimburse the petty cash fund. The vouchers are stamped "paid" so that they cannot be reused.

8. **Reimburse the petty cash fund.** The petty cash custodian cashes the cheque (in this example the cheque is for $85) and replenishes the fund to its original float amount ($100).

Posting Petty Cash to the General Ledger

We have examined the steps that an organization must take when establishing a petty cash fund. Now let us take a closer look at how this process affects the organization's general ledger.

We have already described the transaction that occurs when the petty cash fund is initially established. Cash is credited and petty cash is debited — both for the same amounts, which in our example was $100. Until now, all the activity has been in the physical petty cash box itself, with

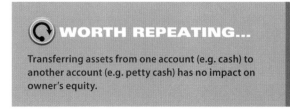

WORTH REPEATING...

Transferring assets from one account (e.g. cash) to another account (e.g. petty cash) has no impact on owner's equity.

no transactions affecting the ledger. When it is time to replenish the fund, we need to increase the cash to $100 and allocate the amounts used to the appropriate expense accounts.

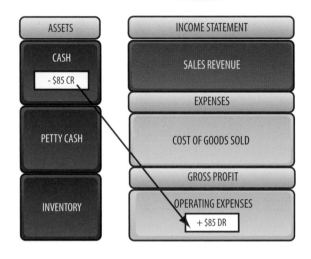

No change is made in the amount of the petty cash ledger account when the reimbursement cheque is issued, and the reimbursed cash is placed in the petty cash box. You may think that the transaction should be recorded by debiting expenses and crediting petty cash, followed by a debit to petty cash and a credit to cash. However, in practice, when the bookkeeper records the cheque, there is *no change to the petty cash account*. The cheque is recorded with a debit to various expenses (parking, freight-in, office supplies, gasoline, cash over and short), and a credit to cash in the amount of $85.

JOURNAL			PAGE 1
Date	**Account Title and Explanation**	**Debit**	**Credit**
2011			
Dec 17	Parking Expense	21	
	Freight-in Expense	24	
	Office Supplies Expense	20	
	Gasoline Expense	18	
	Cash Over and Short	2	
	Cash		85
	Replenish the petty cash fund		

FIGURE 2.27

The cash over and short account behaves like an expense account when there is a shortage. It will be debited in the journal entry. If there is an overage, the cash over and short account behaves like a revenue account. It will be credited in the journal entry.

It is important to note that the *only* time the petty cash account in the ledger is debited or credited is when the account is established or when the float amount is increased or decreased.

Assume that on December 31, the manager decided to increase the petty cash fund to $150. The journal entry to record the $50 increase would be as follows:

JOURNAL			PAGE 1
Date	**Account Title and Explanation**	**Debit**	**Credit**
2011			
Dec 31	Petty Cash	50	
	Cash		50
	Increase the petty cash fund		

FIGURE 2.28

When the petty cash fund is increased, the petty cash account should be debited (increased) and the cash account should be credited (decreased).

Petty cash can also increase at the same time it is replenished. If we combine the transactions from figure 2.27 and 2.28, petty cash would be debited $50 along with the expenses. Cash would then be credited by $135 to replenish and increase the petty cash fund.

A spreadsheet may be maintained listing the various expenses so that each month the general ledger can be updated with the correct allocation of expenses. Here is an example:

HR Clothing
Petty Cash Expenses Paid
July 2011

Description	Receipt #	Amount	Office	Travel	Meals	Marketing
Photo Developing	1	8.07				8.07
Taxis	2	65.00		65.00		
Meals	3	33.00			33.00	
Batteries	4	11.00				11.00
Photocopying - brochures	5	23.32				23.32
Photocopying - general	6	3.05	3.05			
Parking	7	1.87		1.87		
Parking	8	10.26		10.26		
Parking	9	3.00		3.00		
Parking	10	4.00		4.00		
Parking	11	6.50		6.50		
Parking	12	7.00		7.00		
Parking	13	6.00		6.00		
Parking	14	3.94		3.94		
Parking	15	1.00		1.00		
Gas	16	10.00		10.00		
Meals	17	8.10		8.10		
Travel	18	49.01	49.01			
TOTALS		**$254.12**	**$52.06**	**$126.67**	**$33.00**	**$42.39**

Cash will be credited with this amount.

= $254.12
Each of these amounts will be debited to the respective GL expense accounts.

FIGURE 2.29

Petty Cash Controls

Using petty cash funds can be a convenient way to purchase small items. However, the funds also provide opportunities for abuse. It is therefore important to regulate the use of the petty cash fund to ensure that it is not mishandled. Here are four tips to ensure that petty cash is used appropriately:

1. Establish guidelines regarding when and how petty cash may be available.
2. Consistently maintain documentation regarding the use of petty cash.

3. Review the rules regularly with employees.

4. Ensure that petty cash is controlled by one person – the petty cash custodian.

1. **Establish guidelines.** The first step in ensuring that your petty cash is used properly is to draw up a list of items that can be purchased with petty cash. Determine what purchases may be made with purchase orders, and then make a list of other types of regular purchases. The fund should be reserved strictly for small ("petty") expenses and not for items such as long-term assets or inventory, or for paying accounts payable and independent contractors.

2. **Maintain documentation.** It is difficult to keep accurate records unless you have a uniform documentation system. Establish an easy-to-use system and follow it consistently. The easiest way to do this is by keeping track of all receipts, whether they are register receipts or written invoices. Each receipt should have the date of purchase, the name of the vendor, a list of the items or services purchased, the price of each item and the total cost. Accurate recordkeeping also ensures that

- the person who made the purchase signs the receipt.

- all receipts are filed correctly so that they can be checked to determine if there are any discrepancies.

3. **Review the rules with employees.** If the regulations are not well-known, abuse of the petty cash fund becomes easier. Keep everyone up-to-date and do not allow exceptions to the rules.

4. **Ensure that petty cash is controlled by one person – the petty cash custodian.** The appointment of one person to administer and be exclusively responsible for the fund limits the opportunities for mismanagement.

SUMMARY OF PETTY CASH CONTROLS	
Control	**Explanation**
Specific guidelines	Determine what purchases can be made with purchase orders. High value items and regular types of purchases should **never** be made through the petty cash fund. The fund should be strictly reserved for small ("petty") expenses.
Documentation	Track all receipts. Ensure each receipt has the date of purchase, name of company or vendor, list of items or services purchased and total cost. The receipts should be signed by the purchaser and filed correctly.
Rules	Establish a clear and precise method for recording petty cash. Designate a petty cash clerk who prepares petty cash reports each month.
Accountability	Appoint one person as sole petty cash administrator.

FIGURE 2.30

Ethics and Cash Control Guidelines

Cash is very important to a business and it can be tempting for employees to try and misuse cash. Therefore, it is important to have rules for dealing with cash. Three rules are shown below and will be discussed in detail.

- Record cash immediately when it is received
- Protect cash when it is on the premises
- Remove cash from the premises as soon as possible

Record Cash Immediately when it is Received

After the receipt of cash is recorded, its movement through an organization should be tracked and its removal detected and noted.

The method of recording cash depends on the size of the business and the systems used. For a small business, a simple book of pre-numbered receipts will suffice. When the customer offers cash for merchandise, a paper receipt is prepared in duplicate (one copy for the customer, and the other copy retained as a permanent record of the receipt of cash). Proper controls include the recording of the receipts. Receipts are issued in numerical order and are accounted for on a regular basis by a responsible staff member. The amounts shown on the receipts are totaled and compared with the cash on hand on a daily basis.

An improvement to preparing receipts by hand is to use a cash register. The cash register prepares two copies of the receipt, similar to handwritten receipts – one copy being maintained in the cash register itself and the second copy provided to the customer. As with handwritten receipts, individual sales amounts are added and compared to the amount of cash on hand.

For larger companies, the cash register is replaced with a point-of-sale (POS) computer terminal. The terminal connects directly with the company's accounting system, but performs the same functions as a handwritten receipt. Specifically, a receipt is given to the customer and a record is maintained in the system. The sales are totaled and compared with the cash on hand on a regular basis.

All of the above systems require the participation of the customer. When the customer is handed the receipt, he or she is expected to examine the receipt to ensure that it reflects the exact amount of cash paid. For instance, if the amount on the receipt is less than the actual amount on paid, the customer will complain and a correction will be made, ensuring that the receipt for the correct amount is recorded.

The second feature of these systems is a regular summing-up of the sales amounts and comparison of the total with the cash on hand. Cash shortages and overages are dealt with by management. Cash should be deposited intact into a bank account. The total amount of sales should be the amount deposited into the bank, without any deductions being made.

Protect Cash when it is on the Premises

Having cash present on the premises of a business may be a temptation to a dishonest employee. It therefore becomes necessary to protect surplus amounts of cash. When the money reaches a predetermined amount, the overage is placed in a safe area (i.e. a locked office or backroom). In addition, the business may make use of a safe to store the cash until it is deposited in a bank. The combination or key to the safe should only be made available to a limited number of people.

As described previously, cash receipts should be deposited intact. Deposits may be made more than once a day to minimize the amount of cash on the premises. If deposits are to be made after hours, the company can make use of the bank's night deposit box.

For larger companies that have substantial amounts of cash on hand, security guards may be employed to physically protect the premises. Similarly, security firms may be employed when moving large amounts of cash from the company's premises to the bank.

Cheques received, which may be treated like cash, should be stamped "for deposit only" on the back to discourage fraudulent cashing of the cheque.

Remove Cash from the Premises as soon as Possible

Since cash is portable and highly vulnerable to theft, a company should retain minimal cash on site by making regular bank deposits.

In addition, the establishment of a properly controlled bank account is required to keep cash on the premises to a minimum. As all cash receipts are deposited in the bank, all payments are made with cheques, thus removing the need to keep a large amount of cash on the premises. For the few expenses that must be paid in cash, a small amount can be kept as petty cash.

The above information covers only the minimal controls required for internal control over cash. Figure 2.31 provides a sample of detailed controls over cash, some of which were discussed in this chapter.

Control	Explanation
Petty cash custodian	Custodian is responsible for controlling cash.
Use pre-numbered receipts	Review numbers used, accounting for the numerical sequence on a regular basis by a responsible official. Missing receipts can be easily detected.
Stamp "for deposit only"	If cheques and money orders are stamped "for deposit only" (preferably with the bank account number), they cannot be cashed or deposited to another company's bank account.
Count cash	Count cash received and balance with total receipts; deposit daily. Ensures the correct amount is deposited.
Use safe or vault	Keep undeposited cash receipts in a safe place to protect cash.
Bank reconciliation	Locates fraudulent cheques and missing deposits.
Issue receipts	Issuing receipts for *all* sales and other cash received is the key to controlling cash.
Pay by cheque	Pay all disbursements by cheque to avoid keeping cash on hand.
No "cash"	Payee's name on cheque is required, as opposed to cheques written to "cash", for adequate documentation of payments.
Cheque writing	Making two people responsible for signing cheques discourages the writing of fraudulent cheques.
Pay on original documents	Prepare cheques only on presentation of original, approved documents - photocopies not allowed.
Compare invoices	Compare invoices with quotes and contracts before payment - avoids paying inflated/incorrect invoices.
No pre-signed cheques	A supply of pre-signed cheques can be misused.
Stamp invoices "paid"	Invoices cannot be presented a second time for payment.
Bank statement security	Send bank statements directly to the person who prepares bank reconciliations so that statements cannot be tampered with before reconciliation is prepared.

FIGURE 2.31

Short-Term Investments

Businesses sometimes find themselves in the position of having surplus cash on hand. One method of putting this cash to good use would be to reinvest it in the business. It could be used, for example, to upgrade equipment, expand marketing efforts, hire new employees or even buy other corporations. An alternative would be to invest the money outside the company. Instead of investing the cash in a bank account bearing low interest, forward-looking business managers should choose investment options that will provide a good return, even in the short term.

A short-term investment matures within one year. These investments can take various forms, such as loans to individuals, money market instruments and Treasury bills (also known as *T-bills*).

IFRS and GAAP classify investments that will be kept for a short period of time as Held-for-Trading (HFT). The classification differentiates it from other types of investments, and must be

A CLOSER LOOK

In addition to Held-for-Trade investments, IFRS will also classify investments as Held-to-Maturity (HTM) or Available for Sale (AFS). Investments held to maturity can include bonds that will be held until they are due. Available for sale investments can include shares of a corporation that will be held for a long period of time, or any other investments that does not fall into the other categories.

accounted for in a certain manner. Because of the short-term nature of this investment, any gains or losses will be recorded in the income statement in the period they are earned or incurred. Details for this will be shown in the following sections.

Besides held-for-trading investments, there are other classifications that are used for investments. The classifications are listed below, although only held-for-trading investments will be discussed in this textbook.

1. **Held to maturity:**

    These investments have a maturity date with set payments on specific dates. The management should intend to hold the investments to their maturity date.

2. **Held for trading:**

    The company does not plan to hold the investment beyond the short term (12 months) and intends the investment to be sold for the purpose of making a profit during this period.

3. **Available for sale:**

    These are any investments which are not classified as loans, held to maturity investments, or held for trading investments. The management may or may not intend to sell the investment in the short term or is uncertain when it will be sold. These investments earn interest or dividends while they are held and yield a realized gain or loss when they are sold.

Short-Term Investments and the Balance Sheet

We have already examined the role of the balance sheet in terms of the liquidity of assets. Cash is at the top of the order. A short-term investment is not cash, but is expected to be converted into cash within 12 months. For that reason, short-term investments rank immediately after cash in terms of liquidity.

Types of Short-Term Investments

As with the investment market in general, short-term investments usually take the form of either **debt** or **equity**. In other words, a business can try to secure a return in the short term by either lending money to someone else (debt) or buying an ownership stake in another organization (equity). Both forms of short-term investments will be examined thoroughly in this chapter.

FIGURE 2.32

Debt Investments

The Nature of Debt Investments

When a company invests its money in the form of debt, it lends money to a person or business in exchange for interest payments in addition to the return of principal. The terms of the transaction are established in advance, so that both parties to the loan agree upon the amount of the initial loan, the schedule of payments to be made, the interest rate to be charged and the length or term of the loan.

In general, two types of debt investment options are available to a business or organization: traditional loans and bonds.

Traditional Loans and How they are Recorded

Traditional loans represent the most basic form of debt investment and involve financial transactions that are familiar to most people. Just as individuals lend each other money and charge interest on the loan, businesses can lend money to either individuals or other businesses for the purpose of gaining a return on investment.

Our first example will be used to illustrate how to record a short-term debt investment for accounting purposes.

Assume that a business lends $10,000 (the principal) to another business, charging an interest rate of 5% per annum with a repayment term of one year. We

WORTH REPEATING...

Debt involves lending money to someone else in return for interest.

Equity involves investing in another organization in the form of ownership, with the expectation that its value will increase over time while profits are shared in the form of dividends.

first record the initial loan of $10,000 by showing a decrease in cash (CR) and an increase in the short-term investment account (DR).

The journal entry and the accounting map are shown in figure 2.33.

Date	Account Title and Explanation	Debit	Credit
	Short-Term Investment - Loan	10,000	
	Cash		10,000
	Record loan of $10,000		

FIGURE 2.33

Interest Earned

How much money will the business lending the money (the lender) earn on this investment? Since it is a debt investment, which receives interest on a fixed date, the answer is generally known even before the first payment is received. As long as the business that is borrowing the money (the borrower) can meet its required payments, the lender will earn $500, which is 5% interest on the loan. If the loan payments proceed as planned, the $500 in interest revenue needs to be recorded in the lender's financial statements.

The journal entry is: debit cash for $500 and credit interest revenue for $500.

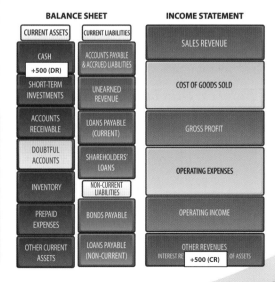

Date	Account Title and Explanation	Debit	Credit
	Cash	500	
	Interest Revenue		500
	Record interest earned on short-term investment		

FIGURE 2.34

It is important to note that the interest earned from the loan is treated as interest revenue in the other revenue section of the income statement.

In our current example, recording the interest earned as general revenue would be misleading. The revenue was not earned as a result of business operations, such as selling goods or services, but by investing surplus cash on hand. Investment decisions are independent of the day-to-day operations of the company and need to be treated as such in the financial statements.

Repayment at Maturity

To complete the process, the repayment of the principal must be recorded. This is done by debiting cash and crediting short-term investments.

BALANCE SHEET

JOURNAL				
Date	**Account Title and Explanation**		**Debit**	**Credit**
	Cash		10,000	
	Short-Term Investment - Loan			10,000
	Record collection of loan principal			

FIGURE 2.35

We have now completed the steps necessary to record the transactions involved in a traditional loan, including the payment of interest and repayment of the principal. In the next section, we will examine the corresponding steps involved in another type of debt investment: bonds.

Bond Purchases and How they are Recorded

Purchasing bonds involves the same basic principle as making traditional loans. Bonds are loans made to institutions, businesses and municipalities with the expectation that the principal will be repaid in full, in addition to the interest agreed upon in the terms of the bond.

A CLOSER LOOK

Let's examine the impact of erroneously recording the interest made from the loan as general revenue. What would this do to the state of the company's finances? In short, it would indicate an increase in revenues without any corresponding increase in the cost of goods sold. This would inflate gross profit and provide management with a distorted picture of the state of the business.

This could have an effect on decisions made throughout the business, such as marketing, pricing and market share. An inaccurate assessment of business finances resulting from overstated general revenues can therefore lead to bad business decisions. This is why it is so important to first record financial transactions accurately. In this case, that means treating income from short-term debt investments as interest revenue, but not general revenue (net sales).

The primary difference between bonds and traditional loans is that there is a market for bonds, whereas traditional loans are negotiated on an individual basis between specific parties. Bonds therefore represent a form of debt that can be readily bought and sold on a bond market. The value of the bond can change depending on its demand. Companies can choose to invest surplus cash in the bond market by buying bonds issued by an institution or resold on the market. A bond is purchased at an initial price and regular payments are received in the form of interest. The bond is held until its term is due or until it is resold on the market.

In addition, when a company hires a broker to make purchases on the bond market, the company pays a brokerage fee. For short-term investments that are classified as held-for-trading, these fees are expensed on the income statement immediately.

> ## A CLOSER LOOK
>
> As we start looking at securities such as bonds and shares, note that various industry terms are used to describe these kinds of assets.
>
> For example, they are often referred to as trade investments, since they are securities that are traded on a market. They are traded by brokers, which is why transactions involving these kinds of investments also come with brokerage fees attached.
>
> Marketable securities is another term used to describe these kinds of assets, especially those that are short term and very liquid in nature. Examples of marketable securities include Treasury Bills (T-Bills), commercial paper and money market instruments.

A business could find itself in the unusual position of having a large amount of surplus cash on hand (e.g. from a large cash sale) and decide to purchase shares or bonds for a short period of time. In this case, since the business is not regularly investing surplus cash in shares and bonds, the brokerage fees can be charged to an expense account.

For example, Big Office Supplies made a large cash sale of office furniture and found itself with surplus cash of $100,000. Rather than keeping the money in a bank account and earn interest at 3% per annum, the accountant invested the cash for a short period in bonds on January 1, 2010. The $100,000 bonds are from ABC Company and pay 5% interest every July 1 and January 1, and the company paid a brokerage fee of $500.

The journal entry to record this investment would be as follows:

JOURNAL			
Date	Account Title and Explanation	Debit	Credit
Jan 1	Short-term Investment – Bond	100,000	
	Brokerage Fees Expense	500	
	Cash		100,500
	Purchase of 100 ABC Company bonds at $1,000 per bond		

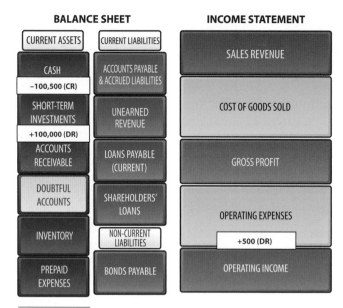

FIGURE 2.36

The purchase is represented by debiting (increasing) the short-term investment and brokerage fees expense accounts, while crediting (decreasing) the cash account. Since this investment is short-term, the brokerage fee must be considered an expense.

IN THE REAL WORLD

Assets on the balance sheet are organized according to their liquidity. That is why making the distinction between short-term and long-term assets is so important. This fact was demonstrated vividly through events that occurred on Wall Street during February, 2008.

Until that time, big investors were treating auction-rate securities as short-term assets on the balance sheet. Auction-rate securities are essentially long-term bonds. However, large financial institutions such as Goldman Sachs, Lehman Brothers and Merrill Lynch were holding monthly auctions that gave investors the opportunity to sell these bonds on an open market — an auction market.

The frequency of these auctions allowed financial institutions to sell these securities as highly liquid short-term assets that were almost as safe as cash. This all fell apart, however, when auctions started to fail and banks stopped supporting them. Investors were stuck with the bonds and unable to sell them in the short term as advertised. In other words they could no longer be classified as short term and had to be moved to the long-term assets section of the balance sheet.

In essence, auction-rate securities were an attempt to change long-term assets into short-term assets. It didn't work, and thousands of big investors were left having to adjust their balance sheets in the process.

A departure from our traditional loan example is the receipt of two interest payments during the course of the year, one of which occurs after the company's year-end of December 31.

Let us first deal with the interest payment received on July 1. The cash account is debited because cash is received. As with the traditional loan, the interest revenue account is credited.

JOURNAL

Date	Account Title and Explanation	Debit	Credit
Jul 1	Cash	2,500	
	Interest Revenue		2,500
	Interest earned from ABC Company bonds ($100,000 x 5% x 1/2)		

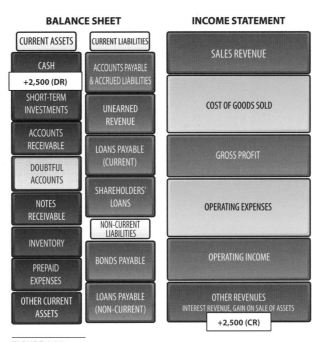

FIGURE 2.37

The interest payment due on January 1 of the next year poses a problem. It will be received after the year-end, but the interest due must be accounted for in the records at the time it is earned. This is done by accruing (recognizing) the interest earned on the bonds up to the year-end reporting date. We need to record it as interest receivable, which could be categorized under the "Other Current Assets" account.

We treat the expected interest payment by recording a debit (or increase) to the interest receivable account, and a credit (or increase) to the interest revenue account, resulting in an increase in assets on the balance sheet, as well as an increase in other revenues on the income statement. The corresponding journal entry is recorded as in figure 2.38:

JOURNAL

Date	Account Title and Explanation	Debit	Credit
Dec 31	Interest Receivable	2,500	
	Interest Revenue		2,500
	To accrue interest earned but not yet received on ABC Company bonds		

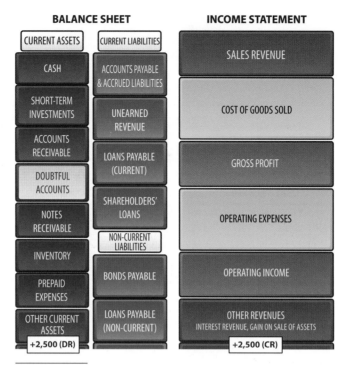

FIGURE 2.38

On January 1, the interest payment must be collected, which means that cash finally gets debited and interest receivable gets credited.

JOURNAL			
Date	**Account Title and Explanation**	**Debit**	**Credit**
Jan 1	Cash	2,500	
	Interest Receivable		2,500
	Received interest on ABC Company bonds		

FIGURE 2.39

Finally, after one year, the bond is sold. The proceeds are what the bonds can be sold for on the open market. If the proceeds are in excess of the cost, a gain will be recorded on the sale of investments as follows:

JOURNAL			
Date	**Account Title and Explanation**	**Debit**	**Credit**
Jan 1	Cash	102,000	
	Short-Term Investments – Bonds		100,000
	Gain on Sale of Investments		2,000
	Sale of ABC Co. bonds at a gain		

FIGURE 2.40

We have demonstrated how to record the purchase of a short-term bond on the financial statements. We now turn our attention to similar procedures involving short-term equity investments.

Equity Investments

The Nature of Equity Investments

Equity investment, as mentioned above, can be a form of short-term investment. Investing in equities is different from investing in bonds. Unlike bonds, which involve lending money in return for interest, equity investment involves buying ownership, usually in the form of shares, in a company.

A CLOSER LOOK

The other current assets account (sometimes called *miscellaneous* or *sundry assets*) on the balance sheet will be dealt with a number of times throughout this course, so we might as well get familiar with the term now.

The term "other" refers to an assortment, variety, or mixture of things. So, it logically flows that an other current assets account will include a mixture of assets. These are miscellaneous items that do not merit a separate account of their own on the balance sheet, but can be represented together as one account. It comes in handy when an accountant doesn't quite know where to place certain assets such as interest receivable, loans to employees, legal matters expected to be resolved favorably, refunds from suppliers, tax refunds, and so on.

Shares represent part ownership of that company and are bought and sold at prices listed on a stock exchange in the case of a publicly traded company. A shareholder can also receive profits in the form of dividends. The size and frequency of dividend payments often reflect the issuing company's profitability.

On the other hand, purchasing shares in a company also involves the risk that its profitability may be reduced leading to a reduction in its value. This could result in smaller dividend payments or no payments at all. Ultimately, owning shares in a company can be risky but has potentially greater rewards than owning a bond, which pays a fixed rate of interest.

To minimize the risks associated with equities, especially in the short term, investors often choose to buy shares in profitable companies that have a history

A vintage share certificate issued in 1913.

of making regular dividend payments and maintaining their share prices. These types of shares are often described as *blue chip stock*s.

How Share Purchases are Recorded

Recording the purchase of shares is similar to recording the purchase of bonds. However, some initial principles need to be kept in mind when buying shares. For example, given that we are dealing with the short-term investment section of the balance sheet,

- The company must intend to sell the shares within one year for it to qualify as a short-term investment.
- The company must hold less than 20% of the voting interest in the invested company.
- The company cannot play an important role in the operations of the business that issued the shares.

IN THE REAL WORLD

Have you heard of Fannie Mae and Freddie Mac? No, they aren't someone's aunt and uncle. They were once large financial giants, and they serve as a perfect example of the risks involved in the equity market.

Putting aside the unusual names, Fannie Mae and Freddie Mac were large government-subsidized private corporations partly responsible for providing low cost mortgages to millions of Americans.

Both of these corporations were hit extremely hard by the mortgage crisis that started in 2007. By September 2008, the government had seized ownership of these two companies. One of the results was the freezing-out of countless shareholders, which involved lost ownership stake, share value and dividend payments. Holders of the company's debt, however, were left protected.

As the saga of Fannie Mae and Freddie Mac shows, the risks associated with equity are very real. Even shareholders in seemingly can't-lose companies can end up with nothing: no value, no dividends, and no protection. It's something to keep in mind when purchasing even the surest looking forms of equity investments.

Furthermore, given that both shares and bonds are purchased through brokers, we must record the brokerage fee expense.

As an example, we will use the purchase of 100 shares in DEF Company Inc. on January 1 at $400 a share, with a brokerage fee of $300. The total price of the shares is $40,000 and the total cost is $40,300. As with the bond purchase demonstrated earlier, this purchase is recorded by crediting (decreasing) the cash account and debiting (increasing) the short-term investment account and the brokerage fees expense account.

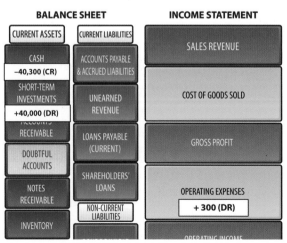

JOURNAL			
Date	Account Title and Explanation	Debit	Credit
Jan 1	Short-Term Investment – Shares	40,000	
	Brokerage Fees Expense	300	
	Cash		40,300
	Purchase of 100 shares of DEF Company Inc. at $400 per share + $300 brokerage fee		

FIGURE 2.41

How Dividend Payments Are Recorded

Let us take the purchase of our shares in DEF Company Inc. to the next level by going through the appropriate steps involved in recording the receipt of a dividend payment (share of the net income).

JOURNAL			
Date	Account Title and Explanation	Debit	Credit
Jul 1	Cash	200	
	Dividend Revenue		200
	Received dividend on 100 shares of DEF Company Inc. ($2 per share x 100 shares)		

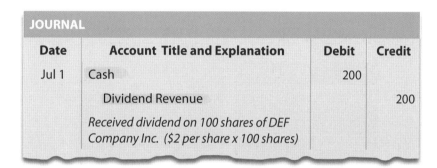

FIGURE 2.42

In our current example, a $2 per share dividend payment was paid to shareholders on July 1. This transaction involves a debit (increase) to cash, and a corresponding credit (increase) to dividend revenue.

Selling Shares and Recording the Sale

There are two ways in which an investor can receive income through owning shares: by receiving dividends (however, not all companies pay dividends) and by selling the shares. When shares are sold for a price higher than its original cost, a gain will be realized and recorded. If the shares are sold for less than its cost, a loss will be realized and recorded.

To go back to our example, our purchase of shares in DEF Company Inc. had an original cost of $40,000. We sell the shares less than a year later on November 1 for a total price of $39,900. The brokerage fee attached to this current transaction is $300.

JOURNAL			
Date	**Account Title and Explanation**	**Debit**	**Credit**
Nov 1	Cash	39,600	
	Brokerage Fees Expense	300	
	Loss on Sale of Investments	100	
	Short-Term Investment – Shares		40,000
	Sale of DEF shares for $39,900 (– loss of $100)		

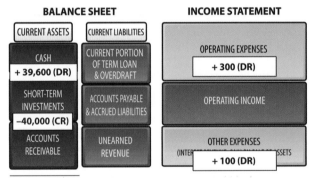

FIGURE 2.43

The proceeds from the sale are $39,600 ($39,900 - $300). The cost of purchasing the shares was $40,000, but the selling price was $39,900. This represents a loss on the sale of $100 ($40,000 - $39,900). A gain or loss on the sale is the difference between the proceeds on the sale and the last carrying value (i.e. the book value).

To record this in the books, we debit cash with $39,600, brokerage fees expense with $300 and loss on sale of investments with $100. We credit the entire original amount of $40,000 to the short-term investment account.

Buying Shares for the Short Term

When a business buys shares in another company, the intention may be to make a profit when selling the shares at a later date. The shares are likely to change in value while being held. This book addresses the sale of shares within a fiscal period. However, if the shares are held for more than one accounting period, the change in the shares' value may require it to be recorded as an unrealized gain or loss.

The accounting treatment would depend on the company's intention when it purchased the shares. If the shares were expected to be held for the long term, the gain in market price would not be recorded as income. If, on the other hand, the share was held for trading in the short term, increases in market price over the accounting period are recorded as income. The details of these transactions are outside the scope of this course.

Controls for Short-Term Investments

Unlike other assets such as cash, accounts receivable and inventory, few are familiar with short-term investments. Nevertheless, it is important that this type of asset be managed properly and that the right controls are in place to ensure its integrity and to safeguard the interests of the business.

Adequate Funds

- Ensure that the appropriate paperwork has been completed.
- Ask the following question: Can the business afford a significant loss in the value of the investment if, for example, the share price falls below the initial purchase price?
- Perform a cash flow analysis to assess whether the business can manage without the cash that would be used to invest.
- When buying or selling shares and bonds, record brokerage fees in the company's books. This means that when shares are purchased, the brokerage fee must be added to the purchase price. When shares are sold, the brokerage fee must be subtracted from the selling price.

Integrity of Information and Bookkeeping

Regular monitoring and controls will help to maintain the integrity of short-term investments.

To adequately safeguard information related to short-term investments, a ledger account should be opened for each investment. If there are numerous investments, a subsidiary ledger should be established and a subsidiary ledger trial balance maintained on a regular basis and reviewed by authorized personnel to ensure that it reconciles with the control account in the general ledger. Each account should adequately describe the nature of the investment. Journal entries for the purchase and sale of investments should be properly authorized. Entries should always be recorded and posted by qualified staff and should be subject to regular review.

The receipt of income from investments should be monitored closely. This is relatively easy with short-term investments, since they often involve regular receipt of interest at fixed rates and on fixed dates.

Personnel

An important control to be used in managing short-term investments is to have the right people assigned to authorize the purchase and sale of investments and to properly record these transactions. Ensure that trustworthy people work for the company and that it employs only reputable brokerage houses and financial institutions when buying and safeguarding investments. It can be tempting for a broker and the company official in charge of investments to share unauthorized commissions, thus reducing the company's income.

Employees involved in investment transactions should always follow established company principles and procedures.

Physical Safekeeping

A business can ensure the physical safety of its short-term investments in various ways. For example, management can choose to leave the share certificates with the brokerage firm used to purchase the investments. Alternatively, the certificates can be kept in a vault on company premises or in a safe deposit box at a bank. Maintain a list of employees who have physical access to certificates. If the certificates are held by the company, they must be registered in the name of the company to avoid potential fraudulent activities.

Safe deposit boxes, like those shown above, can be used to store valuable items like an investment certificate purchased by a company.

Companies should always be in the practice of doing business with people they can trust.

Managerial Oversight

Short-term investments are a good way to make use of surplus cash. Investments of a short-term nature are often in the form of interest-bearing notes, money market funds or other near-cash assets. Regardless of the choice of investments, management must make decisions that are in the best interests of the company.

Setting Company Objectives

Companies should have policies that outline the types of investment to be made on a short-term basis. Although a maximum return is always sought in any form of investment, company assets also need to be safeguarded by the assumption of an appropriate amount of risk. The investments should always be authorized in advance and any investments made should also be reviewed regularly by authorized officers of the company.

On a broader scale, well-managed organizations set strategic goals and objectives, and implement policies to pursue them. This is no different with regard to short-term investments, which can involve large amounts of funds. Goals and objectives should be communicated to the relevant employees, performance reviewed regularly and changes made when corrective action is needed.

The IFRS Perspective

Unrealized gain or loss refers to the difference between an investment's book value and its market value at the end of an accounting period if the investment is not sold. It is "unrealized" because it has not been sold and converted to cash. Under Canadian GAAP standards, only unrealized gains and losses relative to held-for-trading investments are included as part of the income. Under IFRS, the treatment is different. Besides debt investments which are classified as held-to-maturity, all short-term investments are to be updated to the market value when the balance sheet is prepared. IFRS also has a strict choice of policy relative to the transaction costs for held-to-maturity and available-for-sale investments. In addition, if there are gains or losses as a result of the foreign exchange rate on available-for-sale investments, the differences should be accounted for when calculating the value of net income.

In Summary

This chapter has examined how accountants should deal with cash errors, petty cash and short-term investments in the balance sheet. Cash does not always remain in the bank account. It may be set aside for various purposes and invested in the short term. We have also examined the various controls necessary to ensure that such assets are properly safeguarded.

Here is a summary of some of the specific concepts and principles you have learned in this chapter.

- ➪ The bank reconciliation is an internal control that involves comparing and reconciling the items in the company's cash records with the items shown on the bank statement.

- ➪ The petty cash account is established with one accounting transaction. The petty cash custodian deals with specific transactions involving the petty cash fund.

- ➪ While it is easy to think that petty cash is unimportant, small abuses can lead to larger abuses down the line. That is why organizations should establish a formal process to implement a petty cash fund and follow up with controls to ensure that the fund is safeguarded and that employees are informed about its use.

- ➪ When a business has surplus cash, it may choose to invest it for the short term, which, for accounting purposes means less than one year.

- ➪ A short-term investment is a liquid company asset and is located immediately below the cash account on the balance sheet.

- ➪ There are generally two forms of short-term investment: debt, which involves a loan to an individual or business, and equity, which involves buying shares (ownership) in a company.

- ➪ Debt can take the form of a traditional loan to an individual or business or it can take the form of a bond, which is a type of loan that can be bought and sold on the market. Both a loan and a bond earn interest, but a bond can itself change in value and be bought and sold at a lower or higher price.

- ➪ Equity takes the form of shares in a company. Income is earned from the shares, either through an increase in its value or through dividend payments.

- ➪ Brokerage fees are expensed for short-term investments that are classified as held-for-trading.

- ➪ Ensure that income from short-term investments, such as interest, dividends, gains on the sale of investments, is recorded in a special non-operating revenue account, since it is not generated from the day-to-day activities of doing business. Similarly, any losses from short-term investments are recorded in a special non-operating expense account.

Review Exercise 1

Benita Sikorsky is the controller for a medium-sized enterprise that has a July 31 year-end. From time to time, her company has "surplus" cash on hand that it uses to make short-term investments. The types of investments vary from period to period, depending on which investments produce the highest return for the company.

During the past year, the company completed the following transactions:

Jan 1 – Lent $50,000 to another company at an annual rate of 4% and due in 6 months.

Apr 1 – Purchased 1,000 DEF Company bonds priced at $100 each with interest payable semi-annually on July 1 and December 31 at an annual rate of 6%. Also paid for any accrued interest owing.

May 10 – Purchased 1,000 shares of XYZ Company at $50 per share.

Jul 1 – Received the 6-month interest payment on the DEF Company bonds.

Jul 1 – Received full proceeds from the loan of Jan 1, including interest.

Jul 10 – Received the quarterly dividend of $100 on the XYZ Company shares.

Jul 31 – Year end adjustment: Record the interest accrued on the DEF bonds.

Oct 1 – Sold 100 XYZ shares for proceeds of $47 per share.

Dec 15 – Sold 900 XYZ shares for proceeds of $52 per shares.

Dec 31 – Received the second interest payment on the DEF Company bonds then immediately sold the bonds for $102,500.

Required:

Record journal entries for each of the above transactions.

Review Exercise 1 - Answer

Date	Account Title and Explanation	Debit	Credit
Jan 1	Short-Term Investment-Loan	50,000	
	Cash		50,000
	6 month, 4% loan to another company		
Apr 1	Short-Term Investment-Bonds	100,000	
	Interest Receivable (100,000 × .06 × ³⁄₁₂)	1,500	
	Cash		101,500
	Purchased 1,000 bonds at $100 each plus accrued interest		
May 10	Short-Term Investment-Shares	50,000	
	Cash		50,000
	Purchased 1,000 shares of XYZ Co. at $50 per share		
Jul 1	Cash (100,000 × .06 × ⁶⁄₁₂)	3,000	
	Interest Receivable		1,500
	Interest Revenue (100,000 × .06 × ³⁄₁₂)		1,500
	Received 6 months interest on bonds		
Jul 1	Cash (50,000 + 50,000 × ⁶⁄₁₂ × 4%)	51,000	
	Short-Term Investment-Loan		50,000
	Interest Revenue		1,000
	Received proceeds from loan plus interest		
Jul 10	Cash	100	
	Dividend Revenue		100
	Received quarterly dividend on XYZ shares		
Jul 31	Interest Receivable (100,000 × .06 × ¹⁄₁₂)	500	
	Interest Revenue		500
	Accrued interest on bonds at year end		
Oct 1	Cash	4,700	
	Loss on Sale of Investment	300	
	Short-Term Investment-Shares		5,000
	Sale of XYZ shares at a loss $ (47 - 50) × 100 shares = –$300		

Date	Account Title and Explanation	Debit	Credit
Dec 15	Cash	46,800	
	Gain on Sale of Investment		1,800
	Short-Term Investment-Shares		45,000
	Sale of XYZ shares at a gain $ (52 - 50) \times 900 \text{ shares} = \$1,800$		
Dec 31	Cash $(100,000 \times .06 \times {}^6\!/_{12})$	3,000	
	Interest Revenue $(100,000 \times .06 \times {}^5\!/_{12})$		2,500
	Interest Receivable		500
	Received 6 months interest on bonds		
Dec 31	Cash	102,500	
	Short-Term Investment-Bonds		100,000
	Gain on Sale of Investment		2,500
	Sale of DEF bonds at a gain		

Review Exercise 2

The following is the general ledger and bank statement for Martin Furniture Inc.

General Ledger Report May 31, 2010 to June 30, 2010						
Account 1020		Cash				
Date	Comment	Source #	JE#	DR	CR	Balance
Jun 1	Opening Balance					3,100.50
Jun 6	Chicago Hardware Traders Inc.	541	J1		900.50	2,200.00
Jun 9	Reo's Interiors Inc.	700	J3	1,925.00		4,125.00
Jun 10	Air-conditioning Repair & Co.	543	J7		1,600.00	2,525.00
Jun 16	Alex Santiago Payroll	542	J10		400.00	2,125.00
Jun 16	Martin Furnishings Inc.	256	J11	2,000.00		4,125.00
Jun 19	Line-wire Electric	544	J20		110.00	4,015.00
Jun 19	Rice Inc.	545	J21		500.00	3,515.00
Jun 30	Closing Balance					3,515.00

<table>
<tr><td colspan="5">Reserve Bank
146 Lineage Avenue, Chicago

Martin Furniture Inc.
234 Lakeview Drive
Chicago 19112</td></tr>
</table>

Date	Information	Withdrawal	Deposits	Balance
Jun 1	Balance Forward			3,100.50
Jun 8	Cheque #541	900.50		2,200.00
Jun 9	Deposit		1,925.00	4,125.00
Jun 10	Cheque #543	1,600.00		2,525.00
Jun 16	Deposit		2,000.00	4,525.00
Jun 16	Cheque #542	400.00		4,125.00
Jun 18	NSF Cheque #256	2,000.00		2,125.00
Jun 21	Cheque #544	110.00		2,015.00
Jun 27	Deposit Interest		5.00	2,020.00
Jun 29	Service Charge	20.00		2,000.00
Jun 29	Loan Interest	100.00		1,900.00
Jun 30	Ending Balance			1,900.00

You are required to reconcile the ledger and bank statement and record the relevant transactions on the general journal.

Review Exercise 2 – Answer

BANK RECONCILIATION WORKSHEET		
Explanation	**Ledger**	**Bank**
Balance as per records	3,515	1,900
Add: deposit interest	5	
Less: service charge	20	
Less: loan interest	100	
Less: NSF cheque	2,000	
Less: outstanding cheque		500
Corrected balances	1,400	1,400

Date	Account Title and Explanation	Debit	Credit
Jun 18	Accounts Receivable	2,000	
	Cash		2,000
	Reinstate accounts receivable for NSF cheque		
Jun 27	Cash	5	
	Interest Revenue		5
	To record deposit of interest earned		
Jun 29	Bank Service Charges	20	
	Cash		20
	To record payment of bank service charges		
Jun 29	Interest Expense	100	
	Cash		100
	To record payment of bank service charges		

Review Exercise 3

On April 1st, Clayton Company established a petty cash fund of $200.

During the month the custodian paid out the following amounts:

Apr 6	–	Postage	$40
Apr 8	–	Fedex for freight on incoming package	20
Apr 10	–	Public Transit fares for employees on company business	25
Apr 14	–	Coffee and donuts for client during a meeting	8
Apr 15	–	Purchased a package of paper for the copy machine	7

The custodian counted the fund on April 16 and found $95 in the petty cash box.

a) Prepare the journal entry to record the establishment of the fund.

b) Prepare the journal entry to record the reimbursement of the fund on April 16.

Review Exercise 3 – Answer

a)

Date	Account Title and Explanation	Debit	Credit
Apr 1	Petty Cash	200	
	Cash		200
	To establish petty cash fund		

b)

Date	Account Title and Explanation	Debit	Credit
Apr 16	Postage	40	
	Freight-In	20	
	Travel	25	
	Entertainment	8	
	Office Expenses	7	
	Cash Over and Short	5	
	Cash		105
	To reimburse petty cash fund		

Chapter 3
ACCOUNTS AND NOTES RECEIVABLE

LEARNING OUTCOMES:

❶ Understand the importance of accounts receivable

❷ Account for bad debt using the direct method

❸ Account for bad debt using the allowance method

❹ Estimate bad debt using the income statement approach

❺ Estimate bad debt using the balance sheet approach

❻ Calculate financial ratios pertaining to accounts receivable

❼ Record promissory notes and notes receivable

❽ Apply controls and ethics relating to accounts receivable and notes receivable

Accounts Receivable: An Introduction

The next stop on our tour of the balance sheet is accounts receivable, since it ranks immediately after cash and short-term investments in terms of liquidity.

When customers purchase a product or service from a company, they often do so using payment terms. In other words, they receive the product or service, but pay for it later – usually on credit terms established by the company.

FIGURE 3.1

Accounts receivable represents the amounts customers owe as a result of the company exchanging goods or services in return for the promise to pay. This is different to the type of debt we discussed in chapter 2, where money is lent to another party in exchange for interest.

Moving down the current assets section of the balance sheet generally involves not only a decrease in liquidity but also an increase in risk. As far as the company is concerned, accounts receivable are riskier assets to assume than both cash and short-term investments. There is no market for trading accounts receivable since its value does not change over time the way a share price may.

Nevertheless, accounts receivable are an integral part of doing business in a modern economy. Sales may be increased by allowing customers to pay at a later date since some customers may be unable to pay for their purchases immediately.

Since many businesses have accounts receivable on their books, it is important to know how to record and manage them. Throughout this chapter, we will take a closer look at how this is achieved.

Accounts receivable is a different type of asset from those higher up on the balance sheet. One difference involves the way in which information about the asset is collected and managed.

Cash is held in a bank account and the bank provides the account holder with a statement outlining the movement of the cash and the status of the account. Indeed, it is the bank that is essentially responsible for handling the day-to-day administration of the cash being held in the account.

Short-term investments, such as shares and bonds, are traded by expert brokers in a specialized market. The broker provides the investor with all the information related to the account, and the price and status of the investment is determined by the transactions on the market. Investors can readily receive updates on the status of the market. These assets require very limited administration by the company.

Employees need to spend a significant amount of time on the administration of accounts receivable. In fact, perhaps nothing differentiates accounts receivable from other current assets more than their day-to-day administration.

Even a business with a relatively small number of customers has many transactions to record and manage on a daily basis.

In the days before computers, transactions were entered into a journal. While a general journal may be used for transactions that are infrequent, accountants have often used specialized journals for transactions of a specific nature. For example, a purchase journal can be kept to record transactions involving the purchases of the business, and a cash receipts journal can be used to record transactions involving the receipt of money from outside sources.

A CLOSER LOOK

You may recall that income from a short-term investment such as shares or bonds was not considered revenue generated from the business. Instead, this income was classified as "other revenues" in the income statement.

Accounts receivable, on the other hand, form part of the foundation of the business, which is selling products or services to customers. An accounts receivable item represents a sale to a customer and thus generates revenue as part of the routine business of the company. That is why sales generated using credit terms are treated as operating revenue in the income statement.

IN THE REAL WORLD

One of the most prominent business trends of the past decade has been outsourcing, whereby one company hires another company to take over a certain business function — whether it be call center duties or specialized manufacturing capabilities.

The accounts receivable department has not escaped this outsourcing trend. Accounts receivable may represent only a small percentage of a company's total assets; yet the administrative burdens associated with this asset can be overwhelming, and a company's resources in dealing with it are often inadequate.

To handle this challenge, companies have the option of hiring firms that specialize in taking over the accounts receivable function. Such specialists possess the technical hardware, expertise and experience to maximize this important asset.

Outsourcing accounts receivable offers certain advantages, especially for those companies that don't have a good track record in managing this asset. Outsourcing can

- improve a company's profitability by having the asset managed and controlled more efficiently;
- make a company's accounts receivable function more consistently, thereby making customers more satisfied;
- ensure financial reporting is more accurate; and
- allow a company to focus on its core business, while leaving some of the administrative duties to specialists.

Accounts receivable is an important asset for most companies. Leaving it in good hands is necessary for business success, and that may involve outsourcing the accounts.

Before the advent of computers, every sales transaction was entered in the sales journal. Today, sales transactions can be tracked using computer scanning and software, which can generate reports with the click of a mouse. A sample sales report is shown in figure 3.2.

Sales Report		
Archer Limited	Purchased 6 boxes of tiles	$1,000
Beta Company	Purchased 8 boxes of tiles	1,250
Cooper Inc.	Purchased a cord of timber	1,800
Dunwoody Company	Purchased spare parts	200
Archer Limited	Purchased truck of concrete	2,000
Beta Company	Purchased tools	900
	Total Sales	**$7,150**

FIGURE 3.2

If only one account in the general ledger were dedicated to accounts receivable, the general ledger would be overwhelmed with many accounts receivable transactions. This is the reason why accountants use an *accounts receivable subsidiary ledger*, or *sub-ledger*, which is kept separately in order to track each customer's activity. The total of the subsidiary ledger is matched to the balance of the accounts receivable (called the *control account*).

Accounting for Bad Debt: Direct and Allowance Methods

There is an upside and a downside to selling goods and services to customers on credit. The upside is that selling on credit encourages people to buy. For the most part, people pay their bills when they are due. The downside is that there will inevitably be customers who will either delay paying their bills or will never pay. The latter are referred to as ***bad debt***.

All businesses must investigate outstanding accounts receivable in order to identify and account for bad debt. This can be challenging because it is sometimes difficult to know whether the customer is late with the payment or is unable to pay. Assumptions must be made in this regard, because the records need to reflect the company's current financial position as accurately as possible. Generally Accepted Accounting Principles (GAAP) and International Financial Reporting Standards (IFRS) provide two accounting methods for doubtful accounts and bad debt: the direct (write-off) method and the allowance method.

The Direct Method

When a sale is made, it is recorded as a debit to accounts receivable and a credit to sales. This creates an asset that increases the equity of the business while generating what was recorded as revenue at the time.

However, consider this example:

A customer informs you that his company has filed for bankruptcy and is therefore unable to pay its outstanding account balance of $5,000.

When it is determined that the bill will not be paid, the direct method requires a journal entry to increase (debit) *bad debt expense* and decrease (credit) *accounts receivable*. Figure 3.3 shows the required journal entry for this transaction.

BALANCE SHEET

CURRENT ASSETS	CURRENT LIABILITIES
CASH	ACCOUNTS PAYABLE & ACCRUED LIABILITIES
SHORT-TERM INVESTMENTS	UNEARNED REVENUE
	LOANS PAYABLE (CURRENT)
ACCOUNTS RECEIVABLE − $5,000 (CR)	SHAREHOLDERS' LOANS
DOUBTFUL ACCOUNTS	NON-CURRENT LIABILITIES
	BONDS PAYABLE
INVENTORY	LOANS PAYABLE (NON-CURRENT)

INCOME STATEMENT

SALES REVENUE

COST OF GOODS SOLD

GROSS PROFIT

OPERATING EXPENSES | Bad Debt Expense + $5,000 (DR)

OPERATING INCOME

Equity Decreases

One drawback of using the direct method to write off bad debt is that it does not always satisfy GAAP or IFRS, which stipulates that the expense must be recorded during the same period in which the related revenue is generated.

JOURNAL

Date	Account Title and Explanation	Debit	Credit
	Bad Debt Expense	5,000	
	Accounts Receivable - Customer Name		5,000
	Direct write-off of bad debt from accounts receivable		

FIGURE 3.3

The write-off may be made in the same accounting period in which the sale was recorded; however, it is more likely to be made in a later period, which violates the matching principle. For businesses that experience very few bad debt or the dollar amount involved is considered immaterial to the business, the direct method may be used. In the above example, assume that the year-end balance of accounts receivable was $50 million and that credit sales for the year were $650 million, the company experiences very few write–offs and $5,000 is considered by management to be immaterial. In this case, using the direct method may be considered acceptable.

The second drawback to using this method arises if the customer is able to repay the account *after* the account has been written off. Figure 3.4 shows the journal entries that would need to be recorded if this occurs.

JOURNAL			
Date	**Account Title and Explanation**	**Debit**	**Credit**
	Accounts Receivable - Customer Name	5,000	
	Bad Debt Expense		5,000
	To reinstate the customer's account		

JOURNAL			
Date	**Account Title and Explanation**	**Debit**	**Credit**
	Cash	5,000	
	Accounts Receivable - Customer Name		5,000
	To record receipt of payment on account		

FIGURE 3.4

You will need to reinstate the amount into the customer's account. This requires a journal entry to increase (debit) accounts receivable and decrease (credit) bad debt expense, which will cause a reduction in expenses and an overstatement of net income for the current period. Unless the write-off and the subsequent reinstatement occur in the same period, the matching principle is being violated.

After you have reinstated the amount, you would need to make a second journal entry to record the receipt of the payment from the customer.

The Allowance Method

Since the direct method will violate the matching principle if the bad debt is not recorded in the same period as the sale, accountants have devised what is called an ***allowance for doubtful accounts*** (AFDA). It is located directly beneath Accounts Receivable on our Accounting Map™, and is also known as a ***contra account.*** A contra account is linked directly to and is the opposite of another account. In this case, the AFDA contra account is linked directly to accounts receivable, which is the control account in the general ledger.

Under the direct method, a bad debt is recorded by debiting the bad debt expense and crediting accounts receivable. The allowance method, on the other hand, uses the bad debt expense account and the AFDA to record bad debt in the same period in which the revenue is generated; this adheres to the matching principle.

For example, let us assume that at the end of year 1, your customers owe a total of $100,000. After analyzing the existing data and the current economy, it has been determined that $5,000 of the accounts receivable may not be collectable. However, since there is still a chance that you will collect, you will not remove them from the accounts receivable list.

The accounts receivable account of $100,000 does not change (you still hope to collect the full amount). It remains as a debit on the balance sheet. Instead, the AFDA contra account is credited with $5,000, which decreases the combined amount of the accounts receivable and the AFDA by $5,000, resulting in net accounts receivable of $95,000. Bad debt expense is in turn increased, or debited, by $5,000 and this amount is reported as an expense for the period in the income statement. The journal entry at the end of year 1 for this transaction is recorded as follows:

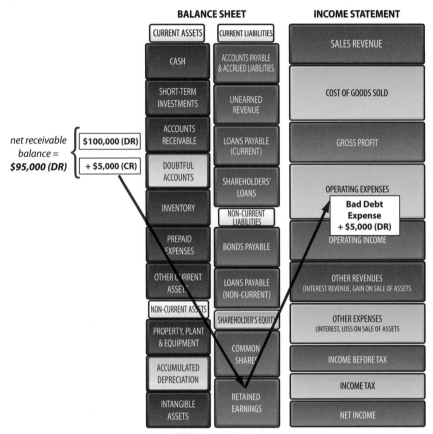

The Accounts Receivable account remains unchanged.
The effect of this transaction decreases equity.

JOURNAL			
Date	**Account Title and Explanation**	**Debit**	**Credit**
	Bad Debt Expense	5,000	
	Allowance for Doubtful Accounts		5,000
	Record an allowance for doubtful accounts		

FIGURE 3.5

The AFDA contra account allows a company to account for the possibility that some of the accounts receivable generated in the current period will not be collected. The debit to bad debt expense supports the matching principle, since this amount will be deducted as an expense in the period during which the sale was recorded.

It should also be noted that according to GAAP and IFRS, any amount of money originally credited to the AFDA contra account, and thus deemed uncollectible, must be justified with backup documentation. In other words, a company must have good reason to believe that an account will not be paid in order to justify the adjustments made to the assets and expenses.

After companies anticipate a bad debt by setting up the AFDA contra account, several scenarios can exist:

1. A customer is unable to pay the debt and the amount is considered uncollectible.
2. After an account is written off as uncollectible, the customer informs you that he or she will pay the amount.
3. The customer will not pay the debt because of a dispute.
4. The customer is unable to pay the debt immediately, but will be able to pay it in the future.

We will now examine each scenario.

Scenario 1: During year 2, a customer who owes you $250, informs you that he is unable to pay his account.

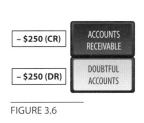

FIGURE 3.6

JOURNAL			
Date	**Account Title and Explanation**	**Debit**	**Credit**
	Allowance for Doubtful Accounts	250	
	Accounts Receivable - Customer Name		250
	To write-off account as uncollectible		

The amount is now considered uncollectible and needs to be written off.

Since the allowance method was used, a debit to the bad debt expense was recorded in the previous period when the sale occurred; therefore, the AFDA account will now be debited and the accounts receivable account credited to remove the amount from the company's records. The above entry will have no impact on the company's equity, since this was already accounted for by the original debit to bad debt expense in year 1.

Scenario 2: The customer in scenario 1 has experienced a windfall and is now eager to pay his account (which you previously wrote off as uncollectible).

This will result in your having to record two journal entries: (1) to reinstate the customer's account balance, and (2) to show the amount being paid.

1. Reverse the previous entry.

JOURNAL			
Date	**Account Title and Explanation**	**Debit**	**Credit**
	Accounts Receivable - Customer Name	250	
	Allowance for Doubtful Accounts		250
	To reinstate amount previously written off		

FIGURE 3.7

2. Record receipt of payment on account.

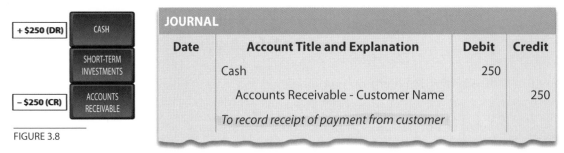

JOURNAL			
Date	**Account Title and Explanation**	**Debit**	**Credit**
	Cash	250	
	Accounts Receivable - Customer Name		250
	To record receipt of payment from customer		

FIGURE 3.8

Scenario 3: The customer will not pay the debt because of a dispute.

This scenario is different from the first two scenarios because it relates to a situation in which the customer believes that he or she has good reason not to pay you (e.g. the customer never ordered the products).

In this scenario, the sale is treated as though it never happened. Assume $1,000 worth of products was mistakenly shipped, and the cost of the products was $600. If the company uses the perpetual inventory system, the following reverse entries should be recorded:

JOURNAL			
Date	**Account Title and Explanation**	**Debit**	**Credit**
	Sales Revenue	1,000	
	Accounts Receivable		1,000
	To reverse the sale		

JOURNAL			
Date	**Account Title and Explanation**	**Debit**	**Credit**
	Inventory	600	
	Cost of Goods Sold		600
	To reverse the cost of goods sold		

FIGURE 3.9

This form of write-off results in a decrease in revenue, not an increase in expenses. This is important because if it is a material amount, the result could affect the way a reader of the statements evaluates the company's performance.

Scenario 4: The customer is unable to pay the debt at present, but will be able to do so in the future.

Even customers with a good credit record sometimes take time to settle their bills. If it is relatively certain that the customer will pay, the company will take no action, except to periodically issue a reminder to the customer. The original amount debited to accounts receivable will remain on the books and will be credited when the account is finally paid.

Approaches to Estimate Bad Debt

Managing accounts receivable includes assessing how much of it will end up as bad debt. This not only has an impact on how a company reflects its financial position on a timely basis, but also has implications for meeting GAAP and IFRS requirements. In other words, businesses should always have good reasons for their treatment of bad debt and should maintain the necessary documentation to justify it.

We will examine two approaches for estimating bad debt: the income statement approach and the balance sheet approach.

The Income Statement Approach

The income statement approach, using percentage of sales, is so called because revenues from the income statement are used as a basis to predict future bad debt. More specifically, a percentage of revenue is used as a basis to estimate the bad debt expense for the current period.

For example, if the collection history of a company suggests that 1% of sales will result in bad debt, that rate is used to estimate the portion of each period's sales that will not be collectible.

Total credit sales for ABC Company amounted to $1,000,000, of which $200,000 is currently owing by customers. On the basis of historical sales, 1% of that amount will be uncollectible. Therefore, the bad debt expense for the period will be:

$$\$1,000,000 \times 1\% = \$10,000$$

JOURNAL			
Date	**Account Title and Explanation**	**Debit**	**Credit**
	Bad Debt Expense	10,000	
	Allowance for Doubtful Accounts		10,000
	To record bad debt expense based on percentage of sale		

FIIGURE 3.10

As previously discussed, the accounts receivable account, or control account, maintains the same debit amount, which in this case is $200,000. Assuming that the AFDA starts with a zero balance, it will now have a $10,000 credit balance. This leaves a net accounts receivable balance of $190,000, which

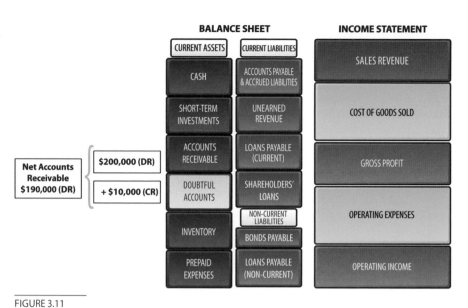

FIGURE 3.11

represents a decrease in the company's assets. The income statement includes a debit balance of $10,000 for bad debt expense.

Even though it is called the income statement approach, the name derives from the way the bad debt expense is calculated. Nevertheless, adjustments must be made to both the income statement and the balance sheet accounts when accounting for the bad debt expense.

The Balance Sheet Approach

The balance sheet approach uses percentage of receivables to calculate bad debt expense. The percentage is applied to the accounts receivable account. Specifically, percentages are often applied to accounts receivable according to groupings based on the age of uncollectible amounts. We will use an example to illustrate this procedure.

The chart in figure 3.12 contains three groups of customers:

1. those who have not paid within 30 days;
2. those who have not paid for 31 to 60 days; and
3. those who have not paid for over 60 days.

Aging Category	Bad Debt % (probability of being uncollectible)	Balance
30 days	2%	80,000
31–60 days	3%	90,000
over 60 days	5%	30,000
Total		200,000

The above percentages are based on historical performance

FIGURE 3.12

A percentage is applied to each aging category. A 2% rate is applied to the first group, 3% to the second group and 5% to the third group. The longer that a customer takes to pay, the less likely he or she will pay; that is the reason why the highest rate is used for the third group.

The Balance column of the chart in figure 3.13 shows the amounts that each group still owes the company. The percentages are applied to these amounts to calculate the expected total bad debt per customer group. These are then added to give us the total amount of bad debt expected in the upcoming period.

Aging Category	Bad Debt % (probability of being uncollectible)	Balance	Estimated Bad Debt*
30 days	2%	80,000	1,600
31–60 days	3%	90,000	2,700
over 60 days	5%	30,000	1,500
Total		200,000	5,800
* Balance x Bad Debt %			

FIGURE 3.13

Uncollectible accounts receivable in the upcoming period is estimated at $5,800. If there is already an amount credited in the AFDA contra account, it needs to be subtracted from the $5,800 total to give us the amount to record our bad debt expense for the period.

Let us assume that the AFDA contra account had a credit balance of $3,000. Subtracting that from the expected bad debt of $5,800 leaves us with a new credit adjustment in the AFDA account of $2,800. In effect, this "tops up" the AFDA contra account, since we are adjusting it to reflect the total amount of bad debt expected.

We need to adjust the amount of the AFDA account with a credit of $2,800. Figure 3.14 shows the journal entry for this transaction.

JOURNAL			
Date	Account Title and Explanation	Debit	Credit
	Bad Debt Expense	2,800	
	Allowance for Doubtful Accounts		2,800
	To adjust the ADFA account to the correct balance		

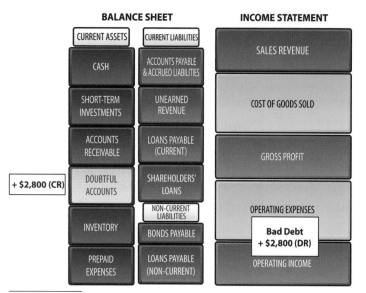

FIGURE 3.14

Note that this net adjustment of accounts receivable adheres to the principle of conservatism under GAAP and IFRS, which requires assets to be valued at the lower amount of possible alternatives and, as a result, reflects a reduced income for the period. This approach allows the business to make decisions based on figures that don't overstate assets, net income or the financial position of the company.

Managing Accounts Receivable Information Using Reports

Much of our analysis of accounts receivable has involved the method of accounting for accounts receivable in the company's books. This is important because these records give management accurate information on which to make good business decisions. This also allows companies to adhere to external reporting standards and principles.

However, another important aspect of accounts receivable is managing or controlling them. It is important for a business to know not only the amount of its accounts receivable but also which policies and procedures will lead to the collection of the maximum possible amount.

Having too many customers owing the company too much money on overdue bills restricts cash flow and working capital. Among other things, it limits the ability of the company to meet its commitments, such as accounts payable and loans.

Since the accounts receivable section of the balance sheet plays such a prominent role in the financial well-being of a company, it is important that information about this asset is efficiently organized.

Fortunately, computer software is available to collect, organize and process information in different ways. Many reports can be produced to give management insight into financial affairs in ways that raw data cannot.

A CLOSER LOOK

A number of strategies will ensure that a company manages and controls its accounts receivable. These include the following:

- Commitment to efficiency. Management commits to ensuring that accounts receivable are handled efficiently.

- Measuring results. After using ratios and reports to manage information, it is essential to determine whether these measures are working.

- Cutting-edge technology. Having the company's technology up-to-date to provide accurate and useful information about accounts receivable will assist in informed decision-making.

The Accounts Receivable Subledger

The list in figure 3.15 is a customer-by-customer list of outstanding amounts owing to a company; these amounts represent the total in the accounts receivable control account.

Accounts Receivable listing as at July 31					
	Current	31-60 days	61-90 days	91 days +	Total
Archer Limited	1,300	900	1,500		3,700
Beta Company	1,200	1,800	1,300	150	4,450
Cooper Limited	1,800	150			1,950
Dunwoody Company	200	500	200		900
Harry's Supplies	4,000	3,000	1,600	1,200	9,800
Lino Inc.	400	600	100		1,100
Total	8,900	6,950	4,700	1,350	21,900
	40.64%	31.74%	21.46%	6.16%	

FIGURE 3.15

Presenting the data in this form facilitates the analysis of accounts receivable by customer. It also highlights the figures that stand out from the others. In this case, the areas of note have been marked in yellow, red and green in the revised chart that follows.

Accounts Receivable listing as at July 31					
	Current	31-60 days	61-90 days	91 days +	Total
Archer Limited	1,300	900	1,500		3,700
Beta Company	1,200	1,800	1,300	150	4,450
Cooper Limited	1,800	150			1,950
Dunwoody Company	200	500	200		900
Harry's Supplies	4,000	3,000	1,600	1,200	9,800
Lino Inc.	400	600	100		1,100
Total	8,900	6,950	4,700	1,350	21,900
	40.64%	31.74%	21.46%	6.16%	

FIGURE 3.16

As the yellow and red areas show, two customers have bills outstanding over 90 days.

The yellow area shows us an amount of $150 from Beta Company that has not been paid for over 90 days. However, this is a relatively small amount, especially in comparison with Beta's total amount owing. It could be the result of an invoice discrepancy or some other minor issue. Although Beta is one of only two customers with balances owing for over 90 days, management should not be too concerned about this balance.

▉▉▉▉ The other customer with a balance exceeding 90 days, Harry's Supplies, should certainly be a cause for concern. The amount marked in red, $1,200, represents a significant portion of its outstanding balance. Furthermore, the amount might be even more problematical, given that the same customer has been given $4,000 credit in the current month. This account is not being well-managed, and management should follow up with the company while also reconsidering the credit policies that have allowed such a situation to develop.

▉▉▉▉ The green area of this chart is notable because, unlike all the other customers on the list, Cooper Limited does not have an outstanding balance for the 61–90 day period. Furthermore, it has only $150 outstanding for the 31–60 day period. Therefore the $1,800 credit given to Cooper in the current period appears to be justified: this customer has paid his bills promptly and providing more credit for that customer would make good business sense.

Alternative Presentation Formats

The preceding examples represent just a few ways in which accounts receivable information can be organized and presented. Computer software provides unlimited possibilities. Management should tailor computer programs to meet the specific needs and objectives of the company with regard to information about accounts receivable, bad debts, internal controls and all other related issues.

The reports that can be generated involving accounts receivable include the following:

- Current active customers
- Past customers not active for the last 12 months
- Customer activities listing value of sales per month
- Customer activities listing value of sales per product
- Categorization of customers according to sales representative or geographic location
- Overdue accounts

Measuring the Effectiveness of Collections Using Ratios

Another approach to measuring the effectiveness of the company's collection efforts is through the use of financial ratios. We examine two types of ratios: **days sales outstanding** and **accounts receivable turnover**.

Days Sales Outstanding

One way of organizing accounts receivable information is to use days sales outstanding (DSO). DSO tracks how long customers take to pay their bills. This is done by using two basic figures from the financial records: net accounts receivable (accounts receivable less allowance for doubtful accounts) and net credit sales for the past 12 months.

The net accounts receivable figure is divided by the credit sales of the past 12 months. The result is then multiplied by 365 (days in the year). The result provides the company with the average number of days that customers take to pay their bills. The following two examples illustrate the use and function of this particular ratio.

Company 1

Let us assume that the total average net accounts receivable amount for Company 1 is $200,000, and the total net credit sales amount for the past year was $1,200,000. Our DSO ratio is calculated as follows:

Days Sales Outstanding = (*Average Net Accounts Receivable ÷ Net Credit Sales) x 365
$$= (200,000 \div 1,200,000) \times 365$$
$$= 61 \text{ days}$$

*Average net accounts receivable is calculated by adding the opening net accounts receivable balance to the closing net accounts receivable balance and dividing the result by 2

* Net credit sales = Total Credit Sales – Sales discount – Sales Returns and Allowances

In other words, it takes an average of 61 days to collect amounts outstanding.

Company 2

Let us assume that the total average net accounts receivable amount for Company 2 is $135,000, and the total net credit sales for the past year were $1,650,000. Our DSO ratio is calculated as follows:

$$(135,000 \div 1,650,000) \times 365 = 30 \text{ days}$$

On the basis of these calculations, Company 2 is collecting its accounts receivable from customers twice as fast as Company 1. Because of the importance of cash in operating a business, it is in a company's best interest to collect outstanding accounts receivable as quickly as possible. By quickly turning sales into cash, a company has the opportunity to effectively use the cash for reinvestment and to produce more revenue. One of the most important factors that affect DSO is the company's credit terms.

If both companies allow customers 30 days to pay for their purchase on account, Company 2 is doing well in terms of collection whereas Company 1 is doing poorly.

Accounts Receivable Turnover Ratio

The accounts receivable turnover (ART) ratio is similar to DSO. It involves dividing a company's net credit sales by the average amount of net accounts receivable.

ART = Net Credit Sales ÷ Average Net Accounts Receivable

Company 3

Company 3 has net credit sales of $1,000,000 and the average amount of its net accounts receivable is $100,000.

$$\text{ART} = \$1,000,000 \div \$100,000 = 10 \text{ times}$$

Company 4

Company 4 has net credit sales of $3,000,000 and the average amount of its net accounts receivable is $400,000.

$$\text{ART} = \$3,000,000 \div \$400,000 = 7.5 \text{ times}$$

A higher ratio indicates a greater ability to convert accounts receivable into cash. In this case, Company 3 is collecting its receivables faster than Company 4.

If a business turns its receivables over 12 times per year, it would mean that it is collecting the average balance of receivables every month.

Accounts Receivable Controls

Now that we have examined various ways of organizing, presenting and managing accounts receivable information, some of the information can be used to implement sound control policies. In other words, there is no value in collecting all that data unless it is used to better manage a company's accounts receivable.

Indeed, this is the purpose of internal controls – to help a company get the most out of one of its largest and most crucial assets. We will look specifically at how a credit policy can serve as a control mechanism to ensure that the accounts receivable asset is managed, protected and maximized in value.

Credit Controls

One of the first issues a company should consider when establishing a credit policy is whether to adopt a lenient or restrictive approach to providing credit. Two broad factors can influence such a decision: the company's own financial position and its market position relative to the competition.

For example, if a company is already financially constrained, it probably cannot afford to extend credit to customers at risk. Similarly, low sales volumes for custom-made products leave a company with less room to extend generous credit terms. A company with little or no competition does not need to increase market share, and therefore has no incentive to adopt lenient credit policies.

Decisions involving credit terms can have a significant impact on sales volume. The more lenient a company's credit policy, the more likely it is to generate additional sales. It provides potential customers with the incentive to buy goods without having to pay for them immediately. Therefore, a more competitive market environment, homogeneous products and high sales volumes provide a company with greater incentive to extend more lenient credit terms to customers.

Credit Approval

Providing payment terms to customers involves making unsecured loans to the customers so that they can buy the company's product or service. Instead of automatically offering these terms, a company can implement various measures to better understand their customers and follow up when necessary. This is the essence of credit approval. It can involve having the customer complete a credit application and update the information regularly. The company can also request a customer's financial statements to ensure that it is in a position to pay its bills.

Credit Information

Of course, customers may not always be completely open about their financial health or ability to pay their bills. Companies therefore get independent credit information about customers from credit reporting agencies, financial institutions and even from other vendors.

Credit agency reports can be very useful in getting up-to-date information on current and potential customers. They can provide payment history, claims against the customer, banking information, existing credit granted, a record of recent inquiries as well as any credit ratings.

Terms of Sale

Another credit control at a company's disposal is setting the terms of sale. A certain period, such as 30 days, can be used and enforced against all customers.

Credit Policy

Finally, deciding on the methods of collecting from customers is yet another control in credit policy. The invoice is always the first tool of collection. If a customer is overdue with his payment, the company can send a second. If that does not prove successful, other measures such as letters, phone calls and even personal visits can be used to put pressure on the customer. If all else fails, a collection agency can be hired to enforce payment, especially when the account is long overdue.

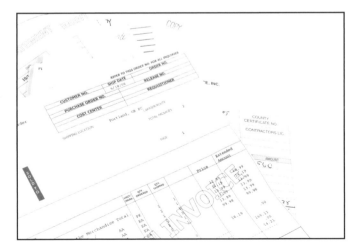

Other controls for accounts receivable that may be implemented are the following:

- Keeping individual records for each customer.
- Following up on large accounts that are overdue.
- Writing off a bad debt when it has been determined that all reasonable measures have been exhausted in collecting the debt.
- Ensuring that the original write-off is reversed when payments are received for a previously written-off account.

Converting Accounts Receivable into Cash

Having too many customers that are not paying on time, or not at all, can create serious problems for a company's cash flow and working capital. Certain measures can be taken to convert a company's accounts receivable into cash in the most efficient manner possible (see "In the Real World" on the next page for a description of one of these measures).

Setting Firm Credit Terms

Perhaps most important, a company should try to assess whether its collection period is stringent enough. Accounts receivable should not be extended more than 10 or 15 days beyond the credit terms. Industry standards differ, so assessing what the competition is doing, then setting a benchmark to meet or surpass those expectations, may be a wise business strategy. Setting a high standard and routinely enforcing it might improve the collection of accounts.

The Promissory Note and Notes Receivable

There is another way to look at accounts receivable. In a sense, the transaction is much like a loan. Since the customers do not initially pay for the goods or services they receive from the company, the selling company is in effect lending customers the money to pay for them until the loan is due. However, this loan usually does not come with interest within the credit period.

WORTH REPEATING...

Two factors are taken into consideration when deciding on how stringent or lenient the company's credit policy should be:

- The company's own financial situation. The stronger it is, the better it can afford to make sales on credit.
- The company's competitive situation. The more competition a company has, the greater the pressure to extend credit in order to increase sales.

A **promissory note**, or **note receivable** makes an account receivable resemble a formal loan by adding precise terms of repayment to which the customer adds his signature.

For example, if a customer is overdue on her account, the company may request that the customer sign a promissory note, which would formalize the arrangements involved in the repayment of the debt – much like a formal loan specifies its terms of repayment. Both a loan and a promissory note can set terms that include naming the parties to the document, the amount to be paid, when the amounts are due, as well as the interest charges related to the payments.

IN THE REAL WORLD

Companies have various means at their disposal to convert their accounts receivable into cash. One that has become more frequent in recent years is known as *factoring*, which can help a company's cash flow and working capital in the short term.

Factoring involves selling accounts receivable assets at a discount price to a third party, the factor. The factor is then responsible for collecting payment from the debtor.

At one time a factor was brought in as a last resort — only after all previous attempts at collecting failed, including the use of a collection agency.

Factoring has, however, now grown from $95 billion in 2000 to $135 billion in 2007.

Today, as it becomes increasingly difficult for businesses to secure loans, factoring is turning into a viable option for raising funds. The cost to the seller involves receiving a discounted price for the total value of accounts receivable. In essence, this amounts to decreasing the value of the company assets. However, it receives cash for its accounts receivable, and the discount price may be worth more than the amount the company could hope to collect from its customers on its own.

A promissory note, or note receivable, is used not only to formalize an accounts receivable item but also to extend unusual credit terms to a specific customer, such as an agreement that may involve lengthening the terms of repayment to more than one year. In addition, the note can be used to extend credit to a customer with no formal credit history. The stronger legal claim associated with a note provides greater protection for the selling company when dealing with uncertain or riskier customer accounts. Provided that the seller is confident the customer will eventually pay the note, there should be no objection to accepting the note.

PROMISSORY NOTE

_____, 201__

At any time after the above date, the undersigned promises to pay the lender the sum of $_____ with _____ % interest until _____ 201__.
The makers, endorsers, and guarantors hereof waive presentment, demand of payment, notice of nonpayment, protest, notice of protest, and all exemptions.

_____   _____
NAME OF LENDER   NAME OF BORROWER

_____   _____
LENDER'S SIGNATURE   BORROWER'S SIGNATURE

For example, on April 1, 2010, Kay Fernandez Alonso has $1,000 of outstanding accounts receivable with Bennet Company. Bennet's year-end is October 31. Kay cannot pay the amount immediately, but is willing to sign a note. The interest is 6% per annum, to be collected when the note is due. Kay promises to pay on April 1, 2011. The entry to record the conversion of the accounts receivable to a note receivable is as follows:

JOURNAL			
Date	**Account Title and Explanation**	**Debit**	**Credit**
Apr 1	Note Receivable	1,000	
	Accounts Receivable		1,000
	Converted accounts receivable to a note receivable		

FIGURE 3.17

On October 31, when Bennet Company prepares its financial statements, it will need to accrue the interest earned from Alonso. Notice that the interest earned is classified as "Other Revenue" rather than regular earned revenue.

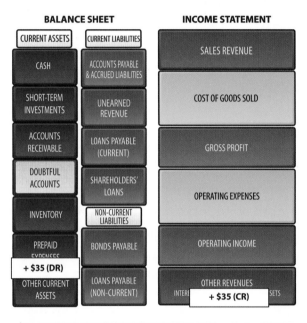

JOURNAL			
Date	**Account Title and Explanation**	**Debit**	**Credit**
Oct 31	Note Interest Receivable	35	
	Note Interest Revenue		35
	To record accrued interest revenue *$1,000 x 6% x 7/12*		

FIGURE 3.18

When Kay pays the amount due on April 1, 2011, the following entry is recorded on the statements of Bennet Company.

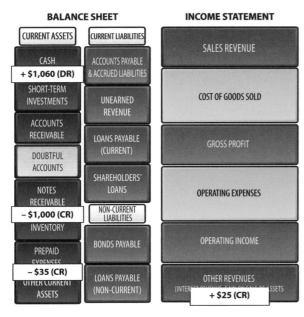

Explanation of this transaction:

- Kay paid $1,060 (debit to cash).
- An amount of $25 was recorded as interest revenue by crediting interest revenue.
- The interest receivable of $35 was eliminated by crediting the account.
- The note receivable of $1,000 was eliminated by crediting the note receivable account.

JOURNAL

Date	Account Title and Explanation	Debit	Credit
Apr 1	Cash	1,060	
	Note Interest Receivable		35
	Note Interest Revenue		25
	Note Receivable		1,000
	Record the receipt of note principal & interest ($1,000 x 6% x 5/12)		

FIGURE 3.19

An Ethical Approach to Managing Accounts Receivable

As some of the discussion in this chapter has already illustrated, a company's accounts receivable asset can be both simple and complex. Its simplicity can be found in the fact that it is represented on the balance sheet as one debit figure in one control account, with a corresponding contra account representing the bad debt allowance. The asset will therefore have one net value, reflecting the balance expected to be collected from customers.

However, the complexity of accounts receivable is revealed by looking at the subledger. This consists of many transactions, which must be regularly updated to reflect ongoing payments or non-payments. Managing these accounts involves different procedures and requires various tools at the accountant's disposal. We looked at some of these tools earlier in the chapter.

The company and its accounting department is responsible for managing these tasks accurately and ethically.

There is little dispute regarding the impact of the value of accounts receivable on the company's financial statements and that the management and accounting of the asset is open to manipulation.

Various ethical principles and standards have been established to prevent or detect manipulation of accounts receivable. Here is a case study that illustrates unethical behavior, which violates the full disclosure principle outlined in GAAP and IFRS.

> *Charles owns a manufacturing business, which has been growing steadily. His bank wants to examine his financial statements before approving his loan to finance his increasing need for additional capital. His records show a total of $450,000 in accounts receivable, and he has earned net income of $80,000 for the current year. Charles is also aware that there is an amount of $50,000 that is likely to be uncollectible; however, he knows that if he allows for the bad debt in his statements, he may not be successful in securing the loan. Charles justifies his non-disclosure by committing himself to allowing for the bad debt the following year because there is a slight chance that he may still get paid.*
>
> *What Charles did was unethical. He deliberately overstated the value of his assets to try to secure the loan. He believed that the debt was not going to be paid, but he represented it otherwise to distort the current value of the accounts receivable.*
>
> *Charles consciously contravened the full disclosure principle by withholding information relevant to the valuing of these assets.*

Let us look at another example of unethical behavior. This time we will examine the importance of maintaining the integrity of the accounts receivable information that a company collects and manages. A failure to do so can put into doubt the accuracy of the company's books, as well as the ethics of the people in charge.

> *Sophie has been hired by the controller, Rick, to manage the company's accounts receivable. Upon assuming the job, Sophie soon notices that the company's accounts receivable have been poorly managed. The computer system was old and the invoices were not detailed enough, thus leading to customers questioning their invoices. Furthermore, the company would increase prices on the date of shipment instead of on the date the order was placed. Customers would complain and did not want to pay invoices showing prices they had not agreed to.*

Sophie brought her concerns to Rick, who told her to keep quiet about her concerns and to do the best she could. Rick was afraid that he would be held accountable if the extent of the problems was made known to upper management, so he tried to hide the problems as much as he could. Sophie did not know what to do about the unethical accounting practices. If she remained silent, the integrity of the company's accounts receivable would be in serious jeopardy.

An accountant is responsible for maintaining the integrity of the information in the books. Rick should have dealt with these problems as soon as he became aware of them. Instead, when these problems were pointed out to him, he tried to hide them and absolve himself of any responsibility. The company's customers were being treated unfairly, the financial information of the company was compromised and the tactics used in response to the problems were ethically unacceptable. Furthermore, he imposed an unacceptable dilemma on his employee, Sophie, requiring her to choose between her job and the proper management of the company's assets.

Unless Rick accepts responsibility for the problems and corrects them, he puts both himself and his company in a vulnerable position both financially and ethically.

A CLOSER LOOK

An important feature of the income statement approach is that the calculation produces an amount for bad debt expense, rather than an adjustment to the amount of the bad debt allowance account, as in the balance sheet approach.

After the amount based on a percent of sales is calculated, bad debt expense is debited and bad debt allowance is credited. The idea behind basing the expense on sales is to appropriately match the bad debt expense with the credit sales of the period.

The total amount of the allowance is essentially ignored. Each period bad debt expense is debited, and bad debt allowance is credited. If the percent of sales used realistically reflects the actual amount of bad debt experienced, the allowance account will reflect a reasonable balance.

On the other hand, if the actual bad debt experienced are materially lower than the estimate (based on a percent of sales), the allowance for doubtful accounts may build to an unrealistically large amount. This would occur because the credit (i.e. the estimate of bad debt) is not matched by a corresponding debit resulting from actual bad debt write-offs.

If you observe that the allowance account is becoming unusually large, you could forego recording additional bad debt expenses (and the corresponding credit to the allowance account), until debits (i.e. actual bad debt write-offs) reduce the allowance account to a reasonable balance once again. What is a reasonable balance? As with many items in accounting, the answer is based on professional judgment.

The IFRS Perspective

Comparing IFRS to GAAP, the accounting approach for accounts receivable and notes receivable is consistent for most of the parts. There are some differences in the more advanced topics such as factoring (selling receivables to a third party for a cash advance). These topics are outside the scope of this course.

 ## In Summary

↪ Accounts receivable often represents a significant percentage of a company's assets.

↪ Since accounts receivable losses usually occur after the end of the fiscal year in which the sale was made, an allowance for doubtful accounts (AFDA) needs to be used. This procedure allows a company to conform to GAAP and IFRS rules.

↪ AFDA is a contra account attached to the accounts receivable account. AFDA entries are recorded in reverse of the entries recorded in accounts receivable.

↪ There are two approaches to evaluate AFDA: The income statement approach and the balance sheet approach.

↪ The effectiveness of accounts receivable collections can be gauged with the use of two ratios: days sales outstanding (DSO) and accounts receivable turnover (ART).

↪ Accounts receivable can be converted into promissory notes, or notes receivable, which are legally binding documents.

↪ Credit controls and policies are necessary to manage and protect the accounts receivable asset.

↪ Reports are used to monitor paying trends by customers and ensure that credit terms are not abused.

↪ Since accounts receivable often represents a significant percentage of a company's assets, there can be a temptation to manipulate its value. Ethical behavior is therefore crucial in maintaining the integrity of a company's financial statements.

Review Exercise 1

Part 1

You are the accountant for Booe company. Your company uses the direct write-off method to account for bad debt. Record the following transactions:

1. Sale to Guy Tygart on account – 1,000 gadgets @ $5 on June 30
2. Collect $4,900 from Guy Tygart on July 10
3. Write off the remaining balance owing from Guy Tygart on July 31
4. Collect 50% of the amount written off on December 15.

Assume the cost of inventory is only updated at the end of the year (i.e. do not consider cost of goods sold for the transactions above).

Part 1 – Answer

Date	Account Title and Explanation	Debit	Credit
Jun 30	Accounts Receivable – Tygart	5,000	
	Sales		5,000
	To record sale on credit		
Jul 10	Cash	4,900	
	Accounts Receivable – Tygart		4,900
	To record receipt of payment in part		
Jul 31	Bad Debt Expense	100	
	Accounts Receivable – Tygart		100
	To record bad debt using the direct write-off method		
Dec 15	Accounts Receivable – Tygart	50	
	Bad Debt Expense		50
	To reinstate customer's account		
Dec 15	Cash	50	
	Accounts Receivable – Tygart		50
	To record receipt of payment		

Part 2

Using the same scenario as above, recalculate all the transactions and record the entries assuming that your company uses the allowance for doubtful accounts method.

Assume that $5,000 had been credited to the allowance account for the year.

Part 2 – Answer

Date	Account Title and Explanation	Debit	Credit
Jun 30	Accounts Receivable – Tygart	5,000	
	Sales Revenue		5,000
	To record sale on credit		
Jul 10	Cash	4,900	
	Accounts Receivable – Tygart		4,900
	To record receipt of payment in part		
Jul 31	Allowance for Doubtful Accounts	100	
	Accounts Receivable – Tygart		100
	To write-off accounts as uncollectible		
Dec 15	Accounts Receivable – Tygart	50	
	Allowance for Doubtful Accounts		50
	To reinstate amount previously written-off		
Dec 15	Cash	50	
	Accounts Receivable – Tygart		50
	To record receipt of payment		

Review Exercise 2

ABC Company uses the allowance method to account for bad debt. During the current year, 2010, the company had $350,000 in sales of which 80% were on account and the remaining 20% were cash sales.

During the year the company received $250,000 from customers as payment on their accounts. In June, it also wrote-off $1,500 for a customer who notified them they were filing for bankruptcy and would not be able to pay. However, the same customer notified them that they had received money from a wealthy relative and would be able to pay their account early in the new year after the account was written off. The company expects that $5,000 of the accounts receivable balance at the end of the year may be uncollectible.

Required:

a) Using the general journal and Dec 31 as the date for all transactions, record the sales, collections for customers on account, write-off of accounts and bad debt expense for 2010. You may omit explanations for each entry.

   Assume accounts receivable had a debit balance of $35,000 and that the AFDA had a credit balance of $2,500 at the beginning of the year (Jan.1, 2010).

b) Show how the above transactions would be posted in the related T-Accounts

c) Show how accounts receivable would be reported on the Dec 31, 2010 balance sheet after the above entries had been posted.

Note: do not consider cost of goods sold in the above transactions.

Review Exercise – Answer

a) Show how the above transactions would be recorded in the journal

Date	Account Title and Explanation	Debit	Credit
Dec 31	Cash	70,000	
	Accounts Receivable	280,000	
	Sales Revenue		350,000
	To record sales for the year		
Dec 31	Cash	250,000	
	Accounts Receivable		250,000
	To record collection of accounts for the year		
Dec 31	Allowance for Doubtful Accounts	1,500	
	Accounts Receivable		1,500
	To write-off uncollectible account		
Dec 31	Accounts Receivable	1,500	
	Allowance for Doubtful Accounts		1,500
	To reverse write-off of account		
Dec 31	Bad Debt Expense	2,500	
	Allowance for Doubtful Accounts		2,500
	To reinstate bad debt for the year		

b) Show how the above transactions would be posted in the related T-Accounts

Cash

$70,000	
250,000	
$320,000	

Sales Revenue

| | $350,000 |

Accounts Receivable

Beg. Bal.: $35,000	$250,000
280,000	1,500
1,500	
$65,000	

Allowance for Doubtful Accounts

$1,500	Beg. Bal.: $2,500
	1,500
	2,500
	5,000

Bad Debt Expense

| 2,500 | |

c) Show how accounts receivable would be reported on the Dec 31, 2010 balance sheet after the above entries had been posted

Current Assets:	Dec 31, 2010	Jan 01, 2010
Accounts Receivable	$65,000	$35,000
Less: Allowance for Doubtful Accounts	5,000	2,500
Net Accounts Receivable	$60,000	$32,500

Chapter 4
INVENTORY

LEARNING OUTCOMES:

❶ Understand the difference between the perpetual and the periodic inventory systems

❷ Record journal entries under the perpetual inventory system

❸ Determine inventory values under the perpetual system

❹ Determine the impact of inventory errors

❺ Use the lower of cost or market to value inventory

❻ Estimate inventory using the gross profit method and the retail method

❼ Calculate ratios to determine inventory efficiency

❽ Apply controls and understand ethics related to inventory

Appendix

❾ Record journal entries under the periodic inventory system

❿ Determine inventory values under the periodic system

Inventory: An Introduction

As our examination of the balance sheet continues, it will become increasingly clear that each type of current asset has its own defining characteristics. For example, cash is the most liquid type of asset and is used to buy other assets, while other assets are sold for cash.

Much like accounts receivable, inventory involves the day-to-day operations of the business; and can also comprise a large portion of the company's current assets. However, unlike accounts receivable and any of the other assets we have studied so far, inventory isn't just a number or monetary concept.

Inventory represents physical goods that a company has bought or manufactured in order to sell to its customers. The inventory has a value that can change unpredictably and even decrease over time. Accountants can make errors in tracking the value of inventory as it moves from receiving to shipping. They can also have a hard time figuring out what inventory to count and how to count it. These are some of the challenges confronting a company in handling its inventory assets.

purchases for resale.

CURRENT ASSETS

CASH

SHORT-TERM INVESTMENT

ACCOUNTS RECEIVABLE

INVENTORY

FIGURE 4.1

Perpetual vs. Periodic Inventory Systems

updated all the time

Under a **perpetual inventory system**, a continuous record of the changes to inventory is maintained. This means all purchases and sales of goods are recorded directly in the inventory account as they occur. With the advent of scanning technology, most retail businesses can now use a perpetual inventory system. With one swipe of the scanner at the point of sale, the value of the specific item can be accounted for and adjusted directly in the company's inventory account. The cost of goods sold is readily available at the end of the period, as the inventory account has been constantly updated.

Updated sometimes ex: restaurant

However, not all companies choose to track their inventory this way. A small grocery store might not have access to scanning technology. In this case, a company can use what is known as the **periodic inventory system**, which determines the quantity of inventory on hand only periodically. Under a periodic inventory system, a physical count is taken at the end of the period to determine the value of the cost of goods sold.

Figure 4.2 highlights the difference between the perpetual and periodic inventory system. It shows sample revenue and expense amounts for a company under both systems over a period of three months. Notice that the perpetual system updates cost of goods sold continuously while the periodic system updates cost of goods sold only when a physical inventory count is performed (at the end of March).

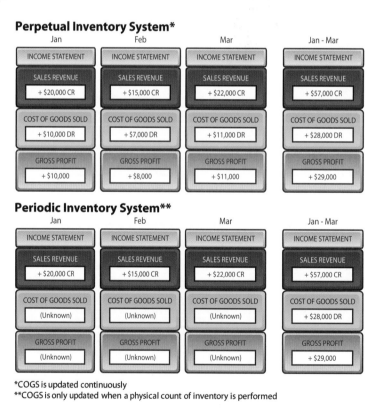

FIGURE 4.2

Since the periodic inventory system is not widely used in today's computerized environment, our discussion will focus on the perpetual inventory system.

The Perpetual Inventory System

As mentioned above, a perpetual inventory system involves recording all transactions affecting the balance of inventory on hand, as they occur. In reality, most businesses have separate, detailed records for each type of product they sell. For simplicity, our examples will focus on one type of product, where all transactions affect a single inventory account directly.

We will demonstrate various inventory-related transactions using an example of a retail store called Tools 4U Inc., which buys and sells various tools. Assume the inventory account has a beginning balance of $20,000 and the following transactions occurred during the accounting period.

Purchases

When inventory is purchased for resale using a perpetual inventory system, the inventory account is debited and the cash or the accounts payable account is credited. Tools 4U Inc. purchased inventory at a cost of $4,800 on January 1, 2011. Assume all purchases and sales are made on account.

JOURNAL			Page 1
Date 2011	**Account Title and Explanation**	**Debit**	**Credit**
Jan 1	Inventory	4,800	
	Accounts Payable		4,800
	Purchased inventory on account		

FIGURE 4.3

Purchase Returns

Goods often need to be returned for reasons such as incorrect product, over-shipments, or inferior product quality.

When the manager of Tools 4U examined the new shipment of inventory from the company's supplier, Roof Tiles Inc., he noticed that there were some damaged goods in the shipment. The damaged goods cost $500. The goods were returned and the journal entry would be the exact reverse of the original purchase transaction.

JOURNAL			Page 1
Date 2011	**Account Title and Explanation**	**Debit**	**Credit**
Jan 2	Accounts Payable	500	
	Inventory		500
	Goods returned to Roof Tiles		

FIGURE 4.4

BALANCE SHEET

CURRENT ASSETS	CURRENT LIABILITIES
CASH	ACCOUNTS PAYABLE & ACCRUED LIABILITIES - $500 DR
SHORT-TERM INVESTMENTS	UNEARNED REVENUE
ACCOUNTS RECEIVABLE	LOANS PAYABLE (CURRENT)
DOUBTFUL ACCOUNTS	SHAREHOLDERS' LOANS
INVENTORY - $500 CR	NON-CURRENT LIABILITIES

Purchase Allowances

Purchase allowances occur when the buyer agrees to keep the undesirable goods at a reduced cost. Continuing with the above example, assume Tools 4U found another $500 worth of unsatisfactory goods and the supplier had offered a 20% allowance for the company to keep the goods, rather than returning them. The journal entry would be recorded by debiting accounts payable and crediting inventory. The transaction amount would be $100 ($500 × 20%).

After recording purchase returns and purchase allowance, a balance of $4,200 ($4,800 - $500 - $100) is still owing to Roof Tiles Inc.

JOURNAL			Page 1
Date 2011	**Account Title and Explanation**	**Debit**	**Credit**
Jan 4	Accounts Payable	100	
	Inventory		100
	Allowance from Roof Tiles *for damaged goods* *(500 × 20% = 100)*		

BALANCE SHEET

CURRENT ASSETS — CASH, SHORT-TERM INVESTMENTS, ACCOUNTS RECEIVABLE, DOUBTFUL ACCOUNTS, INVENTORY - $100 CR

CURRENT LIABILITIES — ACCOUNTS PAYABLE & ACCRUED LIABILITIES - $100 DR, UNEARNED REVENUE, LOANS PAYABLE (CURRENT), SHAREHOLDERS' LOANS, NON-CURRENT LIABILITIES

FIGURE 4.5

Purchase Discounts

Various types of discounts exist when purchasing products or services. Some common reasons for a seller to give discounts are to:

- avoid changes in a price catalogue
- apply price discrimination (i.e. quote different prices for different customers)
- hide the true invoice price from competitors
- encourage customers to purchase more *→ buy one get one free (encourages more sales)*
- encourage early payments

Two types of common discounts given are **trade discounts** and **cash discounts**. Only cash discounts will be discussed in detail for the purpose of this chapter.

Cash discounts are usually given to encourage prompt payment from customers. For example, a seller may offer a 2% cash discount if the payment is made within 10 days of the date of invoice, otherwise the full amount is payable within 30 days. The term for this arrangement is commonly shown as: 2/10, n/30 (read as: a 2 percent discount is applied if paid within 10 days, the net amount owing is due in 30 days). Another example could be: 3/15, n/30, which means a 3 percent discount is applied if paid within 15 days, otherwise the full amount (net amount owing) is payable within 30 days. The following example illustrates how to record a purchase discount.

Tools 4U made the original purchase from Roof Tiles Inc. on January 1, 2011 for $4,800. The amount Tools 4U owes has been reduced by $600 due to returns and allowances, so that only $4,200 must be paid. The supplier (Roof Tiles Inc.) allows 2/10, n/30 on all invoices. Since Tools 4U has excess cash at this time, the manager decides to take advantage of the cash discount by paying the invoice within 10 days.

Assume Tools 4U Inc. made the payment on January 10, the amount for the bill will be $4,200 less the $84 discount ($4,200 × 2%). Since the business is paying less for the inventory, the value of the inventory needs to decrease by the value of the discount. The entry to record the payment is shown in figure 4.6.

Can use purchase discount Acct (handwritten)

JOURNAL			Page 1
Date 2011	**Account Title and Explanation**	**Debit**	**Credit**
Jan 10	Accounts Payable	4,200	
	Cash		4,116
	Inventory		84
	Paid invoice and took discount for early payment		

when not sold (handwritten)

BALANCE SHEET

CURRENT ASSETS	CURRENT LIABILITIES
CASH − $4,116 CR	ACCOUNTS PAYABLE & ACCRUED LIABILITIES − $4,200 DR
SHORT-TERM INVESTMENTS	UNEARNED REVENUE
ACCOUNTS RECEIVABLE	LOANS PAYABLE (CURRENT)
DOUBTFUL ACCOUNTS	SHAREHOLDERS' LOANS
INVENTORY − $84 CR	NON-CURRENT LIABILITIES

FIGURE 4.6

The discount of $84 is credited to inventory because the downward adjustment is made to reflect the true cost of the goods.

If Tools 4U decides not to pay the amount owing within 10 days, then they are not entitled to take the discount. They must pay the full amount of $4,200 within 30 days of the invoice date. This payment is just like paying any other amount that is owed to a supplier. Cash will decrease (credit) and accounts payable will decrease (debit) by the amount owed. The entry is shown in figure 4.7. Notice the date is more than 10 days past the invoice date.

JOURNAL			Page 1
Date 2011	**Account Title and Explanation**	**Debit**	**Credit**
Jan 24	Accounts Payable	4,200	
	Cash		4,200
	Paid amount owing to Roof Tiles		

BALANCE SHEET

CURRENT ASSETS	CURRENT LIABILITIES
CASH − $4,200 CR	ACCOUNTS PAYABLE & ACCRUED LIABILITIES − $4,200 DR
SHORT-TERM INVESTMENTS	UNEARNED REVENUE
ACCOUNTS RECEIVABLE	LOANS PAYABLE (CURRENT)
DOUBTFUL ACCOUNTS	SHAREHOLDERS' LOANS
INVENTORY	NON-CURRENT LIABILITIES

FIGURE 4.7

Freight Cost

When one company purchases goods from another, the items purchased must somehow be transported from the seller's place of business to the buyer's place of business. There are a number of ways to transport goods (sea, rail, truck, etc.). The selling company may have their own fleet of vehicles to deliver goods to customers, or they may use a common carrier. A common carrier in this context is a company that provides shipping service to the general public. Examples would be railroad or trucking companies.

In addition to arranging transport of the goods, at some point ownership of the goods must be legally transferred from the seller to the buyer. The term used to determine when ownership of the goods changes hands is called the FOB point. FOB stands for Freight On Board. There are two possible FOB points: FOB shipping point and FOB destination. Each of these points have implications regarding who pays for shipping, when ownership passes from the buyer to the seller and who bears the risk for the goods during transport.

FOB Shipping Point

FOB shipping point indicates that ownership of the items being purchased changes when the goods leave the seller's place of business. In other words, ownership changes at the point when shipping begins. In this case, a common carrier is often used to deliver the items to the buyer. The buyer will pay for shipping and is responsible to insure the items while they are in transport. If anything were to happen to the items while they are being transported, the buyer bears the risk of loss.

The seller will record revenue earned and the buyer will record an increase to inventory as soon as the goods are loaded on the truck (or other transport). The buyer will also have to record the shipping cost into inventory. The reason the buyer includes shipping costs as inventory is that the value of the goods must include all costs (such as transportation) that were incurred to get the goods ready to sell. Figure 4.8 illustrates who pays the shipping costs.

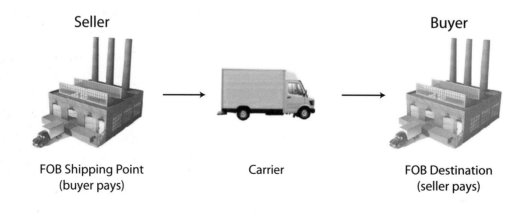

FIGURE 4.8

FOB Destination

FOB destination indicates that ownership of the items being purchased changes when the goods arrive at the buyer's place of business. In other words, ownership changes at the point of destination. In this case, the seller may pay an independent carrier or have a fleet of vehicles and use them to deliver goods to their customers. Thus, the seller pays for the shipping and is responsible for the items while they are in transport. If anything were to happen to the items while they are being transported, the seller bears the risk of loss.

The seller will record revenue earned and the buyer will record an increase to inventory once the goods reach their destination (the buyer's place of business). The seller will also record the cost of shipping the goods as an expense. This expense is part of the sellers cost of doing business.

A summary of FOB shipping point and FOB destination are presented in figure 4.9. Basically, whoever pays for shipping owns the goods while they are being transported and bears the risk of loss.

	FOB Shipping Point	FOB Destination
Ownership Change	When goods leave the seller on a common carrier	When goods arrive at the buyer's place of business
Transportation Costs	Paid by the buyer and recorded in inventory	Paid by the seller and recorded as an expense
Risk of Loss	Buyer bears risk of loss during transport	Seller bears risk of loss during transport

FIGURE 4.9

Assume that Tools 4U had inventory shipped to them FOB shipping point. This means that Tools 4U will have to pay the cost of shipping. If they paid $100 on January 2, that amount would have to be added to the inventory account. The journal entry is shown in figure 4.10.

BALANCE SHEET

JOURNAL			Page 1
Date 2011	Account Title and Explanation	Debit	Credit
Jan 2	Inventory	100	
	Cash		100
	Paid for freight costs		

FIGURE 4.10

Freight Costs → Inventory

Sales

Under a perpetual inventory system, two entries are needed to record the sale of inventory. One entry is needed to record the sale, which involves debiting accounts receivable (or cash) and crediting sales revenue; and another entry is needed to record the cost of goods sold, which involves debiting cost of goods sold and crediting inventory.

Both the COGS and the amount of ending inventory will be updated immediately in the accounting records when using a perpetual inventory system.

Assume Tools 4U Inc. sold $9,000 worth of inventory for $15,000 on January 15. The journal entry is presented as shown in figure 4.11.

JOURNAL			Page 1
Date 2011	**Account Title and Explanation**	**Debit**	**Credit**
Jan 15	Accounts Receivable	15,000	
	Sales Revenue		15,000
	Sales to customer		
	Cost of Goods Sold	9,000	
	Inventory		9,000
	Cost of goods sold for above sale		

FIGURE 4.11

Sales Returns

A business may have to deal with numerous returns from customers, and these returns must be tracked over a period of time. High return levels may indicate serious problems with the products being sold. Therefore, instead of reversing the revenue account with a debit when recording returns, a contra-revenue account called **sales returns and allowances** is used to track the amount of returns.

Sales returns and allowances is a **contra-revenue account** with a normal debit balance. It is generally used to record both sales returns and sales allowances. **Sales returns** occur when undesirable products are returned to the seller. **Sales allowances** occur when the customer decides to keep such undesirable products at a reduced price.

Continuing with our example, if a customer returned Tools 4U Inc. $4,000 of undesirable goods (the cost of the goods is $3,000), the journal entry using the contra-revenue account would be:

There will be a $4,000 increase in the sales returns and allowances account. This amount decreases revenue since the contra revenue account has the opposite normal balance of the revenue account.

In the example in figure 4.12, the inventory that was returned was not what the customer wanted. There was nothing wrong with the product in terms of quality, so it was placed back on the shelf to be sold again. If the items returned by the customer were damaged, then the inventory can not be sold again. Tool 4U would either have to absorb the cost of the damaged items (with an adjusting entry shown later), or return the damaged inventory to their supplier to get their money back (a purchase return).

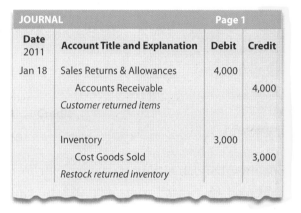

FIGURE 4.12

Sales Allowances

There are circumstances where a reduction to the original selling price is given to a customer.

Assume the customer from January 15 discovered that some goods were damaged during shipping. Instead of returning the items, the customer agreed to accept an allowance of 5% on the price of the goods they kept. The customer kept $11,000 ($15,000 original sale - $4,000 return) of goods, so they will get a $550 ($11,000 × 5%) reduction on what they owe Tools 4U. The journal entry is shown in figure 4.13. The amount is recorded as a debit to sales returns and allowances and a credit to accounts receivable. Since the credit to accounts receivable decrease equity, it must be recorded on the income statement by debiting sales returns and allowances.

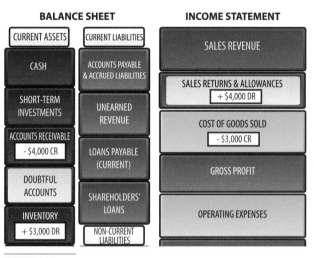

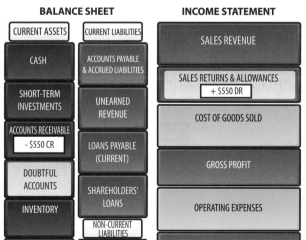

FIGURE 4.13

no adjustment to COGS because no inventory returned.

119

A balance of $10,450 ($15,000 - $4,000 - $550) is still owed by Tools 4U's customer.

Sales Discounts

When selling products or services, it is common to offer sales discounts to customers for early payment. The concept works in the same way as the purchase discount. Assume that Tools 4U offered their customer from January 15 terms of 2/10, n/30 in the invoice. If the customer pays by January 25, they can take a 2% discount on the $10,450 they still owe.

Assume the customer made the payment on January 20; the amount will be for $10,241 ($10,450 less the 2% discount). The journal entry to record this transaction is shown in figure 4.14.

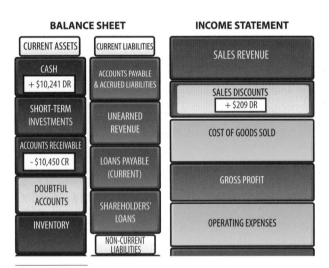

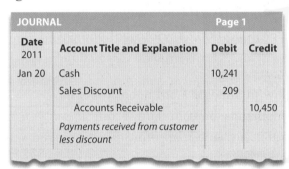

JOURNAL			Page 1
Date 2011	Account Title and Explanation	Debit	Credit
Jan 20	Cash	10,241	
	Sales Discount	209	
	Accounts Receivable		10,450
	Payments received from customer less discount		

FIGURE 4.14

The $209 is recorded as a debit in the **sales discount**. Sales discount is a contra-revenue account which can be increased with a debit and decreased with a credit.

If the customer decides not to pay the amount owing within the discount period, then they are not entitled to take the discount that Tools 4U offers. Instead, the customer will have to pay the full amount of $10,450 within 30 days of the sale. The receipt of cash from the customer is just like receiving cash from any customer that owes the company money. Cash will increase (debit) and accounts receivable will decrease (credit). The entry is shown in figure 4.15. Notice that the date is more than 10 days past the date of the sale.

JOURNAL			Page 1
Date 2011	Account Title and Explanation	Debit	Credit
Feb 2	Cash	10,450	
	Accounts Receivable		10,450
	Payment received from customer		

FIGURE 4.15

Income Statement

A multistep income statement is prepared (shown in figure 4.16) based on the sales transactions that have occurred.

Tools 4U Inc. Income Statement For the Month Ended January 31, 2011		
Sales Revenue		$15,000
Less:		
Sales Returns & Allowances	($4,550)	
Sales Discounts	(209)	(4,759)
Net Sales		10,241
Cost of Goods Sold		6,000
Gross Profit		4,241

(Handwritten notes: "Deed to show breakdown." next to Sales section; "Less:" beside Cost of Goods Sold; "Gross Profit ÷ Net Sales × 100 = Gross Profit margin" beside the totals)

FIGURE 4.16

The sales revenue amount comes from figure 4.11. However, this is not the true value of what was sold. The customer returned some items, was given an allowance for a slightly damaged product, and paid early to receive the discount. Each of these items will reduce the value of sales revenue to provide net sales. **Net sales** is the value of sales after taking into account sales returns and allowances and sales discounts. The gross profit amount represents how much profit is left to pay for operating expenses.

In a situation where a company tracks sales returns and discounts separately, the gross profit margin is calculated using the value of net sales, not sales revenue:

$$\text{Gross Profit Margin} = \text{Gross Profit} \div \text{Net Sales} \times 100\%$$

$$= \$4,241 \div \$10,241 \times 100\%$$

$$= 41.4\%$$

The perpetual inventory system is typically used in the retail sector where the cost of products can easily be identified through technology such as bar coding. In its simplest form, when a product is purchased for resale, the value of goods available for sale is automatically updated. When a product is sold, the inventory is deducted from stock and the value of cost of goods sold is updated immediately. Gross profit can be determined right away since the cost of goods sold is known at any given time. If any adjustment to the value of the inventory is required, it can be determined when a physical inventory count is performed at the end of the year (or from time to time).

Closing Entries

When using a perpetual inventory system, inventory is immediately updated after each purchase and sale transaction. However, the value of inventory on the balance sheet may not accurately represent the value of inventory actually on hand. To verify the accuracy of the accounting records, a physical inventory count should be performed at the end of the reporting period. If the count does not match the records, an adjustment must be made to bring the inventory to its correct balance. This difference is often referred to as "inventory shrinkage", resulting either from an error in recording transactions, theft or breakage.

If the amount is considered immaterial, the following entry would be made where the balance in the inventory account was more than the physical count. Assuming that the amount of shrinkage is $200, the journal entry for this transaction is shown in figure 4.17.

JOURNAL			Page 1
Date 2011	**Account Title and Explanation**	**Debit**	**Credit**
Jan 31	Cost of Goods Sold	200	
	Inventory		200
	Adjust inventory to physical count		

FIGURE 4.17

After this adjustment and all other adjustments have been made, assume Tools 4U has the adjusted trial balance shown in figure 4.18.

Tools 4U Inc. Adjusted Trial Balance January 31, 2011		
Account	**Debit**	**Credit**
Cash	$5,200	
Accounts Receivable	3,750	
Inventory	12,470	
Prepaid Expenses	3,200	
Property, Plant & Equipment	6,840	
Accumulated Depreciation		$340
Accounts Payable		5,260
Unearned Revenue		2,450
Bank Loan		6,500
Common Shares		10,000
Retained Earnings		4,010
Sales Revenue		18,700
Sales Returns & Allowances	2,300	
Sales Discounts	420	
Cost of Goods Sold	7,480	
Salary Expense	3,460	
Rent Expense	2,140	
Total	$47,260	$47,260

FIGURE 4.18

The steps to close the books of a merchandising company are similar to closing a service company. The first step is to close the revenue account and is shown in figure 4.19.

JOURNAL			Page 1
Date	**Account Title and Explanation**	**Debit**	**Credit**
2011			
Jan 31	Sales Revenue	18,700	
	Income Summary		18,700
	Close revenue accounts		

FIGURE 4.19

The second step is to close expenses. In this step, we will also close the two contra-revenue accounts (sales returns and allowances and sales discounts) because they have debit balances like the rest of the expense accounts.

JOURNAL			Page 1
Date	**Account Title and Explanation**	**Debit**	**Credit**
2011			
Jan 31	Income Summary	15,800	
	Sales Returns & Allowances		2,300
	Sales Discounts		420
	Cost of Goods Sold		7,480
	Salary Expense		3,460
	Rent Expense		2,140
	Close expense and debit balance accounts		

FIGURE 4.20

Step 3 closes the income summary account. If this were a proprietorship, the income summary would be closed to the capital account. Since Tools 4U is a corporation, the income summary will be closed to retained earnings.

JOURNAL			Page 1
Date	**Account Title and Explanation**	**Debit**	**Credit**
2011			
Jan 31	Income Summary	2,900	
	Retained Earnings		2,900
	Close income summary		

FIGURE 4.21

The end result, just as in a service company, is that the equity in the business is updated with the net income.

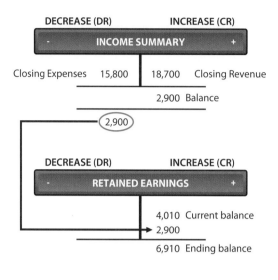

FIGURE 4.22

Methods for Valuing Inventory

Determining the Cost of Inventory

Once an inventory system has been chosen, there are three methods that companies can use, based on the type of business and choice of management, to value the inventory.

Here is a brief description of what they are and under what circumstances they are used:

- **Specific identification** is used when a business wants to value specific items individually. High value items such as cars, houses and diamonds are often valued in this way.
- **The weighted average cost method** is used when a business simply applies an average cost to all its inventory. Homogeneous (standardized) materials, such as plastic used in the making of garbage bags, or oil used in making gasoline, are often valued in this way.
- **The first-in-first-out (FIFO)** method is used when a business assumes that the first items received in inventory are also the first items moved out of inventory. Perishable items that expire within a certain amount of time, such as fruit and vegetables, are often valued in this way.

There are two principles that apply when a company chooses an inventory valuation method:

1. The method chosen can be somewhat arbitrary, since it does not have to actually reflect the physical movement of goods. For example, if a business chooses the first-in-first-out (FIFO) method, a newly received product can still end up being sold before an older product.

2. Once a valuation method is chosen, the company has to stay with it. The reason for this is that a company may be tempted to change the method used in order to impact cost of goods sold and closing inventory values, which can both change depending on the valuation method. (This adheres to the GAAP principle of consistency).

Applying Valuation Methods

Cool Ink Company sells a number of different high quality pens, pencils, markers and highlighters. Let us examine one item from their inventory to illustrate specific identification, weighted average and FIFO inventory valuation methods. Assume that Cool Ink uses a perpetual inventory system to account for purchases and sales.

Cool Ink Company currently has ten collector pens in inventory with a cost of $10 each. During the month of March, the following transactions took place:

Date	Transaction	Quantity	Unit Cost
March 5	Purchase from Pen Distributers	50	$12
March 7	Sale	15	
March 15	Purchase from Promotional Pens	40	$14
March 19	Purchase from Promotional Pens	20	$16
March 27	Sale	50	

FIGURE 4.23

During the month, the cost of the pen changed. This implies that the cost of goods sold applied to each sale will likely be different, based on which pens are actually sold. We can apply the three methods of valuing inventory to the transactions to arrive at different values for inventory and cost of goods sold. This will demonstrate that the choice of inventory valuation method can make a difference on the financial statements of a company.

Using Specific Identification

When using specific identification, it is helpful to list the purchases separately from each other to easily identify the costs associated with each batch of inventory. The opening balance and the transactions from figure 4.23 are listed in figure 4.24. At the bottom of the figure is the value of ending inventory.

Date	Purchases			Sales			Balance		
	Quantity	Unit Cost	Value	Quantity	Unit Cost	Value	Quantity	Unit Cost	Value
March 1							10	$10	$100
March 5	50	$12	$600				10	$10	$100
							50	$12	$600
March 7				8	$10	$80	2	$10	$20
				7	$12	$84	43	$12	$516
March 15	40	$14	$560				2	$10	$20
							43	$12	$516
							40	$14	$560
March 19	20	$16	$320				2	$10	$20
							43	$12	$516
							40	$14	$560
							20	$16	$320
March 27				2	$10	$20	10	$12	$120
				33	$12	$396	25	$14	$350
				15	$14	$210	20	$16	$320
Ending Inventory									$790

FIGURE 4.24

Step 1:   The purchase of 50 pens on March 5 is added to the value of inventory.

Step 2:   The sale of 15 pens on March 7 can be specifically identified. Eight of the pens came from opening inventory and seven of the pens came from the purchase on March 5. As a result, the opening balance of 10 pens is reduced to two and the batch of 50 pens is reduced to 43. The value of cost of goods sold for this sale is $164 ($80 + $84).

Step 3:   The purchase of 40 pens on March 15 is added to the value of inventory.

Step 4:   The purchase of 20 pens on March 19 is added to the value of inventory.

Step 5:   The sale of 50 pens on March 27 can be specifically identified. Two came from opening inventory, 33 from the purchase on March 5 and 15 from the purchase on March 15. The value of the cost of goods sold for this sale is $626 ($20 + $396 + $210).

Step 6:   The value of ending inventory is made up of 10 pens remaining from the March 5 purchase, 25 pens remaining from the March 15 purchase and 20 pens remaining from the March 19 purchase. Total value of ending inventory is $790 ($120 + $350 + $320).

Using First-In-First-Out (FIFO)

When using the FIFO method, it is helpful to list the purchases in the order they were received. This will allow you to easily see which items were the first ones purchased, which will also be considered the first ones sold. The opening balance and the transactions from figure 4.23 are listed in figure 4.25. At the bottom of the figure is the value of ending inventory.

Date	Purchases			Sales			Balance		
	Quantity	Unit Cost	Value	Quantity	Unit Cost	Value	Quantity	Unit Cost	Value
March 1							10	$10	$100
March 5	50	$12	$600				10	$10	$100
							50	$12	$600
March 7				10	$10	$100	45	$12	$540
				5	$12	$60			
March 15	40	$14	$560				45	$12	$540
							40	$14	$560
March 19	20	$16	$320				45	$12	$540
							40	$14	$560
							20	$16	$320
March 27				45	$12	$540	35	$14	$490
				5	$14	$70	20	$16	$320
Ending Inventory									$810

FIGURE 4.25

Step 1: The purchase of 50 pens on March 5 is added to the value of inventory.

Step 2: The sale of 15 pens on March 7 must first use the costs from the opening balance. Since there were only 10 pens in the opening balance, another five will have to be taken from the purchase on March 5. This means that the entire opening balance inventory has been sold and only 45 units remain from the purchase on March 5. The value of cost of goods sold for this sale is $160 ($100 + $60).

Step 3: The purchase of 40 pens on March 15 is added to the value of inventory.

Step 4: The purchase of 20 pens on March 19 is added to the value of inventory.

Step 5: The sale of the 50 pens on March 27 must first use the costs from the purchase on March 5. Since there are only 45 pens left from that purchase, another five will have to be taken from the purchase on March 15. The value of cost of goods sold for this sale is $610 ($540 + $70).

Step 6: The value of ending inventory is made up of 35 pens remaining from the March 15 purchase and 20 pens from the March 19 purchase. Total value of inventory is $810 ($490 + $320).

Using Weighted Average Cost

When using the weighted average cost method, the total inventory value will be divided by the total quantity on hand to arrive at an average cost for each unit. The opening balance and the transactions from figure 4.23 are listed in figure 4.26. At the bottom of the figure is the value of ending inventory.

Date	Purchases			Sales			Balance		
	Quantity	Unit Cost	Value	Quantity	Unit Cost	Value	Quantity	Unit Cost	Value
March 1							10	$10.00	$100
March 5	50	$12	$600				60	$11.67	$700
March 7				15	$11.67	$175	45	$11.67	$525
March 15	40	$14	$560				85	$12.76	$1,085
March 19	20	$16	$320				105	$13.38	$1,405
March 27				50	$13.38	$669	55	$13.38	$736
Ending Inventory									$736

FIGURE 4.26

Step 1:   The purchase of 50 pens on March 5 is added to the quantity on hand. The value of the 50 pens is added to the value of the opening inventory. The unit cost is approximately $11.67 ($700 ÷ 60 units).

Step 2:   The sale of 15 pens on March 7 is taken from inventory. The most recent unit cost of approximately $11.67 per unit is used to calculate the cost of goods sold ($175). Both the quantity and value of inventory decrease, and the unit cost is still approximately $11.67 ($525 ÷ 45 units). The unit cost of inventory will never change after a sale; it can only change after a purchase.

Step 3:   The purchase of 40 pens on March 15 is added to the quantity on hand. The value of the 40 pens is added to current value of inventory. The unit cost is now approximately $12.76 ($1,085 ÷ 85 units).

Step 4:   The purchase of 20 pens on March 19 is added to the quantity on hand. The value of the 20 pens is added to current value of inventory. The unit cost is now approximately $13.38 ($1,405 ÷ 105 units).

Step 5:   The sale of the 50 pens on March 27 is taken from inventory. The most recent cost of approximately $13.38 per unit is used to calculate the cost of goods sold ($669).

Step 6:   The value of ending inventory is 55 pens at the unit cost of approximately $13.38. Total value of inventory is $736.

The Effect of Different Valuation Methods

As the inventory valuation methods demonstrate, different ending inventory figures are produced using different valuation methods. The following chart summarizes these differences when applied to the Cool Ink example:

	Specific Identification	FIFO	Weighted Average
Inventory Available for Sale (beginning inventory + purchases)	$1,580	$1,580	$1,580
Ending Inventory	790	810	736
Value of COGS	790	770	844

FIGURE 4.27

From the above, we can make the following assumptions:

1. In times where product cost increases over the period, FIFO will result in the highest value of ending inventory.
2. While specific identification provides the true value of ending inventory and cost of goods sold, it is costly to implement and therefore not practical for items of small value.

When ending inventory amounts change, so does the cost of goods sold, gross profit and net income. Therefore, companies can dramatically change their financial results by manipulating the inventory valuation method.

Determining the Actual Quantity of Inventory

Goods are moved in and out of inventory all the time, which is why recording the amount and quantities bought and sold is so important. This is done when the goods enter the premises at purchase and when they leave the premises at sale. The reliability of the information recorded at these points must be assured.

For example, the items must be counted when they are received, and these amounts should be compared to the amounts listed on the original purchase order. Any discrepancies must be noted and followed up. Once the inventory count is complete, the company's records should be updated immediately.

Before goods can leave the premises, a release order, such as a packing slip, must be written up and authorized. Just as goods coming in have to be recorded, goods moving out must also be recorded. The shipper should note which goods are leaving and forward the documents to the accounting department to ensure the information is entered into the system.

Some of this paperwork can take time using a manual system. Computer scanning software can eliminate much of the paperwork and time involved in recording the movement of goods in inventory. Whether items are coming in or moving out, a swipe of the scanner can immediately track their location and status while in inventory.

The Physical Inventory Count

As required by GAAP, a business must take a physical count of its inventory accounts at least once a year. While a business may have its own policies and procedures for the process of taking a physical inventory count, the following steps are generally included:

1. Designate an area to a specific person.
2. Count and record each item on pre-numbered sheets that are distributed and controlled by the accounting department.
3. Once completed, the sheets are returned to the accounting department where items are valued and summarized.
4. Where a perpetual system is used, the inventory record (ledger account) is compared to the physical count. Differences are noted and adjustments are recorded accordingly.
5. Where major differences occur between the inventory record and the physical count, further investigation is required.

Effect of Inventory Errors

Inventory is a type of asset that differs somewhat from other assets we have discussed in previous chapters. Unlike cash, the value of which is quite definitive (except when it comes to exchange rates between currencies), or accounts receivable which is also quite definitive, the value of inventory is largely a matter of judgment.

Attaching a value to inventory involves a different kind of challenge. A warehouse can be full of various products which were bought at a certain price and will sold at another price, with no clarity as to which items moved when. As we have already demonstrated, the choice of valuation system often settles the matter. However, even a valuation system only serves to create a snapshot in time, one which management can influence by choosing one valuation system over another.

In other words, matching physical items in inventory to specific dollar values using any valuation method can be complicated. This is why the process is prone to errors, and errors can have an impact on the way that a company presents its financial figures — both internally and externally. Let's examine the impact that an inventory error can have on gross margin percentage and other aspects of financial reporting.

The Impact of Cost of Goods Sold On Gross Profit

*Before we continue, we must first clarify the use of the terms gross profit and gross margin. These terms are used in various ways by different businesses, and there is no right or wrong version. For the purpose of this course, we will refer to **gross profit** as the **dollar amount** calculated by subtracting the COGS from revenues, and **gross margin** as the **percentage** of gross profit divided by sales.*

Although inventory is a balance sheet account, it can have an immediate impact on the income statement, since the cost of goods sold is used to calculate gross profit. Gross profit in turn, is used to calculate the gross margin percentage. The gross margin percentage represents the percentage of sales left to pay the remaining operating expenses of the company.

This relationship between inventory and gross profit is demonstrated in this diagram:

It should become clear that the cost of goods sold serves as a focal point when dealing with inventory on a company's financial statements.

FIGURE 4.28

In a periodic inventory system, COGS is calculated by adding total inventory purchases to the value of inventory on hand at the beginning of the period, then deducting the closing value of inventory at the end of the period. The closing value of inventory is determined by a physical count. An example of the calculation is shown in figure 4.29.

In other words, a company's COGS represents the amount of inventory that is used/sold in a period.

Inventory Calculation	
Opening Inventory	10,000
Plus: Purchases	60,000
Cost of Goods Available for Sale	70,000
Less: Closing Inventory	20,000
Cost of Goods Sold	50,000

FIGURE 4.29

Errors in valuing closing inventory can impact COGS and, as a result, gross profit. Just one broken link in the chain — that of an error in closing inventory — can render many of the other links broken. Beyond affecting COGS and gross profit, an incorrect inventory value impacts opening inventory for the next period. We will examine the impact on gross profit while ignoring the effects on net income for the year.

The Effect of Overstating Inventory

We will use two examples: one set of charts will include the correct amount for closing inventory. The other set of charts will include an incorrect amount for closing inventory.

We will then look at how this error impacts the other important figures on the company's financial statements. Here are the correct numbers:

Inventory Calculation	
Opening Inventory	5,000
Plus: Purchases	75,000
Cost of Goods Available for Sale	80,000
Less: Closing Inventory	9,000
Cost of Goods Sold	71,000

Income Statement Year 1	
Sales	$100,000
Less: Cost of Goods Sold	71,000
Gross Profit	$29,000

FIGURE 4.30

When closing inventory is correctly valued at $9,000, a COGS value of $71,000 is produced. As a result, the gross profit for the year is $29,000. The gross margin for the reporting period would then be: 29,000 ÷ 100,000 = 29%

What happens if we over-value closing inventory by $1,000?

Gross profit for the year is $30,000. Gross margin is then: 30,000 ÷ 100,000 = 30%

Inventory Calculation	
Opening Inventory	5,000
Plus: Purchases	75,000
Cost of Goods Available for Sale	80,000
Less: Closing Inventory	10,000
Cost of Goods Sold	70,000

Income Statement Year 1	
Sales	$100,000
Less: Cost of Goods Sold	70,000
Gross Profit	$30,000

FIGURE 4.31

As a result, COGS is understated by $1,000, gross profit is overstated by $1,000, and gross margin is overstated by 1%. Note that the same error while performing a physical account for a company that uses the perpetual inventory system will lead to the same problem.

If this error is found and corrected before the end of the period, then the following journal entry is made:

JOURNAL			
Date	Account Title and Explanation	Debit	Credit
	Cost of Goods Sold	1,000	
	Inventory		1,000
	Corrected overstated inventory		

FIGURE 4.32

If the error is made after the financial reporting period is over, then an assessment of the materiality of the error must be made.

If the error is considered material, then the company's financial statements would have to be reissued with the amended figures. It is obviously a scenario that companies want to avoid. Such a high profile mistake can only cast doubt on how the company is being run. Nevertheless, if such material errors are found, they must be reported — regardless of any embarrassment they may cause the company.

This is just a snapshot of what errors in valuing inventory can do to a company's financial statements. Both internal and external stakeholders are impacted by inventory errors. Such errors can affect things like business decision-making, tax reporting and adherence to GAAP procedures.

The Impact of Inventory Errors

Overstated gross profits resulting from inflated inventory can give management a false sense of confidence in the company. This could lead to bad decisions when it comes to pricing, discounts, target market share, or other aspects of business performance. The reverse would be true for understated numbers, which could create unnecessary panic and desperation on the part of ownership.

An inaccurate gross profit figure can also have consequences when it comes to paying taxes. A higher gross profit leads to higher net income, which means that a company is paying more tax than it should. Perhaps even more importantly, an understated gross profit figure leads to an understated net income amount, which means that the government is getting less in taxes from the company than it should.

Finally, a company could use its inflated financial figures to create a false impression of its performance on external stakeholders, or even on banks when trying to secure loans. This can represent an ethical breach in violation of GAAP rules of disclosure.

Valuation of Inventory at the Lower of Cost or Market

Market conditions can fluctuate. With regard to inventory, this means that sometimes a company sells its inventory for a lower price than what it was purchased for in the first place (i.e. the selling price is lower than cost).

The GAAP principle of conservatism asserts that, given a choice, the accounting alternative that produces a lower value for assets must always be used. This prevents companies from providing an overly optimistic state of their finances.

As a result, the **lower of cost or market (LCM)** principle must be used when valuing inventory.

So when inventory is sold below cost, it is the selling price that is used to value the inventory — not the purchase price. In other words, an inventory item can never be valued at more than the purchase price.

The LCM principle can be applied on three different levels: individual item; category; and total inventory. We will demonstrate how this is done by using Elan's Camera Shop as an example. The following is a chart detailing the cost and selling price of all their inventory.

	1	2	3	4	5	6	7
					Lower of Cost and Market applied to ...		
	Description	Category	Cost	Selling Price (market)	Individual	Category	Total
	Film type 1	Supplies	$100	$90	$90		
	Film type 2	Supplies	500	520	500		
	Total Supplies		600	610		$600	
	Camera A	Cameras	1,000	1,000	1,000		
	Camera B	Cameras	2,000	2,200	2,000		
	Total Cameras		3,000	3,200		3,000	
	Accessory 1	Accessories	3,000	2,900	2,900		
	Accessory 2	Accessories	4,000	3,500	3,500		
	Total Accessories		7,000	6,400		6,400	
	Total		$10,600	$10,210	$9,990	$10,000	$10,210

FIGURE 4.33

- Column 1 is a description of a particular inventory item.
- Column 2 categorizes the item into supplies, cameras and accessories.
- Column 3 provides the cost of the item.
- Column 4 indicates the market selling price of the item.
- Columns 5, 6 and 7 cover inventory values based on LCM: Column 5 lists the LCM for individual inventory items, Column 6 lists the LCM for each category, and Column 7 simply picks the lower of cost or market after all the inventory items are added together.
- The items marked in grey represent a total cost or selling price per category. For example, the total cost for all supplies is $600, and the total selling price for all supplies is $610.
- The last row of totals, including the items marked in orange, are the final inventory values using the three different methods.

If the LCM is applied to individual items, the total inventory value is $9,990. If applied to the three categories, we get an inventory value of $10,000, and if applied to the total amount of inventory, we get a value of $10,210. You will note that this last number (bottom right-hand corner) is the total selling price of all the inventory. This amount is lower than the total purchase price of $10,600. In other words, it is the most obvious demonstration of the LCM principle at work.

The last step in applying the lower of cost or market principle is to properly reflect the results of figure 4.33 in the accounting records of the company. This is done by recording a journal entry to reduce the value of inventory. For example, suppose Elan's Camera Shop applies LCM to individual items. The entry is a debit to cost of goods sold and

JOURNAL			
Date	Account Title and Explanation	Debit	Credit
	Cost of Goods Sold	610	
	Inventory		610
	To adjust inventory to LCM (on an individual item basis)		

FIGURE 4.34

a credit to inventory. The amount of the adjustment is equal to the original cost of the inventory less the LCM value applied to individual items. In this case, the adjustment is equal to $610 ($10,600 - $9,990). The journal entry is shown in figure 4.34.

In the above journal entry, cost of goods sold is debited. If the amount of the adjustment is deemed material, the company can instead debit another income statement account called "Loss on Write-down of Inventory."

Methods of Estimating Inventory

In a perpetual inventory system, a company maintains a continuous record of the changes to inventory. This means that, at any given point in time, a company can take an instant snapshot of its inventory value, including the amounts for cost of goods sold and ending inventory. That is why modern scanning and computer technology can help a company update its financial situation with the click of the mouse.

Alternatively, a periodic inventory system poses greater challenges in obtaining up-to-date inventory information, since the value of the inventory cannot be tracked from start to finish. Taking a physical count of inventory can be very costly; therefore, the best that a company can hope for under a periodic system is to estimate the inventory values so that the numbers can be used for financial reporting purposes. When it is time to report the company's financial numbers, some value for inventory must be stated. That is where inventory estimation methods come in handy.

We will examine two methods of estimating inventory under a periodic inventory system: the **gross profit method** and the **retail method**.

The Gross Profit Method

As the name suggests, the gross profit method uses a company's gross profit figure in calculating an estimation of inventory value. More specifically, a company analyzes the gross profit numbers of prior years in order to come up with a current gross profit number to apply to estimation figures.

IN THE REAL WORLD

Every now and then, you might come across the term: pro forma financial statements. Simply stated, these are statements prepared by a company that do not adhere to GAAP rules.

There are various reasons why companies might want to prepare such reports. They can be used in an informal way to temporarily guide managerial decision-making. They can also be used to present financial figures in a way that at times might be distorted by GAAP rules. For example, costs associated with a previous accounting scandal have to be included in GAAP reports, yet such numbers may inaccurately reflect how the company is currently performing.

Pro forma statements can provide the public with a clearer snapshot of current organizational performance. In fact, pro forma financial figures were reported publicly and often during the dot.com boom of the late 1990's. However, regulators began to crack down on such practices, since even pro forma statements have their limitations and should not act as a substitute for documents that adhere to GAAP. For example, critics of pro forma statements argue that financial stresses from previous periods happen often and are part of the capitalist economic system. Leaving them out can itself be a distortion of a company's status and not fully reflect its performance.

Nevertheless, pro forma financial statements serve as a tool for company management when they want a financial snapshot of their company that isn't as formal, or potentially cumbersome, as GAAP disclosure principles require.

Other figures that a company needs to complete the gross profit method that can be taken from the general ledger are: sales, opening inventory and purchases. Once an accountant has these numbers, then the rest of the numbers needed to estimate inventory can be filled in one at a time.

Here is an example: Van Der Linden Inc. has to prepare financial statements for the quarter and needs to value its inventory in order to do this. It will use the gross profit method.

Sales	$100,000	
Cost of Goods Sold		
Opening Inventory	3,000	
Purchases	70,000	
Cost of Goods Available for Sale	73,000	
Closing Inventory		
Cost of Goods Sold	?	
Gross Profit	?	50%

FIGURE 4.35

- Based on an analysis of gross margin in previous years, a figure of 50% will be used for current calculations.

- Additionally, the following financial numbers were taken from the accountant's general ledger:

Sales	100,000	
Cost of Goods Sold		
Opening Inventory	3,000	
Purchases	70,000	
Cost of Goods Available for Sale	73,000	
Closing Inventory	?	
Cost of Goods Sold	?	
Gross Profit	$50,000	50%

FIGURE 4.36

Sales: $100,000
Opening Inventory: $3,000
Purchases: $70,000

Van Der Linden Inc.'s accountant will use a pro forma income statement (prepared in addition to those used for reporting purposes) to plug-in these numbers and calculate the others needed in estimating the value of the inventory.

The cells with a question mark are those that need to be calculated step-by-step to complete the estimation process.

If our gross margin is 50% (marked in red) then it is applied to the sales figure (marked in blue). $100,000 \times 50\% = \$50,000$

We now have all the information we need to fill in one of the two remaining question marks: *Cost of Goods Sold*.

Remember:

Sales – Gross Profit = COGS
$100,000 – $50,000 = $50,000

The $50,000 COGS is plugged into the chart and marked in grey.

Sale	100,000	
Cost of Goods Sold		
Opening Inventory	3,000	
Purchases	70,000	
Cost of Goods Available for Sale	73,000	
Closing Inventory		
Cost of Goods Sold	50,000	
Gross Profit	50,000	50%

FIGURE 4.37

There is one question mark left in Van Der Linden Inc.'s pro forma income statement, which is the figure we need to complete the balance sheet for the quarter: *Closing Inventory*.

Closing inventory is calculated by subtracting the Cost of Goods Sold from the Cost of Goods Available for Sale:

Cost of Goods Available for Sale – Cost of Goods Sold = Closing Inventory

$73,000 – $50,000 = $23,000

Therefore, the gross profit method yields a closing inventory estimation value of $23,000, which is marked in grey. This figure will now be used on the quarterly balance sheet for Van Der Linden Inc.

To summarize: The gross profit method starts with historical analysis that yields a gross profit margin. This is applied to sales, which yields a gross profit figure. Each subsequent step fills out another part of the pro forma income statement, until a final figure for closing inventory is obtained. This is the estimation that will be used for the quarterly financial statements.

Sales	100,000	
Cost of Goods Sold		
Opening Inventory	3,000	
Purchases	70,000	
Cost of Goods Sold Available for Sale	73,000	
Closing Inventory	23,000	
Cost of Goods Sold	50,000	
Gross Profit	50,000	50%

FIGURE 4.38

The Retail Method

The retail method of estimating inventory requires less information and fewer steps than the gross profit method. Specifically, it requires two things: (1) the value of sales at retail (which is why it is called the retail method); and (2) the company's cost of goods sold section on the income statement.

Here is an example using Leung Retail Company.

As you can see in figure 4.39, the cost of goods sold section is marked in brown, and the sales figure at retail is marked in red.

The section marked in green, which is the *Cost of Goods Available for Sale*, is calculated by adding *Opening Inventory* and *Purchases*. This section is important because the cost and retail figures for *Cost of Goods Available for Sale* will be used in ratio format as follows:

$$\frac{\text{Cost of Goods Available for Sale at Cost}}{\text{Cost of Goods Available for Sale at Retail}}$$

The ratio for the Leung Retail Company is:

$$\frac{\$73,000}{\$140,000} = 52.1\%$$

This ratio needs to be applied to the *Closing Inventory at Retail* figure, which is marked in blue:

$$\$70,000 \times 52.1\% = \$36,500$$

This is the *Closing Inventory at Cost* figure, using the retail method of inventory estimation, which is added to the bottom of the Leung Retail Company chart.

	At Cost	At Retail
Cost of Goods Sold		
Opening Inventory	3,000	6,000
Purchases	70,000	134,000
Cost of Goods Sold Available for Sale	73,000	140,000
Less: Sales at Retail		70,000
Closing Inventory at Retail		70,000

FIGURE 4.39

	At Cost	At Retail
Cost of Goods Sold		
Opening Inventory	3,000	6,000
Purchase	70,000	134,000
Cost of Goods Sold Available for Sale	73,000	140,000
Less Sales at Retail		70,000
Closing Inventory at Retail		70,000
Closing Inventory at Cost	$36,500	

FIGURE 4.40

Measuring Inventory Using Financial Ratios

Generally speaking, a business wants to be as precise as possible in buying inventory for resale. Ideally, inventory should be sold as soon as it is bought. In other words, the less time that an item spends in inventory, while still meeting customer demand, the better.

A company can measure the extent to which it is moving inventory in this way through the use of two ratios: **inventory turnover ratio** and **days inventory on hand**.

Inventory Turnover Ratio

The extent to which an organization can quickly sell inventory on hand is known as **inventory turnover**. Specifically, the inventory turnover ratio estimates how many times a year a company is buying inventory. The more often a company buys inventory, the less likely it is that the inventory sits for extended periods of time, and the more likely it is that the turnover is high.

The inventory turnover ratio is calculated by taking the cost of goods sold for a year and dividing it by average inventory:

$$\text{Inventory Turnover Ratio} = \frac{\text{Cost of Goods Sold}}{\text{Average Inventory}}$$

beginning balance + ending balance ÷ 2

We'll use a few real life examples to demonstrate how the inventory turnover ratio is applied to a company's inventory numbers.

Research in Motion is the maker of the Blackberry mobile device that people all over the world use for e-mail, the Internet, and even taking pictures. The following is a listing of their relevant inventory numbers for the 2008 fiscal year:

	$ Millions
Inventory – March 31, 2007	$255.9
Inventory – March 31, 2008	$396.3
Cost of Goods Sold	$2,928.8

FIGURE 4.41

Average inventory is calculated by adding the opening and closing inventory numbers and dividing the total by 2.

This number is entered into the inventory turnover ratio as follows:

Average Inventory	$(255.9 + 396.3) \div 2 = 326.1$

FIGURE 4.42

Turnover	$2,928.8 \div 326.1 = 9.0$

FIGURE 4.43

Research in Motion's inventory turnover ratio for fiscal year 2008 is 9.0. This means that the company bought its inventory about 9 times during the year.

As a comparison, we'll calculate the 2007 inventory turnover ratio for NewTech Mobile Corporation, a fictional company in the same industry:

Inventory – December 31, 2010	$501.3
Inventory – December 31, 2011	$428.1
Cost of Goods Sold	$2,882.8
Average Inventory	$(501.3 + 428.1) \div 2 = 464.7$
Turnover	$2,882.8 \div 464.7 = 6.2$

FIGURE 4.44

The inventory turnover ratio is 6.2, which means that for the 2011 fiscal year, NewTech Mobile Corporation bought inventory approximately 6.2 times.

Comparing these two examples, Research in Motion has a higher inventory turnover ratio, which is desirable. These ratios are comparable since both companies are in the same industry.

Inventory Days on Hand

There is another way of looking at inventory turnover. Instead of estimating how often a company sells and replaces inventory over a period of time (which is indicated by the inventory turnover ratio), turnover can be calculated by estimating how many days it takes to move items out of inventory. Expressed in another way: how many days will the inventory last given the current rate of sales?

The number of days in a year (365) is divided by the inventory turnover ratio, resulting in the inventory days on hand.

$$\text{Inventory Days on Hand} = \frac{365}{\text{Inventory Turnover Ratio}} \quad \text{or} \quad \frac{\text{Avg Inventory}}{\text{COGS}} \times 365$$

The inventory days on hand carves up the calendar year into equal sized chunks. The number of chunks equals the inventory turnover ratio. The size of the chunks translates into the inventory days on hand.

For example, if a company's inventory turnover ratio is 10, then the inventory days on hand will have 10 chunks in the year. Since there are 365 days in the year, each chunk will be 36.5 days long.

$$\frac{365}{10} = 36.5$$

Therefore, 36.5 days would be the inventory days on hand ratio.

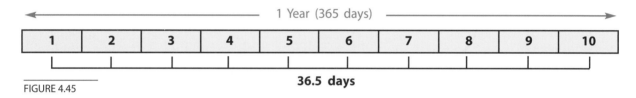

FIGURE 4.45

Here is an example using the inventory turnover ratios we calculated for Research in Motion and the NewTech Mobile Corporation.

If you recall, Research in Motion had the more desirable inventory turnover ratio. The inventory days on hand simply reorganizes the same information as follows:

Research in Motion inventory days on hand: 365 ÷ 9 = 40.6 days

NewTech Mobile Corporation inventory days on hand: 365 ÷ 6.2 = 58.9 days

Another way of calculating inventory days on hand is as follows:

$$\frac{\text{Average Inventory}}{\text{Cost of Goods Sold}} \times 365$$

30,500
500,

Here is the logic of this calculation. The relationship (ratio) is between: (1) how much inventory is in stock; and (2) the amount of inventory used for the year (which is the Cost of Goods Sold). Dividing the average inventory by how much was used and multiplying this number by 365 (number of days in the year) will convert the ratio to the number of days on hand based on how much was used.

Using the Research in Motion inventory and cost of goods sold example below let us test this formula:

$$\frac{\$326.1 \text{ (Average)}}{\$2,928.8} \times 365 = 40.6 \text{ Inventory Days on Hand}$$

The results show that Research in Motion has the more desirable inventory days on hand ratio. A lower number for this ratio means that it takes less time for a company to move its inventory. This is another way of saying that its inventory turnover is better.

	$ Millions
Inventory – March 31, 2007	**$255.9**
Inventory – March 31, 2008	**$396.3**
Cost of Goods Sold	**$2,928.8**

FIGURE 4.46

Management should not be making decisions regarding inventory based on ratios alone. There could be many factors that impact such numbers. For example, some industries might require companies to wait longer periods of time to have goods shipped to them. High turnover in these instances may lead to empty warehouses and customer demands not being met.

As an example, a grocery store will have higher inventory turnover than an appliance store. Alternatively, car engines will move out of an auto plant warehouse much slower than light bulbs in a hardware store.

It is the responsibility of accountants and management to know what inventory levels are best for business. Ratios can help in this regard, but they are only one of many tools that can be used.

Controls Related to Inventory

The way a company handles its inventory can have a major impact on the state of the business. After all, basic economic theory is about supply and demand. If customers demand goods or services, the goal of a business is to meet that demand. In essence, this is what inventory management is about: to manage supply in order to meet demand.

A company with too much inventory on hand risks tying up capital that could be used productively in other areas. A company with too little inventory on hand risks not having enough supply to meet customer demand. Thus there is a delicate balance that needs to be maintained by a company. Perpetual inventory systems help companies to maintain such a balance.

Keeping track of inventory is one of the primary challenges of doing business. This is why transactions need to be recorded properly and relevant information presented in a way that helps company decision-makers.

Keeping track of a company's inventory can be a challenge, but computer software can help mitigate this challenge. However, every accountant should have an understanding of how inventory is tracked and recorded manually.

First, it should be noted that even with the use of technology, errors can be made. It is the responsibility of the accounting department and management to ensure that inventory information is accurate and reliable. The responsibility stops with them.

Second, a thorough knowledge of manual accounting procedures helps the accountant to develop the kinds of controls necessary to ensure that this type of asset is managed responsibly and with integrity.

We will provide examples to show how an accountant can develop a personal method of controlling inventory manually. We will then take a closer look at the kinds of controls needed when dealing with the inventory section of the balance sheet.

Compliance with Plans, Policies, Procedures, Regulations and Laws

All aspects of doing business should be governed by the appropriate plans, policies, procedures, laws and regulations. This is certainly true regarding a company's handling and control of inventory.

All businesses should have plans that are formalized through general policies that lead to specific procedures. These should all comply with the regulations and laws in place within the jurisdiction of the business.

Maintaining the integrity of information is an obligation that companies have when implementing inventory controls.

For example, a company can have a plan to train all inventory personnel. This plan can include detection controls that single out instances of procedures not being followed. An example of such a procedure could be to have all items tagged and scanned at checkout. If this procedure is not followed, then a backup measure could be implemented, with alarms going off upon exit.

All these plans, policies and procedures must adhere to relevant laws and regulations. For example, customers cannot be strip-searched because the alarm goes off as they are leaving the store as this would be a violation of their rights.

FIGURE 4.47

All employees should be trained in the inventory procedures in place. For example, the receiver should count all goods that enter the premises and match the count with the one written on the invoice or packing slip. It should be the job of the supervisor to ensure that this procedure is followed. Internal auditors can engage in field visits to ensure that both the supervisor and the receiver are implementing procedures according to plans and policies in place.

Safeguarding Inventory

All company assets must be physically protected. Cash is generally deposited in a bank; securities can be kept with the brokerage house. Inventory, on the other hand, is often located on company premises in a warehouse or onsite storage facility. The location needs to be easily accessible for receiving or shipping, but it also needs to be protected from the possibility of theft. That is why inventory facilities are usually locked up after closing. The more valuable the inventory, the more elaborate the security measures needed to protect it. These measures can include anything from fences and guard dogs to alarm systems, security guards or even the hiring of an inventory custodian who is charged specifically with protecting the inventory.

The Economical and Efficient Use of Resources

The concept that resources should be used economically and efficiently is especially applicable to inventory. First, financial ratios — which will be examined later in this text — can be used to determine if there is too much or too little inventory on hand. If there is too much inventory, then capital is tied up that could be used more efficiently elsewhere. If there is too little, then customer demand will not be met.

Second, the physical condition of the inventory should be checked regularly. This can be done visually or through inventory reports. Any inventory items that are old or in disrepair, and therefore difficult to sell at market value, can be sold at reduced prices or disposed of so that valuable storage space can be maximized.

Inventory Objectives

All aspects of a business should be guided by the objectives set by management. This not only allows for the accomplishment of specific objectives, but allows all organizational objectives to be properly coordinated. For example, sales objectives can be tied to inventory objectives; and profit objectives can be tied to those set by the marketing department.

All employees should be aware of the company's objectives. For example, if a company wishes to keep items in inventory for only a short period of time before being shipped out, then both the receiver and shipper should be aware of this. This objective would guide much of their short-term and long-term activities.

Meeting inventory objectives needs to be a total team effort. If inventory levels are not close to management's objective, then initiatives should be implemented to ensure that objectives are reassessed or changed. For example, if inventory levels are higher than expected, the sales department can view it as a challenge to get items moving out faster. The more sales increase, the less inventory builds up in the warehouse.

An Ethical Approach to Inventory Estimation and Valuation

As mentioned earlier, management is able to choose how they wish to value inventory. Thus, inventory may be open to manipulation. A company can purchase, store and sell many items throughout the course of a business year, and how all these items are valued can have a significant impact on a company's bottom line.

For example, inventory can sometimes be used as collateral when taking out a bank loan; or employees may steal from the company's inventory. That is why the inventory asset on a company's balance sheet should be subject to ethical guidelines. We will examine some of these guidelines and suggest how organizations should approach estimating and valuing inventory in an ethical manner.

Impact on Financial Statements

The impact of inflating closing inventory is significant. It reduces the cost of goods sold and increases net income for the year. It will also inflate cost of goods sold and reduce net income for the following year. Therefore, any manipulation of inventory value has negative consequences that extend beyond the current fiscal year. The ethical responsibility of management is to ensure this does not happen by detecting errors and the causes behind them.

Who Commits Fraud and Why?

Companies need to know the kinds of inventory fraud that can be perpetrated and understand who would be most likely to commit fraud.

Inventory fraud from the top down

Various methods are used to pad a company's inventory value. One such method is to overstate the value of items deemed obsolete, shop-worn or generally unsalable. This would overstate the overall value of inventory. Similarly, various overhead costs can be attributed to inventory. These figures can also be manipulated in a way that affects the company's bottom line. In addition, a manufacturer might be tempted to overstate the completion of work-in-process inventories and, again, pad the value of its inventory.

Generally speaking, these kinds of attempts to pad inventory numbers tend to come from the top. Unlike determining fixed costs such as rent, determining inventory costs is a more subjective exercise. Accountants and executives can abuse the subjectivity involved in some of these decisions and errors can be rationalized as a matter of opinion.

Such abuses can be avoided by laying out specific policies and guidelines in handling and valuing inventory. Controls should be in place to ensure that these policies are being followed. Companies can also have both internal and external auditors review the design and effectiveness of inventory controls and detect any possible ethical breaches.

In the end, management is responsible for any errors arising from the way its financial situation is being reported. There is no excuse for manipulating the value of inventory. Any wrongful reporting should be dealt with at the earliest opportunity.

Inventory fraud from the bottom up

Lower level employees and thieves can also create havoc with inventory. Their motivation is often associated with greed.

Inventory items are goods that have value and that people want to buy. That is why companies purchase these items and eventually sell them. People who have routine access to such items, such as employees, might be tempted to simply take them without paying for them. Alternatively, an employee might even take funds from the company, buy the inventory, then resell it and pocket the profits. Even borrowing an item without permission, such as a car on a sales lot, is theft, and needs to be prevented.

Some forms of inventory fraud originate from the executive level. Ethical guidelines are needed that detect wrongdoing at any level of the company.

There are various red flags that help a company monitor and prevent inventory shrinkage. One such red flag occurs when sales lag inventory levels. In other words, the company is buying more than it is selling. Some of that inventory is obviously not going to the customer. Another potential inventory red flag should pop up when shipping costs lag inventory. Again, this indicates that the company is not shipping out as many items as it is receiving in inventory. The missing items might well have been taken by thieves.

All companies should be in the practice of noting these red flags and ensuring measures are in place to prevent or detect theft. Furthermore, all businesses should implement security measures that properly safeguard inventory on their premises. Some of these measures were discussed earlier in this chapter.

IN THE REAL WORLD

Perhaps no business philosophy captures the spirit of high inventory turnover more than Just In Time, also known as JIT.

The Japanese first started developing JIT in their manufacturing industries after Word War II. The goal was to gain a competitive advantage by reducing the amount of inventory a company had in storage at any given time, since inventory is often a larger but less liquid asset than others on the balance sheet. JIT eventually made its way to North America and has been used to improve manufacturing efficiency in many different industries.

At the heart of JIT is a comprehensive approach not just to reducing inventory, but to managing a business. Under JIT, it is the customer that drives the manufacturing process. That is why JIT systems are often implemented in conjunction with what is known as Total Quality Management, or TQM. Under such philosophies, everything is done to ensure that the customer gets quality goods and services on time and every time.

To that end, JIT systems mobilize all efforts to coordinate manufacturing processes and reduce waste. This involves the goal of having virtually no excess inventory on hand at any time. This can only be achieved if a company thoroughly understands what the customer wants and when they want it. Receiving and shipping schedules, assembly parts, and labour flexibility are all adapted to ensure that customer demand is met while enhancing organizational efficiency and profitability.

JIT stresses the importance of reducing a company's inventory while enhancing customer service. It is a comprehensive approach that has achieved success on a global scale.

In Summary

↪ Organizations can use a **perpetual system** for valuing inventory, which tracks the value of specific items from purchase to sale, or a **periodic system**, which values inventory items at specific points in time (periodically).

↪ The major differences between the perpetual and periodic inventory systems are in the accounts used to record purchases, sales and returns of merchandise, reporting the **cost of goods sold** on the income statement and the **closing entries**.

↪ Depending on the type of business and the direction taken by management, organizations can also use three specific methods of valuing inventory: **specific identification**, **average cost and FIFO**. Applying different inventory systems can produce different inventory values for the same set of goods.

↪ Various **controls** can be implemented by accountants to preserve the integrity of inventory numbers. Some of these can be personalized and are used on an industry wide basis.

↪ Like most assets on the balance sheet, inventory must be managed and handled in an ethical way. **Fraud** can sometimes occur from the top down so that net income can be unduly inflated. Fraud can also occur from the bottom up when employees or thieves steal items from inventory.

Review Exercise

1. Record the following transactions for Mike's Tikes Toys for the month of March 2011. The company uses a perpetual inventory system and values inventory using the FIFO method. There are 100 items in opening inventory that cost $12 each.

Mar 1	Purchased1,000 items at a cost of $15 each on credit (on account)
Mar 10	Sold 100 items at $45 each on credit
Mar 12	Sold 800 items at $50 each for cash
Mar 20	Purchased 500 items at $20 each on credit

2. Prepare the inventory record to demonstrate the closing inventory after each transaction listed in part 1 above, using the weighted average cost method.

3. Prepare the top portion of the income statement showing Sales, Cost of Goods Sold and Gross Profit for the month ended March 31, 2011. Use the values from the inventory record in part 2.

4. The company physically counted their inventory on March 31st, and found that there was an inventory shortage of $945. Record the adjusting entry required.

5. Prepare the revised income statement reflecting the correct inventory amount from part 2. Calculate the gross profit margin.

Review Exercise 1 - Answers

1.

JOURNAL			Page 1
Date 2011	**Account Title and Explanation**	**Debit**	**Credit**
Mar 1	Inventory	15,000	
	Accounts Payable		15,000
	Purchased inventory on account		
	1,000 units × $15		
Mar 10	Accounts Receivable	4,500	
	Sales Revenue		4,500
	Sale to customer on account		
	100 units × $45		
	Cost of Goods Sold	1,200	
	Inventory		1,200
	Cost of goods sold for above sale		
	100 units × $12		
Mar 12	Cash	40,000	
	Sales Revenue		40,000
	Sale to customer for cash		
	800 units × $50		
	Cost of Goods Sold	12,000	
	Inventory		12,000
	Cost of goods sold for above sale		
	800 units × $15		
Mar 20	Inventory	10,000	
	Accounts Payable		10,000
	Purchased inventory on account		
	500 units × $20		

2.

Date	Purchases			Sales			Balance		
	Quantity	Unit Cost	Value	Quantity	Unit Cost	Value	Quantity	Unit Cost	Value
Mar 1							100	$12.00	$1,200
Mar 1	1,000	$15	$15,000				1100	$14.73	$16,200
Mar 10				100	$14.73	$1,473	1000	$14.73	$14,727
Mar 12				800	$14.73	$11,782	200	$14.73	$2,945
Mar 20	500	$20	$10,000				700	$18.49	$12,945
Ending Inventory									$12,945

3.

Mike's Tikes Toys Income Statement For the Month Ended March 31, 2011	
Sales Revenue	$44,500
Cost of Goods Sold*	13,255
Gross Profit	31,245

*$1,473 + 11,782

4.

JOURNAL			Page 1
Date 2011	**Account Title and Explanation**	**Debit**	**Credit**
Mar 31	Cost of Goods Sold	945	
	Inventory		945
	Adjust inventory to match count		

5.

Mike's Tikes Toys Income Statement For the Month Ended March 31, 2011	
Sales Revenue	$44,500
Cost of Goods Sold	14,200
Gross Profit	30,300
Gross Profit Margin	68.1%

Review Exercise 2

The following information was presented by the bookkeeper for George's Gardening Supplies for the month of December 2011.

DATE	BUSINESS EVENT
Dec 1	Owner George G. deposited $120,000 of his own money into the business account.
Dec 3	The company purchased $50,000 of inventory on account, terms 2/10, net 30.
Dec 6	The company sold $80,000 of inventory to Greenland Care on account, terms 2/10, net 30; cost of goods sold $32,000.
Dec 7	The company purchased $20,000 of inventory on account, terms 2/15, net 30.
Dec 8	The company returned $2,000 of defective merchandise from the purchase on December 7.
Dec 11	The company paid for inventory bought on December 7, less the return and discount.
Dec 12	The customer from December 6 returned $1,000 of goods purchased on account. The cost of goods sold for returned inventory is $600.
Dec 14	The company purchased $10,000 of inventory on account, terms 2/10, net 30.
Dec 15	The company paid $500 freight bill for transportation of inventory purchased in transaction above.
Dec 16	The company collected the amount owing from the customer from December 6.
Dec 19	The company sold $33,500 of goods to Green House Inc. on account, terms 2/10, net 30. The value of cost of goods sold is $13,300.
Dec 22	The company paid for the purchase from December 3.
Dec 28	The following cash transactions were made: prepaid insurance of $3,600; maintenance expense of $600; salary expense of $11,000; rent expense of $6,000; owner's withdrawals of $5,000; property, plant and equipment of $45,000; utility expense of $750; and advertising expense of $2,500.

Assuming that George's Gardening Supplies uses the perpetual inventory system, complete the following exercise.

Part 1

Journalize all the transactions for December.

Part 1 - Answer

JOURNAL			Page 1
Date 2011	**Account Title and Explanation**	**Debit**	**Credit**
Dec 1	Cash	120,000	
	Capital Account		120,000
	Owner invested cash in business		
Dec 3	Inventory	50,000	
	Accounts Payable		50,000
	Purchased inventory on account		
Dec 6	Accounts Receivable	80,000	
	Sales Revenue		80,000
	Sold to customer on account		
	Cost of Goods Sold	32,000	
	Inventory		32,000
	Cost of goods sold for above sale		
Dec 7	Inventory	20,000	
	Accounts Payable		20,000
	Purchased inventory on account		
Dec 8	Accounts Payable	2,000	
	Inventory		2,000
	Purchase return		
Dec 11	Accounts Payable	18,000	
	Inventory		360
	Cash		17,640
	Paid supplier and took discount		
Dec 12	Sales Returns & Allowances	1,000	
	Accounts Receivable		1,000
	Customer returned items		
	Inventory	600	
	Cost of Goods Sold		600
	Return items to inventory		

JOURNAL			Page 1
Date 2011	**Account Title and Explanation**	**Debit**	**Credit**
Dec 14	Inventory	10,000	
	Accounts Payable		10,000
	Purchased inventory on account		
Dec 15	Inventory	500	
	Cash		500
	Paid for freight		
Dec 16	Cash	77,420	
	Sales Discount	1,580	
	Accounts Receivable		79,000
	Customer paid account		
Dec 19	Accounts Receivable	33,500	
	Sales Revenue		33,500
	Sold to customer on account		
	Cost of Goods Sold	13,300	
	Inventory		13,300
	Cost of goods sold for above sale		
Dec 22	Accounts Payable	50,000	
	Cash		50,000
	Paid supplier		
Dec 28	Prepaid Insurance	3,600	
	Maintenance Expense	600	
	Salary Expense	11,000	
	Rent Expense	6,000	
	Owner's Drawings	5,000	
	Property, Plant & Equipment	45,000	
	Utility Expense	750	
	Advertising Expense	2,500	
	Cash		74,450
	Paid cash for various items		

Part 2

Given the trial balance at the end of December, prepare the closing entries.

George's Gardening Supplies Trial Balance December 31, 2011		
Account	**Debit**	**Credit**
Cash	$54,830	
Accounts Receivable	33,500	
Inventory	33,440	
Prepaid Insurance	3,600	
Property, Plant and Equipment	45,000	
Accounts Payable		$10,000
Capital Account		120,000
Owner's Drawings	5,000	
Sales Revenue		113,500
Sales Returns & Allowances	1,000	
Sales Discount	1,580	
Cost of Goods Sold	44,700	
Advertising Expense	2,500	
Maintenance Expense	600	
Rent Expense	6,000	
Salary Expense	11,000	
Utility Expense	750	
Total	**$243,500**	**$243,500**

Part 2 - Answer

JOURNAL			Page 1
Date 2011	**Account Title and Explanation**	**Debit**	**Credit**
Dec 31	Sales Revenue	113,500	
	Income Summary		113,500
	Close revenue account		
Dec 31	Income Summary	68,130	
	Sales Returns & Allowances		1,000
	Sales Discount		1,580
	Cost of Goods Sold		44,700
	Advertising Expense		2,500
	Maintenance Expense		600
	Rent Expense		6,000
	Salary Expense		11,000
	Utility Expense		750
	Close expense and debit accounts		
Dec 31	Income Summary	45,370	
	Capital Account		45,370
	Close income summary		
Dec 31	Capital Account	5,000	
	Owner's Drawings		5,000
	Close drawings account		

Appendix 4A: The Periodic Inventory System

As mentioned in chapter 4, the periodic inventory system determines the quantity of inventory on hand only periodically. A physical count is taken at the end of the period to determine the value of the ending inventory and cost of goods sold.

Thus, a periodic inventory system actually does not update the inventory account on a regular basis, only when a physical count is taken. On a regular basis, the periodic inventory system updates a new list of income statement accounts which are used to calculate cost of goods sold.

Consider the differences between the perpetual and the periodic inventory system. Figure 4A.1 illustrates the perpetual inventory system. A business that has the technology to properly implement the perpetual inventory system will record purchases, discounts, allowances and other adjustments into the inventory asset account. Inventory is then transferred to cost of goods sold when a sale is made. Cost of goods sold is immediately matched to sales and gross profit is reported every month, although gross profit may be slightly incorrect if an inventory count is not performed.

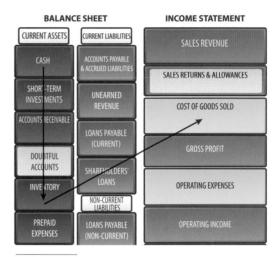

FIGURE 4A.1

A business that does not have the technology to constantly update inventory like in the perpetual inventory system described earlier must instead use the periodic inventory system. Figure 4A.2 illustrates the periodic inventory system. Inventory shows an opening value at the beginning of the period, but will only be adjusted up or down at the end of the period when an inventory count is performed. All purchases, discounts, allowances and other adjustments will be recorded directly into the income statement.

If purchases were recorded in the inventory account on the balance sheet, they would always remain in inventory since inventory is not transferred to cost of goods sold when a sale is made. This would leave a large amount of inventory remaining on the balance sheet and no cost of goods sold on the income statement. It is more practical to record purchases directly on the income statement, and adjust the inventory account only at year end.

Keep the concept of the periodic inventory system in mind as the journal entries are presented. The transactions are very similar to the perpetual inventory system, except that income statement accounts are affected instead of inventory.

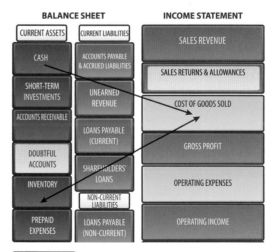

FIGURE 4A.2

Purchases

When inventory is purchased for resale using a periodic inventory system the inventory account is not debited. Instead, we debit an account called *purchases* on the income statement, which is part of cost of goods sold. If the inventory was paid for on credit, then accounts payable is credited. If the inventory was paid for with cash, then the cash account is credited. In this example, Tools 4U Inc. purchased inventory of $10,000 on January 1, 2010. Assume all purchases and sales are made on account.

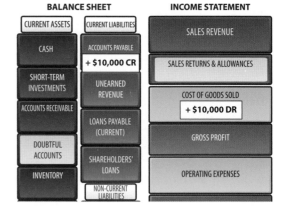

JOURNAL			
Date	Account Title and Explanation	Debit	Credit
Jan 1	Purchases	10,000	
	Accounts Payable		10,000
	Record purchase of inventory		

FIGURE 4A.3

The purchases account is a temporary account located on the income statement. It records all the inventory purchased by a company during a specific period of time under the periodic inventory system.

The value of inventory and cost of goods sold are not adjusted until the end of the period when the physical inventory count is taken. As a result, we need to track the costs related to inventory in separate accounts.

Purchase Returns

Continuing with the example of Tools 4U Inc., assume the company returned $300 worth of inventory to its supplier. Instead of just crediting the purchases account, businesses that use a periodic inventory system track these returns by using a temporary contra-expense account called **purchase returns and allowances**. This new account is also part of cost of goods sold. The following journal entry is recorded to reflect the above return:

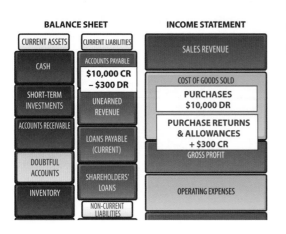

JOURNAL			
Date	Account Title and Explanation	Debit	Credit
	Accounts Payable	300	
	Purchase Returns and Allowances		300
	Record purchase returns		

FIGURE 4A.4

Purchase Allowances

Continuing with the above example, assume Tools 4U found another $300 worth of unsatisfactory inventory. The supplier had offered a 20% **allowance** to Tools 4U to keep the goods, rather than returning them. The transaction resulted in an allowance of $60 ($300 x 20%). When a periodic inventory system is used, the credit will also be recorded in the purchase returns and allowances account as shown in figure 4A.5:

JOURNAL			
Date	**Account Title and Explanation**	**Debit**	**Credit**
	Accounts Payable	60	
	Purchase Returns and Allowances		60
	Record purchase allowance for a supplier		

BALANCE SHEET

CURRENT ASSETS — CASH, SHORT-TERM INVESTMENTS, ACCOUNTS RECEIVABLE, DOUBTFUL ACCOUNTS, INVENTORY

CURRENT LIABILITIES — ACCOUNTS PAYABLE **$10,000 CR – $300 DR – $60 DR**, UNEARNED REVENUE, LOANS PAYABLE (CURRENT), SHAREHOLDERS' LOANS, NON-CURRENT LIABILITIES

INCOME STATEMENT

SALES REVENUE

COST OF GOODS SOLD — PURCHASES **$10,000 DR**, PURCHASE RETURNS & ALLOWANCES **+ $300 CR + $60 CR**

OPERATING EXPENSES

FIGURE 4A.5

Purchase Discounts

The supplier may offer credit terms and a discount period to encourage early payments. In a periodic inventory system, the amount of the discount is credited to a contra-expense account called **purchase discounts**. This is another account that is part of cost of goods sold. By crediting this account, instead of simply crediting the inventory account like we did in the perpetual inventory system, management is able to track the amount they are saving in paying their suppliers within the discount period. We will now show the journal entries for both the purchase and payment from Tools 4U Inc. who bought goods from Roof Tiles Inc. in the amount of $4,200 on January 10. The supplier allows 2/10, n/30 on all invoices. Since Tools 4U had excess cash at this time, the manager chose to take advantage of the cash discount by paying the invoice within 10 days.

The original entry for the purchase is:

JOURNAL			
Date	**Account Title and Explanation**	**Debit**	**Credit**
Jan 10	Purchases	4,200	
	Account Payable		4,200
	Purchase of goods from Roof Tiles		

BALANCE SHEET

CURRENT ASSETS — CASH, SHORT-TERM INVESTMENTS, ACCOUNTS RECEIVABLE, DOUBTFUL ACCOUNTS, INVENTORY

CURRENT LIABILITIES — ACCOUNTS PAYABLE **+ $4,200 CR**, UNEARNED REVENUE, LOANS PAYABLE (CURRENT), SHAREHOLDERS' LOANS, NON-CURRENT LIABILITIES

INCOME STATEMENT

SALES REVENUE

COST OF GOODS SOLD — PURCHASES **+ $4,200 DR**

GROSS PROFIT

OPERATING EXPENSES

FIGURE 4A.6

The payment amount for the bill would be $4,200 less the $84 discount ($4,200 × 2%). Since the business was paying less for the purchases of inventory, the value of the purchase needed to decrease by the discount amount. The entry to record the discount when the payment was made to Roof Tiles Inc. on January 12 is:

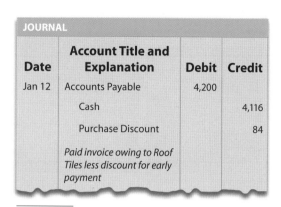

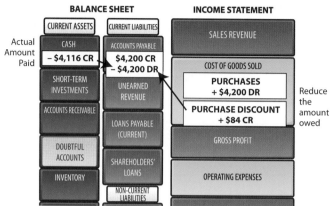

FIGURE 4A.7

Both purchase returns and allowances and purchase discounts are known as contra accounts as they have the opposite balance to the account to which they are related to. They reduce the balance of purchases when reported on the financial statements.

Calculation of Net Purchases

From the above journal entries, the amount of net purchases is determined in figure 4A.8.

Purchases		$14,200
Less: Purchase Returns and Allowances	$360	
Purchase Discounts	84	444
Net Purchases		$13,756

FIGURE 4A.8

Freight-In

In a periodic inventory system, freight-in is recorded by debiting the **freight-in** account which is an income statement account that is part of cost of goods sold. Assume Tools 4U Inc. paid $100 freight cost for the inventory on January 10, the journal entry is shown in figure 4A.9.

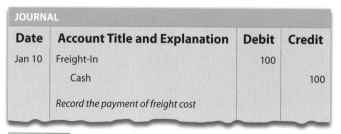

FIGURE 4A.9

Sales

The major difference between the periodic and perpetual system occurs at the point of sale. Unlike the perpetual system which immediately records cost of goods sold when revenue from the sale of inventory is recognized, the periodic system calculates cost of goods sold at the end of the period when ending inventory is determined with a physical count. Assuming inventory is sold on account, the entry should be recorded by debiting accounts receivable and crediting revenue.

Assume Tools 4U Inc. sold $13,000 worth of goods for $20,000 on January 15. In a periodic system, this transaction would be recorded as shown in figure 4A.10:

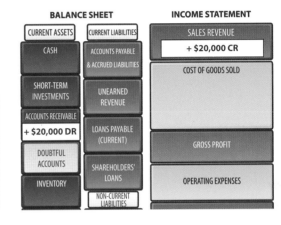

JOURNAL			
Date	Account Title and Explanation	Debit	Credit
Jan 15	Accounts Receivable	20,000	
	Sales		20,000
	Record sales on account		

FIGURE 4A.10

The entry is recorded by debiting accounts receivable and crediting sales. The cost of goods sold and inventory accounts are not updated immediately. Instead, they will be updated at the end of the period when the physical count is taken.

Sales Returns

If a customer returns goods, in a periodic inventory system, only one journal entry is required to record the sales return and credit the amount owing from the customer (assuming the goods were sold on account). The journal entry for a return of $4,000 worth of goods by a customer is shown in figure 4A.11.

The entry is recorded by debiting sales returns and allowances and crediting accounts receivable. Unlike the perpetual inventory system, the cost of goods sold and inventory are not updated immediately.

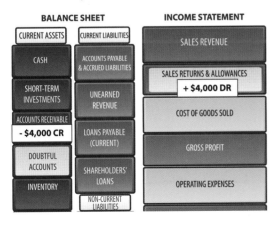

JOURNAL			
Date	Account Title and Explanation	Debit	Credit
	Sales Returns and Allowances	4,000	
	Accounts Receivable		4,000
	Record return of items by customer for credit		

FIGURE 4A.11

Sales Allowances

Sales allowances are recorded in the same way as when a perpetual inventory system is used. Referring to the sales allowances example from the previous section, we recall that Tools 4U granted a $300 sales allowance. The journal entry is recorded as shown in figure 4A.12 in a periodic inventory system.

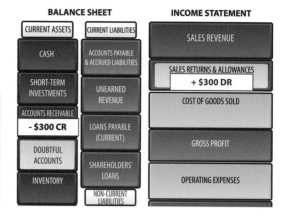

JOURNAL			
Date	Account Title and Explanation	Debit	Credit
	Sales Returns & Allowances	300	
	Accounts Receivable		300
	Record sales allowances provided for customer		

FIGURE 4A.12

Sales Discounts

Sales discounts are recorded in the same way as when a perpetual inventory system is used. In our example, the customer paid within the discount period and received a $250 discount as shown in the following journal entry:

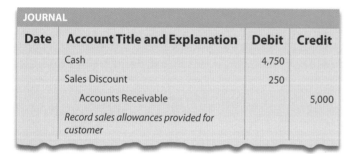

JOURNAL			
Date	Account Title and Explanation	Debit	Credit
	Cash	4,750	
	Sales Discount	250	
	Accounts Receivable		5,000
	Record sales allowances provided for customer		

FIGURE 4A.13

Net sales is determined by deducting sales returns & allowances and sales discounts from sales revenue as follows:

$$\$15,000 + \$5,000 + \$2,000 - \$4,000 - \$300 - \$250 = \$17,450$$

Reporting the Cost of Goods Sold

In a periodic system, the cost of goods sold is not known until the end of the period, when the ending inventory is known. This is because, unlike the perpetual system where all costs flowed through the inventory account, the costs that make up the cost of goods available for sale are kept in separate accounts (beginning inventory, purchases, and freight-in). Once ending inventory is determined, it is subtracted from the cost of goods available for sale to determine the cost of goods sold. Assuming the ending inventory in our example is $22,856, the cost of goods sold is determined on the income statement as shown in figure 4A.14.

Cost of Goods Sold		
Beginning Inventory		$20,000
Net Purchases	$13,756	
Freight-In	100	13,856
Cost of Goods Available for Sale		$33,856
Less: Ending Inventory		22,856
Cost of Goods Sold		$11,000

FIGURE 4A.14

Using the same numbers as the perpetual example, assume the business had ending inventory of $22,856. The ending inventory is counted and the cost of goods sold is calculated as follows:

Cost of Goods Sold = Beginning Inventory + Net Purchases − Ending Inventory

$$= \$20,000 + \$13,856 - 22,856$$

$$= \$11,000$$

The freight-in is added to net purchases to determine cost of goods available for sale. The value of ending inventory is determined by a physical count and subtracted from cost of goods available for sale to determine cost of goods sold. The amounts included in the inventory and cost of goods sold is no different from the example under the perpetual inventory system. It is mainly a timing difference regarding when these amounts are updated.

FOB and Inventory Counts

The terms of shipping items will have an impact on period end inventory counts. An inventory count is supposed to include all inventory that is owned by the company, and this can include items that are not physically at the place of business. All companies must pay careful attention to items in the process of being shipped when counting inventory.

For example, suppose Company A purchases items with a cost of $10,000 with terms of FOB shipping point. This means that Company A takes ownership of the goods as soon as they are loaded onto the carrier, and should include these as part of their inventory. While these goods are in transit, Company A performs an inventory count and does not include the inventory that they just purchased. This means that the value of their ending inventory on their balance sheet will be too low, or understated by $10,000. If Company A uses the periodic inventory system, an understated ending inventory will cause COGS to be overstated and net income to be understated. This is shown in figure 4A.15.

	Correct		Incorrect
Sales	$160,000		$160,000
Cost of Goods Sold			
Beginning Inventory	50,000		50,000
Net Purchases	65,000		65,000
Cost of Goods Available for Sale	115,000		115,000
Less: Ending Inventory	45,000		35,000
Cost of Goods Sold		70,000	80,000
Gross Profit		90,000	80,000
Operating Expense		50,000	50,000
Net Income		$40,000	$30,000

FIGURE 4A.15

Similar problems would occur if a company sells inventory with terms of FOB destination. Although the items are not in the seller's warehouse, the seller still owns the items while they are in transit and must include them as part of their inventory.

To summarize the differences between the perpetual and periodic journal entries, the following table indicates which accounts are affected by the types of transactions we have learned.

Transaction	Perpetual*		Periodic*	
	Debit	Credit	Debit	Credit
Purchase	Inventory (B/S)	Cash or Accounts Payable	Purchases (I/S)	Cash or Accounts Payable
Purchase Return	Cash or Accounts Payable	Inventory (B/S)	Cash or Accounts Payable	Purchase Returns & Allowances (I/S)
Purchase Allowance	Cash or Accounts Payable	Inventory (B/S)	Cash or Accounts Payable	Purchase Returns & Allowances (I/S)
Payment with Discount	Accounts Payable	Cash Inventory (B/S)	Accounts Payable	Cash Purchase Discounts (I/S)
Freight	Inventory (B/S)	Cash or Accounts Payable	Freight-In (I/S)	Cash or Accounts Payable
Sales	Cash or Accounts Receivable Cost of Goods Sold (I/S)	Sales Revenue (I/S) Inventory (B/S)	Cash or Accounts Receivable	Sales Revenue (I/S)

Transaction	Perpetual*		Periodic*	
	Debit	**Credit**	**Debit**	**Credit**
Sales Returns	Sales Returns & Allowances (I/S) Cost of Goods Sold (I/S)	Cash or Accounts Receivable Inventory (B/S)	Sales Returns & Allowances (I/S)	Cash or Accounts Receivable
Sales Allowance	Sales Returns & Allowances (I/S)	Cash or Accounts Receivable	Sales Returns & Allowances (I/S)	Cash or Accounts Receivable
Receipt with Discount	Cash Sales Discounts (I/S)	Accounts Receivable	Cash Sales Discounts (I/S)	Accounts Receivable

*B/S = Balance Sheet and I/S = Income Statement

FIGURE 4A.16

In essence, the mechanisms behind recording these transactions under both inventory tracking methods are the same. They only differ in the way that no "inventory" and "cost of goods sold" accounts are present under the periodic inventory system.

A CLOSER LOOK

The accurate financial performance of a company that uses the periodic system can only be calculated when an inventory count is performed and the cost of goods is calculated. If a business wanted to see how they were performing between inventory counts, they may have to make some adjustments to the reports before the numbers can be useful for decision making.

For example, a nursery selling flowers and other plants may operate from May to October. After closing in October, they perform a physical count of inventory and prepare formal financial statements.

Before they open in May, they have to purchase soil and seeds and start growing plants in their greenhouses in preparation for spring. These purchases are made before any sales are made. Recall that under a periodic inventory system, cost of goods sold = beginning inventory + purchases - ending inventory. If the company uses the periodic inventory system and wanted to see their performance after one month of operations (May), without counting inventory, only the beginning inventory and purchases amount would be available for the purposes of calculating cost of goods sold. That is, ending inventory would be missing. By not deducting ending inventory, the information presented would be distorted and it would appear that they are operating at a loss.

To prevent the distortion of the financial statements, management can instead estimate what cost of goods sold was using the gross profit method discussed earlier in chapter 4.

For example, if the nursery typically operates at 40% gross profit during their sales season, the following figure illustrates how the income statement could be estimated without doing a physical inventory count.

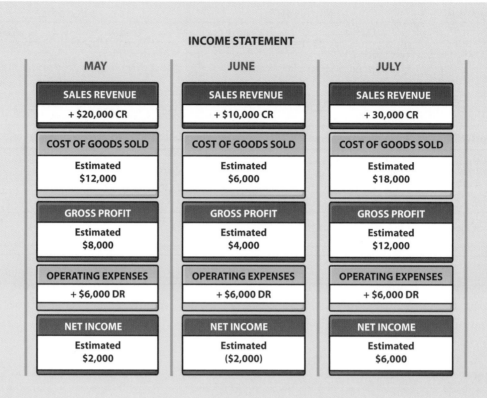

This estimation can only be used for management purposes and interim statements. Formal financial statements can only be prepared after a physical count has been performed.

Closing Entries

Closing Entries and Inventory in a Periodic System

Although there are a few variations of how inventory is adjusted through the closing entries when a periodic system is used, the main objective is the same - to remove the beginning inventory balance and add the new ending inventory balance.

Here is one approach that is frequently used as shown in figure 4A.17.

JOURNAL			
Date	Account Title and Explanation	Debit	Credit
Mar 31	Revenue	20,000	
	Inventory	22,856	
	Purchase Returns & Allowances	360	
	Purchase Discounts	84	
	Income Summary		43,300
	To close revenue and other income statement credit balance accounts and to set up ending inventory balance for the period		

FIGURE 4A.17

When closing the accounts with a credit balance on the income statement, the new ending inventory balance of $22,856 is debited to the inventory account. To understand the logic of this entry, refer to the detailed cost of goods sold section above. The ending inventory is deducted from the cost of goods available for sale to determine the amount of cost of goods sold because ending inventory represents the amount a company still has on hand at the end of the

JOURNAL			
Date	**Account Title and Explanation**	**Debit**	**Credit**
Mar 31	Income Summary	40,360	
	Inventory		20,000
	Sales Returns & Allowances		4,300
	Sales Discounts		250
	Purchases		14,200
	Freight-in		100
	Operating Expenses		1,510
	To close expense and other debit balance income statement accounts and to remove beginning inventory for the period		

FIGURE 4A.18

accounting period. It is available for sale at the beginning of the next accounting period.

In closing the expense accounts, notice that the beginning inventory balance of $20,000 is credited. Refer to figure 4A.14, the detailed cost of goods sold section is shown. What effect does the beginning inventory have on the cost of goods available for sale? It is added together with purchases and therefore represents an expense of the period. The logic is: expenses are credited through the closing entries; therefore, the beginning Inventory balance of $20,000 must be credited.

After the closing entries are posted to the accounts, the inventory account will be updated to reflect the actual amount of inventory on hand, $22,856.

The final step of the closing entry process is to close the Income summary account to the owners' capital (proprietorship) or retained earnings (corporations). Assuming the company operates as a proprietorship, the journal entry on January 31 is shown in figure 4A.19.

JOURNAL			
Date	**Account Title and Explanation**	**Debit**	**Credit**
Jan 31	Income Summary	2,940	
	Owner's Capital		2,940
	To close income summary and transfer net income to owner's capital account		

FIGURE 4A.19

The T-Accounts below summarize the closing entries under the periodic inventory system. Note how the inventory account is updated following the physical inventory count.

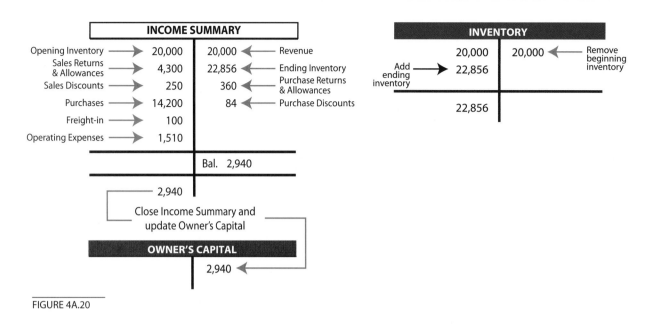

FIGURE 4A.20

Methods for Valuing Inventory: Periodic

Cool Ink Company sells a number of different pens, pencils, markers and highlighters. Let us examine one item from their inventory to illustrate specific identification, weighted average and FIFO inventory valuation methods. Assume that Cool Ink uses a periodic inventory system to account for purchases and sales.

Cool Ink Company currently has 10 pens in inventory with a cost of $10 each. During the month of March, the following transactions take place:

Date	Transaction	Quantity	Unit Cost
March 5	Purchase from Pen Distributers	50	$12
March 7	Sale	15	
March 15	Purchase from Promotional Pens	40	$14
March 19	Purchase from Promotional Pens	20	$16
March 27	Sale	50	

FIGURE 4A.21

During the month, the cost of the pen changed. This implies that the cost of goods sold applied to the sales will likely be different, based on which pens are actually sold. We can apply the three methods of valuing inventory to the transactions to arrive at different values for inventory and cost of goods sold. This will demonstrate that the choice of inventory valuation method can make a difference on the financial statements of a company.

The main difference between the perpetual and the periodic inventory system is when costs are assigned to the sales. The perpetual system, as illustrated in chapter 4, assigns costs to the sales as the sales are made. The perpetual system only assigns costs at the end of the period, when a physical count of the inventory is made.

Using Specific Identification

When using specific identification, list the purchases separately from each other to easily identify the costs associated with each batch of inventory. The opening balance and the transactions from figure 4A.21 are listed in figure 4A.22. At the bottom of the figure is the value of ending inventory.

Date	Purchases			Sales			Balance		
	Quantity	Unit Cost	Value	Quantity	Unit Cost	Value	Quantity	Unit Cost	Value
March 1							10	$10	$100
March 5	50	$12	$600				10	$10	$100
							50	$12	$600
March 15	40	$14	$560				10	$10	$100
							50	$12	$600
							40	$14	$560
March 19	20	$16	$320				10	$10	$100
							50	$12	$600
							40	$14	$560
							20	$16	$320
Sales for the Month				10	$10	$100	10	$12	$120
				40	$12	$480	25	$14	$350
				15	$14	$210	20	$16	$320
Ending Inventory									$790

FIGURE 4A.22

Step 1: The purchase of 50 pens on March 5 is added to the value of inventory.

Step 2: The purchase of 40 pens on March 15 is added to the value of inventory.

Step 3: The purchase of 20 pens on March 19 is added to the value of inventory.

Step 4: The sales are tallied at the end of the month and are identified based on which batch of inventory they came from. In this example, the entire amount of opening inventory was sold, 40 items from the March 5 purchase were sold and 15 items from the March 15 purchase were sold. Total cost of goods sold is $790 ($100 + $480 + $210).

Step 5: The value of ending inventory is made up of 10 pens remaining from the March 5 purchase, the 25 pens remaining from the March 15 purchase and the 20 pens remaining from the March 19 purchase. Total value of inventory is $790 ($120 + $350 + $320).

Using First-In-First-Out

When using the FIFO method, list the purchases in the order they were received. This will allow you to easily see which items were the first ones purchased and will be the first ones to be sold. The opening balance and the transactions from figure 4A.21 are listed in figure 4A.23. At the bottom of the figure is the value of ending inventory.

Date	Purchases			Sales			Balance		
	Quantity	Unit Cost	Value	Quantity	Unit Cost	Value	Quantity	Unit Cost	Value
March 1							10	$10	$100
March 5	50	$12	$600				10	$10	$100
							50	$12	$600
March 15	40	$14	$560				10	$10	$100
							50	$12	$600
							40	$14	$560
March 19	20	$16	$320				10	$10	$100
							50	$12	$600
							40	$14	$560
							20	$16	$320
Sales for the Month				10	$10	$100	35	$14	$490
				50	$12	$600	20	$16	$320
				5	$14	$70			
Ending Inventory									$810

FIGURE 4A.23

Step 1: The purchase of 50 pens on March 5 is added to the value of inventory.

Step 2: The purchase of 40 pens on March 15 is added to the value of inventory.

Step 3: The purchase of 20 pens on March 19 is added to the value of inventory.

Step 4: There was a total of 65 items sold (15 units + 40 units). Costs will be taken from the list of inventory, starting with the first item at the top of the list. The entire amount of opening inventory, the entire amount of the March 5 purchase, and five items from the March 15 purchase are considered sold. Total cost of goods sold is $770 ($100 + $600 + $70).

Step 5: The value of ending inventory is made up of 35 pens remaining from the March 15 purchase and the 20 pens remaining from the March 19 purchase. Total value of inventory is $810 ($490 + $320).

Using Weighted Average Cost

When using the weighted average cost method, the average cost per unit only has to be calculated at the end of the period. The opening balance and the transactions from figure 4A.21 are listed in figure 4A.24. At the bottom of the figure is the value of ending inventory.

Date	Purchases			Sales			Balance		
	Quantity	Unit Cost	Value	Quantity	Unit Cost	Value	Quantity	Unit Cost	Value
March 1							10		$100
March 5	50	$12	$600				60		$700
March 15	40	$14	$560				100		$1,260
March 19 .	20	$16	$320				120	$13.17	$1,580
Sales for the Month				65	$13.17	$856	55	$13.17	$724
Ending Inventory									$724

FIGURE 4A.24

Step 1:   The purchase of 50 pens on March 5 is added to the quantity on hand. The value of the 50 pens is added to the value of the opening inventory.

Step 2:   The purchase of 40 pens on March 15 is added to the quantity on hand. The value of the 40 pens is added to current value of inventory.

Step 3:   The purchase of 20 pens on March 19 is added to the quantity on hand. The value of the 20 pens is added to current value of inventory.

Step 4:   At the end of the month, there are 120 pens available for sale with a total cost of $1,580. The average cost per pen is approximately $13.17 ($1,580 ÷ 120 units). This average cost will be applied to the total sales of 65 pens for the month. Total cost of goods sold is $856 (65 units X $13.17).

Step 5:   The value of ending inventory is 55 pens at the unit cost of approximately $13.17. Total value of inventory is $724.

The Effect of Different Valuation Methods: Periodic

As the previous example with Cool Ink Company demonstrates, different ending inventory figures are produced using different valuation methods. The following chart summarizes these differences when applied to the Cool Ink examples:

Periodic Inventory System	Specific Identification	FIFO	Weighted Average
Inventory Available for Sale (beginning inventory + purchases)	$1,580	$1,580	$1,580
Ending Inventory	790	810	724
Value of COGS	790	770	856

FIGURE 4A.25

From the above, we can make the following assumptions:

1. In times where product cost increases over the period, FIFO will result in the highest value of ending inventory.

2. While specific identification provides the true value of ending inventory and the cost of goods sold, it is costly to implement and therefore not practical for items of small value.

When ending inventory amounts change, so does the cost of goods sold, gross profit and net income. Therefore companies can dramatically change their financial results by manipulating the inventory valuation method.

When comparing inventory valuation methods between the perpetual and periodic systems in figures 4A.25 and 4A.26, notice the following figure of ending inventory and cost of goods sold. Specific identification will always provide the same values since the company is able to specifically identify which items are being sold, regardless of the inventory system being used. FIFO will also provide the same values because the most recent purchases are always in ending inventory.

Perpetual Inventory System	Specific Identification	FIFO	Weighted Average
Inventory Available for Sale (beginning inventory + purchases)	$1,580	$1,580	$1,580
Ending Inventory	790	810	736
Value of COGS	790	770	844

FIGURE 4A.26

The weighted average method shows different values for ending inventory and COGS. This is because the perpetual inventory system assigns costs as the items are sold, whereas the periodic inventory system only assigns costs at the end of the period.

Review Exercise

The following information was presented by the bookkeeper for George's Gardening Supplies for the month of December 2010.

DATE	BUSINESS EVENT
Dec 1	Owner George G. deposited $120,000 of his own money into the business account
Dec 2	The company purchased $50,000 of inventory on account, terms 2/10, net 30.
Dec 3	The company sold $80,000 of inventory to Greenland Care on account, terms 2/10, net 30; cost of goods sold $32,000.
Dec 4	The company purchased $20,000 of inventory on account, terms 2/15, net 30.
Dec 5	The company returned $2,000 of defective merchandise to the suppliers.
Dec 6	The company paid for inventory bought on Dec 4, less $400 discount.
Dec 7	A customer returned $1,000 of goods purchased on account. The cost of goods sold for returned inventory is $600.
Dec 8	The company purchased $10,000 of inventory on account, terms 2/10, net 30.
Dec 9	The company paid $500 freight bill for transportation of supplies purchased in transaction above.
Dec 9	The company collected $39,000 outstanding accounts receivable less approved sales discount of $780.
Dec 10	The company sold $33,500 of goods to Green House Inc. on account, terms 2/10, net 30. The value of cost of goods sold is $13,300.
Dec 11	The company paid $48,000 for inventory bought previously less a $960 discount.
Dec 12	The following cash transactions were made: Prepaid insurance of $3,600; Repairs and maintenance of $600; Salary expense of $11,000; Rent expense of $6,000; Withdrawals of $5,000; Equipment of $45,000, Utility expense of $750, and Advertising Expense of $2,500.

Assume that George's Gardening Supplies uses the periodic inventory system. Complete the following exercises.

Part 1

Journalize all transactions.

Part 1 - Answer

Journal			
Date	**Account Title and Explanation**	**Debit**	**Credit**
Dec 1	Cash	100,000	
	G. George, Capital		100,000
	Owner's initial investment in business		
Dec 2	Purchases	50,000	
	Accounts Payable		50,000
	Purchase of inventory on account, terms 2/10, net 30		
Dec 3	Accounts Receivable	80,000	
	Sales Revenue		80,000
	Record sales on account, terms 2/10, net 30		
Dec 4	Purchases	20,000	
	Accounts Payable		20,000
	Record purchase of inventory on account, 2/15, net 30		
Dec 5	Accounts Payable	2,000	
	Purchase Returns & Allowance		2,000
	Returned defective merchandise for credit		
Dec 6	Accounts Payable	20,000	
	Purchase Discounts		400
	Cash		19,600
	Paid for merchandise less return and discount		
Dec 7	Sales Returns & Allowances	1,000	
	Accounts Receivable		1,000
	Customer returned goods bought on account		
Dec 8	Purchases	10,000	
	Accounts Payable		10,000
	Purchase of inventory on account, terms 2/10, net 30		
Dec 9	Freight-in	500	
	Cash		500
	Paid freight bill on above purchase		

Date	Account Title and Explanation	Debit	Credit
Dec 9	Cash	38,220	
	Sales Discounts	780	
	Accounts Receivable		39,000
	Received payment on account, less return and discount		
Dec 10	Accounts Receivable	33,500	
	Sales Revenue		33,500
	Sales on account, terms 2/10, net 30		
Dec 11	Accounts Payable	48,000	
	Purchase Discounts		960
	Cash		47,040
	Paid for merchandise, less return and discount		
Dec 12	Prepaid Insurance	3,600	
	Repairs and Maintenance	600	
	Salary Expense	11,000	
	Rent Expense	6,000	
	Withdrawals	5,000	
	Equipment	45,000	
	Utilities Expense	750	
	Advertising Expense	2,500	
	Cash		74,450
	Record payment of various items		

Part 2

Given the following year-end trial balance (prior to closing entries), prepare the schedule of cost of goods sold and close the accounts at the period end. Assume the physical count determined the value of ending inventory to be $39,940.

George's Garden Centre Trial Balance December 31, 2010		
Account Title	DR	CR
Cash	$16,630	
Accounts Receivable	73,500	
Inventory	7,500	
Prepaid Insurance	1,800	
Equipment	45,000	
Accumulated Depreciation-Equipment		$9,000
Accounts Payable		17,500
Salary Payable		1,000
G. George, Capital		120,000
G. George, Withdrawals	5,000	
Sales Revenue		113,500
Sales Discounts	780	
Sales Returns and Allowances	1,000	
Purchases	80,000	
Purchase Discounts		1,360
Purchase Returns and Allowances		2,000
Freight-in	500	
Salary Expense	12,000	
Rent Expense	6,000	
Advertising Expense	2,500	
Utilities Expense	750	
Repairs & Maintenance	600	
Depreciation Expense-Equipment	9,000	
Insurance Expense	1,800	
Totals	$264,360	$264,360

Part 2 – Answer

Schedule of COGS:

Beginning inventory		$7,500
Purchases	$80,000	
Less:		
Purchase returns & allowances	2,000	
Purchase discounts	1,360	
Add:		
Freight-in	$500	
Net purchases		77,140
Cost of goods available for sale		86,640
Less:		
Ending inventory		39,940
Cost of goods sold		$44,700

Part 3

Prepare the closing entries for the company at the end of December.

Part 3 – Answer

Date	Account Title and Explanation	Debit	Credit
Dec 31	Inventory (Ending)	39,940	
	Sales Revenue	113,500	
	Purchase Discounts	1,360	
	Purchase Returns & Allowances	2,000	
	Income Summary		156,800
	To close revenue and other income statement credit balance accounts and to set up ending inventory balance for the period		
Dec 31	Income Summary	122,430	
	Inventory (Beginning)		7,500
	Sales Discounts		780
	Sales Returns & Allowances		1,000
	Purchases		80,000
	Freight-in		500
	Salary Expense		12,000
	Rent Expense		6,000
	Advertising Expense		2,500
	Utilities Expense		750
	Repairs & Maintenance Expense		600
	Depreciation Expense-Equipment		9,000

Date	Account Title and Explanation	Debit	Credit
	Insurance Expense		1,800
	To close expense and other debit balance income statement accounts and to remove beginning inventory for the period		
Dec 31	Income Summary	34,370	
	G. George, Capital		34,370
	To close income summary and transfer net income to owner's capital account		
Dec 31	G. George, Capital	5,000	
	G. George, Withdrawals		5,000
	To close the withdrawal account		

Chapter 5

PREPAID EXPENSES AND OTHER CURRENT ASSETS

LEARNING OUTCOMES:

❶ Understand the purpose of prepaid expenses

❷ Record transactions relating to prepaid expenses

❸ Define other current assets

❹ Apply controls and ethics relating to prepaid expenses

Prepaid Expenses and Other Current Assets: An Introduction

Our discussion of accounting for current assets has followed the logic and sequence of the balance sheet itself. Cash is the most liquid of all company assets and is therefore found at the top of the assets in the balance sheet. The assets listed below *cash* possess certain defining characteristics and often make up a significant proportion of the value of the business's assets.

As we reach the last of the list of current assets in the balance sheet, the items may not be as easy to define or as prominent as those listed above; but they do constitute assets owned by the company and need to be listed as such in the balance sheet.

The last items listed on our Accounting Map™ are *Other Current Assets* and *Prepaid Expenses*. Unlike other balance sheet items, these accounts rarely contain sub-ledgers (subsidiary ledgers) or detailed lists of entries. Instead, assets listed in these accounts are often totaled and summarized in one amount. They are nevertheless real assets that the company must account for, control, safeguard and apply accounting principles to – as with every other balance sheet item.

FIGURE 5.1

Prepaid Expenses

Prepaid expenses pose a different kind of challenge to the assets we have dealt with to date. Funds are taken out of the company's bank account to pay for an expense. However, the expense does not occur until a future period.

For example, if a company pays its insurance premiums one year in advance, it is paying for services not yet received. The insurance company is paid in advance of the periods in which the expense will occur. The premiums should only be expensed in the months to which they apply

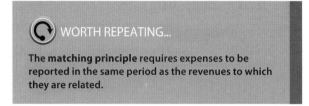

WORTH REPEATING...

The **matching principle** requires expenses to be reported in the same period as the revenues to which they are related.

– hence they are called *prepaid expenses*. They serve as a good example of the matching principle. An insurance premium is an expense that must be matched to the period in which it occurs.

A premium for the month of January is part of the cost of revenue generated in that month. This holds true not only for insurance payments but also for any prepaid expense such as web-hosting fees or maintenance contracts.

If a prepaid amount was treated as an expense at the time, this would incorrectly reduce the company's equity without any benefit being received in return. To deal with this situation, accountants create an asset account – namely, prepaid expenses. In effect, the company is lending the cash used to prepay expenses. The provider of the service that is being prepaid is simply holding the money until the service is provided.

The prepaid expense is a company asset and must be recorded in the company's books as such. The amount used to prepay an expense is credited to cash and debited to prepaid expenses, thereby transferring the amount from one asset account to another.

Note that in figure 5.2, the amount of $1,200 is prepaid on December 20, which is in the fiscal year prior to the year when the expenses will be incurred.

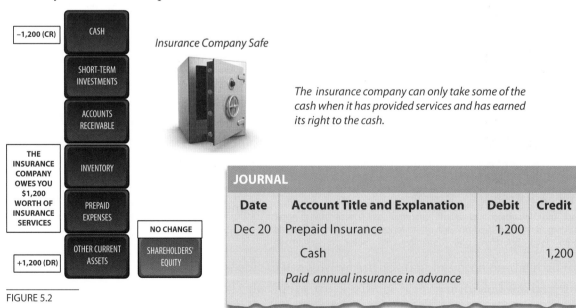

Insurance Company Safe

The insurance company can only take some of the cash when it has provided services and has earned its right to the cash.

JOURNAL			
Date	**Account Title and Explanation**	**Debit**	**Credit**
Dec 20	Prepaid Insurance	1,200	
	Cash		1,200
	Paid annual insurance in advance		

FIGURE 5.2

During the next fiscal year, the prepaid insurance premiums will be expensed on a monthly basis. In January, the journal entry that reflects the expense will look like this:

Prepaid insurance is credited with $100 for the month of January, and insurance expense is debited with the same amount. The existence of prepaid expenses in the balance sheet allows a company to adhere to the matching principle by crediting the prepaid asset account and debiting the expense account in the month the service is provided.

JOURNAL			
Date	**Account Title and Explanation**	**Debit**	**Credit**
Jan 31	Insurance Expense	100	
	Prepaid Insurance		100
	Recognize $100 prepaid insurance for the current month		

Another accounting principle that must be taken into consideration when dealing with a company's prepaid expenses is *materiality*. In other words, is the prepaid amount significant enough to warrant debiting the prepaid expense account in advance and crediting it regularly thereafter? It is a duty that comes with some administrative responsibilities. If the amount is deemed immaterial, the company can expense the entire amount in advance and not be concerned about administering the prepaid expense account.

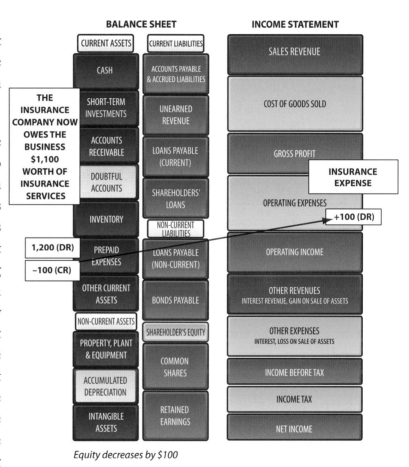

FIGURE 5.3

For example, if a prepaid expense amounts to only $100 for the whole year, the entire amount would be expensed immediately. Cash would be credited, expenses would be debited and prepaid expenses would not be affected.

In addition to prepaid expenses such as prepaid insurance, there are prepaid expenses of a tangible nature, such as office supplies. Depending on the materiality of the value, companies may choose to allocate office supplies as an asset and expense them as they are used. For example, a business would expense a few erasers, but may record a large quantity of expensive laser printer toner as assets. This is largely a matter of judgment.

Assume that Moya Company had $2,000 worth of office supplies on hand on January 1, 2010. At the end of January, the office clerk calculated that $1,200 worth of supplies remained on hand. The adjustment for the $800 supplies expense ($2,000 - $1,200) on January 31, 2010 would be recorded as follows:

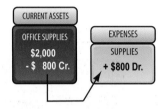

JOURNAL			
Date	**Account Title and Explanation**	**Debit**	**Credit**
Jan 31	Supplies Expense	800	
	Office Supplies		800
	Record supplies used		

FIGURE 5.4

The supplies expense account is debited and the office supplies account is credited to reflect an increase in expenses and a decrease in assets.

A CLOSER LOOK

The International Accounting Standards Board's Framework for the preparation and presentation of financial statements defines materiality as follows:

"Information is material if its omission or misstatement could influence the economic decision of users based on the financial statements. Materiality depends on the size of the item or error judged in the particular circumstances of its omission or misstatement. Thus, materiality provides a threshold or cut-off point rather than being a primary qualitative characteristic which information must have if it is to be useful."

Other Current Assets

Most of the asset accounts on the balance sheet that we have studied so far represent well-defined types of assets. However, many companies own an asset that does not fit into any of these clearly defined categories. These are usually referred to as *miscellaneous assets*, *other assets* or *sundry assets*.

For example, interest due on a loan is called *accrued revenue*. The interest has been earned, but has yet to be received and would be categorized as a *miscellaneous, other* or *sundry asset*.

Prepaid expenses and miscellaneous assets usually make up a relatively small proportion of a company's assets. Separate accounts may be kept for items such as prepaid insurance or office supplies in order to make them easier to manage.

Controls for Prepaid Expenses and Other Current Assets

Prepaid expenses and other current assets are generally not vulnerable to fraud, since they are not liquid and cannot be readily sold.

However, as with all of the company's financial information, the company has an ethical duty to ensure that these types of assets are accounted for and accurately presented to both internal and external stakeholders.

A company should ensure that policies and procedures are in place to effectively control prepaid expenses and other current assets and that errors are not made with respect to these assets. For example, a refund from prepaid tax expense could be allocated to the incorrect account. Other current assets may include physical items such as tanks of heating oil or boxes of photocopy paper; these should be physically protected as well as appropriately recorded and documented. For example, furniture that is no longer being used and is awaiting disposal should be classified as *other current assets* since the cost and accumulated depreciation will have already been removed from the capital asset account. Since other current assets can include many types of items, the accountant should ensure that unusual items are dealt with according to the local laws and regulations. Controls over prepaid expenses and other current assets can serve as a benchmark for the way a company is implementing accounting controls. In assessing the effectiveness of these controls, questions such as the following should be asked: "Are effective review procedures being implemented? Is the appropriate software being used to account for transactions involving these kinds of assets?"

No matter what shape a miscellaneous asset is in, like the old office furniture pictured above, it needs to be stored, protected, and accounted for with the proper paperwork.

An Ethical Approach to Prepaid Expenses and Other Assets

Miscellaneous and other current assets can be small and constitute one line on the balance sheet. This does not mean that the section should be used to hide material assets from public view.

As has already been stated, prepaid expenses and other current assets do not normally make up a large proportion of the assets on a company's balance sheet. They also do not represent the most obvious examples of assets that can be manipulated for financial gain. For these reasons, it may be imagined that it is easier to get away with manipulating such assets. Prepaid expenses, such as insurance policies, are sometimes cancelled, resulting in a refund to the company. These refunds should be made payable to the company (not to an individual, who might be tempted to pocket the amount).

Executive level ethical breaches are not as likely with prepaid expenses since they are often not considered material. Nevertheless, a company's net income can be improperly inflated if an expense is classified as a prepaid expense. This would overstate the value of the company's assets and result in an inaccurate presentation of the company's financial status.

At the executive level, the temptation with miscellaneous and other assets might be to hide an item in that account without disclosing more information to stakeholders. On a company's balance sheet, the account is often labeled "sundry," "miscellaneous," or "other," and simply contains one amount. If an asset is worth a material amount, shareholders and auditors should be informed of its nature.

IN THE REAL WORLD

Independent ethics watchdogs are often set up by governments to oversee the conduct of various public institutions. But who watches the watchdog? And what happens when the ethics watchdog commits ethical breaches? This is precisely the situation that the state of Connecticut was facing as events transpired in 2004. The alleged ethical breaches included the manipulation of a prepaid expense item.

The Ethics Commission of Connecticut was the state's independent agency established to oversee ethical conduct in the government. The Auditors of Public Accounts was responsible for ensuring that the watchdog's money was being spent properly and according to accepted ethical procedures.

The auditors began looking into two hirings made by the Ethics Commission to improve technology. During the investigation, the Ethics Commission began withholding requested information pertaining to new hires, whose salaries totaled $202,000. Predictably, this is where the Commission's troubles began.

Upon further investigation, the Ethics Commission was found to have withheld timesheets and other requested information relating to the hired personnel. Furthermore, the Commission's executive director had signed a letter stating that all requested records had been disclosed and were accurate. Since the timesheets were withheld, the letter raised the prospect that the ethical duty to represent all facts accurately had been breached. As with many ethical controversies, one alleged breach led to the discovery of another — relating to the way a prepaid expense was handled on the Commission's financial records.

The Commission had sent six people to a conference on ethics laws in San Francisco during 2004. Yet this was classified as a prepaid expense for the 2003 fiscal year, instead of a direct expense for 2004. The Auditors said that this transaction was an attempt by the Commission to avoid having the expenditure scrutinized during the year in which it was made.

Many lessons were learned during this incident. First, even an ethics watchdog needs to be watched. Second, all organizations — even watchdogs — need to accurately report on all public disclosures. Third, the prepaid expenses section of the balance sheet cannot be used to hide assets or expenses from public scrutiny. This can only lead to further scrutiny and embarrassment for organizations engaging in the practice — even ethics watchdogs.

The IFRS Perspective

The accounting approach for prepaid expenses is the same between the IFRS and the newly updated Canadian GAAP standards (2008).

 ## In Summary

- ↪ The challenge with prepaid expenses is to adhere to the matching principle. Since expenses need to be linked to associated revenues, a prepaid expense account is established in the balance sheet, treated as an asset and credited when the expense is made.

- ↪ Materiality comes into play when dealing with both prepaid expenses and other current assets. Since many of these assets are deemed to be immaterial, they tend to be lumped together in one amount and summarized as one item in the balance sheet. Material amounts are sometimes specified in the notes section of the financial statements.

- ↪ The other current assets section of the balance sheet, also referred to as miscellaneous or sundry assets, is an area to account for items that do not fit the neatly defined criteria of other balance sheet accounts. For example, accrued interest revenue is not a billed amount, so it cannot be considered part of accounts receivable. Instead, it should be categorized as a miscellaneous asset.

- ↪ Controls related to prepaid expenses and other current assets ensure that the money goes where it is supposed to go at the correct time; that calculations are accurate; and that any corresponding paperwork is done properly and in accordance with established policies and regulations.

- ↪ Both prepaid expenses and other current assets must be accounted for and accurately presented to both internal and external shareholders. For example, refunds of prepaid expenses should be made payable to the company itself. Any physical assets in this category need to be protected with all the security measures at the company's disposal.

Review Exercise

Wachowiak Company is a small manufacturing company with a year-end of June 30. During the year, the following transactions occurred.

- July 5 – paid cash for maintenance contract for the quarter July 1 to September 30 - $3,000.

- August 28 – paid yearly insurance premium of $24,000 for one year commencing September 1.

Required:

1. Record the required journal entries for the period July 1 – Sept 30 of the current year.

2. Prepare the Prepaid Maintenance and Prepaid Insurance ledger accounts for the period July 1 – Sept 30 of the current year.

Review Exercise – Answer

Part 1   **J1**

Date	Account Title and Explanation	Debit	Credit
Jul 5	Prepaid Maintenance	3,000	
	Cash		3,000
	Paid maintenance contract for quarter July 1 to September 30		
Jul 31	Maintenance Expense	1,000	
	Prepaid Maintenance		1,000
	Recognize $1,000 prepaid maintenance for July		
Aug 28	Prepaid Insurance	24,000	
	Cash		24,000
	Paid insurance premium for one year commencing September 1		
Aug 31	Maintenance Expense	1,000	
	Prepaid Maintenance		1,000
	Recognize $1,000 prepaid maintenance for August		
Sep 30	Maintenance Expense	1,000	
	Insurance Expense	2,000	
	Prepaid Maintenace		1,000
	Prepaid Insurance		2,000
	Recognize prepaid maintenance and insurance for September		

Part 2

PREPAID MAINTENANCE					
DATE	DESCRIPTION	PR	DR	CR	BALANCE (DR/CR)
Jul 5		J1	3,000		3,000 (DR)
Jul 31		J1		1,000	2000 (DR)
Aug 31		J1		1,000	1,000 (DR)
Sep 30		J1		1,000	0 (DR)

PREPAID INSURANCE					
DATE	DESCRIPTION	PR	DR	CR	BALANCE (DR/CR)
Aug 28		J1	24,000		24,000 (DR)
Sep 30		J1		2,000	22,000 (DR)

Notes

Chapter 6
NON-CURRENT ASSETS

LEARNING OUTCOMES:

❶ Define non-current assets

❷ Record the acquisition and changes in value of non-current assets

❸ Apply the three methods of depreciation of non-current assets

❹ Account for the gain or loss on the sale of non-current assets

❺ Account for natural resources

❻ Define intangible assets and describe the different types of intangible assets

❼ Account for intangible assets

❽ Calculate asset turnover and return on asset ratios

❾ Understand controls and ethical approach related to non-current assets

Non-Current Assets: The Big Picture

You will recall from our examination of the *current assets* section of the balance sheet that current assets are defined as those owned for less than a year. On the other hand, *non-current assets* are those that will be owned and will be used by the company as part of normal operations for longer than a year. Non-current assets are also commonly referred to as **long-term assets**. Non-current assets comprise tangible assets, which have physical substance – that is, they can be perceived with our senses, especially by touch; and intangible assets, which have no physical substance and can only be perceived by the mind or imagination; intangible assets represent amounts paid for "rights" of ownership. We will cover each group of assets in this chapter.

Non-current assets tend to be worth large amounts of money and constitute major items on a company's balance sheet. Accountants often face the challenge of classifying, recording and monitoring the value of non-current assets. In this chapter, we will have a detailed discussion on how accountants perform these tasks.

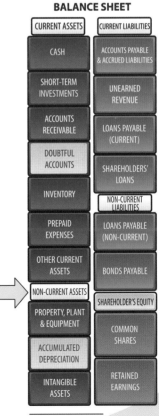

FIGURE 6.1

The *Non-Current Assets* section of the Accounting Map™ is divided into two parts. The first part, labeled *Property, Plant & Equipment*, pertains to a company's non-current assets that are of a tangible nature. The second part is labeled *Intangible Assets* and we will discuss these later in the chapter.

A company has to have non-current tangible assets in order to get physical tasks accomplished – for example, machines that package bottles, trucks that deliver catalogues and computers that scan and compute inventory data. Indeed, non-current tangible assets often form the physical backbone of a company. Without them, a business will not have the property, buildings and machinery it needs to deliver goods and services to its customers. This is particularly true for manufacturers or companies involved in the transportation industry whose capital assets are often the largest on the balance sheet.

FIGURE 6.2

For example, look at figure 6.3, which shows an excerpt of the balance sheet for Amtrak for the years ended September 30, 2008 and September 30, 2007.

National Railroad Passenger Corporation and Subsidiaries (Amtrak) Consolidated Balance Sheet For the Year Ended September 30 (In Thousands of Dollars, Except Share Data)		
ASSETS	**2008**	**2007**
Current Assets:		
Cash and cash equivalents	329,813	223,949
Restricted Cash	10,012	10,393
Short-term investments	-	9950
Accounts receivable, net of allowances of $4,794 and $7,397 at September 30, 2008 and 2007, respectively	100,892	141,645
Materials and supplies – net	155,583	174,897
Other current assets	40,927	44,026
Total current assets	637,227	604,860
Property and Equipment:		
Locomotives	1,365,541	1,405,200
Passenger cars and other rolling stock	2,642,830	2,650,963
Right-of-way and other properties	8,693,663	8,363,818
Leasehold improvements	331,314	310,503
Property and equipment, gross	13,033,348	12,730,484
Less - Accumulated depreciation and amortization	(4,592,516)	(4,424,569)
Total property and equipment, net	**8,440,832**	**8,305,915**
Other Assets, Deposits, and Deferred Charges:		
Escrowed proceeds on sale-leasebacks	894,752	874,744
Deferred charges, deposits, and other	327,057	379,942
Total other assets, deposits, and deferred charges	**1,221,809**	**1,254,686**
Total Assets	**10,299,868**	**10,165,461**

FIGURE 6.3

You can see that for both fiscal years 2008 and 2007, the company's largest assets were its property, plant and equipment. These are obviously important investments for the business and need to be properly managed to achieve long-term success.

Defining a Non-Current Asset

Various components distinguish a non-current asset from a current asset. An asset can be considered to be non-current (or long-term) if it contains certain characteristics related to time, money and purpose. In fact, these characteristics can be determined by the accountant who asks three questions when presented with the purchase of an item:

1. How long will the company use the item?
2. How much does the item cost?
3. What will the item be used for?

1. How long will the company use the item?

As already mentioned, a period of one year is the dividing line between current and non-current assets. If a business intends to use an item for more than a year, it meets one of the criteria for defining a non-current asset.

Different types of capital assets tend to have different life spans – all exceeding one year. Office equipment, such as computers and printers, tend to have life spans averaging five years. The life span of buildings can often be measured in decades. Land can be considered to have an infinite life span; it can be used for as long as the company is in business.

2. How much does the item cost?

When one hears the term *capital* being used, it usually refers to items worth large sums of money that are integral to the finances of an organization, industry or even the country. This certainly holds true for non-current tangible (capital) assets, which normally make up a large portion of the value of the assets on a company's balance sheet. Yet, how much does something have to cost for it to be classified as a capital asset in the financial statements? The short answer is this: it depends. It depends on the size of the organization and the guidelines used to classify capital assets. The accounting principle of *materiality* should be applied – that is, companies need to decide the dollar amount they will use as the basis on which amounts will either be set up as non-current assets or expensed during the current accounting period.

What a large multinational corporation considers to be a significant amount of money will almost invariably differ from the amount a small business would consider significant. A large organization could, for example, establish the guideline that something needs to cost at least $2,000 to be considered a tangible non-current asset. A small business might set $500 as a threshold. For businesses large and small, if an item is less than the threshold, it is recorded as an expense on the income statement.

It is important to keep in mind that once a rule is chosen, a company should adhere to it. This is what the GAAP rule of consistency is about, and it seeks to prevent accountants from manipulating the numbers after the fact.

3. What will the item be used for?

For something to be considered a capital asset, an organization should acquire it for the purpose of generating income (i.e. it must be used for business purposes). Businesses buy land in order to build factories; they buy buildings in order to set up stores; they buy trucks in order to deliver goods; and they buy machines in order to make products. All these items should be considered capital assets as long as they meet the first two criteria discussed.

The Acquisition of Non-Current Assets

When companies purchase physical items such as land, buildings and equipment, the accountant must consider the cost, purpose and expected useful life of the item. According to the materiality principle, an item can be considered a capital asset on the balance sheet instead of an expense in the income statement if it satisfies the following: it has material value relative to the size of the business and it is expected to last for longer than one year.

Once the decision has been made to record the item as a capital asset, focus shifts to the cost principle to ensure that all the costs associated with acquiring the asset are properly recorded. A company pays not only for the asset in question

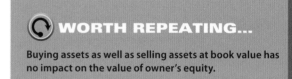

WORTH REPEATING...

Buying assets as well as selling assets at book value has no impact on the value of owner's equity.

but also for all the costs associated with acquiring the asset – for example, the freight that was paid to bring a machine to the factory; the infrastructure upgrades involved in connecting electricity and water lines; and the installation fees paid to set up the machines and have them ready for operation.

Note that since these costs are directly related to the asset itself, they are not treated as expenses but as part of the cost of the asset. This cost is then recorded on the company's balance sheet.

For example, the Sunshine Juice Company has purchased a new bottling machine for its orange juice line. It was purchased at a price of $120,000 and shipped at a cost of $5,000, with installation costs amounting to $2,000. Assuming one invoice for all these costs, here is the journal entry for the acquisition of this capital asset:

JOURNAL			
Date	Account Title and Explanation	Debit	Credit
	Machine	127,000	
	Accounts Payable		127,000
	Record the purchase of a machine for $120,000 + $2,000 for installation, and $5,000 for shipping		

BALANCE SHEET

FIGURE 6.4

When totaled, the costs amount to $127,000. This amount is debited to an account that is part of property, plant and equipment and credited to accounts payable, since the company was invoiced and owes this amount to the bottling machine manufacturer. Of course, once the bill is paid, accounts payable will be debited and cash will be credited.

Although financial statements may just show a single property, plant and equipment line item, there are actually separate accounts for each capital asset within that category. In this text, we will journalize each capital asset by using the asset's specific name.

Lump Sum Purchases of Capital Assets

Unique circumstances can throw a wrench in the way transactions are recorded. This also holds true for capital assets. Companies sometimes purchase capital assets in bundles, or what is known as a "basket of assets." Instead of buying capital assets individually from different vendors, a company may get a good price for a basket of assets by buying them from the same vendor.

The challenge with this type of transaction is that by paying a lower price for the assets, the buyer acquires them for less than their appraised value. Accountants find creative ways to resolve conflicting principles like this. In this case, the lump sum paid for all the assets will be divided and allocated to each item according to percentages based on the appraised values. For example, the Huge Bargain Store has purchased land, a building and a parking lot for the purpose of opening a new store. It bought all these assets in a bundle for the lump sum payment of $800,000. However, each asset has its own appraised value, as listed in the following chart:

Item	Appraised Value
Property	600,000
Building	300,000
Parking Lot	100,000
Total	1,000,000

FIGURE 6.5

As you can see, the total of all the appraised values is $1,000,000, which is $200,000 more than the purchase price. The first step is to take each appraised value and divide it by the total appraised values. This produces a percentage that should be allocated to each asset.

Property	600,000 ÷ 1,000,000	60%
Building	300,000 ÷ 1,000,000	30%
Parking Lot	100,000 ÷ 1,000,000	10%

FIGURE 6.6

These percentages are now allocated to the amount actually paid, which was $800,000.

We have based the amounts to be recorded for each asset on the appraised values, and these will be recorded as follows:

Property	800,000 × 60%	480,000
Building	800,000 × 30%	240,000
Parking Lot	800,000 × 10%	80,000
		800,000

FIGURE 6.7

The specific capital asset accounts are debited and cash is credited.

JOURNAL			
Date	Account Title and Explanation	Debit	Credit
	Land	480,000	
	Building	240,000	
	Parking Lot	80,000	
	Cash		800,000
	Record the purchase of land, building and parking lot		

FIGURE 6.8

Changes in a Capital Asset

Capital assets can change in value as a result of two factors: depreciation, which we will examine shortly, and changes made to the capital asset itself. As already mentioned, a challenge with capital assets is determining whether an item should be classified as a non-current asset or whether it should simply be recorded as an expense in the current year. This challenge is made even more difficult when a change to the asset takes place. Is this an example of maintenance, which can be recorded as a routine expense? Or does the change alter the nature of the asset itself so that it is worth more, lasts longer or undergoes a change in function?

These determinations are important every time money is spent on a capital asset. Is the expenditure considered to be an asset or an expense? To make the assessment, ask four questions:

1. Does the expenditure extend the life of the asset?
2. Does the expenditure improve the productivity of the asset?
3. Does the expenditure reduce the company's operating costs?
4. Is the expenditure a material amount?

We will examine each question separately through examples.

1. Does the expenditure extend the life of the asset?

A company has a large stamping press that runs on an electric motor. The maintenance department has been adding replacement parts to keep the motor in operation. The head of the maintenance department tells the owner that these replacement parts are becoming harder to find and that the motor has only one year of operation left. The maintenance manager recommends that the company buy a new motor for the stamping press, which would extend the life of the machine by about 10 years.

If the maintenance department continues buying new parts for the motor, no material changes or upgrades are made to the stamping press; the motor's life span is not extended. These expenditures are therefore classified as expenses in the income statement. However, if the company buys a new motor, a material improvement will be made to the stamping press. Its life span will significantly increase, as will its total cost as a non-current asset on the balance sheet.

2. Does the expenditure improve the productivity of the asset?

Assume that a company originally bought a machine without a lighting system (which could be purchased as an option). The lighting system would have enabled the machine to be operated at night. Management later decided to have a night production shift, and therefore needed to install the lighting system at a substantial cost. This installation significantly increased the machine's productivity, since it could produce more products within the work week. The lighting system, along with all additional costs associated with its delivery and installation, should be considered an improvement, and added to the original cost of the machine.

3. Does the expenditure reduce the company's operating costs?

Many pieces of equipment require routine maintenance by paid staff or by outsourced help – for example, a company's Internet server, which stores web page information. Technicians periodically check the server to ensure that everything is running smoothly. However, technology is available to enable the server itself to perform many routine checks. If the company were to purchase such technology, it would reduce some of the expenses involved in having personnel perform the maintenance, thereby reducing operating costs of the company. The new technology would be classified as a capital expenditure and added to the cost of the server on the company's balance sheet.

4. Is the expenditure a material amount?

As mentioned earlier, the amount of expenditure should be capitalized (added to the cost of the asset) if the money was spent for one of the purposes described in items 1 to 3 above. However, accountants need to consider whether the expenditure is a material amount. Companies often have accounting policies that determine what dollar amount is considered to be material. If the amount is material, the cost is capitalized. If the amount is immaterial, the cost is expensed.

For example, a company that owns a $50 million capital asset may decide that any asset-related cost below $600 is automatically expensed. Therefore, when a $100 addition is made to the capital asset providing a $12,000 benefit, the cost will be considered immaterial and expensed. It is management's responsibility to decide what amount is considered material for their company.

Changes to a capital asset that increases its productivity, such as the addition of an overhead light, which extends the production time of the machine, is considered a material improvement and needs to be added to its total cost.

The Concept of Depreciation

In any discussion of expenses arising from assets, the matching principle needs to be considered. Expenses associated with assets need to be matched with associated revenues. As a company generates annual revenue from using a capital asset, it also generates annual expenses. Capital assets are typically used for long periods of time and their value tends to decrease with use; in other words, as with a car, the more a capital asset is used, the less value it will have on the market, when it is eventually sold. This decrease in value is considered an expense of "using" the asset and is referred to as *depreciation*. We will examine various aspects of depreciation and how capital assets on the balance sheet are affected.

Residual Value

Before discussing specific methods of depreciation, we should first examine what a capital asset's **residual value** is and how it affects depreciation calculations. As already mentioned, depreciation is the process by which accountants reduce the value of a capital asset over time. At the end of its useful life, the asset might still be worth something. This is called its *salvage value*, since it is possible that the asset can be salvaged for a certain amount of money. It is also called *residual value*, since the asset is considered to have some value, despite no longer being useful to the company.

New capital assets like company trucks can gradually turn into old capital assets. Depreciation is the process by which gradual decreases in value are estimated and recorded over time.

For example, a company may no longer be able to use a delivery truck that has been on the road for six years. A buyer might see some residual value in the truck, salvage it for a price and sell its spare parts or the scrap metal it contains, or even donate it to a museum. In fact, people might want an item for a number of purposes, which is the reason why a capital asset might carry a residual or salvage value even after it is unable to do what it was designed for.

The total amount to be depreciated for a capital asset is affected by the residual value that is expected to remain at the end of the asset's useful life. In other words, if a company purchases a capital asset for $5,000, and determines that its residual value will eventually be $1,000, the amount to be depreciated over the useful life of the asset is $4,000. Even though the capital asset can no longer be used for business after its useful life expires, somebody may salvage it for a price; this price should be subtracted from the depreciation calculations made by the company.

Actual Salvage Value

One of the realities confronting accountants is that depreciation is a theoretical concept. The value of a capital asset does not decrease according to a depreciation schedule. It will decrease on the basis of the price it actually fetches on the market. In other words, depreciation involves an accountant's best estimate, which requires justified calculations of a capital asset's value over its useful life with the company.

For example, a capital asset might be purchased at an initial cost of $100,000. The accountant will examine the asset, study its potential worth over time, and make an educated guess at what someone might eventually be willing to pay to salvage it. This is not an easy task.

Let us assume that the accountant estimates a residual value of $10,000. Ten years later, the item is salvaged for $5,000. It would appear that the accountant overestimated the residual value. This is in order as long as the accountant was justified in making the initial estimate and adjusts for a loss once the asset is salvaged. The book value was initially recorded as $10,000, though the selling price ended up being $5,000. As a result, the accountant will have to record a loss of $5,000. Similarly, if a capital asset is eventually sold for more than its estimated residual value, the difference would be recorded as a gain.

Three Methods of Depreciation

As time goes by and an asset is used, its value on the market will decline. The capital asset's book value should reflect this decline. Since no one knows what an asset will be worth until it is actually sold, an accountant must estimate how much a capital asset is depreciated while being used by the company.

This process is similar to the one used when estimating a capital asset's residual value. In other words, it is somewhat of a guessing game. The difference with depreciation, however, is that some method should be used to calculate a relatively gradual decline in the asset's worth, period after period. Additionally, once this method is chosen, adherence to the consistency principle requires that the same method be used for the entire time the company uses the asset (unless special conditions are met).

The simplest method of depreciating a capital asset is to take its total cost, deduct any residual value it is expected to have, and divide the balance by the amount of years the asset is expected to be useful. This would produce the same depreciation amount year after year.

This is called the *straight-line depreciation* method, which we will examine in further detail shortly. Its attraction is that it is simple. Its fault is that it may not reflect a realistic decline in the value of the asset. That is why other methods of depreciation have been developed, which we will also discuss.

We will now examine three methods of depreciation related to capital assets:

The Straight-Line Method

The Straight-Line Method	Uses simple average
The Declining-Balance Method	Try to reflect a more realistic decline in asset value
The Units-of-Production Method	

FIGURE 6.9

Let us recap what the straight-line method of depreciation does. It takes the entire cost of the capital asset, less any estimated residual value, and divides it by the number of years of its estimated useful life. This produces an average depreciation expense, which is applied each year until the asset is sold or reaches the end of its useful life.

Any method of depreciation involves changing the book value of an asset as realistically as possible

In our first example, we will apply the straight-line method to an asset that is expected to have a residual value once its useful life is over. Remember, only the value related to an asset's useful life is depreciated. This means that the residual value is subtracted from the initial cost before the depreciation method is applied.

Total Cost of Asset - Residual Value = Amount Depreciated

Smith Tools buys a machine for $5,000. The machine is expected to have a useful life of five years and its residual value is estimated to be $1,000. The amount to be depreciated is:

$$\$5,000 - \$1,000 = \$4,000$$

Under the straight-line method, the average is calculated by dividing the amount to be depreciated (cost − residual value) by the number of years of the asset's useful life:

$$\text{Yearly Depreciation} = \frac{\text{Amount Depreciated}}{\text{Years of Useful Life}} = \frac{\$4,000}{5}$$

$$= \$800 \text{ depreciation per year}$$

This annual depreciation would be applied to the capital asset as follows:

Year	Cost of Capital Asset	Depreciation Expense	Accumulated Depreciation to Date	Net Book Value
0	5,000	-0-	-0-	5,000
1	5,000	800	800	4,200
2	5,000	800	1,600	3,400
3	5,000	800	2,400	2,600
4	5,000	800	3,200	1,800
5	5,000	800	4,000	1,000

FIGURE 6.10

Depreciation of $800 is accumulated each year until the end of the asset's useful life. At that time, all that is left of the asset's book value is its residual value. In this case, the amount is $1,000, being the final net book value at the bottom right hand corner of the table.

Continuing with the Smith Tools example, we will assume this time that the asset will have no residual value at the end of its presumed useful life. This means that the total amount to be depreciated will be $5,000 (the original cost of the asset) instead of $4,000, which included a $1,000 residual value deduction from the original cost. The annual depreciation amounts would be recorded as shown in figure 6.11:

As is common in accounting, the calculations are only part of the process. The subsequent challenge is to record the results of those calculations in the financial statements.

You will recall from our examination of accounts receivable in chapter 3 that a contra account was established that allowed bad debt to be written off for the period before the debt was proved to be bad. In other words, the company expected some loss of assets during the course of the year, and a contra account was established to mark a negative change in the value of the asset without distorting the company's net worth.

Year	Depreciation Expense
1	1,000
2	1,000
3	1,000
4	1,000
5	1,000

FIGURE 6.11

A similar process is implemented with a company's capital assets. On the one hand, accountants like to see the original value of the asset remain on the balance sheet. On the other hand, the value of the asset does change over time, as does the company's equity. Contra accounts allow both the asset's original value and the book value to be reflected on the balance sheet. Remember, a contra-asset account is linked to another asset account, but works in reverse. Any addition to the contra account serves to decrease the value of the asset. The contra account for a capital asset is called *accumulated depreciation*. It reflects the decrease in value of the capital asset over time. The original cost in the capital asset account remains constant. The net value of the original cost and the accumulated depreciation equals the book value of the asset.

Figure 6.12 shows the corresponding journal entry for recording $1,000 of depreciation expense of a capital asset:

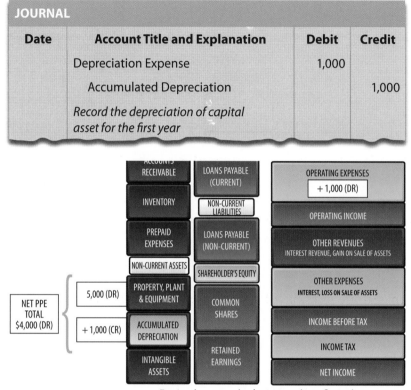

FIGURE 6.12

We now continue with our Smith Tools example to demonstrate how the contra account is used to depreciate capital assets on the balance sheet. The initial purchase of the capital asset is recorded as a debit of $5,000 to property, plant and equipment, with no change to equity. Using the straight-line method, we calculate each year's depreciation as $1,000. This amount is credited in the accumulated depreciation contra account. As you can see, this reduces the net value of the capital asset to $4,000 in the first year, but does not change the original $5,000 value recorded in the property, plant and equipment account. In the income statement, the depreciation expense of $1,000 is recorded as a debit because equity decreased by $1,000.

Each year depreciation is recorded, the amount of accumulated depreciation increases and the net book value of the capital asset decreases. This is illustrated in the following table, which can also be referred to as an *asset register*.

Year 0 marks the beginning of the year in which the capital asset is purchased. Although the $5,000 cost remains the same from year to year, as does the $1,000 amount of depreciation expense, notice that the accumulated depreciation increases annually by $1,000, while the net book value decreases annually by the same amount.

Year	Cost of Capital Asset	Depreciation Expense	Accumulated Depreciation to Date	Net Book Value
0	5,000	-0-	-0-	5,000
1	5,000	1,000	1,000	4,000
2	5,000	1,000	2,000	3,000
3	5,000	1,000	3,000	2,000
4	5,000	1,000	4,000	1,000
5	5,000	1,000	5,000	-0-

FIGURE 6.13

The Declining and Double-Declining-Balance Method

The commonly discussed drawback to the straight-line method is that it may not reflect how asset values actually decrease over time because capital assets do not normally decrease in value by the same amount each year. Alternative depreciation methods have been developed by the accounting profession. One of them is known as the *declining–balance method*.

The most common real life example of asset depreciation is the car. Think about how that asset depreciates over time. It is common knowledge that the largest decrease in a car's value occurs the moment the car is driven off the dealership's lot. In other words, the value of the car depreciates the most during the early years of its useful life and depreciates the least during its later years. This principle is applicable for most capital assets and that is why the declining-balance method is used (and is so called): the amount depreciated on an annual basis declines over time.

The procedure used for the declining-balance method differs from the straight-line method in two ways:

First, the straight-line method simply calculates an average annual depreciation rate. It achieves this by dividing the amount to be depreciated by the number of years of the asset's useful life.

As an example, let us consider the purchase of a capital asset worth $10,000 that has a useful life of 5 years with no residual value.

It is often said that the value of a new car tumbles the second it is driven off the dealership lot. The declining method of depreciation tries to capture this more dramatic decline in the early years of the useful capital assets.

Straight–Line Method

$$\text{Annual Depreciation} = \frac{\text{Cost - Residual Value}}{\text{Years of Useful Life}} = \frac{\$10,000}{5} = \$2,000$$

Declining-Balance Method

For the declining-balance method, instead of using an equal annual depreciation amount, an annual percentage is used, which is calculated as follows:

$$\text{Annual Depreciation} = \frac{100\%}{\text{Years of Useful Life (5)}} = 20\%$$

If the useful life of an asset is 10 years, then the base depreciation rate to be applied would be 10% (100% divided by 10). If the useful life is 20 years, the depreciation rate applied each year would be 5% (100% divided by 20).

There is one more step: the ***double-declining-balance method***, by which twice the depreciation rate is used each year. With the same percentages already calculated, a double-declining depreciation rate of 40% (20% × 2) would be used when the useful life of an asset is 5 years. When the useful life is 10 years, a double-declining depreciation rate of 20% would be used (10% × 2). For a useful life of 20 years, an annual rate of 10% would be used (5% × 2).

Formula for calculating double-declining balance rate:

Double-Declining Rate = Yearly Depreciation Rate Using Declining Balance Method × 2

In essence, using a double-declining rate amounts to exaggerating the declining effect by the order of two. This ensures that much of the rate of depreciation occurs during the early years of an asset's life span. This effect will be demonstrated in figure 6.14.

Second, the reason that the double-declining method amplifies the depreciation effect in the early years of an asset's useful life is that, unlike the straight-line method, the declining method applies depreciation to the remaining balance of the book value of the asset. In other words, it does not apply the same amount of depreciation every year. Instead, it applies the same depreciation percentage rate to the remaining balance at the beginning of every year.

Continuing with our example of a capital asset purchased for $10,000, that has an estimated useful life of 5 years, the depreciation for the first year would be

$10,000 x 40% = $4,000

The remaining book value for the beginning of the second year would be

$10,000 - $4,000 = $6,000

The double-declining depreciation rate of 40% is now applied to this new balance to determine the depreciation amount for the second year:

$6,000 x 40% = $2,400

The same double-declining rate is applied to a decreasing book value on an annual basis. This means that over the years, the depreciation amounts are reduced substantially, which generally reflects the way capital assets decline in value.

The rest of the depreciation amounts in our example are shown in the following chart:

Year	Beginning of Year Book Value		@ 40% Double Declining Depreciation Rate		Remaining Book Value
1	$10,000	minus	$4,000	equals	$6,000
2	$6,000		$2,400		$3,600
3	$3,600		$1,440		$2,160
4	$2,160		$864		$1,296
5	$1,296		$518.40		$777.60

FIGURE 6.14

Applying a percentage rate to a balance every year means that there will always be a remaining balance when the double-declining method is used; for this reason, a residual value estimation is not necessary with this method. In this example, the remaining book value at the end of five years is $777.60. However, if the asset has a residual value when the declining-balance (or double-declining-balance) method is used, it should not be depreciated below the residual value. For example, if the residual value is $1,000 for the example shown above, the last year's depreciation should amount to $296 ($1,296 - $1,000 = $296).

The Units-of-Production Method

The **units-of-production method** involves a different procedure for depreciating a capital asset – asset usage as the basis for calculating depreciation. The methods we have studied so far use a predetermined formula that is not based on usage. The first step in the units-of-production method is to choose a unit for measuring the usage of the capital asset. If the asset is a vehicle, the unit can be the number of kilometers driven. If the asset is a machine, the unit can be the number of hours operated. These measures are known as *units of production* – hence the name of this method.

Once the type of unit is chosen, the next step is to estimate the number of units to be used for the entire life of the asset. The total cost of the asset is then divided by this number to arrive at a cost per unit. This cost per unit is then applied to the number of units produced in a year to determine that year's depreciation amount. The same procedure is followed each year until the end of the asset's estimated useful life.

Here is an example to illustrate how the units-of-production method can be applied in depreciation of a capital asset.

Deliveries Are Us bought a truck for $110,000 to be used for deliveries. The truck has an estimated residual value of $10,000. The company wants all its trucks to be in top condition, so it retires them after 200,000 kilometers of usage.

1. The unit of production to be used will be kilometers.

2. The number of units to be used for the life of the truck is 200,000 kilometers.

3. The cost per unit to be used in calculating annual depreciation is:

$$\frac{\text{Cost} - \text{Residual Value}}{\text{Total Units of Production}} = \frac{\$110,000 - \$10,000}{200,000} = 50\text{¢ per unit}$$

4. If the truck is driven 30,000 kilometers for the first year, the depreciation for that year would be:

$$\text{Units of Production Used for Year} \times 0.50 = 30,000 \times 0.50 = \$15,000$$

The amount of depreciation for a year is entirely dependent on its usage. For example, if in the second year, the truck was driven for 25,000 kilometers, the depreciation for that year would be:

$$25,000 \times 0.50 = \$12,500$$

If in the third year, the truck was driven for 35,000 kilometers, the year's depreciation would be:

$$35,000 \times 0.50 = \$17,500$$

This depreciation procedure would be applied annually until the truck had been driven for 200,000 kilometers, the initial estimation for the life of the truck. However, when the usage exceeds the estimated units of production, no additional depreciation expense should be allocated to the units produced.

Which Depreciation Method Should Be Used?

As is common in accounting, no single method of calculating a balance sheet item is necessarily better or preferable than another. The challenge for the accountant is to choose a method that best reflects the nature of the asset involved. Perhaps most important, the accountant must continue to use the initial method chosen. This is what the consistency principle dictates, so that manipulation of financial figures after the fact is prevented.

However, the consistency principle does not prevent an accountant from using different methods of depreciation for different types of company assets — so long as the same method is used for the life of the particular asset. For example, a company might use the straight-line-method to depreciate an advertising sign, but use the declining-balance method to depreciate a company-owned vehicle, since the value of cars and trucks decreases most during their early years.

Depreciation For Partial Years

Our examination of depreciation has been based on the assumption that capital assets are purchased at the beginning of a year and sold at the end of a year. Of course, business executives do not allow depreciation methods to dictate when capital assets are bought and sold. Various tactics can be employed to accommodate the realities of the calendar year when depreciating a company's capital assets. Once a capital asset has been purchased, the accountant must choose a depreciation schedule that accommodates the timing of asset ownership. The accountant may decide that no depreciation will be recorded in the year of purchase, and a full year's depreciation will be recorded in the year of sale. Alternatively, she may decide to depreciate the asset for the full month of purchase, depreciate monthly thereafter until the asset is sold, and not depreciate for the month of sale.

A number of possible combinations are available to the accountant to depreciate during the year of purchase or sale, or month of purchase or sale. These combinations provide the accountant with the flexibility to develop a depreciation schedule that best reflects the business reality of the company.

Let us examine the situation that arises from the purchase of a $120,000 packaging machine by the Jones Cookie Factory on March 27, 2001. The company determines that the packager will have a useful life of 10 years, after which it will not be salvageable; thus no residual value needs to be estimated. The machine will be depreciated by $12,000 annually and $1,000 monthly. The machine is eventually sold on October 1, 2008 at a price of $32,000. The fiscal year-end for the Jones Cookie Factory is November 30.

The company decides to use the following depreciation rules: no depreciation in the month of purchase and monthly depreciation thereafter, including the month of sale.

Figure 6.15 displays the annual depreciation calculated after the application of the chosen schedule. For fiscal years 2002–2007, each year includes 12 full months and will have $12,000 of annual depreciation at $1,000 per month. That is the easy part. The challenge is dealing with the partial years of 2001 (year of purchase) and 2008 (year of sale).

In fiscal year 2001, the month of purchase was March. The chosen schedule dictates that there is no depreciation in that month. That leaves eight months of depreciation in the fiscal year, or $8,000.

	Months	Depreciation
2001	8	8,000
2002	12	12,000
2003	12	12,000
2004	12	12,000
2005	12	12,000
2006	12	12,000
2007	12	12,000
2008	11	11,000
	Total	91,000

FIGURE 6.15

Fiscal Year 2001

FIGURE 6.16

In fiscal year 2008, the month of sale was October. The chosen schedule dictates that even though the sale occurred on the first day of the month, depreciation for the entire month is calculated. This means that there will be 11 months of depreciation for the fiscal year amounting to a total of $11,000.

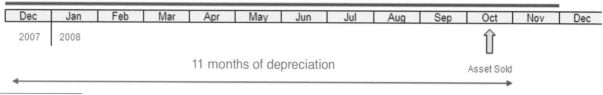

Fiscal Year 2008

Dec	Jan	Feb	Mar	Apr	May	Jun	Jul	Aug	Sep	Oct	Nov	Dec
2007	2008											

11 months of depreciation   Asset Sold

FIGURE 6.17

As figure 6.18 shows, the total amount depreciated for the packaging machine is $91,000. Subtracting this amount from the original purchase price of $120,000 produces a net book value of $29,000. The machine was sold for $32,000, generating a gain of $3,000 on disposal. As is often true in accounting, the method chosen will affect net income. It is therefore incumbent on the accountant to choose the most appropriate method.

Packaging Machine

$91,000 Depreciated

$32,000 Sale Price - $29,000 Book Value = $3,000 Gain

FIGURE 6.18

Disposal, Revision And Depreciation

When a capital asset is disposed of, a gain or loss will be generated from disposal of the asset. The accountant must remove from the books all the accumulated depreciation for the asset in question, since the company no longer owns the item. For example, a company has equipment (capital asset) that cost $5,000, with a useful life of 5 years and a residual value of $1,000. The asset is eventually sold for precisely that value: $1,000. The journal entry needed to record the transaction at sale would be:

JOURNAL			
Date	Account Title and Explanation	Debit	Credit
	Cash	1,000	
	Accumulated Depreciation - Equipment	4,000	
	Equipment		5,000
	To record the sale of used asset for $1,000		

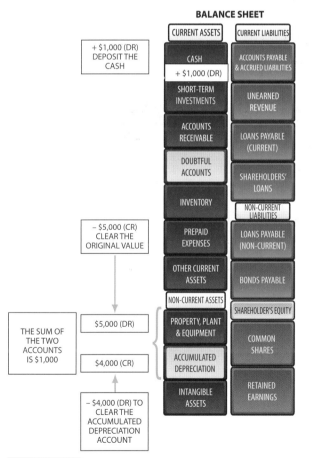

FIGURE 6.19

The amount of $1,000 is received for the asset and debited to cash; $4,000 is debited to the accumulated depreciation account, which was initially set up to record the systematic write-off of the asset each year through the adjusting entry (debit depreciation expense, credit accumulated depreciation). The amount of $5,000 is now credited to the property, plant and equipment account, since the company no longer owns the capital asset.

Now let us assume that the equipment was sold for $500, half the estimated residual value. Since only $500 was received for the asset, this amount is debited to cash and the $500 loss is debited to *other expenses* in the income statement. The $4,000 in accumulated depreciation is still debited to that account, and the initial cost of $5,000 is still credited to the property, plant and equipment asset account.

JOURNAL			
Date	**Account Title and Explanation**	**Debit**	**Credit**
	Cash	500	
	Accumulated Depreciation - Equipment	4,000	
	Loss on Disposal of Asset	500	
	Equipment		5,000
	To record the sale of used asset		

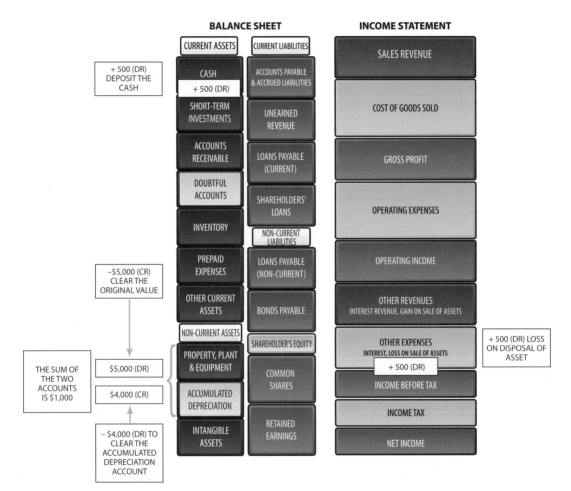

FIGURE 6.20

If the equipment was sold for $1,500, the $500 gain would change the journal entry:

JOURNAL			
Date	**Account Title and Explanation**	**Debit**	**Credit**
	Cash	1,500	
	Accumulated Depreciation - Equipment	4,000	
	Gain on Disposal of Asset		500
	Equipment		5,000
	To record the sale of used asset for $1,500		

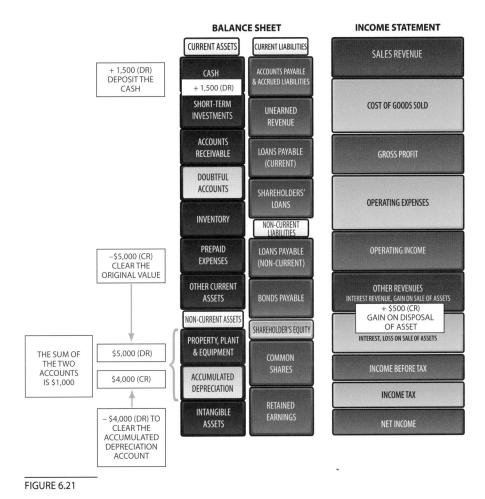

FIGURE 6.21

Debit $1,500 to cash and credit $500 to *other revenue* in the income statement.

Instead of trying to sell the capital asset, a company may decide to donate it to charity. The transaction would involve a loss for the company and would be recorded as a donation expense. Assume the company donated the equipment from the previous example to a local charity.

JOURNAL			
Date	**Account Title and Explanation**	**Debit**	**Credit**
	Accumulated Depreciation - Equipment	4,000	
	Donation Expense	1,000	
	Equipment		5,000
	To record the donation of used asset		

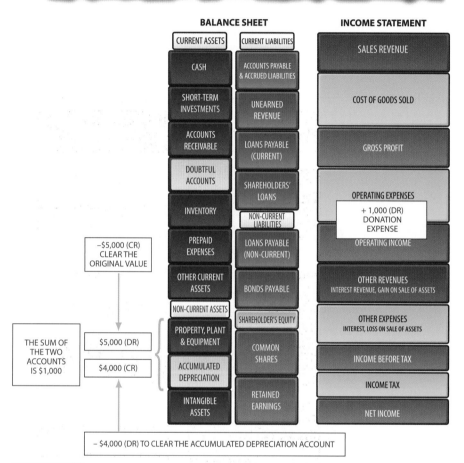

FIGURE 6.22

A capital asset can be disposed of in many ways that do not involve selling the item. For the purpose of this book, we have discussed only the routine methods of disposal and provided a solid foundation for understanding the accounting concept in general. Here is one final change to our initial example in this section. Instead of 5 years, the life of the equipment ends up being 4 years, and the asset is sold for $500.

JOURNAL			
Date	**Account Title and Explanation**	**Debit**	**Credit**
	Cash	500	
	Accumulated Depreciation - Equipment	3,200	
	Loss on Disposal of Asset	1,300	
	Equipment		5,000
	To record the sale of used asset for $500		

FIGURE 6.23

When the useful life was 5 years, $4,000 of total depreciation had to be spread out over those 5 years, using the straight-line method. This amounted to $800 of depreciation per year. If the actual life of the asset ends up being four years, then only 4 years' worth of depreciation was accumulated, for a total of $3,200 ($800 × 4). The remaining book value, or amount yet to be depreciated, increases to $1,800. Since the asset was sold for $500, this results in a loss of $1,300.

In summary, $500 is debited to cash; $3,200 in accumulated depreciation is taken off the books by debiting that amount; $1,300 is debited as a loss in the income statement; and the original cost of the asset ($5,000) is removed from the books by crediting that amount to the account.

One final note: going back to our original example, if the company uses the capital asset for longer than the estimated useful life of 5 years, the remaining book value would be $1,000, which is the estimated residual value. In this case, no adjustments would be made and the company would continue to use the asset without further depreciation.

Revising Depreciation

Our examination of depreciation in this chapter has included numerous references to estimates. We have also looked at examples in which the residual value or the asset's useful life, or both, were incorrectly estimated. Let us take a closer look at these scenarios with a more comprehensive example.

Brian's Bricks bought a new oven for its factory at a cost of $300,000. It was expected to have a useful life of 10 years and a salvage value of $20,000.

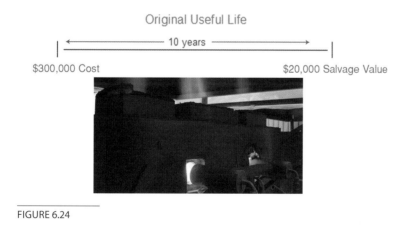

FIGURE 6.24

After five years of use, the oven shows that it is not deteriorating as quickly as expected. After consulting with the oven manufacturer, management determines that the useful life of this capital asset could be extended to 15 years, and the salvage value increased to $40,000.

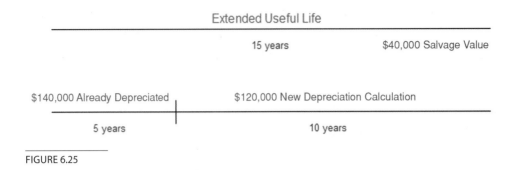

FIGURE 6.25

Using the straight-line method, the company's accountants had recorded depreciation of [($300,000 – 20,000) ÷ 10] × 5 = $140,000, which produced a net book value of $300,000 – 140,000 = $160,000.

Brian's Bricks then started a new depreciation schedule, assuming the straight line method again, in which the amount to be depreciated for the rest of the asset's new useful life would be $160,000 - $40,000 (new salvage value) = $120,000. This amount is divided by the number of years left in the new useful life (15 years - 5 years already recorded = 10 years), to produce an annual depreciation amount of $12,000.

Note that the company should not change the depreciation already accumulated during the first five years of using the oven. An accountant should only make or change depreciation estimates for the future. Any changes that are made need to be justified with the appropriate documentation. In this case, that documentation would include consultation with the asset's manufacturer.

Natural Resources

Natural resources have a physical nature, but one that is different from the nature of other capital assets. In fact, some companies place natural resources in a separate asset category on the balance sheet. For our present purpose, we will examine these types of assets in our broader discussion of non-current assets and how we account for natural resources in the company's books.

First, as with most other assets we study in this book, natural resources come at a cost. This cost includes any expenditure made in acquiring the asset. In the case of natural resources, this cost includes expenditures involved in preparing resources for extraction. It also includes any expenditure for restoring the land upon completion of use. The total cost is to be recorded in the appropriate asset account on the balance sheet.

Second, like other capital assets we have studied, natural resources represent items that will decrease in value as a result of use. In this case, natural resources are *depleted* over time, and this depletion needs to be accounted for in the books. This is done through the process of depreciation, just as with other non-current assets. However, the term depreciation is replaced with *depletion*.

Special note:

- Some companies still use the term *amortization* or *depreciation*.
- Not all companies use the accumulated depreciation or depletion account. Instead, they credit the natural resource account directly and debit the expense.

Our examination of depreciation introduced us to the *units-of-production method* of depreciation: the method that involves actual usage of an asset. It is therefore most appropriate for use in depleting natural resources; the actual units depleted – such as cubic meters, barrels, and tons – can be used in the calculation.

We will use the example of the Standing Tall Timber Company to illustrate how the units-of-production method is applied to a natural resource asset. The company has bought land to be harvested for timber, at a total cost of $10 million. It estimates that once all the land is harvested, it will be worth $2 million. This is the asset's residual or salvage value. Furthermore, the company estimates that the total timber to be harvested will amount to 80 million MFBM (thousand board feet).

$$\frac{\text{Total Cost - Residual Value}}{\text{Total Units}} = \frac{\$10,000,000 - \$2,000,000}{80,000,000 \text{ MFBM}} = \$0.10 \text{ per MFBM}$$

If 2 million MFBM were harvested in the first year, the depletion for the year would be:

$$2,000,000 \times \$0.10 = \$200,000$$

JOURNAL			
Date	**Account Title and Explanation**	**Debit**	**Credit**
	Depletion Expense	200,000	
	Accumulated Depletion - Standing Tall Timber		200,000
	To record depletion expense for the year for Standing Tall Timber		

The three figures above (total cost, residual value and total units) will be used to calculate a per unit depletion cost that is to be applied for every unit of timber depleted within a year.

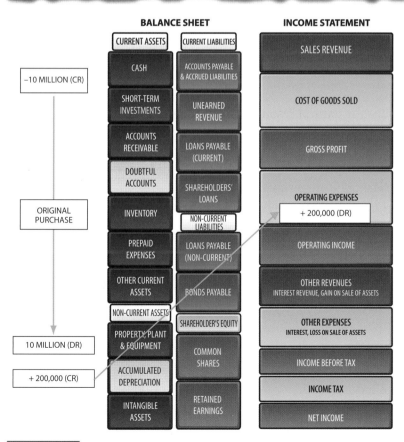

FIGURE 6.26

The rate per year is $200,000 and the whole asset will be depleted over 40 years at that rate. To record this amount, $200,000 is credited to the accumulated depreciation account, and $200,000 is expensed as depletion on the income statement. The timber that is yet to be harvested remains a separate asset on the balance sheet and is valued at cost less any depletion. Any harvested timber that a company still has on hand is now considered inventory and is valued at the per unit rate that was used for depletion. In this case, it was $0.10 per MFBM.

The following table represents the components of property, plant and equipment for Wausau Paper.

2008 Annual Report of WAUSAU PAPER Note 3: Supplement Balance Sheet Information		
Property, plant, and equipment	**2008**	**2007**
Buildings	$122,224	$124,465
Machinery and equipment	985,452	983,937
	$1,107,676	$1,108,402
Less: accumulated depreciation	(748,916)	(713,820)
Net depreciated value	$358,760	$394,582
Land	6,868	7,386
Timber and timberlands, net of depletion	5,675	5,064
Construction in progress	34,105	6,264
Total property, plant and equipment	$405,408	$413,296

FIGURE 6.27

Wasau Paper is a US paper manufacturer headquartered in Wisconsin. Figure 6.27 shows the balances included in Note 3 in the Notes to the Financial Statements section of their 2008 annual report. Given that Wausau owns and manages thousands of acres of timberland, it follows that a large portion of the company's assets are tied up in land used to harvest timber. Note that the timber and timberlands are reported "net of depletion".

Intangible Assets

Our previous discussion of capital assets covered *tangible assets*, which are physical in nature and can be touched or sensed. The value of these types of assets often constitute a large proportion of the total value of a company's assets.

In contrast, intangible assets do not have a physical form, are conceptual in nature and do not usually constitute a large component of the company's total net assets. Nevertheless, *intangible assets* (like tangible non-current assets) occupy the *non-current assets* section of the balance sheet and should remain with a company for more than a year.

A company's intangible assets largely constitute intellectual property. A large portion of the costs involved with such assets include research and development costs and legal fees to protect the intellectual property from imitation and theft, fees to obtain the necessary documentation or the purchase price to obtain certain rights from someone else. Most intangible assets have their values amortized over time.

FIGURE 6.28

All the components of a company's intangible assets will be examined more thoroughly as we progress through this chapter. The topic is the final one dealing with the assets side of a company's balance sheet.

Goodwill

Since goodwill is perhaps the most misunderstood business asset, it may be the perfect place to begin when examining the intangible assets section of the balance sheet. The value of goodwill is often not fully appreciated even by experienced business people.

Goodwill arises when a company purchases another company at a cost that is greater than the book value of that company's net assets. The excess of the cost of the company over the total of the book value of its assets, less its total liabilities, must be recorded as goodwill.

Goodwill can be attributed to factors such as a recognizable brand name, experienced management, a skilled workforce or a unique product. Unlike other company assets, items representing goodwill do not come with an easily determinable market price to be amortized over time. Nevertheless, businesses are willing to pay for goodwill, and it increases equity on the balance sheet. We will use an example to explain how goodwill works and how accountants should record such items in the company's books.

Vicky's Entrepreneurial Enterprises decides to buy Jack's Sweets, a relatively new, but established, candy maker. The purchase price amounts to $1 million. At the time of purchase, Jack's Sweets had assets worth $1.5 million and liabilities totaling $700,000, giving the purchased company a net book value of $800,000.

The remaining $200,000 in the company's purchase price constitutes goodwill. Vicky was willing to pay for the brand name, because Jack's Sweets had become known for great tasting candies. Jack's Sweets' low budget, but memorable, commercials featured a fictional "Uncle Jack" handing out treats to beloved customers. Indeed, Vicky considers $200,000 for this brand to be a bargain and is more than willing to pay this amount for goodwill. However, she also expects a good return on her investment for the premium paid for the business. The accountant for Vicky's Entrepreneurial Enterprises records the purchase of Jack's Sweets in two steps:

First, the net book value portion of the purchase price is recorded as follows:

Vicky pays $800,000 (a credit to cash) for $1,500,000 in assets from Jack's Sweets. This is a debit in assets and assumes $700,000 of Jack's Sweets' liabilities, which is recorded as a credit in Vicky's balance sheet.

JOURNAL

Date	Account Title and Explanation	Debit	Credit
	Assets	1,500,000	
	Liabilities		700,000
	Cash		800,000
	Paid for net book value of Jack's Sweets		

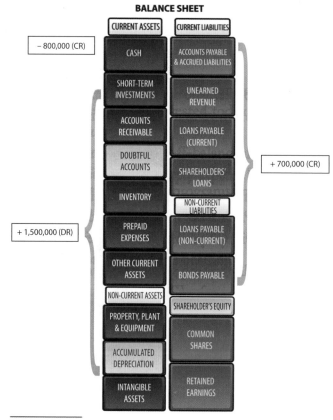

FIGURE 6.29

Second, Vicky's accountant records the portion of the purchase price involving goodwill, with the following entry:

JOURNAL

Date	Account Title and Explanation	Debit	Credit
	Goodwill	200,000	
	Cash		200,000
	Paid for goodwill		

FIGURE 6.30

Unlike tangible assets, goodwill does not have a value in the books of the company, and that is the reason why a separate entry is made and a different account – *intangible assets* – is debited on the balance sheet.

Alternatively, both components of the transaction can be recorded using a compound entry like the following:

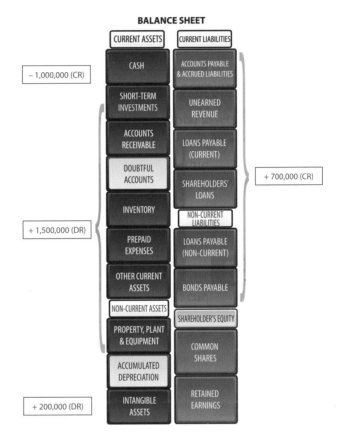

JOURNAL			
Date	**Account Title and Explanation**	**Debit**	**Credit**
	Assets	1,500,000	
	Goodwill	200,000	
	Liabilities		700,000
	Cash		1,000,000
	Paid cash for net assets and goodwill		

FIGURE 6.31

Unlike other company assets, items categorized as goodwill do not have their value amortized over time. In essence, there is no book value to amortize. However, this does not mean that the value of goodwill cannot decrease. In other words, events may occur that would impair the value of goodwill.

Note: we use the title "Assets" and "Liabilities" in this journal for demonstration purpose. In reality, each asset and liability would be recorded in its specific account.

For example, let us assume that Company A bought Company B because the latter was producing a unique product that the rest of the market could not match. The uniqueness of the product is considered to be goodwill and is worth $150,000. However, since the purchase, advances in technology led to the creation of a new product to compete with the one produced by Company B. The new product is still undergoing development and testing, but will almost certainly enter the market within a decade.

In other words, the value of goodwill associated with the innovative quality of Company B's product will be seriously reduced. But it will not be negated altogether, since it is estimated that the product will still be competitive, even after the introduction of an alternative product.

A decrease in the value of goodwill for the current year is estimated at $50,000. The journal entry to record this would be as follows:

JOURNAL			
Date	**Account Title and Explanation**	**Debit**	**Credit**
	Loss on Impairment of Goodwill	50,000	
	Goodwill		50,000
	Loss on impairment of goodwill		

The value of goodwill should *never* be adjusted upward, above cost. This would violate the GAAP principle of conservatism, which we previously covered. You

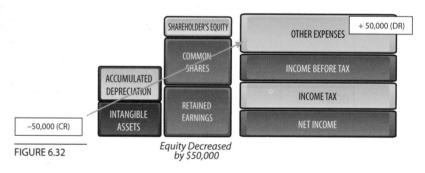

FIGURE 6.32

should now be more familiar with GAAP principles and how they apply to examples and situations highlighted in this book.

Patents

Individuals and companies invent and develop innovative products, usually at enormous cost in terms of both money and time. Inventors need to protect their intellectual property and this is achieved through patenting.

A **patent** grants the patentee the exclusive right, for a set period of time, to prevent others from making, using, selling or distributing the patented invention without permission. In most international jurisdictions, a patent term lasts for about 20 years, but the duration can differ according to the type of patent. This gives the inventor or inventing company the right to enjoy the rewards of creating a new and successful product.

The costs associated with many intangible assets involve legal fees paid in acquiring them. With regard to patents, the application process typically requires the use of patent lawyers (as does the defense and management of a patent). Depending on the product, development costs that are incurred in developing the product may be capitalized (considered as part of the cost of patent) or expensed. All legal and associated costs in acquiring a patent are recorded in the non-current assets section of the balance sheet. The value of the assetS is then amortized for the remaining term of the patent.

Another aspect of a patent is that it can be bought and sold. A purchaser can buy the rights to the patent, thereby giving the new owner of the patent the same exclusive rights that originally belonged to the inventor). The price of the patent would then be amortized for the amount of time left in the patent's term.

Here is an example to illustrate this point. Henry's Lights purchases a patent from Crazy Larry Light Bulb for $28,000. The patent has seven years remaining in its term. The entries to record the purchase, as well as one year's amortization would be recorded as follows:

JOURNAL			
Date	**Account Title and Explanation**	**Debit**	**Credit**
	Patents	28,000	
	Cash		28,000
	To record purchase of patent from Crazy Larry Light Bulbs. Remaining life is seven years.		

JOURNAL			
Date	**Account Title and Explanation**	**Debit**	**Credit**
	Amortization Expense - Patents	4,000	
	Accumulated Amortization - Patents		4,000
	To record amortization expense for one year		

FIGURE 6.33

The $4,000 annual amortization amount is calculated using the straight-line method. The straight-line method involves taking the entire amount to be amortized or depreciated and dividing it by the number of years remaining; this calculation produces the annual amortization expense accurately reflecting amortization over time.

Copyright

Copyright is similar to a patent in that it gives exclusive rights of ownership to a person or group that has created something. The difference with copyright, however, is that it applies to artistic works such as music and literature. In addition, copyright can exist even if the work has not been registered. For example, it is automatically assumed that an article or photo posted on the Internet is protected by copyright. A person cannot simply assume that he has unlimited rights to use or copy a work from the Internet. Registration with the Canadian Intellectual Property Office, however, puts a copyright holder in a better position if litigation arises over the copyright. In Canada, the laws regarding copyrights are governed by the Copyright Act which states that, generally, the life of a copyright lasts the life of the author plus 50 years from the end of the calendar year of his death. This means that estimates of a copyright's useful life depend on when the work was first created and how long the author of the work lived.

Overall, copyright is treated in much the same way as a patent. The costs may include legal fees paid to register the copyright, the purchase price in obtaining the copyright from someone else or any other fees involved in its acquisition. When a copyright is purchased, the remaining value of the copyright is amortized over the number of years of its term.

Trademark and Trade Name

A **trademark** is similar to a patent and copyright except that it grants ownership rights for a recognizable symbol or logo. A **trade name** grants exclusive rights to a name under which a company or product trades for commercial purposes, even though its legal or technical name might differ. Some corporations have numerous trademarks and trade names that they protect on a continuing basis. For example, *McDonald's* is not only a trade name that the company protects at all costs, but it serves as an umbrella brand for numerous other trademarks, such as the *Golden Arches*, the *Extra Value Meal* and *Hamburger University*. McDonald's finds itself in countless legal battles in fending off pretenders and imitators.

Any costs in developing and maintaining a trademark or trade name, such as those involved with advertising, are expensed during the year they are incurred. However, just as with patents and copyrights, legal fees for registering the name or logo are capitalized. Alternatively, trademarks and trade names can be purchased from someone else. The purchase cost is capitalized, which means it will be amortized for the remainder of its term.

Leasing Non-Current Assets

Instead of owning non-current tangible assets, a company can choose to lease them.

The contract that specifies the terms of the lease is known as a **lease agreement**. The owner of the asset to be leased is known as the *lessor*. The user of the leased asset is known as the *lessee*. In essence, the lessee buys the right to use the asset from the lessor. Such assets usually constitute some form of land or property.

Sometimes the lease agreement requires the lessee to pay an amount of cash in advance. In some jurisdictions, the government can even grant a 99-year lease to a lessee for a stipulated amount.

Whatever amount is paid upfront for lease should be debited to the appropriate account under non-current assets on the balance sheet, and the value amortized for the remaining term of the lease.

Non-Current Assets, Total Assets And Financial Ratios

Since we are nearing the end of our examination of company assets, and non-current assets often form a large proportion of the value of these assets, we will end this chapter by examining financial ratios dealing with company assets. This should provide an understanding of the way large sections of the company's balance sheet can provide useful financial information and the significance that non-current assets play in analyzing such important data. We will specifically examine two financial ratios that measure company performance relative to total assets: **asset turnover** and **return on assets**.

Asset Turnover

As discussed in previous chapters, a turnover ratio measures how rapidly an asset's status changes and becomes productive. For example, inventory turnover measures how quickly an asset converts from inventory to becoming a sale. Asset turnover, on the other hand, measures how quickly a company converts its total assets, including non-current assets, into revenue.

To calculate asset turnover, the first figure needed is *Revenue*. The second figure needed is *Average Total Assets*, which is produced by taking the average of beginning and ending total assets:

$$\text{Average Total Assets} = (\text{Beginning of Year Total Assets} + \text{End of Year Total Assets}) \div 2$$

$$\text{Asset Turnover} = \frac{\text{Revenue}}{\text{Average Total Assets}}$$

Return on Assets

A company's return on assets is similar to asset turnover except that its focus is on net income, instead of revenue. This ratio seeks to measure the relationship between net income and assets. In other words, is the company making enough money from investment in its non-current assets? Since the two ratios involve similar analyses, they also involve similar calculations.

$$\text{Return on Assets} = \frac{\text{Net Income} \quad \text{Revenue (Sales)}}{\text{Average Total Assets}}$$

As you can see, the ratios have the same denominator: Average Total Assets. It is their numerators that differ. One uses revenue, the other uses net income. Another difference between the two ratios, which will be illustrated in the example to follow, is that turnover is expressed as a decimal number, while return is expressed as a percentage.

Using the Ratios

Let us apply these two ratios by using the financial information made available by Amtrak and Union Pacific, two U.S. companies in the same industry; railway transportation. Using the formulas we have already outlined, the ratios have been calculated for us in the accompanying chart.

Selected Financial Information			
Year 2008	(in millions)	Amtrak	Union Pacific
A	Revenue	$ 2,453	$17,970
B	Total assets-beginning of year	$10,166	$39,722
C	Total assets-end of year	$10,300	$38,033
D=(B+C) ÷ 2	Average total assets	$10,233	$38,878
E=A ÷ D	Asset Turnover	0.24	0.46
F	Net income	-1,133	2,338
G=F ÷ D	Return on Assets	-11.07%	6.01%

FIGURE 6.34

For Amtrak and Union Pacific, both revenue and net income were divided by average total assets to produce the two financial ratios we have been examining.

With regard to asset turnover, Amtrak has a figure of 0.24 and Union Pacific has a figure of 0.46. What this means is that Union Pacific was able to generate more revenue dollars per investment in assets than Amtrak.

With regard to return on assets, Amtrak has a rate of -11.07% and Union Pacific's rate is 6.01%. This essentially means that Union Pacific was able to generate significantly more net income per investment in assets than Amtrak.

All financial ratios represent a simple snapshot of company performance. They tend to focus on one aspect of a business and give us different kinds of information about how well a company is doing. In this case, Union Pacific appears to be using its investment in assets to generate revenue and net income more effectively than Amtrak.

Controls Related To Non-Current Assets

Tangible assets, which by definition are physical in nature, are purchased by the company, used to earn an income and eventually disposed of. In the meantime, the value of a capital asset is depreciated over the period of its estimated useful life. Accounting procedures are used to control and safeguard all tangible assets while the company possesses them. Different companies and industries depend on capital assets to varying degrees. For instance, auto manufacturers General Motors and Ford rely heavily on capital assets such as machines, robots and factories. It is sometimes possible for criminals to steal large assets of a company. Security measures such as physical barriers and security personnel can be used to protect large items from theft.

Insurance is an even more useful measure to protect large capital assets. Insurance can protect a company's capital assets not only in the event of theft, for example, but also in the event of catastrophic situations such as extreme weather or unforeseen breakdowns. It is therefore incumbent upon management to make sure that the best possible insurance policies are in place and are updated or adjusted when needed. Some companies may even want to consider some self-insurance options to help protect their capital assets from catastrophic risk.

A company's largest and most protected capital assets can be lost as a result of catastrophe. Even though physical barriers can help, insurance should also be used to safeguard a business from undue risk and loss.

Big or small, pricey or inexpensive, all types of tangible assets should be tracked properly and relevant transactions recorded accurately in the company's books. Experienced accountants should be on hand to perform these control procedures. Capital assets should be tagged in some way, perhaps by bar code and scanner. The tags should be read, compared with accounting records and vice versa. Physical audits should be performed on a regular basis to ensure that all assets on the books are on the premises and accounted for.

For all company assets, paperwork and records should be completed correctly and handled securely. The first priority is to record the correct amount of cost for the capital asset. As always, any costs related to the acquisition of the asset must be included in the total cost. These can include freight, installation and even invoicing costs related to the asset.

As has been emphasized throughout our discussion of asset controls, policies, plans and procedures need to be in place, and regulations and laws followed. For example, a large company may have a policy of classifying items as capital assets only if they cost more than $1,000. A smaller company may institute a lower threshold for its policy. These policies need to be clearly communicated to the staff responsible for seeing their implementation. Adherence to all related policies, plans, procedures and regulations should be monitored, with audits when necessary.

Economic and efficient use of tangible assets involves purchasing assets at the best possible price. It also means that internal controls should include a bidding process for suppliers, which helps to ensure the best possible price is obtained. Financial ratios, which we discussed earlier in this chapter, can be used on a regular basis to monitor the efficient use of a company's capital assets. If the ratios indicate an inefficient use of these assets, measures can be taken to either dispose of or make better use of them. If sales are sluggish, this may mean that capital assets are not being used to their full capacity. A business may also find that too much money has been invested in its capital assets. Leasing them could free up some capital. As always, company goals and objectives related to capital assets should be stated, implemented, reviewed and changed when necessary.

Controls related to intangible assets are not very different from those relating to tangible assets. As always, qualified staff should be available to ensure that transactions are recorded and classified properly in the company's books and all payments are properly documented. Costs should be objectively verified and any supporting documentation should be properly maintained. The procedures involved are similar for both tangible and intangible assets.

However, with intangible assets, the only physical evidence of their existence often comes in the form of contracts, accompanying invoices and supporting cost documentation. That is why it is so important to physically protect such documents. They can be placed in a vault on the premises or a safe deposit box in a bank. These documents can be referenced when changes are made or when the company's books need updating.

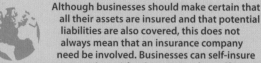

IN THE REAL WORLD

Although businesses should make certain that all their assets are insured and that potential liabilities are also covered, this does not always mean that an insurance company need be involved. Businesses can self-insure to cover various risks. Companies that self-insure are sometimes regarded as being uninsured. In other words, "self-insurance" can be seen as an attempt to avoid paying for insurance. Indeed, this can be true, since some companies fail to adequately self-insure.

Proper self-insurance involves a company setting aside enough capital reserves to cover itself in case of a catastrophic event. If something happens to a company's capital assets, these capital reserves can be used to cover the loss. The advantage of self-insurance is that a company will avoid paying premiums that are often very high as a result of insurance company administrative costs or poor underwriting.

The disadvantage of self-insurance is that a company needs to tie up a certain amount of its capital to cover a disaster, and even that is sometimes insufficient. To minimize this disadvantage, alternative self-insurance strategies can be undertaken. For example, a business can still buy some insurance, but add self-insurance. Alternatively, businesses can form collaborative self-insurance groups, whereby a group of companies contributes to a pool of funds that can be used if one or more of them suffer a catastrophic event.

As with most aspects of today's business environment, various innovative solutions can be found to resolve inadequacies in the market. Self-insurance is an example of one of those innovations.

Beyond initial registration or purchase, ongoing valuation of intangible assets needs to take place. For example, market conditions may affect the value of goodwill, or competing trademarks may diminish the value of a brand name. Furthermore, companies that own patents, copyright and trademarks should be on the lookout for entities that are using such intellectual property without permission. Any such use will diminish the value of the protected asset. All proper legal avenues should be pursued, including legal action or the threat of legal action, when improper use of protected intellectual assets has taken place.

An Ethical Approach To Non-Current Assets

Accounting for a firm's capital assets is vulnerable to manipulation to produce fraudulent figures, as has been mentioned in earlier chapters dealing with abuses of other assets. Decisions regarding classifying capital assets, depreciating them and calculating residual values can have a significant impact on a company's financial statements. It is therefore important for accountants to understand the ethical principles that exist to help prevent abuse.

Almost any accounting decision is open to abuse. Beyond GAAP principles and other accounting industry standards, the question that any accountant should ask when facing a decision is this: Should this be done because it is an accurate reflection of the business or for some other reason?

These other reasons could be to protect one's own incompetence, to seek financial gain, to succumb to pressure from management or to meet public expectation of company performance.

In other words, a good accountant should always raise a red flag when the answer to the question is anything other than, "This is being done because it is an accurate reflection of the financial condition of the business."

With regard to capital assets, figures can be manipulated to present a financial picture that does not accurately reflect the financial state of the company. For example, one of the first decisions that an accountant must make regarding capital assets is whether it is in fact a capital asset. An attempt to falsely classify the item as an expense would lead to reducing company net income. Conversely, an attempt to classify an expense as a capital asset will not reduce the company's equity. Either way, any result that does not reflect the true nature of the asset is an ethical breach and should always be avoided.

Estimating the useful life of a capital asset is another accounting decision that is open to manipulation. For example, intentionally shortening an asset's life span can unduly increase the annual depreciation charges recorded in the company's books. Similarly, intentionally increasing a capital asset's residual value will decrease the amount to be depreciated, thus decreasing those depreciation charges. An accountant has an ethical obligation to detect and avoid these abuses at all times.

Accountants are presented with a different kind of challenge when dealing with intangible assets. These assets, such as trademarks and goodwill, will only be amortized if it can be demonstrated that the value of the assets has been impaired.

Ethical considerations with respect to intangible assets relate mostly to their correct reporting in financial statements. This includes ensuring that the appropriate cost is determined, that the correct amount of amortization is calculated and that all amounts are reported accurately in the statements of operation and financial position.

Companies should always set up internal controls to ensure that ongoing transactions involving intangible assets are expensed or capitalized properly. Review procedures should be in place to ensure that annual amortization is verified and properly reported. Any review procedure should be the joint responsibility of both management and company auditors. As corporate scandals have shown, executives and accountants must take responsibility for the company's books; not doing so could lead to serious consequences.

IN THE REAL WORLD

The year 2001 saw the beginning of numerous corporate and accounting scandals, amounting to breaching ethical standards. Authorities began investigating some of America's largest corporations regarding, among other things, accounting fraud. The corporations investigated included three telecommunications companies: Global Crossing, Qwest and WorldCom.

Some of these investigations found a distortion of gains and expenses as a result of misclassifying capital assets. These errors may have been a result of incompetence. Alternatively, they may have been a deliberate attempt to mislead the public. Either way, GAAP violations were found in numerous instances. For example, both Global Crossing and Qwest engaged in billions of dollars of what are known as swaps. These companies purchased telecom capacity from customers who then bought it back from the companies. These were falsely treated as capital expenses rather than as current operating expenses. The result was that both companies recorded the revenue upfront, then expensed the amount over a period of time. This violates, among other things, the matching principle.

In addition, WorldCom classified billions of dollars of current operating expenses as capital assets. This was done over a period of 15 months. The auditing firm Arthur Andersen failed to raise any red flags over the practice.

The IFRS Perspective

There are both similarities and differences in accounting policies related to capital assets under GAAP and IFRS. One of the main differences is the valuation rule. Under the existing Canadian standards, capital assets are reported at their book value. IFRS not only permits reporting capital assets at book value but also allows revaluation for long-lived capital assets (e.g. building) to market value if certain criteria are met. This means companies would have the opportunity to report its assets at an amount higher than the historical cost.

In Summary

⇨ A company's tangible non-current assets, also called *long-term assets* or *capital assets*, often constitute a significant proportion of the value of its assets.

⇨ To determine whether an item is a capital asset, the accountant must ask three questions: How long will the company have the item? How much does the item cost? What will the item be used for? If an item does not qualify as a capital asset, it is recorded as an expense on the income statement.

⇨ Three more questions can be asked to determine if any actions performed on a capital asset constitute routine maintenance or a material improvement: Does the expenditure extend the life of the asset? Does the expenditure improve the productivity of the asset? Does the expenditure reduce company operating costs?

⇨ Depreciation is the process by which accountants reflect changes in the book value of a capital asset. It also allows expenses related to capital assets to be matched with the periods in which related revenue is generated. One of the first tasks in depreciating an item is determining its residual value or salvage value, which is deducted from the total amount to be depreciated over the useful life of the asset.

⇨ Accountants can use three different methods of depreciation. The straight-line method calculates an annual average to be depreciated over the course of an asset's useful life. Two other methods have been developed to ascertain a more realistic depreciation schedule: declining-balance method (and the double-declining-balance method) and units-of-production method.

⇨ A capital item can be disposed of in various ways, including selling it or donating it to charity. The transaction will involve either a gain or loss relative to the item's book value. Revisions can also be made to a depreciation schedule. However, proper justification should always be used and prior depreciation deductions should never be changed. This would violate the *consistency principle*.

⇨ Various controls can be implemented to protect a company's capital assets, ranging from accurate recording and tracking procedures to proper insurance in case of catastrophic events.

Although different industries require different controls, qualified accounting personnel should always supervise the policies and measures that a company implements.

↪ An ethical approach to non-current assets involves decisions that accurately reflect the nature of the asset. Net income figures and net asset values can be distorted by manipulating decisions regarding the classification of non-current assets, the estimation of residual value and useful life, and other aspects of depreciation.

↪ A company's non-current assets usually constitute a large proportion of the total value of its assets. That is why financial ratios involving total company assets are useful when discussing performance related to non-current assets. Asset turnover measures the revenue a company generates relative to its investment in total assets. Return on assets measures the net income a company generates relative to total assets.

↪ The natural resources that a company owns – such as minerals, oil or timber – are physical in nature, but are not classified as tangible assets on the balance sheet. Some companies categorize them separately from other non-current assets. The value of natural resources gets amortized over time, using the units-of-production method.

↪ Goodwill represents the portion of a company's purchase price, above and beyond its net asset value, that is considered valuable in its own right – for example, the company's good name or its experienced and dedicated workforce.

↪ A patent gives an inventor exclusive rights to use a product. The costs related to most intangible assets are generally for legal fees or the purchase of rights from someone else. This cost is amortized over the remaining term of the patent, defined by the applicable jurisdiction. Other expenses are recorded as incurred.

↪ Copyright gives exclusive rights of a creation to its creator. Copyright is granted automatically to works produced and published. However, copyright is time limited and does not cover fair use privileges to others.

↪ A trademark gives exclusive rights to logos and other company symbols. A trade name provides exclusive rights to names of companies and products. Large corporations often engage in extensive efforts to legally protect the various trademarks and trade names that they own.

↪ Leasehold involves a lessor lending an asset (usually land or property) to a lessee. Any upfront fees are capitalized in the appropriate non-current asset account on the balance sheet.

Review Exercise 1

Nelson Rugasa is an entrepreneur who has just started a consulting business. During the first month of business, Nelson purchased a laptop computer for $3,000 and office equipment for $10,000.

Required:

a) Record the purchase of non-current assets, assuming Nelson paid with cash.

Research Component
to be done outside of class time

Research the useful life of capital assets, and suggest the useful life for the computer and office equipment.

Research the way in which the value of capital assets decline, and suggest the depreciation method(s) that should be used for the computer and office equipment.

Based on your research on useful life, and the ways in which the value of capital assets decline, prepare a table showing the cost, depreciation, accumulated depreciation, and net book value of the computer, and office equipment for the first three years.

b) Explain how you calculate the profit or loss on disposal of a non-current asset.

Review Exercise 1 – Answer

a)

Date	Account Title and Explanation	Debit	Credit
	Computer	3,000	
	Office Equipment	10,000	
	Cash		13,000
	Purchase of computer and office equipment for cash		

A reasonable life for a computer would be 3 years, for equipment 5-10 years. Students will arrive at various numbers based on their research.

Because computers are upgraded quickly, a declining balance method would be appropriate with large amounts of depreciation early on. For office equipment, straight-line depreciation would be reasonable.

Year	Cost	Depreciation	Accumulated Depreciation	Net Book Value
0	$3,000.00	$0.00	$0.00	$3,000.00
1	3,000.00	1,000.00	1,000.00	2,000.00
2	2,000.00	666.67	1,666.67	1,333.33
3	1,333.33	444.44	2,111.11	888.89

Year	Cost	Depreciation	Accumulated Depreciation	Net Book Value
0	$10,000.00	$0.00	$0.00	$10,000.00
1	10,000.00	2,000.00	2,000.00	8,000.00
2	8,000.00	2,000.00	4,000.00	6,000.00
3	6,000.00	2,000.00	6,000.00	4,000.00
4	4,000.00	2,000.00	8,000.00	2,000.00
5	2,000.00	2,000.00	10,000.00	0.00

b) The profit or loss on disposal of a non-current asset is the difference between the amount received, and the net book value of the asset at the time of disposal.

Review Exercise 2

Rulison Company had the following transactions during the year:

DATE	DESCRIPTION
Jan 1	Paid $250,000 to purchase Regnier Limited. Regnier Limited had $500,000 in assets and $300,000 in liabilities.
Jan 1	Purchased patents from Saundra Arneson for $50,000. The remaining life of the patents is 4 years.
Jan 1	Purchased a trademark, which will be applied to the patented product for $20,000. Management believes that the trademark will be useful for double the life of the patent, at which time it will have a value of $100.
Jan 30	Purchased mineral rights for $100,000. The company needs to extract a mineral that goes into the patented product. Rulison Company expects to extract 500,000 kg of mineral before the rights expire.
Jun 30	Rulison Company's senior executives resigned en-masse. The directors felt that the loss of the senior executives seriously affected the company's goodwill. In fact, they felt that the decrease in the value of goodwill was estimated to be $25,000.

Rulison Company prepares its financial statements with a year end of December 31. Amortization policy states that one half year's amortization is taken in both the year of purchase and year of sale. Depletion is based on units extracted. The company extracted 10,000 kg of mineral from the beginning of February to the end of December. Assume all purchases are made with cash and that the straight-line method of depreciation is used for the patent and trademark.

Required: Prepare the journal entries to record the above transactions. Also prepare the year-end adjusting entries associated with the non-current assets.

Review Exercise 2 – Answer

Date	Account Title and Explanation	Debit	Credit
Jan 1	Assets	500,000	
	Goodwill	50,000	
	Liabilities		300,000
	Cash		250,000
	Purchase of assets and liabilities of Reigner company		
Jan 1	Patents	50,000	
	Cash		50,000
	Purchase of patents for cash		
Jan 1	Trademarks	20,000	
	Cash		20,000
	Purchase of trademarks for cash		
Jan 30	Mineral Rights	100,000	
	Cash		100,000
	Purchase of mineral rights for cash		
Jun 30	Loss Due to Impairment of Goodwill	25,000	
	Goodwill		25,000
	To record impairment of goodwill		
Dec 31	Amortization Expense – Patents	6,250	
	Accumulated Amortization – Patents		6,250
	Amortization for the period (50,000 ÷ 4) × ½ year		
Dec 31	Amortization Expense – Trademarks	1,244	
	Accumulated Amortization – Trademarks		1,244
	Amortization for the period ((20,000 – 100) ÷ 8) × ½ year		
Dec 31	Depletion – Mineral Rights	2,000	
	Accumulated Depletion – Mineral Rights		2,000
	Depletion for the period 10,000 × (100,000 ÷ 500,000)		

Notes

Chapter 7
CURRENT LIABILITIES

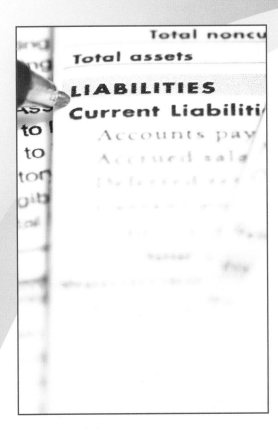

LEARNING OUTCOMES:

❶ Understand different types of current liabilities

❷ Record accounts payable

❸ Record transactions with sales tax

❹ Record unearned revenue

❺ Record short–term notes payable

❻ Understand the current portion of long-term liabilities

❼ Record shareholders' loans

❽ Record estimated liabilities

❾ Calculate financial ratios relating to current liabilities

❿ Apply controls and ethics relating to current liabilities

A Company's Current Liabilities

FIGURE 7.1

The earlier chapters of this book dealt with the assets side of the balance sheet and we examined each type of asset, both current and non-current.

This chapter deals with current liabilities. The main difference in the way that assets and liabilities are listed on the balance sheet is that the order of liabilities is dictated by the timing of the amount owed, whereas assets are placed in the order of their liquidity. Figure 7.1 illustrates this difference. In this example, the blue side represents current assets. Accounts payable and accrued liabilities are listed first among the current liabilities. Also, the current portion of loans are listed as current liabilities. Current liabilities need to be paid out sooner than the non-current liabilities.

A company's liabilities can be divided into two categories: known liabilities and unknown liabilities. These categories are sometimes referred to as *determinable liabilities* and *non-determinable liabilities*.

Determinable liabilities have a precise value. Most businesses know exactly how much they owe and when they are supposed to pay. Amounts owed to suppliers (trade payables), employees (payroll liabilities) and the government (e.g. sales taxes) constitute a debt that a company has agreed to pay. The failure to pay off debts is one of the first signs of serious financial trouble.

A company's unknown or non-determinable liabilities include estimated liabilities. They are non-determinable because the exact amount owing is unknown. This is similar to a topic we studied on the assets side of the balance sheet, where the amount of bad debt for the year was also unknown in advance.

All known company liabilities should leave an easily recognizable and traceable paper trail, and may include documents such as invoices and contracts. The exact amounts due, and when they are due, should be clearly identified.

Accounts Payable

In many ways, the liabilities side of the balance sheet is a mirror of the assets side. This concept is perhaps best reflected when companies purchase items on credit from other companies.

When a company sells product using payment terms, the asset is called *accounts receivable*. When a company purchases product from another company using payment terms, the liability is called *accounts payable*.

In chapter 4, we pointed out that selling an item on account means debiting *accounts receivable* and crediting *sales*. With accounts payable we see a mirror transaction: accounts payable is credited and the asset or expense account is debited.

Here is an example of a purchase on credit. A company buys a repair service on credit from Plumbers Inc. for an amount of $1,000.

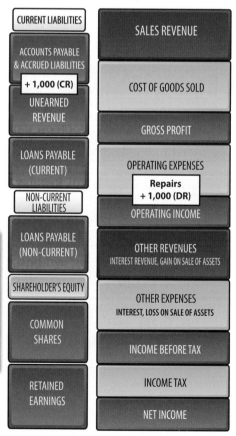

JOURNAL			
Date	Account Title and Explanation	Debit	Credit
	Repairs Expense	1,000	
	Accounts Payable		1,000
	Record invoice #1425 owing to Plumbers Inc.		

FIGURE 7.2

Equity decreases

This increase in accounts payable is offset by a decrease in equity (caused by an increase in expenses). However, the increase in accounts payable could also have been offset by an increase in an asset, with no impact on equity.

It is necessary to control the amount of money owed by customers by using an accounts receivable subledger (subsidiary ledger). The same principle applies when maintaining control of the amount of money owed to suppliers. This is controlled by using the accounts payable subledger.

For accounts payable, the control account in the general ledger includes the total amount of credit balances in the individual subledgers.

Here is an example of a purchases journal used to record transactions on a daily basis:

	Purchase Journal		Repairs & Maint	Legal	Supplies	Inventory Purchases	Accounts Payable
Date	Vendor/Account Name	Vendor Invoice No.	Debit	Debit	Debit	Debit	Credit
Jan 2	Antonio's Electrical	5125	82.65				82.65
Jan 2	Vander Berkel Distributors	2089				1,707.60	1,707.60
Jan 3	Wong Imports Limited	2360				1,498.80	1,498.80
Jan 8	Yonge Office Supplies	5890			76.14		76.14
Jan 9	Designer's Choice	1925				1,137.00	1,137.00
Jan 15	Designer's Choice	1966				1,862.40	1,862.40
Jan 16	Rawlston Equipment Suppliers	6091			25.89		25.89
Jan 18	Sanders Multi-Media Ltd.	26				1,915.20	1,915.20
Jan 21	Yonge Office Supplies Limited	6198			91.26		91.26
Jan 22	Western Plumbers	121	536.23				536.23
Jan 30	Becker & Partner - Lawyers	7001		468.46			468.46
	Totals		618.88	468.46	193.29	8,121.00	9,401.63

The total of $9,401.63 will be recorded in the control account in the general ledger.

FIGURE 7.3

Expense and inventory debits are recorded when amounts are payable for invoices received from vendors. The corresponding credits are recorded in the accounts payable control account.

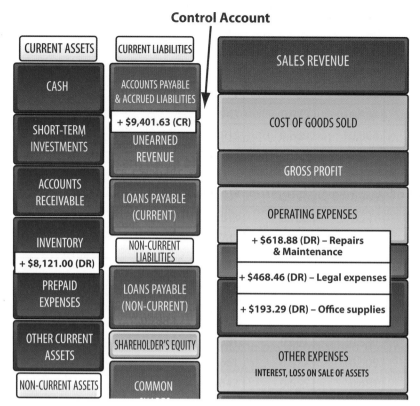

Equity decreases by $1,280.63

FIGURE 7.4

Note that the total amount of $9,401.63 owing is recorded in the accounts payable control account. The subledger contains various levels of detail pertaining to the purchase of products or services. Examples are listed below.

	Antonio's Electrical	Invoice	Current #	60 days	90 days	90 days +	Total
Dec 20	Service performed on transformer	5035		426.22			
Jan 1	Replace light fitting	5126	86.78				
	Total		86.78	426.22	0	0	513.00

	Vander Berkel Distributors	Invoice	Current #	60 days	90 days	90 days +	Total
Dec 14	Purchased product	2010		5,312.23			
Jan 1	Purchased product	2089	1,792.98				
	Total		1,792.98	5,312.23	0	0	7,105.21

FIGURE 7.5

The circled amounts would be totaled for each supplier and eventually represented as one credit increase in the accounts payable account in the general ledger.

WORTH REPEATING...

It should be noted that equity decreases when the expense actually occurs — even though cash has yet to exchange hands. This concept adheres to the matching principle.

Alternatively, if an automated system were used, all these transactions would be entered into the general ledger, which essentially serves as a database from which all related reports are generated.

The Accounts Payable Subledger Report

One of the reports that could be generated from general ledger database information is the **accounts payable subledger report**, which presents specific information related to vendors and amounts owing to them.

Keeping accounts payable subledgers is important for forward-looking businesses for a number of reasons. The subledgers:

- help monitor the amounts owing to specific suppliers and their corresponding due dates;
- provide the company with information regarding when to pay its bills, which allows for important planning relating to cash flow – for example, if it is found that a company has surplus cash, early payments of bills may lead to discounts;
- enable company accountants and managers to look up specific information related to suppliers and purchases made from them;
- allow for trend analysis to help in negotiating volume discounts with the suppliers;
- provide decision makers with the information that allows for better planning and implementation of goals.

Accrued Expenses

Accounts payable is a known liability. A company purchases goods or services from a vendor and that vendor issues the company an invoice, which must be paid by a certain date. The terms of the liability are easily recognized and recorded by the company.

An **accrued charge** is a known liability that is recognized for a current period, but is not paid until the period expires. An example of an accrued charge would be fees charged by an accountant for services rendered in preparing the business's year-end financial statements.

Even though the payment of an accrued charge is delayed, the delay in payment is, for the most part, predictable and occurs on a schedule. This is why accrued charges are usually categorized as known liabilities.

We will use the example of accounting fees to demonstrate how an accrued charge is to be recorded in the company's books. Let us say that we need to accrue the year-end fee of $10,000 charged by the company's accountant on December 31, which is paid on January 10 of the following year:

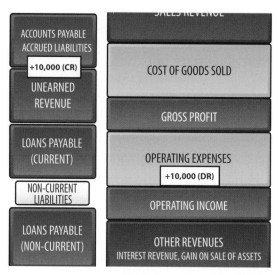

change

JOURNAL			
Date	**Account Title and Explanation**	**Debit**	**Credit**
Dec 31	Accounting Fees Expense	10,000	
	Accounting Fees Payable		10,000
	Record accrued accounting fees expense		

FIGURE 7.6

The company must record the transaction in the period in which the service was rendered. To satisfy this requirement, the accounting fees expense is debited with $10,000 and accrued accounting fees payable is credited with $10,000 in the current period. On January 10 of the next year, the company pays the accountant the amount owing. This is how the payment is recorded:

payment

JOURNAL			
Date	**Account Title and Explanation**	**Debit**	**Credit**
Jan 10	Accounting Fees Payable	10,000	
	Cash		10,000
	Record payment for accrued accounting fees		

FIGURE 7.7

Note that since equity did not change, there is no effect on the income statement.

The $10,000 debit to accounting fees payable (accrued liabilities) takes that amount owing off the books, and the $10,000 credit to cash represents the payment to the accountant. Again, note that the decrease in equity had already occurred when the accrual was recorded in the previous year. No change in equity occurs when the payment is finally made.

Another area in which accrued liabilities commonly occur is sales tax discussed in the next section.

Sales Tax

Sales tax is a tax that is applied by the government to goods or services that are sold. Sales taxes can be applied by both the federal and provincial government. They are calculated as a percentage of a sale, and the percentages can vary from province to province. Some provinces have a provincial sales tax (PST) that is applied by the provincial government. The federal government applies a federal sales tax called the goods and services tax (GST). Some provinces have partnered with the federal government and combined both the provincial and federal sales tax into a harmonized sales tax (HST). The figure below shows some examples of provinces and the sales taxes they charge.

FIGURE 7.8

Although sales tax must be paid to the government, it would be impractical, if not impossible, for individual customers to send the sales tax money to the government every time they bought something. Imagine buying a coffee and having to send the government a few cents in sales tax.

Instead, businesses act as tax collectors for the government by collecting the sales tax from their customers and sending it to the government. Businesses must be careful and accurate in collecting sales taxes from customers. These taxes collected are not money that the business can spend; the money does not belong to them, it belongs to the government.

For example, if a business receives $1,500 from a customer, which included $150 in sales tax, the business must make sure it does not spend the $150. This money must eventually be sent to the government.

FIGURE 7.9

The due date for a business to send the collected sales tax to the government can vary from business to business. Companies that have a very small amount of sales may be required to send in the sales tax once a year. As the amount of sales increase and the amount of sales tax collected increase, the business may be required to send in the money on a quarterly or monthly basis. Failure to send this money, or sending the money late, will result in interest and penalties being charged to the business by the government.

Provincial Sales Tax

A **provincial sales tax** (PST) is paid by the final consumer of a product. This means a retailer buying inventory for resale from their supplier would not pay the PST since the retailer is not the final consumer of the inventory. But when the retailer sells the inventory to their customers, the customers will pay the PST.

The retailer is responsible for collecting the PST from the customer and eventually sending (remitting) the amount collected to the provincial government. The amount collected will be recorded in a current liability account until it is remitted.

As an example, assume Hardware Store Inc. sells inventory to a customer for $1,000 cash on June 15, 2012. The provincial sales tax rate is 6%. The transaction is shown in figure 7.10. For this example, we will ignore the cost of goods sold.

Each sale would gradually increase the amount in the PST payable account until it is time for the company to send it to the provincial government. Assume the payment is made on August 31, 2012 and the account only has a $60 credit balance. Figure 7.11 shows the transaction.

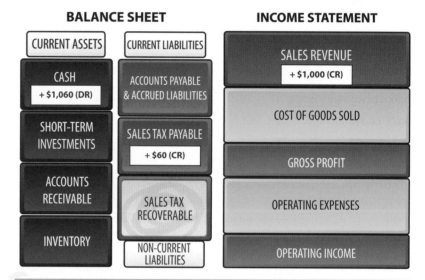

FIGURE 7.10

The PST payable account essentially acts as a clearing account. It accumulates the PST collected over a period of time, and then is cleared to $0 when a payment is made to send the sales tax to the provincial government.

The retailer would have to pay PST on purchases that will not be resold to customers. In this case, the retailer is considered to be the final consumer of the product and will have to pay the PST. In cases like this, the PST is calculated and added to the cost of the asset or expense that is being purchased.

BALANCE SHEET

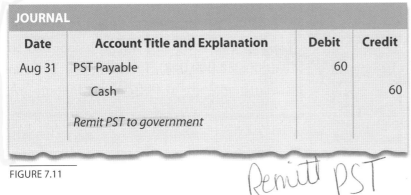

JOURNAL			
Date	Account Title and Explanation	Debit	Credit
Aug 31	PST Payable	60	
	Cash		60
	Remit PST to government		

FIGURE 7.11

Goods and Services Tax

The **goods and services tax** (GST) is a sales tax that is imposed by the federal government on most transactions between businesses and between businesses and consumers. The GST rate is currently 5% of the sales amount. Similar to the provincial sales tax, the business that is selling a product or service must collect the GST on the sale and record it in a liability account.

Where the GST differs from the provincial sales tax is that it is considered a recoverable sales tax. This means that a business is able to reduce the amount of GST that must be paid to the government by the amount of GST the business spends. The amount of GST that the business spends is usually recorded in a contra liability account called GST Recoverable. The following transactions will illustrate how these accounts are used.

Suppose Hardware Store Inc. purchases some inventory for resale on June 1. As discussed above, they do not have to pay PST on the purchase, but they will have to pay GST. The GST will be recorded in the contra liability account to eventually reduce the amount owing to the government. The transaction is shown in figure 7.12.

BALANCE SHEET

JOURNAL			
Date	Account Title and Explanation	Debit	Credit
Jun 1	Inventory	600	
	GST Recoverable	30	
	Cash		630
	Purchased inventory		

FIGURE 7.12

239

Now, Hardware Store Inc. makes a sale to a customer for $1,000 cash. This was already shown in figure 7.10, but now we will include the GST as part of the sale.

As we focus on the GST, Hardware Store Inc. owes the government $50 from the sale. However, they can reduce the amount owing by the $30 they spent earlier during the month. To make the payment to the federal government on June 30, the transaction shown in figure 7.14 must be made.

The cash payment is for the difference between the two accounts ($20). Both GST accounts act as clearing accounts. They accumulate the GST collected and GST paid over a period of time, and then they are cleared to $0 when a payment is made to send the sales tax to the federal government.

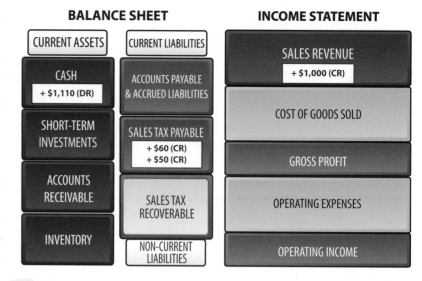

FIGURE 7.13

(handwritten) GST collected

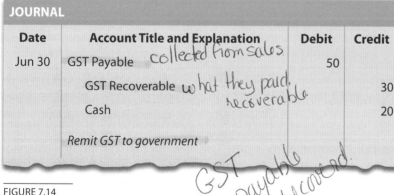

FIGURE 7.14

(handwritten) collected from sales / what they paid, recoverable / GST payable recovered

In the end, the customer will ultimately pay the entire amount of GST, but the amount sent to the government will be sent by different companies. In the example, the customer paid $50 GST to Hardware Store Inc. Hardware Store Inc. sent only $20 to the government and their supplier of inventory would send the other $30 to the government.

Harmonized Sales Tax

The **harmonized sales tax** (HST) is a sales tax that is a combination of the provincial and federal taxes into one sales tax amount. The provinces that have the HST will not charge separate PST or GST amounts. Instead they just charge a single HST amount.

JOURNAL			
Date	Account Title and Explanation	Debit	Credit
Jun 1	Inventory	600	
	HST Recoverable	78	
	Cash		678
	Purchased inventory		

FIGURE 7.15

Harmonized sales tax is applied to almost all of the same transactions that GST is applied to, and is sent to the federal government. HST is also a recoverable sales tax, just like GST. Using the Hardware Store Inc. example and assuming an HST rate of 13%, a purchase would be recorded as shown in Figure 7.15.

The cash sale for $1,000 is shown in figure 7.16.

The payment to the federal government is very similar to the way the GST is paid. Both the HST recoverable account and the HST payable account are cleared when the payment is made.

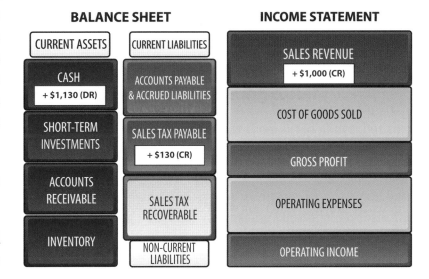

JOURNAL			
Date	Account Title and Explanation	Debit	Credit
Jun 15	Cash	1,130	
	HST Payable		130
	Sales Revenue		1,000
	Sold inventory		

FIGURE 7.16

The cash payment is for the difference between the two accounts ($52). Both HST accounts act as clearing accounts. They accumulate the HST collected and HST paid over a period of time, and then they are cleared to $0 when a payment is made to send the sales tax to the federal government.

BALANCE SHEET

CURRENT ASSETS	CURRENT LIABILITIES
CASH – $52 (CR)	ACCOUNTS PAYABLE & ACCRUED LIABILITIES
SHORT-TERM INVESTMENTS	SALES TAX PAYABLE (balance) $130 – $130 (DR)
ACCOUNTS RECEIVABLE	SALES TAX RECOVERABLE (balance) $78 – $78 (CR)
INVENTORY	NON-CURRENT LIABILITIES

JOURNAL

Date	Account Title and Explanation	Debit	Credit
Jun 30	HST Payable	130	
	HST Recoverable		78
	Cash		52
	Remit GST to government		

FIGURE 7.17

In the end, the customer will ultimately pay the entire amount of HST, but the amount sent to the government will be sent by different companies. In the example, the customer paid $130 HST to Hardware Store Inc. Hardware Store Inc. sent only $52 to the government and their supplier of inventory would send the other $78 to the government.

Sales Tax Remittances

When making the remittances, or payments, to the government, some business will use government forms and make the payment by cheque. Others will use an online form and electronically transfer the funds.

The sales tax forms have various lines, all of which are numbered, which must be filled out. Instructions are available on the form or online regarding which information must be entered in each line and how to calculate the amount of HST owing.

The purpose of the HST remittance form is to have companies report the total HST they collected and the total HST they paid out during the period. If the total HST collected is greater than total HST paid out, then the difference is a balance owing to the government. On the other hand, if HST collected is less than HST paid out, the difference is a refund for the company that the government will pay out. The company's total sales before tax is also listed on the form for informative purposes and to reconcile the amount of HST collected.

Returning to the example with Hardware Store Inc., we will determine the company's HST balance owing or refund. From figure 7.16, the HST collected is $130. From figure 7.15, the HST paid is $78. The difference, also known as net tax, is $52 ($130 - $78). There are various adjustments that might be made after this point that may change the balance owing or refund. In this particular case, assuming there are no adjustments, the $52 is a balance owing and a cheque or electronic payment must be sent to the government.

Unearned Revenue

We have already discussed accruals when matching expenses: expenses are recognized during the period in which they are incurred, and not when they are actually paid. The accrual concept is the same for unearned revenue. For example, a publishing company might receive payment in advance for a one-year subscription to its magazine. The money is paid, but the magazine has not yet been supplied to the customer. Until the product exchanges hands, the amount paid in advance cannot be recognized as revenue. The payment is therefore considered unearned revenue (a liability).

Businesses sometimes misunderstand how accruals work. This can lead to mistakes and bad decisions. For example, management may be tempted to treat unearned revenue as though it is already earned. Using the example of a magazine subscription again, what would happen if a customer later decided to cancel his or her subscription and the magazine publisher had considered the money as earned? Until the product has been delivered, no transaction has been finalized with the customer. The money still belongs to the customer.

With a non-refundable subscription, the same principle would apply. It is still the obligation of the company to deliver goods or services that have already been paid for and to treat the money as unearned until completion of the transaction.

If a customer voluntarily cancels his or her rights to the goods or services and notifies the company to that effect, the revenue will be treated as earned and classified as such on the books. An example of this might be a subscriber moving overseas and informing the publisher that delivery of the magazine is no longer necessary. If the subscription is non-refundable, the customer would have no right to demand repayment. Of course, if the subscription were refundable, the publisher would have to reverse the initial transaction and refund the subscriber. This is another example of why the publisher should treat the cash received as a liability instead of earned revenue.

There is one more principle to keep in mind with regard to earned and unearned revenue: an expense is recognized in the month in which it occurs – not when it is finally paid. As a consequence, the change in company equity occurs in that same month.

The same principle applies to earned and unearned revenue. Since the revenue is not earned until later, it is only at that time that company equity changes. In other words, equity does not change at the time of payment, since this is not when the revenue is recognized.

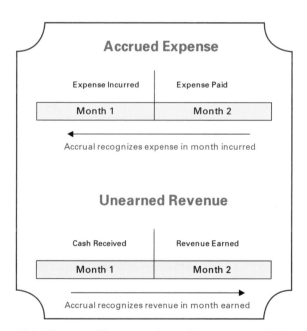

This diagram illustrates how the concept of the accrual works for both expenses (e.g. salaries) and revenues (e.g. magazine subscriptions).

FIGURE 7.18

Here is an example to illustrate the above concept of accruals and revenue. Tracking Time Inc. is the publisher of a magazine with a fiscal year-end of December 31. In December, Tracking Time receives $120,000 from subscribers to cover the delivery of magazines for one year starting on January 1. The delivery will be made on a monthly basis.

The transaction should be recorded in the company's books as follows.

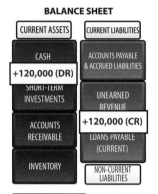

BALANCE SHEET

JOURNAL			
Date	**Account Title and Explanation**	**Debit**	**Credit**
Dec 31	Cash	120,000	
	Unearned Revenue		120,000
	Record the deposit of subscription sales		

Received in Dec   subscription starts in Jan.

FIGURE 7.19

The money is received and debited in the cash account in December. However, the money is yet to be earned, so the amount is credited to the unearned revenue account. Since revenue is not yet earned, there is no change in the company's equity. $120,000 \div 12 \text{ mo} = 10,000/\text{m}$

On January 1, the magazine is delivered to customers for that month. This means that Tracking Time's obligation to the customer has been met for the month and the corresponding revenue is now earned (equity increased). One month of subscriptions equals 1/12th of the whole year subscription; therefore, the amount of $10,000 is recognized as revenue for the month of January.

JOURNAL			
Date	**Account Title and Explanation**	**Debit**	**Credit**
Jan 1	Unearned Revenue	10,000	
	Sales Revenue		10,000
	Record delivery of magazines from January		

Unearned revenue originally had a credit balance of $120,000. Of that amount, $10,000 is now debited to the unearned revenue account and credited to the revenue account in the income statement. Although cash remains the same, the recognition of the unearned revenue means that equity has increased by the amount of $10,000. The obligation that Tracking Time now has to its customers is reduced to $110,000 from the original total of $120,000.

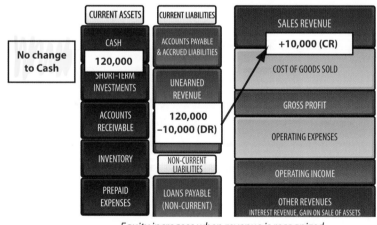

Equity increases when revenue is recognized

FIGURE 7.20

This example reinforces the fact that an increase in cash does not necessarily mean an increase in revenue or profits. Not all businesses recognize revenue in such a precise fashion. For example, a business might hire a management consulting firm for a period of four months and pay the entire fee upfront. Of course, the consulting firm should not classify this as earned revenue; it needs to be accrued.

Many businesses, such as consulting firms, do not operate on a fixed fee schedule. They charge on the basis of hours worked, material produced or any other method; the fee to be charged is often unknown beforehand. The firm essentially categorizes any upfront fee as unearned and then reclassifies it as earned as the work is performed. For example, if the firm counts the hours it works on behalf of a company for a month, the value of those hours is used to credit the revenue account in the income statement for the month. If the firm worked 100 hours in a month and charged $100 per hour, then $10,000 of revenue would be earned for the month. This amount gets debited from the original amount in the unearned revenue account and credited to revenue.

Of course, industries that charge customers upfront are not limited to magazine publishing or management consulting. Many types of businesses receive money from customers and accrue the related revenues until goods are produced or services rendered. Examples include health clubs that charge annual memberships, insurance companies that receive annual premiums and lawn care companies that receive retainers for future services.

 For any company that charges for work in advance, the amount received must be recorded as unearned revenue and only recognized as revenue when the goods or services are delivered. This is an important accounting principle.

Short-Term Notes Payable

With regard to accounts receivable, companies sometimes want greater assurance that a customer will pay its bill. To achieve this, instead of issuing an invoice and creating an account receivable, a company might make a more formal arrangement in the form of a note receivable.

In the same way that a company can have a customer agree to the terms of a note receivable, a supplier can have a company agree to the terms of a note payable. These notes are in essence the flip side of the same document. They are legally binding documents that obligate the borrower to certain terms, much like a loan.

FIGURE 7.21

Such documents outline the amount owed, when it is due and the interest payable. They are signed by the parties involved and constitute a more formalized arrangement than a basic account payable. A separate account on the balance sheet is established with short-term notes payable placed in the current liabilities section of the balance sheet. This is an example of a note payable.

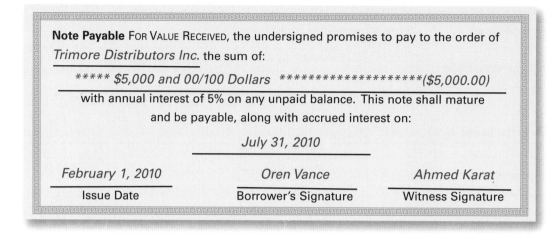

FIGURE 7.22

In the note payable presented above, Oren Vance borrowed $5,000 from Trimore Distributors Inc. on February 1, 2010. The interest rate is 5% and both principal and interest are payable in six months. The journal entry used to record the note payable is shown below:

loan

JOURNAL			
Date	Account Title and Explanation	Debit	Credit
Feb 1	Cash	5,000	
	Notes Payable		5,000
	Record a 6-month, 5% note payable		

FIGURE 7.23

Accrued Interest and Notes Payable

Using the above example, let us assume the borrower has a June 30 year-end date. As we have seen in previous chapters, the matching principle dictates that we must report expenses in the period in which they helped to earn revenue; since no payment has been made or interest expense recognized, we must accrue the interest owing on the note to June 30. The following journal entry would be required:

In addition to the note payable for $5,000, the company would report Interest payable of $104 on its June 30 year-end balance sheet.

JOURNAL			
Date	Account Title and Explanation	Debit	Credit
Jun 30	Interest Expense	104	
	Interest Payable		104
	Record interest on a 6-month, 5% note payable ($5,000 x 5% x 5/12 = $104.17)		

record interest expense @ Year End

FIGURE 7.24

On July 31, both principal and interest will be paid to Trimore Distributors Inc. The entry to record repayment of the note, plus interest, would be as follows:

Note that the interest payable account is debited to remove the accrual recorded in the previous period and interest expense is debited with $21, which represents the interest expense for the month of July. In total, six months worth of interest has been recorded: five months in the previous period and one month in the current period.

JOURNAL

Date	Account Title and Explanation	Debit	Credit
Jul 31	Interest Payable *5 mos*	104	
	Interest Expense *1 mo owing*	21	
	Notes Payable *borrowed*	5,000	
	Cash		5,125
	Record interest and payment for a 6-month, 5% note payable ($5,000 x 5% x 1/12 = $21, $5,000 + $5,000 x 5% x 6/12 = $5,125) *interest / mo*		

FIGURE 7.25

Current Portion of Non-Current Liabilities

When the term of a note payable (loan payable) is longer than one year, the liability should be classified as a non-current liability called *loans payable*. If a portion of the loan will be paid within the next 12 months, that portion would be considered current. Although the entire portion will be contained within the non-current loans payable account, the current portion must be reported separately when the balance sheet is prepared.

For example, a company manufactures a wide range of products for consumers. It wants to purchase a new processing machine to keep up with growing demand for its product. The company has insufficient cash reserves on hand to finance the purchase. Management decides to engage in a common business practice, which is to obtain a loan from a bank to finance an important capital investment.

To that end, on January 2 of the current year, the company negotiates a loan from the bank of $50,000 with a term of five years, bearing an annual interest rate of 5%. Of that debt, $10,000 plus interest is payable every December 31.

Here is how the loan from the bank is recorded in the company's books:

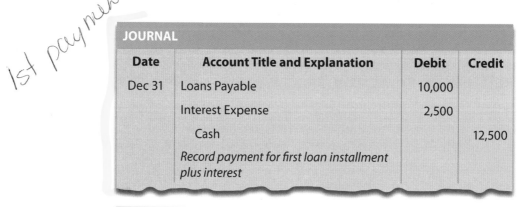

JOURNAL

Date	Account Title and Explanation	Debit	Credit
Jan 2	Cash	50,000	
	Loans Payable		50,000
	Borrowed $50,000 term debt payable over 5 years		

FIGURE 7.26

On December 31, the first installment plus interest was paid. The transaction would be recorded as follows:

1st payment

JOURNAL

Date	Account Title and Explanation	Debit	Credit
Dec 31	Loans Payable	10,000	
	Interest Expense	2,500	
	Cash		12,500
	Record payment for first loan installment plus interest		

FIGURE 7.27

After the first payment, the balance of the loan decreases to $40,000, $10,000 of which is still considered current. When the balance sheet is prepared at the year end, $10,000 will show as part of current liabilities and $30,000 will show as part of non-current liabilities.

Shareholders' Loans

The liabilities section of a company's balance sheet indicates sources of company financing by listing and categorizing where the company is borrowing money from. Current liabilities or short-term liabilities are those that need to be repaid within one year.

A shareholder is someone who owns all or some of the equity in the company. Shareholders help a company to raise finances by buying a part of the company, or shares, in exchange for part ownership.

There is another way in which shareholders can help a company to obtain financing. They can lend the company money in the form of a shareholder loan. If the loan is to be repaid to the shareholder within a year, it is considered a short-term or current liability. However, shareholder loans are sometimes loaned to a company for the long term, in which case it should be regarded as a non-current liability.

BALANCE SHEET

CURRENT ASSETS	CURRENT LIABILITIES
CASH **+50,000 (DR)**	ACCOUNTS PAYABLE & ACCRUED LIABILITIES
SHORT-TERM INVESTMENTS	UNEARNED REVENUE
ACCOUNTS RECEIVABLE	LOANS PAYABLE (CURRENT)
INVENTORY	SHAREHOLDERS' LOANS **+50,000 (CR)**
PREPAID EXPENSES	NON-CURRENT LIABILITIES
OTHER CURRENT ASSETS	LOANS PAYABLE (NON-CURRENT)
NON-CURRENT ASSETS	

For example, let us look at a transaction for an initial shareholder loan of $50,000:

As with all loans, a debit to cash (an asset) is offset by an equal credit to shareholder loan (a liability), with no change to equity. The repayment of a portion of the money from the shareholder loan is recorded as follows:

JOURNAL

Date	Account Title and Explanation	Debit	Credit
	Cash	50,000	
	Shareholders' Loan		50,000
	To record a shareholder loan		

FIGURE 7.28

BALANCE SHEET

CURRENT ASSETS	CURRENT LIABILITIES
CASH **50,000 −10,000 (CR)**	ACCOUNTS PAYABLE & ACCRUED LIABILITIES
	UNEARNED REVENUE
ACCOUNTS RECEIVABLE	LOANS PAYABLE (CURRENT)
INVENTORY	SHAREHOLDERS' LOANS **50,000 −10,000 (DR)**
PREPAID EXPENSES	NON-CURRENT LIABILITIES
OTHER CURRENT ASSETS	LOANS PAYABLE (NON-CURRENT)
NON-CURRENT ASSETS	

FIGURE 7.29

The shareholder loan (a liability) decreases and cash (an asset) also decreases with no change to equity.

JOURNAL

Date	Account Title and Explanation	Debit	Credit
	Shareholders' Loan	10,000	
	Cash		10,000
	To record the withdrawal from the Shareholders' Loan account		

Estimated and Contingent Liabilities

We have already discussed various forms of known liabilities, also referred to as *determinable liabilities*, which are debts taken on by the company for which the terms are readily known. In other words, known liabilities leave a paper trail of invoices, contracts and purchase orders that tell the company exactly how much is due, to whom and when.

However, some company liabilities exist for which the exact terms are not precisely known and cannot be determined until future events occur. These unknown liabilities are also referred to as *non-determinable liabilities*, and can be divided further into two more categories: **estimated liabilities** and **contingent liabilities**.

Estimated liabilities are financial obligations that a company cannot exactly quantify. Examples of estimated liabilities include income and property taxes and warranties. A company needs to adhere to the matching principle when it makes an estimate of the amount of the upcoming liability.

In our discussion of accounts receivable in chapter 3, we described a company faced with the same challenge of matching expenses with the period in which linked revenues were generated. To meet that challenge, the company set up an allowance account based on the estimated bad debts for the period. A similar process can be established for a company's estimated liabilities.

Product Warranties

Just as a company needs to estimate how much bad debt it will have in the upcoming period, when a company sells products with warranties it needs to estimate how much warranty liability it will have. By doing this, the company can expense this liability in the period in which linked revenues are generated. Any errors in estimation can then be adjusted once the actual figures are known.

For example, Star Inc. is a manufacturer of industrial labeling machines. It offers customers a warranty of three years on the purchase of each machine. If a machine breaks down during this warranty period, it is Star Inc.'s obligation to repair it, provide necessary parts and, if necessary, replace the machine.

On the basis of an analysis of historical company trends, the company's accountant determines that an average of $100 per machine is paid out in warranty obligations. The company has sold 50 of these labeling machines during their 2009 fiscal year; therefore, the following journal entry is made to recognize the warranty expense for 2009:

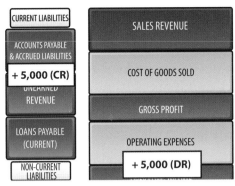

Equity decreases by $5,000.

JOURNAL			
Date	**Account Title and Explanation**	**Debit**	**Credit**
	Warranty Expense	5,000	
	Estimated Warranty Liability		5,000
	To record estimated warranty expense		

FIGURE 7.30

The $5,000 is expensed for this period in the income statement (since these estimates cover expected warranties for the year) and the estimated warranty liability of $5,000 is credited in the corresponding liability account.

During the next year, Star Inc. will receive some warranty claims and make some actual expenditure in meeting those claims. Let us assume that Star Inc. uses $500 in parts from its own inventory, and maintenance staff report $1,500 worth of billable hours related to warranty claims. Here is how their accountant would record these transactions:

JOURNAL			
Date	**Account Title and Explanation**	**Debit**	**Credit**
	Estimated Warranty Liability	2,000	
	Inventory (Parts)		500
	Cash		1,500
	To record inventory and wages for warranty work		

FIGURE 7.31

The category of estimated warranty liability is debited with $2,000, leaving a balance of $3,000 to satisfy warranty claims over the remaining two-year period. On the credit side, $500 worth of inventory is taken off the books, and $1,500 is recorded as a decrease in the bank account.

There is no change to the income statement, since the estimated warranty has already been expensed in the year the machine was sold. The company will calculate and record a debit to warranty expense and credit to estimated warranty liability accounts on the basis of the number of machines sold that year.

Assuming that this amount does not change for the remainder of the warranty period (i.e. no one else makes any warranty claims), Star Inc. would have to reconcile the original estimate with the actual claims made. This is how that process would be transacted.

The remaining $3,000 in the estimated warranty liability account is removed with a debit. In the income statement, $3,000 in expenses is removed from the books with a credit (decrease) of that amount. The company is reversing the original expense for the amount that remains in the estimated warranty liability account.

Of course, no company wants to find itself in a position of significantly erring in estimating certain liabilities as this would result in large adjustment entries after the fact.

Accountants should provide an accurate snapshot of company finances. Large errors in estimating liabilities will distort that snapshot.

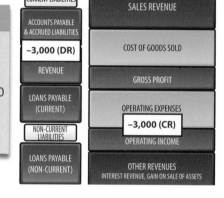

JOURNAL			
Date	**Account Title and Explanation**	**Debit**	**Credit**
	Estimated Warranty Liability	3,000	
	Warranty Expense		3,000
	To decrease the balance of estimated liability owing		

FIGURE 7.32

To avoid such difficulties, a company should always closely monitor its estimated liability accounts. If estimates are continually and significantly wrong, then reviews should be conducted and changes made to historical and other analyses that are producing these errors. For example, if liabilities keep increasing, it would indicate that a manufacturing problem exists.

The example above demonstrated a situation of embedded warranty. Embedded warranty is provided with a product or service with no additional fee required from the customer. However, sometimes companies sell warranties separately to customers. In those cases, revenue generated on the sale of these warranties is initially recorded as unearned warranty revenue. The unearned warranty revenue is recognized throughout the life of the warranty contract.

Let us assume that Star Inc. sold $60,000 worth of three-year warranties as a separate product to its customers on June 1, 2010. This is how the transaction would be recorded in the company's books:

JOURNAL			
Date	**Account Title and Explanation**	**Debit**	**Credit**
Jun 1	Cash	60,000	
	Unearned Warranty Revenue		60,000
	Record the sale of the 3-year warranties		

FIGURE 7.33

The receipt of $60,000 is recorded as a debit to cash and as a credit to unearned warranty revenue. Since this is a three-year warranty, $20,000 will be recognized at the end of each year. At the end of the first year, the company recorded the appropriate adjustment (see figure 7.34).

JOURNAL

Date	Account Title and Explanation	Debit	Credit
May 31	Unearned Warranty Revenue	20,000	
	Warranty Revenue		20,000
	Recognize one year unearned warranty revenue as earned		

FIGURE 7.34

1 yr of warranty recognized

The $20,000 is recorded as a debit to the unearned warranty revenue and as a credit to the warranty revenue account. The rest of the revenue will become earned as the warranty periods elapse. At present, the unearned warranty revenue account has a $40,000 balance because there are two more years left in the warranty period. Note that only the unearned revenue in the next twelve months is counted as current liabilities.

Contingent Liabilities

Unlike estimated liabilities, a company's contingent liabilities involve a financial obligation that will occur only if a certain event takes place. As a result, not only are contingent liabilities estimated, but they are also dependent upon another event taking place.

According to the accounting rules, a company will only establish a contingent liability if payment is likely and the amount of liability can be reasonably estimated. Since it is difficult to determine what is and what is not possible, and how much of a contingency should be estimated, these items usually involve discretion and judgment by the accountants on behalf of the company.

Perhaps the most common reason to establish a contingent liability is to anticipate a costly lawsuit. If such a lawsuit does happen, it could seriously affect a company's bottom line. It would be prudent to include a note in the company's financial statements outlining any contingencies that may lead to a liability.

Current Liabilities and Financial Ratios

Earlier in this chapter, we discussed the importance of a company's assets covering its liabilities. A company's current assets should always be used to cover its current liabilities. The ratio of current assets to current liabilities may be considered acceptable if it is at least 2:1. In other words, for every dollar of current liabilities, a business should have two dollars of current assets. However, this is just a rough guideline and should not be relied upon as a strict rule. The acceptable current ratio often depends on the company's industry. This helps to ensure that a company has enough liquidity to cover its short-term financial obligations.

Another business practice often used to ensure that a company can pay its short-term liabilities is for it to have enough assets that can be liquidated within three months. For every dollar of current liabilities, a company should have about one dollar of liquid assets, excluding current assets such as inventory.

These basic business guidelines are encapsulated in some widely used financial ratios. The current ratio (also known as the working capital ratio) and the quick ratio are used to measure and assess a company's ability to maintain a proper balance between current assets and current liabilities.

Current Ratio

The current ratio simply tracks current assets against current liabilities.

Current Assets: Current Liabilities

In this example, the current ratio is $50,000:$50,000 or 1:1. Since a company usually needs its non-current assets to run the business over the long term, they are not included in the current ratio.

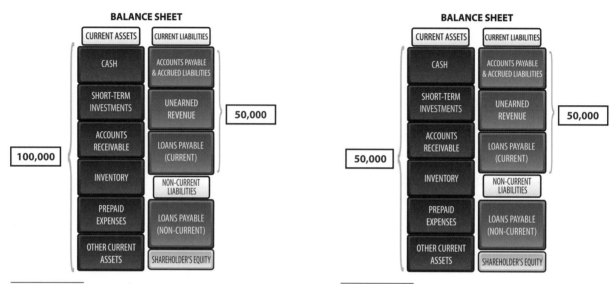

FIGURE 7.35   FIGURE 7.36

A current ratio of 1:1 is undesirable and impractical. It means that all of a company's current assets would need to be liquidated to pay all its current liabilities. (see figure 7.36 above).

As figure 7.35 illustrates, a ratio of 2:1 is far more desirable. It means that a company will likely have enough liquid assets on hand to cover its short-term financial obligations with some reserve in case not all accounts receivable are collected or not all inventories are sold.

Quick Ratio

One of the drawbacks of the current ratio is that it does not tell us how liquid the assets are that are being used to cover current liabilities. That is where the quick ratio is more helpful. It is also known as the ***acid test***.

The quick ratio is based on current *liquid* assets: current liabilities. The equation is:

$$\text{Quick Ratio} = \frac{\text{Cash + Short-Term Investments + Net Accounts Receivable}}{\text{Current Liabilities}}$$

Figure 7.37 shows a further breakdown of the current assets section of the Accounting Map™. As illustrated, the entire current assets section totals $100,000, indicating a current ratio of 2:1. This should be an ideal situation. However, the breakdown reveals that only $40,000 of the current assets can be considered liquid. This gives us a quick ratio of less than 1:1 ($40,000:$50,000). An amount of $60,000 of the company's current assets is tied up in inventory and prepaid expenses, which are unlikely to be converted to cash in the immediate future. The company would have to sell some of its assets to get closer to the desirable quick ratio of 1:1. It would then be in a better position to cover its current liabilities with its liquid current assets.

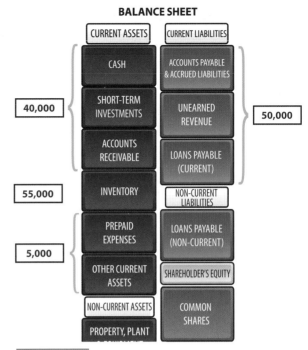

FIGURE 7.37

Controls Relating to Current Liabilities

One of the first and basic controls over a company's liabilities involves a simple principle: keep track of company bills and budget well enough to pay them on time. The inability to pay suppliers could cause serious inventory shortages. Even more important, not paying suppliers risks a company's reputation and ability to do business with others.

Ensuring that bills are paid involves implementing controls to ensure that the right bills are paid. To that end, all relevant documents should be gathered, such as purchase orders, receipts and original invoices, to ensure the legitimacy of the invoices.

After an invoice is paid, it should be marked as such and kept on file for verification purposes. The last thing that a company wants to do is pay the wrong bills or pay the same bills more than once in error. Controls related to invoices should prevent this from happening.

Accounting controls also involve ensuring that a company's resources are used efficiently and economically. This includes paying bills on time and making use of any payment discounts that may be available. Automated systems can alert the appropriate personnel when payments should be made. Manual systems can make use of "tickler files," which allow for the placement of time-sensitive documents in labeled folders that are to be reviewed on important dates.

An Ethical Approach to Current Liabilities

Much of our discussion of accounting ethics has focused on how the books can be manipulated to alter some aspect of a company's financial results. A company's current liabilities are no different in this regard. For example, management might want to understate current liabilities by classifying them as long-term liabilities because this might be helpful in securing a bank loan.

The nature of liabilities can make them a source of fraud that is difficult to detect by both internal and external auditors. In essence, a liability involves a financial obligation to another party, usually as a result of being loaned money. Yet if you're a third party looking for evidence that the transaction took place in the manner alleged, sometimes all that exists is a copy of an invoice or an entry in the books. Experienced auditing teams will know how to follow the money.

IN THE REAL WORLD

Many people, even those experienced in the business world, usually do not give invoices a second thought. They receive a bill, take a look at how much they owe, and send the money before the due date. This is how honest people, both in business and private life, deal with their financial obligations. However, there is one potential problem with paying invoices this way: they may in fact be phony!

One of the oldest scams in business, yet one that continues to deliver success for fraudsters, is sending a phony invoice to a company. In other words, a company is sent a bill for goods or services they never asked for nor received. Nevertheless — and as strange as it may seem — honest businesses often get fooled by this practice and end up wasting their money in the process.

In a sense, it is an honest mistake. Many of these invoices look real. They often use names similar to businesses dealt with on a regular basis, such as an Internet service provider or a club offering membership. Furthermore, the people who pay these bills are often not the people responsible for making the purchases.

There are various ways in which such fraud can be detected. Collecting all necessary internal documentation is one approach. Relying on a copy of an invoice without a purchase order is a mistake. Another approach is to simply call the number provided on the invoice to see if it is a legitimate business.

Businesses have enough of a challenge to meet financial obligations they actually owe. So ensuring that phony invoices are detected and dealt with appropriately not only makes good business sense but also helps prevent one of the oldest and most embarrassing scams around.

Liability fraud often involves a company being on the receiving end of a phony invoice. That is, companies receive invoices from various suppliers and vendors, and an accounting department that doesn't implement some of the controls already discussed might be in the practice of paying any invoice that looks legitimate. It is an old scam, and one that can only be prevented through proper accounting controls.

The IFRS Perspective

The Balance Sheet is called the Statement of Financial Position under IFRS. On the statement of financial position, current liabilities are listed after the non-current liabilities. A liability is classified as current if it is held for the purpose of trading and expected to be paid within 12 months after the reporting period. A company uses the term contingent for liabilities that are not yet recognized because of uncertain future events. When the company determines the payment is probable, the contingent liability will be recognized as an actual liability. IFRS defines the word probable as more likely than not whereas GAAP defines it as likely.

In Summary

↪ A company's balance sheet should be structured in a way that its assets are used to cover its liabilities. This means that current assets should cover current liabilities, and non-current assets should cover non-current liabilities.

↪ A company's known liabilities, or determinable liabilities, are financial obligations with fixed terms that can be traced using documentation (e.g. accounts payable).

↪ An accounts payable is the flip side of an accounts receivable. Instead of sending a customer a bill, an accounts payable involves receiving an invoice for goods or services received.

↪ An accrued charge is how expenses are reconciled with the matching principle. Even though an expense such as an employee's salary may not be paid until the next period, the expense itself must be recognized in the current period with an accrual.

↪ Sales taxes are charged on sales. The amount collected by the business must be sent to the government.

↪ Unearned revenue relates to the way revenues are reconciled with the matching principle. Even though an amount, such as magazine subscriptions, may already have been paid by customers, the revenue itself can only be recognized in a later period when goods or services are delivered.

↪ Notes payable are the flip side of a promissory note from a customer. They represent a more formalized contract between a company and a supplier after a sale has been made, as opposed to a standard bill or invoice.

↪ A shareholder loan occurs when an owner of a company makes a loan to the company.

↪ Estimated liabilities, such as product warranties, represent financial obligations whose specific amount will not be known until some future time. Contingent liabilities represent a financial obligation that will need to be met only if a certain event occurs. The possibility of a lawsuit might necessitate the establishment of a contingent liability.

↪ The current ratio (also known as the working capital ratio) compares a company's current assets with its current liabilities.

↪ The quick ratio (also known as the acid test) compares a company's current liquid assets with its current liabilities.

↪ Controls related to current liabilities should include proper tracking and monitoring of invoices and all related documentation. This ensures that the correct bills are paid on time, which is a crucial part of maintaining the company's finances.

↪ Ethics related to current liabilities should ensure that liabilities are not understated for the purpose of overstating net assets.

Review Exercise

Elnora Yearby Limited buys and resells machines. During the year, the following transactions took place:

Jan 15 – Bought a machine for resale for $105,000 plus 13% HST. The amount is payable in 30 days. The company uses a perpetual inventory system.

Jan 30 – Sold the machine for $214,000 plus 13% HST cash including a five-year warranty. Based on past experience, the accountant determines that an amount of $20,000 will probably be paid out in warranty obligations.

Jan 30 – Paid the HST amount owing to the federal government.

Feb 15 – Paid for the machine purchased on Jan 15.

Mar 1 – The company is short on cash, so shareholders loan the company $100,000, interest free, to be paid back by the end of the year.

Mar 27 – Elnora Yearby must repair the machine under warranty. The company uses $200 in parts from its own inventory.

Required:

Record the journal entries for the above transactions.

Review Exercise - Answer

Date	Account Title and Explanation	Debit	Credit
Jan 15	Inventory	105,000	
	HST Recoverable	13,650	
	Accounts Payable		118,650
	Bought machine for resale		
Jan 30	Cash	241,820	
	Cost of Goods Sold	105,000	
	HST Payable		27,820
	Inventory		105,000
	Sales Revenue		214,000
	Sold machine for cash		
	Warranty Expense	20,000	
	Estimated Warranty Liability		20,000
	Accrued for estimated warranty costs		
Jan 30	HST Payable	27,820	
	HST Recoverable		13,650
	Cash		14,170
	Paid HST to the government		
Feb 15	Accounts Payable	118,650	
	Cash		118,650
	Paid for machine bought on account on Jan 15		
Mar 1	Cash	100,000	
	Shareholders' Loan		100,000
	To record shareholders' loan, interest-free, to be repaid by end of year		
Mar 27	Estimated Warranty Liability	200	
	Inventory		200
	To record inventory for warranty work		

Notes

Chapter 8
NON-CURRENT LIABILITIES

LEARNING OUTCOMES:

❶ State the characteristics and different types of bonds

❷ Apply the concept of present value

❸ Record bonds issued at par

❹ Record bonds issued at a discount or a premium

❺ Record the retirement of bonds

❻ Calculate debt-to-total assets and debt-to-equity ratios

❼ Apply controls and ethics related to non-current liabilities

Non-Current Liabilities: An Introduction

The liabilities side of the balance sheet contains two main sections: current liabilities and non-current liabilities. Current liabilities were the focus of our discussion in chapter 7. This chapter focuses on non-current liabilities (liabilities paid after a period of more than 12 months). Non-current liabilities are also called long-term liabilities. Two common types of non-current liabilities of business organizations are term loans and bonds payable.

The most common form of long-term financing used by a company is a loan. Term loans were partly covered in chapter 7 because the portion of the loan due within one fiscal period is presented as a current liability on the balance sheet.

Another source of long-term financing for companies includes the issuance of bonds. Due to the pervasiveness of this type of financing, it is important for bookkeepers to be familiar with the principles involved in recording such transactions.

FIGURE 8.1

Characteristics and Types of Bonds

Companies cannot always secure sufficient long-term financing from a bank or from private investors. Instead, large companies may borrow money by issuing bonds to interested investors.

The company is called the bond issuer since it issues the bond. The bondholder is the investor who purchases the bond. There a number of complexities involved with bonds but essentially, it is a contract, whereby a bondholder loans money (the principal) to a bond issuer. In return, the bond issuer promises to provide regular interest payments to a bondholder and after a set time (when the bonds mature), the principal is returned to the bondholder. Bond investors are often large organizations such as pension funds but can also include smaller institutions or individuals. The primary difference between a bond and a loan is that there is a market in which bonds are actively traded. On the other hand, a loan is usually a private agreement between two parties that is non-tradeable.

There are several types of bonds:

- Term bonds mature on a specific date, whereas serial bonds are a set of bonds that mature at different intervals.
- Companies may issue secured or mortgage bonds whereby they put up specific assets as collateral (like loans) in the event that it defaults on interest or principal repayments.
- Unsecured or **debenture bonds** are backed only by the bondholder's faith in the company's good reputation.
- Bonds may have a callable feature whereby the company has the right to buy back the bonds before maturity at a set or "call" price.
- If the bonds are convertible, bondholders have the option of converting or exchanging the bonds for a specific number of the company's common shares.
- Registered bonds list the bondholders as registered owners who receive regular interest payments on the interest payment dates.
- Coupon bonds contain detachable coupons that state the amount and due date of the interest payment. These coupons can be removed and cashed by the holder.

An organization that issues bonds faces the challenge of competing with other investments in the market. A bond is an interest-bearing investment vehicle whereby money is received from investors in exchange for interest payments. For example, a 5% interest rate on a bond means that 5% annual interest on the principal balance outstanding will be paid back to the investor. A company that has issued a five-year bond, with annual interest of 10% (payable twice per year) and having a $100,000 principal value, is obligated to make semi-annual (twice per year) interest payments to bondholders totaling $5,000 ($100,000 × 10% × ½). The interest rate on a bond must compete with market interest rates in general – that is, investors can earn interest through a number of other investments on the market, including bonds issued by other organizations.

That is why companies generally issue bonds at the going market interest rate. For example, if the market rate is 10%, the company is likely to issue the bond with a 10% interest rate; this is known as issuing a bond at par. Since it takes time to arrange the printing and distribution of bonds, however, rates of existing bonds can differ significantly from current market rates. We will examine what issuing companies do under these circumstances; but first, a discussion on the time value of money is necessary.

The Concept of Present Value

In our discussion of accounting methods, we have been using round figures to demonstrate various procedures. We have also assumed that the value of money remains constant. One dollar in a person's hand at one moment has been assumed to be equal in value to a dollar in that person's hand at a later time.

This, however, is not so. In fact, the value of money changes over time. This is what interest rates are all about.

In other words, money itself has a price. If it is lent, it gets repaid with interest. A deposit in a bank account is essentially a loan to a bank — with interest. Of course, a loan from a bank also comes with a price tag (in the form of interest).

The world of finance often refers to this phenomenon as the **time value of money**. It is important for accountants to be familiar with the time value of money because it is a basic principle of economics and finance. Furthermore, it almost certainly affects the amounts in transactions that an accountant records over time. If a company keeps money in a bank, for example, its value will change, even if nothing is done to it.

In the context of our current discussion of **bonds payable**, the time value of money matters because it will help determine the price the bonds will sell for when the market rate of interest differs from the stated rate. We begin with a simple example to show how a company can pay both the principal and interest over time. This involves making calculations concerning the value of money at some future point in time. We will look closely at this issue.

We will start with the basics. If you have one dollar and you invest it for one year at an interest rate of 10%, you will have made 10 cents in interest and have a total in the account of $1.10 at the end of the year.

At the start of the second year, you start with $1.10. The interest for the year will amount to 11 cents ($1.10 × 10%) and produce a year-end balance of $1.21.

You should see a pattern developing. The more money that is left in an interest-bearing account, the more the interest grows each year. In the first year, interest was 10 cents. In the second year, it was 11 cents. The following chart represents the interest that would accumulate in the account over a period of 10 years.

Year	Opening Balance	Interest at 10%	Closing Balance
1	1.000	0.100	1.100
2	1.100	0.110	1.210
3	1.210	0.121	1.331
4	1.331	0.133	1.464
5	1.464	0.146	1.611
6	1.611	0.161	1.772
7	1.772	0.177	1.949
8	1.949	0.195	2.144
9	2.144	0.214	2.358
10	2.358	0.236	2.594

FIGURE 8.2

As you can see, the amount of interest earned in year 10 is over 23 cents, more than double the amount of interest earned in Year 1.

This phenomenon is commonly referred to as *compound interest*, which refers to the piling on effect that applying the same interest rate has on an account over a period of time. Essentially, with each passing period, the interest rate is applied to interest on top of the principal.

The amount in the bottom right-hand corner of our chart ($2.59) will be the value of the money in the account after Year 10. It can also be referred to as the *future value*. *after 10 years.*

Following this basic logic, the future value of the money after Year 2 is $1.21. After year 5, it is $1.61, and so on.

Of course, calculating the value of money can work in reverse, too. In other words, an accountant can try to calculate what amount needs to be invested today to produce a certain amount in the future. This is known as the *present value*.

The formulas used to calculate present value are beyond the scope of this textbook. They are not used often by accountants since most spreadsheet programs and calculators come with functions to calculate both present value and future value. Accounting and finance textbooks, however, can be used as a reference to verify or understand the calculations being made.

The following chart indicates calculations showing present values of $1.00 over 10 years, given an interest rate of 10%. The factors shown in the table are calculated using a formula that is beyond the scope of this book. However, these factors can be found in many mathematical textbooks, and are commonly included as tables in professional accounting exams. Most business calculators include functions which use the factors, as do common spreadsheet programs.

The chart provides answers for the following question: What amount needs to be invested now to create $1 in x number of years, with x representing Years 1 to 10 in this particular chart?

10%

Year	Factor
1	0.909
2	0.826
3	0.751
4	0.683
5	0.621
6	0.564
7	0.513
8	0.467
9	0.424
10	0.386

FIGURE 8.3

For example, an investor requiring $1.00 after one year would have to invest about 91 cents (as indicated on the first line of the chart). If the investor wanted $1 after 10 years, it would necessitate investing about 39 cents now (as shown on the last line of the chart). Indeed, the difference between the amounts is a testament to the power of compound interest. That is, waiting 9 years to get the same payoff means initially investing less than half the money. The greater the interest rate, and the longer this interest rate is applied, the more compound interest is earned.

It should be noted that the chart provided applies only to an interest rate calculation of 10%. Separate charts need to be used when other interest rates are involved in calculating present and future values.

Time Value of Money and Bonds Payable

Now that we have some understanding of how the time value of money works, we can start applying its principles to bonds payable.

When bonds are sold at their par or face value, both the present value of the principal, and future interest payments, can be calculated. One point regarding the interest payments needs to be mentioned before we proceed. In the above calculations, interest was stated at an annual rate and paid once per year. Interest on bonds is normally paid semi-annually. Therefore, when applying present value concepts, we need to <u>double</u> the <u>number of periods</u> and <u>divide the interest rate by</u> two.

(handwritten: ÷ 2 = 5)   *(handwritten: 10)*

Using our $100,000 bond issue with 10% interest payable semi-annually over the next 5 years, we provide the following:

(handwritten: Principle = Periods)
(handwritten: Interest = Annuity)

$$\text{Interest payments} = \$100,000 \times 5\% \ (10\% \times \tfrac{1}{2}) = \$5,000$$
$$\text{Number of Periods} = 5 \times 2 = 10$$

The present value of the $100,000 principal repayment is:

$$\$100,000 \times 0.614 = \$61,400$$

5%

Periods	Factor
1	0.952
2	0.907
3	0.864
4	0.823
5	0.784
6	0.746
7	0.711
8	0.677
9	0.645
10	0.614

FIGURE 8.4

The interest payments are different from the principal repayment in that they represent an **annuity** because they are periodic and recurring fixed payments. To calculate the present value of the interest payment annuity, we can use one of two methods:

1. We can calculate, individually, the present value of each interest payment. For example, we take the first interest payment of $5,000 in 6 months and multiply it by the 6-month factor to determine the present value of that particular payment. To this amount, we then add the second $5,000 payment in 12 months and multiply it by the 12-month factor. After this, we then add the third $5,000 payment in 18 months and multiply it by the 18-month factor. This goes on for all ten interest payments. As you can see, this can get tedious and is prone to error. For a 5-year bond, we would have to repeat this calculation 10 times (once for each interest payment) to determine the present value of all the interest payments.

2. Fortunately, annuities are a common occurrence in the financial industry and, so, tables containing factors for annuities, in particular, have been developed (see figure 8.5). Using this table, we can calculate the present value of ALL interest payments in just one calculation.

Calculate the present value of the future interest payments:

Present value of $5,000 payments (annuity) made over 10 periods
= $5,000 x 7.722 = $38, 610 (round to $38,600)

5%

Periods	Factor
1	0.952
2	1.859
3	2.723
4	3.546
5	4.329
6	5.076
7	5.786
8	6.463
9	7.108
10	7.722

FIGURE 8.5

Summary

Present value of principal	= $61,400
Present value of interest payments	= $38,600
Total proceeds	$100,000

Note: the present value of the interest payments is rounded to $38,600 for illustrative purposes.

It is important to note that the present value of the principal and the interest payments equal the face value of the bond ($100,000). This occurred because we have discounted the 5% bond using the 5% interest rate. This shows that the face value of the bond is equal to the present value of the payments when the market rate is equal to the interest rate of the bond.

Issuing Bonds at Par

Business Time Inc., a publisher of investment-related books, magazines and newspapers, wants to raise money for long-term financing by issuing bonds. On December 31, 2009, the company issues 1,000, 10-year bonds at par at a price of $100 each with 5% annual interest. Here is how the entire transaction is recorded by the company's accountant:

JOURNAL			
Date	Account Title and Explanation	Debit	Credit
Dec 31	Cash	100,000	
	Bonds Payable		100,000
	Issue of $100,000 worth of bonds at par (due in 2019)		

FIGURE 8.6

BALANCE SHEET

CURRENT ASSETS	CURRENT LIABILITIES
CASH	ACCOUNTS PAYABLE & ACCRUED LIABILITIES
+ $100,000 (DR)	
INVESTMENTS	UNEARNED REVENUE
ACCOUNTS RECEIVABLE	
DOUBTFUL ACCOUNTS	LOANS PAYABLE (CURRENT)
INVENTORY	SHAREHOLDERS' LOANS
PREPAID EXPENSES	NON-CURRENT LIABILITIES
OTHER CURRENT ASSETS	BONDS PAYABLE
NON-CURRENT ASSETS	+ $100,000 (CR)

FIGURE 8.6

The total amount of $100,000 is debited in the cash account. A corresponding liability on the other side of the balance sheet involves a credit increase of $100,000 in the bonds payable account. Since the principal for the bonds is due in 10 years, the liability is classified as long term and placed in that section of the balance sheet.

Issuing the bond for a 10-year term means that a company will have to make interest payments to its bondholders every year for 10 years. Most bonds call for semi-annual (twice per year) interest payments. For the sake of simplicity, we will assume interest is paid annually in this illustration.

A $5,000 credit represents a decrease in cash, while a $5,000 debit represents an increase in bond interest expense.

During the 10-year term that Business Time Inc. is making interest payments to its bondholders, the year-end may occur before the payment is made. A portion of the payment may be due, but the interest is actually paid in the following period.

The company is, therefore, required to expense the interest during the period in which it was incurred; this is regarded as an accrual and represents a decrease in the company's equity for the period. According to the matching principle, this keeps the company's books in good standing until the payment is made in the following period.

JOURNAL			
Date	**Account Title and Explanation**	**Debit**	**Credit**
Dec 31	Bond Interest Expense	5,000	
	Cash		5,000
	Record interest on bonds ($100,000 × 5%)		

FIGURE 8.7

The previous journal entry was made on the anniversary date of the bond. Assume for a moment that the company's year end is October 31, but the bond anniversary date is December 31. On October 31, when the company prepares its financial statements, it will accrue only 10/12 of the annual interest:

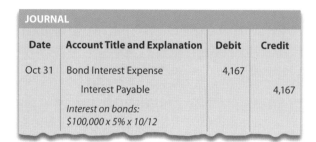

JOURNAL			
Date	Account Title and Explanation	Debit	Credit
Oct 31	Bond Interest Expense	4,167	
	Interest Payable		4,167
	Interest on bonds: *$100,000 x 5% x 10/12*		

As with the other interest payments on the bond, $4,167 is expensed as a debit (increase) to bond interest on October 31. However, unlike the previous transaction, interest payable (accrued liabilities) is credited instead of cash.

Continuing the above example, when interest is paid on December 31, the payment should be recorded with the following entry:

JOURNAL			
Date	Account Title and Explanation	Debit	Credit
Dec 31	Bond Interest Expense	833	
	Interest Payable	4,167	
	Cash		5,000
	Interest on bonds: *$100,000 x 5%*		

The logic of the transaction:

1. Cash was paid to the bondholder for $5,000.

2. The $833 applied against this period means that it is considered to be an expense in this period.

3. However, the $4,167 amount belongs to the previous period, so it cannot be regarded as an expense at this time, even though it is being paid now. It therefore needs to be recorded as a debit to accrued liabilities.

FIGURE 8.8

FIGURE 8.9

There is another principle involved in making annual interest payments on bonds: on the first day of every year, the company knows that interest payments will be due before the end of the year. Therefore, that year's interest payable gets classified as a current liability.

On the other hand the original principal (which will be paid back at the end of the 10-year term of the bond), is classified as a non-current liability by the company. This is like a 10-year term loan where you only pay the interest.

We have demonstrated how a bond issue is treated *at par*. However, the period from the time that a business decides to issue the bonds to the time they are printed for distribution can be several months. In the meantime, the market rate is likely to have changed. This means that the interest rate on the bond may end up being higher – or lower – than that of the market. This will affect the demand for the company's bonds. The price of the bond must, therefore, be adjusted accordingly.

A bond's **face value** is the price at which it was originally sold and is printed on the face of the bond. Another way of putting it is that the face value is the same as the principal. The principal amount gets paid back to the bondholder, regardless of any changes in market price. In other words, *regardless of the price paid for the bond*, the business needs to pay the full face value of the bond to the bondholder when payment is due.

However, the market value and the face value of a bond are not always the same. There are two scenarios to consider when such situations occur.

Scenario 1: Market value is less than face value. The bond will be sold at a discount.

Scenario 2: Market value is more than face value. The bond will be sold at a premium.

Issuing Bonds at a Discount

Continuing with our Business Time Inc. bond issue when the bonds were sold at par (or face value), the resulting transaction was relatively simple. The company received a lump sum of $100,000 and established a bonds payable for that same amount.

Things change somewhat when market interest rates rise above the interest rate attached to the bond. When that happens, investors can receive higher interest payments from other bonds and market investments.

To deter investors from those other investments and to attract them to Business Time's bonds, the company should offer the bonds at a more attractive price – at a **discount**.

But what should that discount price be? The answer is logical. The company sets a discount price which compensates the investor for the money lost with the bond's lower interest rate. Here is a demonstration of how this is done.

We know that the interest rate on the Business Time bonds is 5%. The principal is $100,000, which means that the annual interest payment is $5,000. Payment of the full amount of principal, or face value of the bond, returns a yield of 5%.

However, when the market rate is 6%, receiving a yield of 5% is not high enough. In that case, the company must essentially lower the price of the bond to below face value so that the buyer can get an effective interest rate of 6%. It is important to understand that the buyer still expects to get $100,000 for the bond when it matures plus the $5,000 interest in the last year regardless of what was paid. Using the same present value concepts as shown above, here is how the price of the bond is determined:

> Note: Use table 8-1 and table 8-2 at the end of the chapter for factors used in the following calculations.

Present value of the principal = $100,000 x 0.558 = $55,800
(Market interest rate of 6%, 10 periods)

Present value of future interest payments =$5,000 x 7.360 = $36,800
(6% interest, 10 periods)

Total price bondholders are willing to pay for their investment = $55,800 + $36,800 = $92,600

The price investors are willing to pay is lower than the par value because the market rate is 6%, meaning the investors can easily get return higher than 5% elsewhere in the market. Therefore, the price they are willing to pay will be lower.

The difference between the price paid and the par value is known as the *discount*.

Here is how the receipt of $92,600 for the issue of Business Time Inc. bonds (at discount), is entered into the company's books:

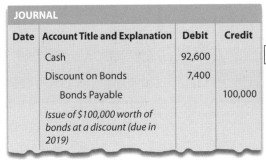

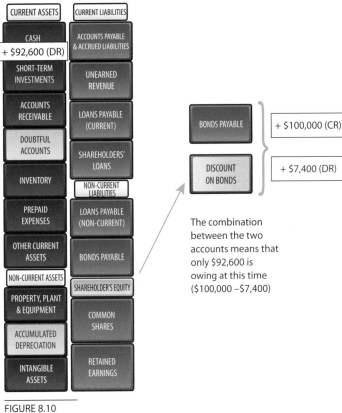

FIGURE 8.10

Here is the logic behind the entry:

1. The business deposits $92,600 instead of $100,000, due to the discount. This is recorded by debiting cash.

2. Though only $92,600 was paid by the bondholder, the full amount of $100,000 must be paid when the bond matures in 10 years. Therefore, $100,000 must be regarded as a long-term liability. This is recorded by crediting bonds payable (a long-term liability).

Consider the following possibilities of recording the discount:

a. Debit an asset: This is not possible since there is no future benefit associated with the discount.

b. Debit an expense: This is incorrect because the discount pertains to the 10 year term of the bond so expensing immediately would violate the time period concept. The discount, in fact, should be amortized over the term of the bond.

c. Solution: Debit a contra liability account called discount on bonds, and amortize the discount as an expense over the life of the bond (refer to the Accounting Map™ above).

The discount is amortized (using the straight-line method) and added to interest expense each year. At the end of 10 years, the discount on the bond will be cleared to a zero balance. The principle involved is very similar to amortizing the purchase price of property, plant and equipment, a concept we discussed in chapter 6, which is why a discount on a bond is also amortized over the life of the bond. In this example, the discount will be amortized at $7,400 ÷ 10 = $740 per year.

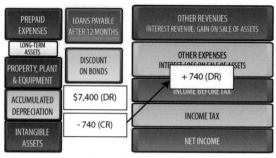

Journal entry each year when amortizing the discount

FIGURE 8.11

Each year, the company that issues the bond will pay $5,000 interest on the bond (in cash to the bondholder). The amortization of the discount of $740 is just a book entry; the total expense related to the bond for the period is $5,740.

JOURNAL

Date	Account Title and Explanation	Debit	Credit
	Interest Expense	5,740	
	Discount on Bonds		740
	Cash		5,000
	Record interest and the depreciation of the discount for the current year.		

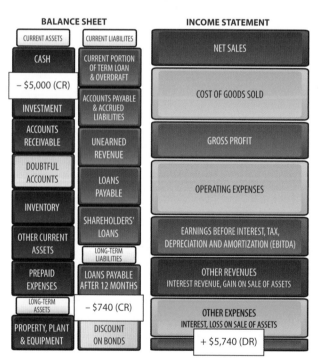

$5,000 of the expense is cash and the balance relates to the depreciation of the discount (not cash)

FIGURE 8.12

Over the period of 10 years, the journal entry shown in figure 8.12 will be repeated. As this happens, the value of the discount on the bonds will decrease and the book value (or carrying value) of the bond will increase. By the end of the 10 years, the discount will be reduced to zero and the book value of the bond will be the face value, $100,000. Figure 8.13 shows an amortization table of the bond for 10 years. Notice how the discount balance decreases while the bond book value increases.

Year	A Interest Payment ($100,000 × 5%)	B Discount Amortization (D ÷ 10 years)	C Interest Expense (A + B)	D Discount Balance (D − B)	E Bond Book Value ($100,000 − D)
0				$7,400	$92,600
1	$5,000	$740	$5,740	6,660	93,340
2	5,000	740	5,740	5,920	94,080
3	5,000	740	5,740	5,180	94,820
4	5,000	740	5,740	4,440	95,560
5	5,000	740	5,740	3,700	96,300
6	5,000	740	5,740	2,960	97,040
7	5,000	740	5,740	2,220	97,780
8	5,000	740	5,740	1,480	98,520
9	5,000	740	5,740	740	99,260
10	5,000	740	5,740	0	100,000

FIGURE 8.13

FIGURE 8.14

At the end of the 10-year term, cash is credited in the amount of $100,000, and the same amount is debited to non-current debt, thereby clearing the liability. Any outstanding interest payments will be included with this final payment. The journal entry is presented as shown below:

JOURNAL			
Date	Account Title and Explanation	Debit	Credit
	Bonds Payable	100,000	
	Cash		100,000
	Repay $100,000 to bondholder		

Issuing Bonds at a Premium

We have already discussed why companies issue bonds at a discount. The higher market interest rate makes the bond's interest rate less competitive, so the selling price is reduced to make up the difference with potential investors.

Of course, there is a flip side to that coin. By the time a company's bond issue reaches the market, the market interest rate may decline. This means that the bond's interest rate would be higher than that of the market, and produce a higher rate of return for an investor than what the market is currently offering. This creates a greater demand for the company's bond, which means the company can now sell the bond at a premium (at a price that is higher than its face value).

IN THE REAL WORLD

When using the straight line method of amortization, the calculation doesn't necessarily produce a result that accurately reflects the changes over time in the value of an item. This is true with regard to the value of assets, and is also true with regard to the value of bonds issued at a discount or premium.

In the real world, accountants often use a method which applies a fixed interest rate to the changing value of a bond, which more accurately reflects the way that bond issues work. This is often called the Effective Interest Method of Amortization. The interest rate used is seen as a reflection of market rates in general. The changing value of the bond reflects the fact that the carrying value (or value incorporating amortization on the books) changes, even though the bond's face value remains the same.

At this level of accounting, it is not necessary to know all the details. What students should know, however, is that amortization schedules for bond discounts and premiums can get complicated. For now, the straight line method introduces us to bond amortization. Future courses will expand on how other methods are used to more accurately reflect the value of a bond issue.

A company that issues bonds at a premium takes the same steps in recording the transaction as it would with a discount, except in reverse. Let us review those steps with an example using the Business Time Inc. publishing company again.

The interest rate for Business Time Inc. bonds is 5%. A market rate of 5% meant that the bonds could be issued at par. A market rate of 6% meant that the bonds were issued at discount. What happens when the market rate is 4%?

> Note: Use table 8-1 and table 8-2 at the end of the chapter for factors used in the following calculations.

Present value of the principal = $100,000 x 0.676 = $67,600
(Market interest rate of 4%, 10 periods)

Present value of future interest payments =$5,000 x 8.111 = $40,555
(4% interest, 10 periods)

Total price bondholders are willing to pay for their investment =
$67,600 + $40,555 = $108,155

The price investors are willing to pay is higher than the par value because the market rate is 4%, meaning it is difficult for investors to get return higher than 5% elsewhere in the market. Therefore, the price they are willing to pay will be higher.

This is how this bond issue is recorded on the company's books:

JOURNAL

Date	Account Title and Explanation	Debit	Credit
	Cash	108,155	
	Premium on Bonds		8,155
	Bonds Payable		100,000
	Issue of $100,000 worth of bonds at a premium (due in 2019)		

FIGURE 8.15

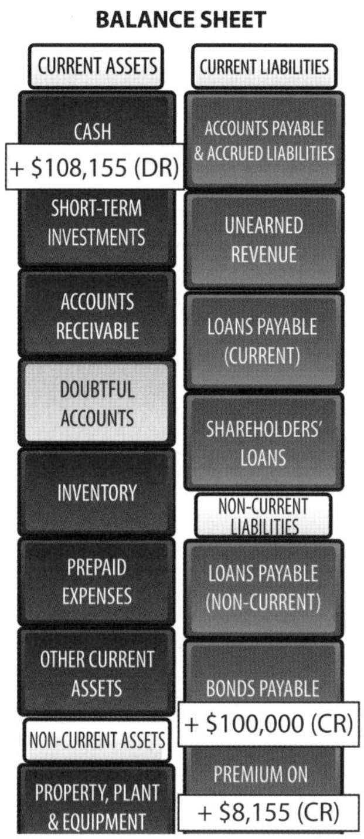

As always, proceeds from the sale are deposited and recorded as a debit to the cash account. On the other side of the balance sheet, the principal amount of the bond ($100,000) is credited to bonds payable (a non-current liability) account. Finally, the premium on the bond of $8,155 is recorded as a credit in an account called premium on bonds. Premium on bonds appears in the other liabilities section of the balance sheet. So far, there is no change to equity; therefore the income statement is not impacted.

Unlike the discount on a bond, which is recorded in a contra liability account, the premium is recorded in a separate liability account. Since it is credited, it represents an amount owing. Intuitively you may think that because a discount is considered as an expense, why should a premium not be regarded as revenue? A discount is an increase to an expense (DR) and the premium simply offsets the same account and decreases the expense (CR).

Similar to a discount on a bond issue, a premium must be amortized as periodic interest payments are made. In other words, the premium liability of $8,155 should be amortized over the term of the bond. Using the straight line method again, this amount comes to $8,155 ÷ 10 = $816 (rounded). Therefore, $816 is debited to premium on bonds every year until the amount is zero upon maturity of the bond.

Here is how that transaction would be recorded each year if the straight line method is used:

The $5,000 interest payment is recorded each year, and is represented by a credit to cash. The expense to the company is now only $4,184, and the rest of the debit is taken care of by the $816 annual amortization premium calculated using the straight-line method.

JOURNAL			
Date	Account Title and Explanation	Debit	Credit
	Interest Expense	4,184	
	Premium on Bonds	816	
	Cash		5,000
	Payment of interest and depreciation of premium 1/10 x 8,155		

FIGURE 8.16

When financial statements are prepared, the premium on bonds is added to the face value of the bonds. The balance sheet would look like this at the end of the first year, after 1/10 of the discount had been charged to expense:

Bonds payable	$100,000
Added: unamortized premium	7,339
Book value	$107,339

FIGURE 8.17

At the end of 10 years, the company will only pay the bondholder $100,000 instead of the $108,155 that was originally received.

Over the period of 10 years, the journal entry shown in figure 8.16 will be repeated. As this happens, the value of the premium on the bonds will decrease and the book value (or carrying value) of the bond will decrease. By the end of the 10 years, the premium will be reduced to zero and the book value of the bond will be the face value, $100,000. Figure 8.18 shows an amortization table of the bond for 10 years. Notice how the premium balance and the bond book value decrease.

Year	A Interest Payment ($100,000 x 5%)	B Premium Amortization (D ÷ 10 years)	C Interest Expense (A - B)	D Premium Balance (D - B)	E Bond Book Value ($100,000 + D)
0				$8,155	$108,155
1	$5,000	$816	$4,184	7,339	107,339
2	5,000	816	4,184	6,523	106,523
3	5,000	816	4,184	5,707	105,707
4	5,000	816	4,184	4,891	104,891
5	5,000	816	4,184	4,075	104,075
6	5,000	816	4,184	3,259	103,259
7	5,000	816	4,184	2,443	102,443
8	5,000	816	4,184	1,627	101,627
9	5,000	816	4,184	811	100,811
10	5,000	811*	4,189	0	100,000

*$811 is due to rounding

FIGURE 8.18

Retiring Bonds

Regardless of the price at which a bond was issued, whether at par, discount or premium, the underlying terms of the bond remain the same. That means that an interest payment is made every year according to the rate on the bond. It also means that the principal amount is paid back in full. In other words, the original investor essentially loans the issuing company the principal amount.

When the bond matures, that principal amount is paid back to the current owner of the bond. This transaction is also referred to as *redeeming* the bond, or buying it back. At a basic level, it is nothing more than paying back the original amount loaned to the company.

Using our example of Business Time Inc. bonds, at par, discount, or premium, this is how the final bond redemption is recorded:

JOURNAL			
Date	**Account Title and Explanation**	**Debit**	**Credit**
	Bonds Payable	100,000	
	Cash		100,000
	Redemption of $100,000 worth of bonds at par due in 2019		

FIGURE 8.19

Cash is credited in the amount of $100,000. The original bonds payable, created 10 years earlier at the time of bond issue, is finally taken off the books with a $100,000 debit to that account.

This transaction takes care of the redemption of the bond. However, a company sometimes issues what are known as **callable bonds**. These give the issuing company the option to buy back the bonds before the stated maturity date. The issuer might want to do this to take advantage of lower market interest rates, which would allow for the issuance of new bonds to match those lower rates. In other words, the company could now make lower annual payments on its bonds.

We have just demonstrated how bond redemption is recorded. You may realize that there is another issue that needs to be resolved when a bond is redeemed before maturity. The issue is that any remaining discount or premium must also be removed from the books. We will stay with our Business Time Inc. bonds example to see how this is achieved.

Consider our earlier example of Business Time Inc. bonds which were issued at a discount. If the company was to exercise a call option on the bonds at the end of 2017 (which includes 8 years of paid interest), the unamortized discount would amount to:

$$\$7,400 - [8 \times (\$740)] = \$1,480$$

This is how the transaction would be recorded:

JOURNAL

Date	Account Title and Explanation	Debit	Credit
	Bonds payable	100,000	
	Discount on Bonds		1,480
	Cash		98,520
	Redemption of $100,000 worth of bonds at par due in 2019		

The cash payment of $98,520 represents the fair value paid to the present bond holder.

FIGURE 8.20

The cash payment of $98,520 represents the fair value paid to the present bondholders. This involves removing both the bonds payable and the discount on bonds accounts off the books. The transaction is recorded by debiting bonds payable of $100,000, crediting discount on bonds with $1,480 and crediting cash by $98,520. The $1,480 amount is what was left in the discount account after annual credits of $740 have been applied to amortize the initial amount.

If we use the bonds which were issued at a premium, then the same type of transaction would take place, except that a debit would be recorded to the premium on bonds to close the account.

Financial Ratios Related to Liabilities

Debt-to-Total Assets Ratio

Debt-to-total-assets ratio measures how much of a company's assets are financed through debt. The higher the ratio, the greater the difficulty a company will have in repaying its creditors. A high debt-to-total assets ratio indicates that the company is at a greater risk of being unable to meet debt obligations. On the other hand, a low debt-to-total assets ratio is desirable to creditors.

Debt-to-Equity Ratio

Debt-to-equity ratio is used to assess how much of a company is being financed by lenders, and how much is being financed by the owners or shareholders. In other words, it measures the extent to which a business is indebted to lenders.

Ideally, a business should have a debt-to-equity ratio of 1:2. In other words, the company has $1 of debt for every $2 of equity. Like other ratios, though, make note that the debt-to-equity ratio must be compared to industry benchmarks to draw sound conclusions.

Controls Related to Non-Current Liabilities

Controls related to balance sheet items should include:

- Hiring qualified staff to handle transactions accurately
- Compliance with all relevant policies, plans, procedures, laws and regulations
- Setting appropriate goals and objectives that are reviewed regularly for proper implementation

Although liabilities are different from assets, the controls for both tend to mirror each other since both involve an exchange of money. With regard to loans, this means that all documents pertaining to the loan should be reviewed by legal counsel. Strong controls surrounding the negotiation of non-current liabilities should result in obtaining the best possible interest rates. The lower interest rates will increase cash flow which can be used in the operating activities of the business.

In addition, robust cash controls ensure that interest and principal payments are made on time. Other controls include verifying that interest and principal payments have been received by lenders.

An Ethical Approach to Non-Current Liabilities

We will now examine ethical violations related to non-current liabilities.

Companies assume non-current liabilities to finance large items and projects that often take years to complete. This type of financing usually takes the form of term loans and bond issues. The sheer magnitude of these transactions makes them vulnerable to abuse.

First, where large sums are concerned, management is usually closely involved. This level of company operations often has fewer internal controls, so those in place must be thorough and complete. They should include reviews by top-level executives and audits performed both internally and externally.

One cannot assume that individuals will not be tempted when dealing with large amounts of money that could possibly be siphoned off or redirected by clever

IN THE REAL WORLD

In the fall of 2008, the world was hit by the worst financial crisis since the Depression. In a nutshell, global financial institutions had too much money invested in bad credit, especially sub-prime mortgages. The economy started to slow down when these bad debts went unpaid and the credit market crashed as a result.

In the aftermath of the crash, leading financial minds started looking for solutions to problems that had gone unsolved for years. Although many experts looked for ways to better regulate the markets, some analysts started pointing fingers at the accounting profession.

Specifically, a long-running criticism of accounting standards is that they do not require an appropriate level of disclosure. A perfect example of this is off-balance-sheet financing - the practice of keeping some forms of long-term financing off the company books.

Another example of poor disclosure practices comes in the form of reporting pension fund assets and liabilities only in footnote form. Recent standards are now forcing companies to disclose a net amount on the balance sheet itself.

Critics of the accounting profession believe that it is only through fair and open reporting that companies can gain the trust of investment markets in general. How can companies expect people to trust them with money if they are not fully open about what is reported in the financial statements?

Open and fair accounting practices can help bring back some stability and trust in world markets at a time when it is most needed.

fraudsters. Staying alert and attentive to these risks is one of the primary responsibilities of those who own and run the company.

Second, it is always necessary to be vigilant with transactions conducted with financial institutions, where the possibility of unauthorized commissions may exist. That is, some part of the loan money might end up in the hands of individuals who work out a side deal for themselves. That is why it is always important for companies to keep track of all the money.

Finally, another type of fraud related to a company's non-current liabilities involves something called off-balance sheet financing. Some businesses engage in accounting practices that keep some large financing schemes off the books. Examples include joint ventures, research and development partnerships and operating leases.

The practice of off-balance sheet financing allows a business to keep its debt to equity and leverage ratios low, which might artificially inflate share prices by overstating a company's equity position.

Operating leases were once a common example of off-balance sheet financing. Instead of owning the asset in question, a company could lease it and simply expense any rental fees involved. Accounting rules have been changed so that the leases, depending on their terms, are actually treated as a form of financing. This forces the company to book an asset and the accompanying liability to their balance sheet. This, in turn, increases their debt-to-equity ratio and gives users of their financial statements a better idea of the company's financial position.

The IFRS Perspective

The accounting treatment for non-current liabilities under the current Canadian standards and IFRS is similar. The differences in certain terminologies and approaches are outside the scope of this course.

In Summary

⇨ A company usually has two basic options when it comes to long-term financing: bank loans and bond issues.

⇨ A current year's payable amount for a term loan is listed in the current liabilities section of the balance sheet, while the balance of the amount payable is listed under non-current liabilities.

⇨ When a company needs a source of long-term financing other than a bank loan, an option would be a bond issue. A bond is a contract that a company establishes with an investor. The investor provides principal loan to the issuing company. In return, the company makes interest payments to the investor, in addition to eventually repaying the principal.

⇨ When the bond rate equals the market rate, the company can sell the bond at par.

⇨ When the bond rate is lower than the market rate, the company sells the bond at a discount.

⇨ When the bond rate is higher than the market rate, the company can sell the bond at a premium.

⇨ Both the discount and premium attached to the bond price should be amortized over the term of the bond until maturity.

⇨ When the bond reaches maturity, it is time for the issuing company to repay the principal to whoever holds the bond at the time. This is also called redemption. The issuing company may have the option to redeem a bond early. Such securities are referred to as callable bonds.

⇨ The time value of money involves the principle that interest attached to an investment compounds the rate of increase in the value of the investment. That is why it is called compound interest. This principle is important for accountants when breaking down amounts to be paid on loans and other non-current liabilities.

⇨ Future value determines the value of an investment in the future if an amount is invested today. Present value determines the amount invested today to produce a certain amount in the future.

⇨ Debt-to-total-assets ratio measures how much of a company's assets are financed through debt. Debt-to-equity ratio is used to assess how much of a company is being financed by lenders, and how much is being financed by the owners or shareholders.

⇨ Controls related to non-current liabilities should ensure that all documents are in order and that cash flow planning accommodates future payments for loans and bonds.

⇨ Ethics related to non-current liabilities should ensure the integrity of large amounts of cash that upper management has the responsibility of handling. Unauthorized commissions are always a risk when dealing with financial institutions. Off-balance-sheet financing is also a practice that can skew the way in which company finances are reported to the public.

Table 8-1

Present Value of $1

Periods	1%	2%	3%	4%	5%	6%
1	0.990	0.980	0.971	0.962	0.952	0.943
2	0.980	0.961	0.943	0.925	0.907	0.890
3	0.971	0.942	0.915	0.889	0.864	0.840
4	0.961	0.924	0.888	0.855	0.823	0.792
5	0.951	0.906	0.883	0.822	0.784	0.747
6	0.942	0.888	0.837	0.790	0.746	0.705
7	0.933	0.871	0.813	0.760	0.711	0.665
8	0.923	0.853	0.789	0.731	0.677	0.627
9	0.914	0.837	0.766	0.703	0.645	0.592
10	0.905	0.820	0.744	0.676	0.614	0.558
11	0.896	0.804	0.722	0.650	0.585	0.527
12	0.887	0.788	0.701	0.625	0.557	0.497
13	0.879	0.773	0.681	0.601	0.530	0.469
14	0.870	0.758	0.661	0.577	0.505	0.442
15	0.861	0.743	0.642	0.555	0.481	0.417

Table 8-2

Present Value of Annuity $1

Periods	1%	2%	3%	4%	5%	6%
1	0.990	0.980	0.971	0.962	0.952	0.943
2	1.970	1.942	1.913	1.886	1.859	1.833
3	2.941	2.884	2.829	2.775	2.723	2.673
4	3.902	3.808	3.717	3.630	3.546	3.465
5	4.853	4.713	4.580	4.452	4.329	4.212
6	5.795	5.601	5.417	5.242	5.076	4.917
7	6.728	6.472	6.230	6.002	5.786	5.582
8	7.652	7.325	7.020	6.733	6.463	6.210
9	8.566	8.162	7.786	7.435	7.108	6.802
10	9.471	8.983	8.530	8.111	7.722	7.360
11	10.368	9.787	9.253	8.760	8.306	7.887
12	11.255	10.575	9.954	9.385	8.863	8.384
13	12.134	11.348	10.635	9.986	9.394	8.853
14	13.004	12.106	11.296	10.563	9.899	9.295
15	13.865	12.849	11.938	11.118	10.380	9.712

Review Exercise

Hohl Company is planning to expand its facilities by constructing a new building, and installing new machines. In order to complete this project, the company has decided to issue $2,000,000 worth of 20-year 4% callable bonds, with interest paid every six months.

On April 1, the company completed all the necessary paperwork, and is now ready to issue the bonds. Fortunately, just as Hohl Company was issuing its bonds, the current market rate dropped to 3.5%. Their financial advisor recommended issuing the bonds at a premium of $142,124.

On March 31 of year 10, interest rates dropped to 2%. At this point, the company issues $2,200,000 of 10-year 2% bonds at par to redeem all outstanding 3.5% bonds.

Required

a) Record the journal entry for the issuance of bonds on April 1, year 1.

b) Record the payment of interest on September 30.

c) Record any required journal entries as of the company year-end, February 28, year 2. Note that the company pays interest semi-annually.

d) Record journal entries for retirement of the 3.5% bonds and issue of new 2% bonds.

e) Record the first interest payment on the 2% bonds.

Review Exercise – Answer

Premium bond price = 2,000,000 + 142,124 = 2,142,124

Date	Account Title and Explanation	Debit	Credit
Apr 1 yr. 1	Cash	2,142,124	
	Premium on Bonds		142,124
	Bonds Payable		2,000,000
	Issue of $2 million worth of bonds at a pre-mium, due in 20 years		
Sep 30 yr. 1	Interest Expense	36,447	
	Premium on Bonds	3,553	
	Cash		40,000
	Payment of interest and amortization of premium $142,124 ÷ 20 × ½ = $3,553 *$2,000,000 × 4% × 6/12 = $40,000*		
Feb 28 yr. 2	Interest Expense	30,372	
	Premium on Bonds	2,961	
	Accrued Interest		33,333
	To recognize accrued interest at year-end *$2,000,000 × 4% × 5/12 = $33,333* *$142,124 ÷ 20 × 5/12 = $2,961*		
Mar 31 yr. 10	Cash	2,200,000	
	Bonds Payable		2,200,000
	Issuance of new bonds		
Mar 31 yr. 10	Bonds Payable	2,000,000	
	Premium on Bonds	71,062	
	Cash		2,071,062
	Redemption of bonds		
Sep 30 yr. 10	Interest Expense	22,000	
	Cash		22,000
	To record interest *$2,200,000 × 2% × 6/12 = $22,000*		

Chapter 9
PARTNERSHIPS

LEARNING OUTCOMES:

❶ Describe the advantages and disadvantages of a partnership

❷ Understand different types of partnerships

❸ Record the formation of a partnership

❹ Record the division of income or loss and partners' drawings

❺ Account for the addition or withdrawal of a partner

❻ Record the liquidation of a partnership

Proprietorships, Partnerships and Corporations

There are three primary options for structuring the ownership of a business:

1. In a proprietorship, only one person owns the business and keeps all the earnings, which are taxed at the personal level. The owner is personally responsible for all the liabilities of the business. This means that if creditors are looking for payment, they will pursue the owner's personal assets.

2. A **partnership** is an association of two or more people who jointly own a business, its assets and liabilities, and share in its gains or losses; earnings are taxed personally. Some partners may be brought in for their technical expertise and others for their ability to raise capital.

3. In a corporation, there can be a large number of owners known as *shareholders*, many of whom may not participate in the running of the business. A corporation has many rights and duties, because it is a legal entity distinct from its owners. All earnings are taxed at the corporate level when they are earned and at the personal level when dividends are distributed to shareholders. Corporations can raise funds from the general public by issuing shares. The *shareholders* (owners) of a corporation are not personally responsible for the company's debt, and are only responsible for paying any unpaid amount owing on their shares.

In most of the examples in this book, we have focused, primarily, on proprietorships and corporations. In this chapter, we will examine the characteristics of partnerships in detail.

We now turn our attention to the partnership form of business as we demonstrate the effect of transactions and financial reporting on the asset, liability and owners' equity accounts and how various accounting principles are applied.

If a corporation were to sell all its assets and pay its debt, the remaining cash would be divided amongst all the shareholders, according to how many shares they own. There is only one equity account.

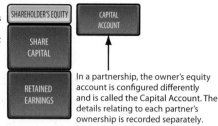

In a partnership, the owner's equity account is configured differently and is called the Capital Account. The details relating to each partner's ownership is recorded separately.

FIGURE 9.1

Advantages and Disadvantages of Partnerships

Many professional businesses are structured as partnerships – for example, consulting firms, law firms and accounting firms. In addition to the characteristics listed above, certain advantages and disadvantages are associated with conducting a business as a partnership.

Advantages

Instead of one person owning and operating a business, as is the case with a proprietorship, a partnership involves two or more people combining resources, both human and financial. This provides two advantages. First, the combination of human resources means that the business should benefit from the skills and experience of each partner. To illustrate, assume two lawyers, Helen White and Greg Harris, decide to form the partnership White & Harris, Attorneys at Law. Helen specializes in family law and Greg specializes in criminal law. Together they are able to service twice as many clients in two different areas of law. Second, due to their combined financial resources, they are more likely than a proprietorship to be able to provide sufficient cash flow to the business without having to rely on external financing.

Another advantage of the partnership form of business is the relative ease of formation. A partnership can be formed with a simple handshake; however, most partnerships employ the services of a lawyer to have a partnership agreement drawn up to formalize the arrangement for sharing profits and losses and for other eventualities such as the addition or withdrawal of a partner or terminating the partnership.

Some contend that there is also an income tax advantage to the partnership form of business in that the partnership itself does not pay income tax. Any income or loss is taxed in the hands of the partners personally. This means that the partnership does not need to file a separate tax return or concern itself with an income tax liability.

Disadvantages

Perhaps the most serious disadvantage of the partnership form of business is the fact that each partner is responsible for the liabilities of the business; this is referred to as having *unlimited liability*. Let us assume that Partner A has no personal assets other than what she invested in the partnership. Partner B, on the other hand, owns his own home, a rental property, a cottage, a sailboat and several valuable paintings. The business suffered losses for several years and was then sued by a dissatisfied client for $1.5 million. As the partnership has very little remaining cash or assets, the partners were personally liable for the $1.5 million liability. Since Partner A had no assets, Partner B, because of unlimited liability, was required to pay the debt on behalf of the partnership.

Other disadvantages include the limited life of a partnership, which means that changes would have to be made for accounting and income tax purposes if any of the following events were to occur: death of one of the partners, bankruptcy or the addition or withdrawal of a partner. Another disadvantage is mutual agency – that is, each partner can authorize contracts and transactions on behalf of the partnership provided the activity is within the scope of the partnership's business. This is viewed as a disadvantage because it places the other partners at risk if the authorizing partner does not act in the best interests of the partnership.

Characteristics	Proprietorship	Partnership
# of owners	One	Two or more
Control	Owner has complete control	Decisions are shared among partners, with possibility of disagreement and conflict
Raising capital	Small - since only one person raising money	Larger - since more than one person is responsible for raising money
Earnings	Proprietor receives 100% of earnings	Partners share earnings in proportion to terms of the partnership agreement
Formation	Relatively simple to set up	Simple to set up, but details require close attention
Liability	Proprietor is responsible for all debts and/or legal obligations	Partners are responsible jointly and individually for actions of other partners
Skills	Reliance on the skills of the proprietor alone	Partners offer different skills in various areas of the business
Dissolution	Relatively simple to dissolve	May be dissolved upon death or withdrawal of a partner - partnership has limited life
Taxation	Earnings are taxed whether or not cash is withdrawn from the business	Partners share earnings and are taxed whether or not cash is withdrawn

FIGURE 9.2

Types of Partnerships

General Partnership

A general partnership means that all partners share the responsibility for the liabilities of the business – that is, they have unlimited liability.

Limited Partnership

Businesses sometimes find themselves in the position of being legally obligated to pay other parties a considerable amount of money. These obligations can take the form of debt owed to creditors or financial sums awarded to other parties in a lawsuit. In other words, a business is liable to others for its actions. Proprietorships and partnerships generally extend unlimited liability to all the owners of the business. Unlimited liability in a partnership can be particularly damaging because if one partner is unable to meet liability obligations that are related to the partnership, the other partners are obliged to pay. This could mean having to sell off personal assets such as houses, cars and cottages. Limited partnerships resolve the potential problem of unlimited liability by creating two categories of partners within the business: the **general partner** and the **limited partner**.

Unlimited liability is assigned to a general partner, who is responsible for the day-to-day operations of the business and is legally responsible for decisions made on behalf of the business.

Limited liability is assigned to a limited partner, who is responsible only for providing the capital to finance the business. This partner should not be involved in day-to-day operations and is therefore not considered liable for decisions made by the business that can lead to a liability. As a result, limited partners are liable only for the amount they have invested in the business.

Limited Liability Partnership

Another business legal entity – the **limited liability partnership** or **LLP** – has been developed in some jurisdictions to deal with liability. Unlike in a limited partnership, a general partner is not required in an LLP and the limited partners usually participate in managing the business. LLPs are primarily used in professional partnerships to protect one partner from another partner's negligence. For example, if a lawyer is sued for malpractice, other lawyers in the firm are not automatically considered liable; however, as was indicated in limited partnerships, partners usually cannot escape liability entirely. In the case of LLPs, this means that all partners are still liable for any unpaid debts to creditors. An LLP can protect partners from some forms of liability, but not all.

Formation of a Partnership

Once a decision has been made to form a partnership, the next step is to record the initial journal entries to set up the asset, liability and owners' equity accounts. The partners may have assets (other than cash) and liabilities that they would like to bring into the business. An independent market evaluation, or appraisal, of the items is required. Assume Lee Wang and Kim Chow decide to form the partnership Wang & Chow. The following is a summary of the amounts contributed by each partner:

Lee Wang

Cash	$2,500
Accounts receivable	5,340
Allowance for doubtful accounts	890
Equipment	10,500
Accumulated depreciation	2,000
Accounts payable	1,240
Note payable	5,000

Kim Chow

Cash	$20,000
Building	175,000
Bank loan	80,000

FIGURE 9.3

An independent appraiser determined that the allowance for doubtful accounts should be $1,200 and the market value of the equipment is $5,000. All other assets are recorded at their fair market values.

The journal entry in the books of the partnership would include the following amounts:

	DR	CR
Cash (2,500 + 20,000)	$22,500	
Accounts receivable	5,340	
Allowance for doubtful accounts		$1,200
Equipment	5,000	
Accumulated depreciation – equipment		0
Building	175,000	
Accumulated depreciation – building		0
Accounts payable		1,240
Note payable		5,000
Bank loan		80,000
Lee Wang, capital		5,400
Kim Chow, capital		115,000

FIGURE 9.4

The amount of accumulated depreciation is not set up in the books of the partnership because the market value of the equipment, $5,000, represents the cost of the asset in the new business. A method of depreciation, useful life and residual value will all need to be determined in order to calculate depreciation for current and future years. Each owner's opening capital is calculated by deducting the total amount of liabilities from the total amount of assets.

Lee Wang, Capital = $2,500 + $5,340 - $1,200 + $5,000 - $1,240 - $5,000 = $5,400

Kim Chow, Capital = $20,000 + $175,000 - $80,000 = $115,000

Division of Income or Loss

A key difference between a partnership, a proprietorship and a corporation is the way in which earnings are distributed. In a proprietorship, the proprietor simply receives all the earnings. In a corporation, earnings are distributed in the form of dividend payments (earnings paid out to shareholders). If all the assets are sold and all debts paid, the remaining cash would be distributed among the shareholders in proportion to the number of shares owned. For example, a shareholder with 10 times more shares than another shareholder would receive 10 times more of the remaining cash.

In a partnership, earnings are distributed differently than they are in a proprietorship or a corporation. Since partners are involved, earnings must be shared, not always on an equal basis. A partnership agreement sets out the terms of ownership, including how earnings are to be divided. A partnership's equity account on the balance sheet is referred to as the *capital account*. Here is an example of such an account:

	J. Witner	R. Pierce	Total
Capital balance (beginning)	25,000	50,000	75,000
Add: Additional contribution	0	0	0
Share of partnership net income for the period	50,000	100,000	150,000
Subtotal	75,000	150,000	225,000
Less: Drawings	40,000	80,000	120,000
Capital balance (ending)	35,000	70,000	105,000

FIGURE 9.5

The partnership's capital account is broken down by partner. In this case, J. Witner had a beginning capital balance of $25,000 and R. Pierce had a beginning capital balance of $50,000. During the year, they did not contribute additional capital to the business. At the end of the year, J. Witner's share of net income is $50,000 and $40,000 was withdrawn. R. Pierce's share of net income is $100,000 and $80,000 was withdrawn. The closing capital account balance is the net worth of the partnership.

One of the primary purposes of a partnership agreement is to stipulate how earnings are to be divided. In fact, the partners can choose any method they wish, as long as they are willing to abide by the terms of the partnership agreement.

The typical methods of dividing earnings in a partnership include the following:

- equally
- according to an agreed-upon ratio
- according to the capital contribution of each partner
- according to agreed-upon salaries, plus a share of the remainder

We will examine each of these methods separately.

Dividing Earnings Equally

The simplest method of dividing earnings is on an equal basis. For example, Partners A and B own a consulting practice that earned $100,000 net income for the year. The net income is credited in the income summary account after the revenue and expense accounts have been closed. For the partners to share the earnings equally, a debit is then made to the income summary account for the entire amount, while credits of $50,000 each are made to the capital accounts of the two partners, as shown in the journal entry.

JOURNAL			
Date	**Account Title and Explanation**	**Debit**	**Credit**
	Income Summary	100,000	
	Capital - Partner A		50,000
	Capital - Partner B		50,000
	To close income summary account		

Equal.

FIGURE 9.6

Dividing Earnings According to an Agreed-Upon Ratio

The allocation of business earnings can be done according to an agreed upon ratio. For example, if Partner A is to get 60% of the earnings and Partner B is to get 40%, the split would be recorded in the books as follows:

JOURNAL			
Date	**Account Title and Explanation**	**Debit**	**Credit**
	Income Summary	100,000	
	Capital - Partner A		60,000
	Capital - Partner B		40,000
	To close income summary account		

60%
40%

FIGURE 9.7

Dividing Earnings According to the Capital Contribution of Each Partner

Another method of allocating the earnings among partners is to base it on the amount that each partner invested in the business. For example, if Partner A contributed $10,000 (one-quarter) of the capital and Partner B contributed $30,000 (three-quarters), they would be entitled to their proportion of the earnings.

based on contribution

JOURNAL			
Date	Account Title and Explanation	Debit	Credit
	Income Summary	100,000	
	Capital - Partner A		25,000
	Capital - Partner B		75,000
	To close income summary account		

FIGURE 9.8

Dividing Earnings According to Agreed-Upon Salaries, Plus a Share of the Remainder

Earnings can also be divided by using a fixed salary for each partner, and then dividing the remaining earnings equally. For example, if the partnership agreement stipulates that Partner A's salary is $25,000, and Partner B's salary is $40,000, then those are the first amounts to be deducted from the net income of the business and distributed to the partners. These amounts are shown in orange in figure 9.9.

	Total	Partner A	Partner B
Net Income	$100,000		
Salary to A	-25,000	25,000	
Salary to B	-40,000		40,000
Remainder	35,000		
Remainder - to A	-17,500	17,500	
Remainder - to B	-17,500		17,500
Capital balance (ending)		42,500	57,500

Salary / Remainder divided =

FIGURE 9.9

The $35,000 remaining after the salaries are distributed is divided equally among the partners. These amounts are shown in green on the chart.

If the distributed amounts are added up for each partner, the totals come to $42,500 ($25,000 + $17,500) for Partner A, and $57,500 ($40,000 + $17,500) for Partner B, as marked in red on the chart. These payments are the earnings to be recorded in the capital account of the business.

JOURNAL

Date	Account Title and Explanation	Debit	Credit
	Income Summary	100,000	
	Capital - Partner A		42,500
	Capital - Partner B		57,500
	To close income summary account		

Net Income.
} Salary + balance.

FIGURE 9.10

The number of ways that earnings can be divided between partners is unlimited. For example, interest can firstly be paid (out of net income) at a fixed rate on each partner's capital account. The remaining amount of net income could then be divided according to a predetermined ratio or salary. The method chosen should meet the needs and interests of the partners involved and be clearly stated in the partnership agreement. These amounts are not to be deducted from the partnership's revenues in determining net income for the period.

Partner Drawings

The amount reported as owner's drawings does not represent the amount that has been earned by the partner during the period, but the amount that has been withdrawn from the partner's equity. During the year, partners may withdraw cash or other assets from the business for personal use. The journal entries to record the withdrawals and related year-end closing entries for the Witner and Pierce Partnership are as follows:

not earned

JOURNAL

Date	Account Title and Explanation	Debit	Credit
	Drawings - Witner	40,000	
	Drawings - Pierce	80,000	
	Cash		120,000
	To record owner drawings during the year		

Record drawings

JOURNAL

Date	Account Title and Explanation	Debit	Credit
	Capital - Witner	40,000	
	Capital - Pierce	80,000	
	Drawings - Witner		40,000
	Drawings - Pierce		80,000
	To close the owner drawings account		

To close drawing accts to Cap.

FIGURE 9.11

293

Addition and Withdrawal of a Partner

The legal basis for any partnership is the partnership agreement. Once a partner leaves, or another is added, a new partnership agreement should be prepared and signed by all parties. However, this does not mean that the business needs to open a new set of books. Instead, adjustments can be made to the current set of books to reflect any change in partner status.

In figure 9.12, the first row of opening balances reflects the capital introduced by each partner plus the net income that the owners have earned to date.

	Partner A	Partner B	Partner C	Partner D	Total
Balance before admitting new partner (includes all earnings to date)	120,000	150,000	50,000		320,000
Admission of new partner				100,000	100,000
Balance after admitting new partner	120,000	150,000	50,000	100,000	420,000

FIGURE 9.12

Partner D is the new addition, therefore his opening balance is zero. The total of all the opening balances is $320,000. Partner D contributes $100,000 to the partnership, which creates a new balance of $420,000.

Here is how the admission of the new partner is recorded in journal format:

JOURNAL			
Date	**Account Title and Explanation**	**Debit**	**Credit**
	Cash	100,000	
	Capital - Partner D		100,000
	To record admission of new partner		

FIGURE 9.13

The receipt of $100,000 represents a debit in the company's cash account, and a corresponding credit of $100,000 is made in Partner D's section of the capital account.

This illustrates what occurs when a new partner invests cash into the business. However, the new partner could also purchase all or part of the investment (equity) held by another partner in the partnership. For example, Partner D may have bought a $100,000 share of the business from Partner A. In that case, the new partnership account would look as follows:

Buy from other Partner

	Partner A	Partner B	Partner C	Partner D	Total
Balance before admitting new partner (includes all earnings to date)	120,000	150,000	50,000		320,000
Admission of new partner	- 100,000			100,000	0
Balance after admitting new partner	20,000	150,000	50,000	100,000	320,000

FIGURE 9.14

As you can see in the second row, $100,000 is deducted from Partner A's balance, and added to Partner D's balance. The journal entry would be as follows:

Record new partner buy from another.

JOURNAL

Date	Account Title and Explanation	Debit	Credit
	Capital - Partner A	100,000	
	Capital - Partner D		100,000
	To record admission of new partner		

FIGURE 9.15

Instead of being debited to cash, Partner A's section of the capital account is debited with the amount of $100,000, leaving Partner A with a balance of $20,000, since Partner D bought a $100,000 share of the business from Partner A.

The partnership's total net assets therefore remain at $320,000, instead of the $420,000 shown in figure 9.12. The reason should be clear. Instead of adding new cash to the partnership, Partner D purchased most of Partner A's capital (equity). Partner A would receive the cash personally from Partner D.

When Market Value Differs from Book Value

As much of our discussion has indicated, the value of items on the books for a business may not necessarily reflect their current market values. This principle can also apply to partnerships. When new partnership agreements are negotiated, the partners usually come to an understanding of what the business is really worth, relative to its stated book value. This understanding can then form the foundation of how much new partners must pay to receive a percentage or share of ownership in the business.

Here are two examples to build upon those we have already looked at in this chapter. Our opening balance originally looked like this:

	Partner A	Partner B	Partner C	Partner D	Total
Balance before admitting new partner (includes all earnings to date)	120,000	150,000	50,000		320,000

FIGURE 9.16

In our first example, we are going to assume that Partner D (the new partner) is willing to pay a premium for a share of the business. He would be willing to do this because the business could have a value that is not reflected in the capital account, such as an increase in the value of the good name of the business (goodwill), or a higher market value for assets such as land or copyright.

After negotiating the new partnership agreement, Partner D agrees to contribute $200,000 to receive a $130,000 share of the business's book value, which amounts to a quarter of the business. Here is how that transaction could be recorded:

	Partner A	Partner B	Partner C	Partner D	Total
Balance before admitting new partner (includes all earnings to date)	120,000	150,000	50,000		320,000
Admission of new partner	23,334	23,333	23,333	130,000	200,000
Balance after admitting new partner	143,334	173,333	73,333	130,000	520,000

FIGURE 9.17

The addition of Partner D's $200,000 contribution raises the total level of net assets from $320,000 to $520,000. One-quarter of this total amounts to $130,000, which is Partner D's new share. The remaining balance of Partner D's $200,000 investment, amounting to $70,000, is divided equally among the other partners.

JOURNAL			
Date	**Account Title and Explanation**	**Debit**	**Credit**
	Cash	200,000	
	Capital - Partner A		23,334
	Capital - Partner B		23,333
	Capital - Partner C		23,333
	Capital - Partner D		130,000
	To record admission of new partner		

FIGURE 9.18

In our second example, we are going to assume that Partner D is a partner who adds value to the business. Perhaps Partner D has a client list that would considerably increase the value of the business once the new partnership is formed. This time we will see what happens when Partner D pays $100,000 to receive a quarter share of the business, for a value of $105,000.

	Partner A	Partner B	Partner C	Partner D	Total
Balance before admitting new partner (includes all earnings to date)	120,000	150,000	50,000		320,000
Admission of new partner	- 1,666	- 1,667	- 1,667	105,000	100,000
Balance after admitting new partner	118,334	148,333	48,333	105,000	420,000

FIGURE 9.19

The contribution made by Partner D of $100,000 creates total net assets of $420,000. One-quarter of this amount is $105,000, which is Partner D's share. Since Partner D only paid $100,000 for this share, the $5,000 difference is essentially paid for by the other partners – split three ways. This means that approximately $1,667 is deducted from the account balances of partners A, B and C.

JOURNAL			
Date	Account Title and Explanation	Debit	Credit
	Cash	100,000	
	Capital - Partner A	1,666	
	Capital - Partner B	1,667	
	Capital - Partner C	1,667	
	Capital - Partner D		105,000
	To record admission of new partner		

Paid.

÷5,000 difference between.

Share.

FIGURE 9.20

Liquidation of a Partnership

Partnerships may end for a variety of reasons, including the death of one partner or by agreement between the partners. When a partnership is liquidated, the main challenge is to establish who receives whatever remains of the business after the assets are sold and liabilities have been paid. In figure 9.21, the balance sheet of ABC Partnership is shown after liquidation. Since the only remaining asset consists of $100,000 in cash, this is distributed to the partners in proportion to their equity in the business.

The balance sheet would appear as follows:

JOURNAL

Date	Account Title and Explanation	Debit	Credit
	Capital - Partner A	35,000	
	Capital - Partner B	40,000	
	Capital - Partner C	25,000	
	Cash		100,000
	To record cash distribution among partners		

ABC Partnership Balance Sheet As at mm/dd/yy	
Cash	**$ 100,000**
Partners' Equity	
Partner A	35,000
Partner B	40,000
Partner C	25,000
Total	**$ 100,000**

FIGURE 9.21

This was a relatively simple example. The amounts of cash received by the partners were equal to their share of equity. This example also assumes that assets were sold at their book value. As we already know, this rarely happens. If the business's net assets are sold for $70,000, representing a loss of $30,000, the following entry would appear:

Assets 700,000
Liabilities 600,000
Assets 100,000
Sold Assets 70,000 (cash)
Loss (30,000)

JOURNAL

Date	Account Title and Explanation	Debit	Credit
	Cash	70,000	
	Liabilities	600,000	
	Loss on sale of net assets	30,000	
	Assets		700,000
	To record the sales of assets		

Net Assets sold
Liabilities
loss from sale

FIGURE 9.22

As you can see, total business assets were valued at $700,000; total liabilities amounted to $600,000. This produced a net book value of $100,000. Since the assets were sold for only $70,000, a loss on sale of net assets of $30,000 must be recorded as an additional debit.

This loss is then allocated to the partners according to the same formula that would be used when distributing earnings, or whatever terms were agreed upon in the partnership agreement. For the purpose of this example, we assume that the earnings (or losses) are distributed equally.

JOURNAL

Date	Account Title and Explanation	Debit	Credit
	Capital - Partner A	10,000	
	Capital - Partner B	10,000	
	Capital - Partner C	10,000	
	Loss on sale of net assets		30,000
	To allocate loss on sale of net assets		

FIGURE 9.23

The cash is then distributed to the partners in proportion to their closing share of equity in the partnership.

This example involved allocating a loss on sale of assets. Any earnings would be allocated in the same manner – equally, unless otherwise provided for – and the cash would be divided according to each partner's equity contribution to the partnership.

JOURNAL			
Date	Account Title and Explanation	Debit	Credit
	Capital - Partner A	25,000	
	Capital - Partner B	30,000	
	Capital - Partner C	15,000	
	Cash		70,000
	To record cash distrubuion among partners		

FIGURE 9.24

IN THE REAL WORLD

One of the lesser known facts of the business world is that some of the world's most famous ventures and corporations started out as partnerships.

Wilbur and Orville Wright were brothers who received a toy helicopter from their father in 1878. They went into business with one another, which led to ventures in building a printing press and publishing a newspaper. In 1886 the brothers made their own brand of bicycles. However, the toy helicopter from their father always inspired visions of machines and flight for the young men, which is why they ended up building gliders and a wind tunnel. In 1903 they built and flew the first airplane in history. Six years later they incorporated the Wright Co. and continued their pioneering work in the field of aeronautics.

Richard and Maurice McDonald were brothers from New Hampshire who decided to move to California in the late 1920s to seek their fortune. They eventually fine-tuned their hot dog stand and barbecue restaurant to limit the number of items on the menu, eliminated utensils and plates, and made the kitchen more efficient. After having sold 21 franchises by the mid-1950s, Ray Kroc came along and purchased all the rights to the business for $2.7 million. There are now approximately 31,000 McDonald's restaurants around the globe with sales of over $22 billion a year.

Bill Hewlett and David Packard graduated with engineering degrees from California's Stanford University in 1934, forging a friendship that would last a lifetime. A few years later, they started working together on a technical sound device; Disney Studios bought eight of these devices. Their partnership was formalized in 1939 and they went on to innovate in the fields of technology and management style. Today, Hewlett-Packard generates over $100 billion in sales from computer-related equipment. The name of the company was decided on a coin toss. You can guess who won.

The IFRS Perspective

The full adoption of IFRS is only applicable to publicly accountable enterprises (publicly traded companies). Partnerships are considered privately held businesses which are not subject to the IFRS conversion. However, private businesses can still be impacted by IFRS as some of the IFRS principles are embedded in the new GAAP.

In Summary

- ⇨ A partnership differs from a proprietorship in the number of owners, the way in which earnings are divided, and the manner in which disagreement and conflict are settled.

- ⇨ The characteristics of a partnership reveal several advantages and disadvantages, all of which must be carefully considered before choosing this form of business.

- ⇨ A general partnership means that all partners have unlimited liability.

- ⇨ A limited partnership divides a company's partners into two categories: general partners and limited partners. Unlimited liability extends to general partners because they are involved in the day-to-day decision making of the business. Limited partners, on the other hand, are only liable for the amount of capital they invest in the business. This is known as limited liability.

- ⇨ A limited liability partnership or LLP is a legal ownership structure, used in some jurisdictions, that usually protects professionals from a partner's negligence. If one of the partners gets sued, the others are not necessarily liable. However, all the partners are liable for any debts owed to regular "day-to-day" creditors.

- ⇨ A partnership's earnings can be divided in a number of different ways; these are usually outlined in the partnership agreement. Four common methods of dividing earnings are the following: equally; based on a ratio; based on the capital contribution of each partner; and drawing salaries before dividing the rest.

- ⇨ Various stipulations can be made in a partnership agreement to accommodate the addition or withdrawal of partners. For example, a new partner can simply add in a new portion of partner's equity, or purchase some or all of another partner's share.

- ⇨ The negotiated value of a partner's worth to a business might differ from what eventually appears in the books. On one hand, a partner may pay more than book value because goodwill or other factors make it worth more. On the other hand, other partners may require a new partner to pay less, as the new partner may bring added value to the business, such as a distinguished client list.

- ⇨ Partnerships may eventually be liquidated. The partnership agreement should stipulate how this should be done. If assets are sold above or below book value, the corresponding earnings or losses are shared among the partners. The remaining cash can be distributed according to a ratio based on each partner's capital contribution.

Review Exercise

Zelma Rapoza, Serena Dennen and Sharron Throop have decided to set up a spa and operate it as a partnership. They will each contribute $10,000 to buy equipment and help pay for lease expenses. Zelma is also contributing $25,000 of her own equipment.

They agreed to pay themselves a yearly salary of $5,000 each. Since Zelma contributed the equipment, she expects $3,000 "rent" per year on the equipment for ten years. Each partner is to earn 5% on their investment (cash contribution). The net income for the year was $25,000. The profit remaining after salaries, rent, and interest is to be distributed at ratio of their cash contribution.

Required:

a) Prepare a schedule showing the changes in capital during the year.

b) Provide the journal entries that:

   i)   Record the initial cash contribution

   ii) Record the equipment contribution

   iii) Record the division of partnership income. Assume that revenues and expenses have already been closed to the income summary account."

Review Exercise - Answer

Part a)

	Total	Zelma	Serena	Sharron
Cash Contribution	$30,000	$10,000	$10,000	$10,000
Contribution of Equipment	25,000	25,000		
Partner Contributions	$55,000	$35,000	$10,000	$10,000
Net Income	$25,000			
Salaries	-15,000	5,000	5,000	5,000
Equipment Rental	-3,000	3,000		
Interest	-1,500	500	500	500
Division of Income	5,500	1,834	1,833	1,833
Addition to Partners' Capital		$10,334	$7,333	$7,333
Closing Capital Balance	$80,000	$45,334	$17,333	$17,333

Part b)

Date	Account Title and Explanation	Debit	Credit
	Cash	30,000	
	Capital - Rapoza		10,000
	Capital - Dennen		10,000
	Capital - Throop		10,000
	To record set up of partnership		
	Equipment	25,000	
	Capital - Rapoza		25,000
	To record contribution of equipment		
	Income Summary	25,000	
	Capital - Rapoza		10,334
	Capital - Dennen		7,333
	Capital - Throop		7,333
	To adjust partners' capital accounts for their share of net income		

Chapter 10

CORPORATIONS: SHARE CAPITAL AND DIVIDENDS

LEARNING OUTCOMES:

❶ Describe the characteristics of corporate organizations

❷ Outline the advantages and disadvantages of corporations

❸ Understand financial statements and shareholders' equity

❹ Record the issuance of shares

❺ Describe the differences between common shares and preferred shares

❻ Record the payment of dividends

❼ Record share dividends and share splits

The Professionalization of the Ownership Structure

Almost everyone has heard of **corporations**, shares and stock markets but few may know what it all means and how various components interact with one another. This chapter will bring clarity and understanding to the various issues involved with corporations — especially where ownership issues are concerned.

In essence, the corporation brings business ownership to the next level. We have already discussed how partnerships involve adding more owners to a business. In this chapter, we will demonstrate the various ways in which corporations are different from both proprietorships and partnerships. Corporations come with many advantages, but they also come with some additional responsibilities.

Proprietorships and partnerships have a common characteristic of not separating the owner from the business in a legal sense. Owners are ultimately responsible for the debts of the business, and can be held accountable. On the other hand, any corporation, large or small, is legally separate from the owners. This means the owners are not responsible for the debts of the business. In some cases, owners of a corporation may have very little to do in managing the business.

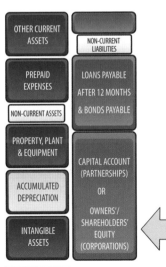

FIGURE 10.1

At the heart of a corporation is the separation of ownership and management. In a large publicly traded company, the company's shareholders do not necessarily run the business. Generally speaking, the business is run by executives hired by representatives of the shareholders: the board of directors. This three-way relationship within a corporation can be complex and can sometimes lead to turmoil. However, it is also one of the foundations of our current economic system, which is why accountants need to be intimately familiar with how corporations work and how their finances are managed.

Public vs. Private Corporation

A corporation can be classified as either a public or private corporation. A **public corporation** has shares listed on a stock exchange. That is, its shares are available to be traded "publicly" from one member of the general public (the current shareholder) to another (the purchaser). "Trading" simply means buying or selling. Microsoft, Apple, and Toyota are only a few of many well-known public corporations. The

WORTH REPEATING...

Recall that the three main forms are organizations are sole proprietorships, partnerships and corporations. A sole proprietorship is a small business owned and generally operated by one owner. A partnership is a non-corporation owned by two or more partners. Lastly, a corporation is a business that is registered with the government as a separate legal entity from its owners.

shares of Microsoft and Apple are traded on the NASDAQ stock exchange and Toyota shares are traded on the New York Stock Exchange (NYSE).

On the other hand, a **private corporation** does not offer its shares to the general public in a stock market exchange. The company's shares are, instead, owned and exchanged privately. For example, a private company may have a single owner who wishes never to sell his shares publicly. Another common example of a private corporation is a company with several owners that belong to the same family, who have no intentions of selling shares on a stock exchange. A private corporation is also commonly known as a closed corporation or a privately held corporation.

The following table shows the classification of various entities.

Entity or Individual	Classification
Toyota	Public Corporation
IKEA[1]	Private Corporation
PricewaterhouseCoopers	Partnership[2]
Bill Gates	Shareholder
Jim's Corner Bread Bakery[3]	Sole Proprietorship

(1) IKEA's few shares are held privately
(2) All partnerships are essentially "privately-owned"
(3) Assume that Jim is the single owner of the company

FIGURE 10.2

IN THE REAL WORLD

In Canada, a private corporation can be regarded as a Canadian-controlled private corporation (CCPC). Keep in mind that not all private corporations that operate in Canada are classified as CCPCs. Certain requirements must be met for a private company in Canada to qualify as a CCPC.

Before discussing the requirements to qualify as a CCPC, it is important to briefly mention why a private enterprise would to choose to become a CCPC. A CCPC has corporate tax advantages. A discussion of the specific tax benefits are outside the scope of this course. However, some corporate tax advantages include: additional time to pay some taxes, higher investment tax credits and potential capital gains exemptions.

There are several requirements for a company to qualify as a registered CCPC in Canada. Shown below are a few of these requirements:

- The company's shares are not traded on a stock exchange (i.e. it must be a generic private corporation)
- The corporation is a resident in Canada
- The corporation is not directly or indirectly controlled by a non-resident shareholder

The financial reporting requirements for private companies are different from those of public companies. The reporting standards for public corporations are generally more strict and detailed than those for private companies since more external users depend on the financial statements of public corporations. We will explore these differences in the following sections.

Public vs. Private Corporations: Implications under IFRS

In Canada, all publicly traded companies were required to adopt International Financial Reporting Standards (IFRS) by January 1, 2011. All public corporations have no other option but to be IFRS-compliant at this point.

On the other hand, private corporations are given an option. They can decide to either adopt IFRS, or they can use Accounting Standards for Private Enterprises (ASPE), which is embedded in GAAP. ASPE is also commonly referred to as Private Enterprise GAAP.

Private Corporation Reporting Method

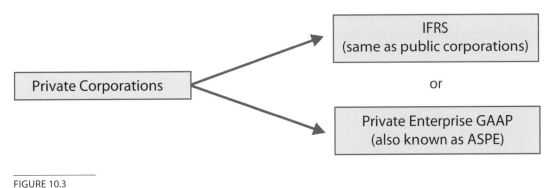

FIGURE 10.3

Some of the reasons that a private corporation may choose to continue to use private enterprise GAAP is because they are resistant to change or do not wish to incur the high costs of transitioning to IFRS. Also, since IFRS can be quite technical and strict when compared to ASPE, staying with private enterprise GAAP reduces the amount of work that must be done to prepare financial statements.

On the other hand, a private corporation may choose to switch from GAAP to IFRS because they are considering becoming a public corporation in the near future and would have to adopt IFRS anyway. Switching to IFRS may also be a good option if the corporation has international operations or wishes to compare its own financial statements to international competitors.

Most private corporations are ultimately deciding to remain with GAAP and not switch to IFRS. Whatever the corporation's final decision may be, it should also consider the specific technical differences between private enterprise GAAP and IFRS. A few of the differences are listed below:

- IFRS allows capital assets (property, plant and equipment) to be measured at fair value at each balance sheet date; GAAP does not.

- Shares, bonds and other investments can have different values reported on the balance sheet between GAAP and IFRS, depending on how they are classified.

- The value of goodwill may be stated differently under GAAP and IFRS due to differences in recognizing any impairment.

At this time, no specific section exists tailored for private companies within IFRS (whereas one does exist under GAAP, called ASPE, as discussed earlier). Therefore, if a private corporation chooses to adopt IFRS, they would be following the same rules as a public corporation. The International Accounting Standards Board (IASB) is the entity responsible for developing and maintaining IFRS. IASB is currently working on designing a specific section for private companies within IFRS. This is being done in an attempt to meet the reporting needs of private organizations and to move towards the full harmonization of IFRS.

The focus of this chapter and the next will be public corporations and how to account for the various aspects of them. As such, statements will be shown in accordance to IFRS guidelines in addition to GAAP guidelines. But first, we must discuss the characteristics of corporations in detail.

Corporate Structure: Separating Management from Ownership

Corporations are legal entities whose primary characteristic is the legal separation of those who run the business from those who own the business. Specifically, owners of a corporation consist of the people who own shares in the company. Alternatively, management consists of people hired to protect the interests of shareholders, while delivering the goods or services provided by the company. The board of directors is established to ensure that management is accountable to ownership.

When examining proprietorships, partnerships, and corporations, it becomes clear that the ownership structure is taken to the next level in the way that money is raised and the company is managed.

> **WORTH REPEATING…**
>
> There are three primary options for structuring the ownership of a business:
> 1. In a proprietorship, only one person owns the business and keeps all the earnings which are taxed on the personal level.
> 2. A partnership is an association of two or more people who jointly own a business, its assets and liabilities, and share in its gains or losses; earnings are taxed personally
> 3. In a corporation, there can be a large number of owners known as shareholders, many of whom may not participate in the day-to-day activities of the business. Earnings are taxed twice. Once at the corporate level and then, again, at the personal level (e.g. dividends).

With respect to how money is raised, corporations do not rely solely on the finances of the proprietor, or on the financing capability of its partners. Instead, corporations can potentially raise large sums of money by issuing shares to the public. Indeed, large corporations can issue many shares in order to raise large sums of money. This basic principle of corporate finance is what drives the shares market. The people who buy and sell shares on *Wall Street* are essentially exchanging a share of ownership in some of America's largest companies — and they're doing it on a daily basis.

To manage and run the business, corporations are not necessarily dependent on the brilliance of one proprietor, or on the specialties exhibited by various partners. In fact, large corporations don't rely on the business expertise of those who actually own the business: the shareholders.

Instead, large corporations rely on the expertise of hired management to run the business for them. This is why corporations have a board of directors to hire the management team, usually headed by the company's chief executive officer (CEO). In turn, the CEO presides over a team of executives responsible for various aspects of running the business.

Generally, executives are specialized and often well-trained professionals who graduate from business school and make their way up the corporate ladder. At medical school, people can learn to become doctors; at business school, they can start learning to become corporate executives.

Chapter 9 included a chart which summarized the advantages and disadvantages associated with a partnership. The following chart provides something similar with respect to corporations:

Advantages of Corporations

- *Fixed organizational structure.* The board of directors represents the interests of shareholders and is responsible for hiring executives and setting the broad direction of the organization.
- *The power to raise money.* Shares can be issued to raise amounts of money that would be much more difficult to obtain solely using the resources of proprietors or partners.
- *Limited liability.* Shareholders are only held liable for the value of the shares they hold.
- *Liquidity of shares.* The ability to sell shares quickly on the market makes them attractive investment vehicles, without affecting the stability of the business. In other words, management continues to function even while shares continue to be traded.
- *Tax treatment.* Although the business itself pays taxes, shareholders do not, until dividends are paid out.
- *Unlimited life.* The corporation remains an entity regardless of the comings and goings of shareholders. This is unlike proprietorships and partnerships which end when an owner leaves the company (with the exception of Limited Partnerships).
- *Professional management.* With proprietorships and partnerships, the owners may or may not possess specific or specialized expertise. With corporations, the board of directors ensures the hiring of experts exhibiting specialties in countless fields.

Disadvantages of Corporations

- *Red tape.* Although the corporate structure brings with it many advantages, the structure also comes with legalities that can require lawyers to be hired, forms to be completed and documents to be prepared and filed.
- *Annual requirements.* Many obligations need to be met on an annual basis, including: corporate fees, audits, financial reports, shareholder meetings, board meetings, etc.
- *Double Taxation.* Governments tax corporate earnings; shareholders who receive some of those earnings in the form of dividends are also taxed.

In a nutshell, the corporate form of ownership allows businesses to do things on a bigger scale and in a professional manner. Yet these advantages come with regulatory and bureaucratic responsibilities that can be costly and time consuming.

Financial Statements and Shareholders' Equity

As the ownership structure gets more complicated, so does the way owners' equity is divided and reported on the balance sheet. With a proprietorship, owner's equity is literally a simple figure that represents net worth. With partnerships, owners' equity gets divided into capital accounts that outline each partner's stake in the business. With corporations, things are more complicated.

When referring to corporations, the term **shareholders' equity** is used in place of owners' equity since the shareholders actually own the company. Shareholders' equity is further divided into **share**

capital (or paid-in capital) and **retained earnings**. Both get reported separately in the shareholders' equity section of the company's financial statements.

Share capital includes all the information related to a company's shares, including the types or "*class*" of shares issued, the number of shares authorized, and the number of shares that is issued or "*outstanding*".

Retained earnings is relatively simple to define. It represents the part of a company's earnings that have not been distributed to shareholders in the form of dividends. In other words, the earnings *not* paid out to shareholders are *retained* in the business. Retained earnings can then be used for business purposes in the future.

As an example, let us take a look at the shareholders' equity section of a sample company for the fiscal year 2011 as shown in figure 10.4.

Sample Company Statement of Shareholders' Equity As at December 31, 2011	
Shareholders' Equity	(in thousands of $)
Share Capital	
Preferred shares, $2, 10,000 shares authorized, 3,000 shares issued and outstanding	$12,000
Common shares, unlimited shares authorized, 50,000 shares issued and outstanding	5,000,000
Total Share Capital	5,012,000
Retained Earnings	240,000
Total Shareholder's Equity	$5,252,000

FIGURE 10.4

To properly create the shareholders equity portion of a corporation, several values must be calculated. The quantity of shares that have been sold (issued) through the stock market must be shown for all classes of shares (common and preferred). The characteristics of common and preferred shares will be discussed later in this chapter. Also, the total value that the shares were sold for must be shown. This is considered the book value of the shares, and the value does not change as market prices for the shares increase or decrease.

Retained earnings must be calculated at the end of each period. The calculation for retained earnings is:

Ending Retained Earnings = Beginning Retained Earnings + Net Income – Dividends

A dividend is a distribution of the profits to shareholders, and will be covered in more detail later in this chapter. As an example to calculate retained earnings, suppose a company started 2011 with $100,000 in retained earnings. During the year, they earned a net income of $40,000 and paid dividends to shareholders in the amount of $15,000. Figure 10.5 shows how to calculate the value of retained earnings at the end of 2011.

Sample Company Statement of Retained Earnings For the Year Ended December 31, 2011	
Retained Earnings – January 1, 2011	$100,000
Add: Net Income	40,000
Less: Dividends	15,000
Retained Earnings – December 31, 2011	$125,000

FIGURE 10.5

You may notice that calculating the ending value of retained earnings is quite similar to calculating the ending value of owner's equity in a proprietorship.

The figure below presents the equity portion of Bombardier's consolidated balance sheet for their year-end 2011 and how they calculated the change in retained earnings for 2011. Bombardier's equity section is composed of common shares, preferred shares, retained earnings and other equity items that are beyond the scope of this course.

Bombardier Consolidated Balance Sheet (an excerpt) As at January 31, 2011 (in millions of U.S. dollars)	
Equity	
Preferred shares	347
Common shareholders' equity	3,927
Equity attributable to shareholders of Bombardier Inc.	4,274
Equity attributable to non-controlling interests	78

Bombardier Consolidated Statement of Changes in Equity (an excerpt) For the Fiscal Year Ended January 31, 2011 (in millions of U.S. dollars)	
Retained earnings	
Balance at beginning of year	2,087
Net income attributable to shareholders of Bombardier Inc.	755
Excess of price paid over carrying value of repurchased Class B Shares	(13)

Dividends:
    Common shares
    Preferred shares, net of tax
	
	(173)
	(24)

Balance at end of year	2,632

Taken from Bombardier Annual Report, Year Ended January 31, 2011, pages 162 and 167.

Accessed from the website ir.bombardier.com, October, 2011.

FIGURE 10.6

There are various terms regarding corporate shares and the shares market that all financial personnel, including accountants, need to familiarize themselves with. For example:

Company shares represent a stake in ownership. In essence, a share represents a claim to assets, if liquidated, once all debts have been paid. However, the share price is often more of a reflection of shares market forces than of the book value of assets.

Authorized shares refer to the way a company issues shares. Some authorize an unlimited number of shares - they issue as many as they like when they feel the time is right. Others authorize a limited amount, and additional authorization is required in order to issue more.

Outstanding shares are those that have already been issued and are eligible to be traded on the secondary market by those who hold them. Although a company can authorize an unlimited amount of shares, they are only created upon issue and entry into the market in some way.

Par value for shares is essentially the same as par value for bonds - their original value is actually printed on the issued certificate itself. Since the market has become accustomed to setting the price of shares, par value shares are now less common.

The corporate charter of a company is essentially its founding document, which lists details that are necessary to its operation, including its name, purpose, and general objectives. The charter will also stipulate the number of shares authorized for issue by corporate representatives.

Issuing Shares

One of the strengths of adopting a corporate form of ownership involves the amount of money that can be raised by issuing and selling shares to the public. However, shares can also be issued in exchange for something other than money.

We will outline three ways in which shares can be issued and examine how they are accounted for on the company's books.

Issuing shares in exchange for cash

The most common reason for issuing shares is for the purpose of raising capital. Suppose a company issues 1,000 common shares, at $10 each, to raise a total of $10,000.

Here is how the transaction would be recorded:

JOURNAL			
Date	Account Title and Explanation	Debit	Credit
	Cash	10,000	
	Common Shares		10,000
	Issue of 1,000 common shares for cash		

BALANCE SHEET

CURRENT ASSETS	CURRENT LIABILITIES
CASH **+ 10,000 (DR)**	LOANS PAYABLE (CURRENT)
SHORT TERM INVESTMENT	SHAREHOLDERS' LOANS
ACCOUNTS RECEIVABLE	NON-CURRENT LIABILITIES
DOUBTFUL ACCOUNTS	LOANS PAYABLE (NON-CURRENT)
	SHAREHOLDER'S EQUITY
INVENTORY	SHARE CAPITAL **+ 10,000 (CR)**
PREPAID EXPENSES	RETAINED EARNINGS

FIGURE 10.7

In fact, the transaction is relatively straightforward. The receipt of $10,000 is recorded as a debit to cash, and the corresponding credit is made in the common shares account within the Share Capital section of the balance sheet.

However, not every type of shares issuance is as straightforward as this exchange for cash.

Issuing shares in exchange for assets

Shares represent ownership in a company that has some value. Although that value can be determined by issuing and selling shares on the market, it can also be determined by an exchange of some other kind. An example of such an exchange might involve assets instead of cash.

In other words, a company might issue shares for the purpose of receiving assets in return. For example, here's the transaction to be recorded if a company issues 1,000 shares in exchange for land that is valued at $1,000,000.

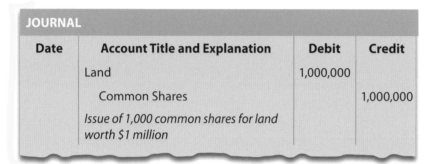
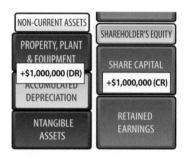

FIGURE 10.8

The receipt of the land is *capitalized* and recorded as a debit in the appropriate fixed asset account, which in this case falls under *property, plant & equipment*. The corresponding $1,000,000 credit is recorded in the common shares account.

Note that the $1,000,000 amount for the land should represent its fair value, and be determined by some objective appraisement.

Issuing shares in exchange for services

In the past, it was commonplace for shares to be issued in exchange for services rather than assets. Nowadays, however, the opposite is true. Nevertheless, it may be beneficial to show an example that involves share issuance in exchange for services rendered.

Example: A new corporation obtained the services of an accountant. The services amounted to a cost of $10,000. Given that this is a new corporation, $10,000 expenditure might be considered quite costly. As an alternative, the company offers the accountant an issuance of shares worth $10,000. The accountant accepts because he's an experienced investor and is confident that the shares will be worth much more in the not-too-distant future. Here is how that transaction is recorded on the company's books:

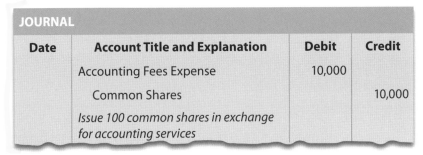

JOURNAL			
Date	**Account Title and Explanation**	**Debit**	**Credit**
	Accounting Fees Expense	10,000	
	Common Shares		10,000
	Issue 100 common shares in exchange for accounting services		

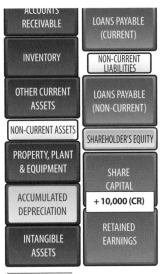

FIGURE 10.9

In this example, $10,000 is expensed in the form of a debit to the appropriate income statement account. As in the other examples, the share capital account receives the corresponding credit. Given the nature of such a transaction, the cash account remains untouched.

Issuing Shares that are Common or Preferred

As we have already mentioned, one of the justifications for establishing a corporate form of ownership is to raise more money. By giving the public the opportunity to buy a stake in the company, the company has access to potentially large amounts of financing.

However, as with most aspects of modern business and finance, methods have been developed to sweeten the pot even further for potential investors, while at the same time giving corporations some flexibility in the way they finance their business. With regard to company shares, this involves offering different classes of shares: **common** versus **preferred**.

Typically, when people discuss company shares, they are referring to a company's **common shares**. Common shares represents ownership in the company, which means that they come with voting rights that involve selection of a board of directors and establishment of corporate policies.

Investors purchase common shares with the expectation that the corporation will remain or become profitable and, thus, pay out dividends. These dividends, however, are paid out at the discretion of the board of directors. So it is possible for an investor in a profitable company to not receive dividends.

In order to sweeten the pot for some investors, some corporations will issue what are called **preferred shares**. In essence, preferred shares addresses the primary disadvantage that comes with common shares (that dividend payments are not guaranteed). Preferred shares come with regular and fixed dividend payments. It is this characteristic of preferred shares that makes them similar to bonds (making regular payments in the form of interest).

Preferred shares have other attributes that are similar to bonds. Specifically, they both rank ahead of common shares with regard to a claim on assets. In the event of liquidation, bondholders have a claim on assets before preferred shareholders, who, in turn, have a claim before common shareholders. However, as with bondholders, preferred shareholders have no voting rights regarding the direction of the company. In this sense, it is only common shareholders that maintain this specific right of company ownership, and it is an important one.

Features of common shares

- Represent ownership in the corporation
- Owners elect the board of directors
- Owners vote on corporate policy
- Owners rank after bondholders and preferred shareholders in the event of a liquidation
- Owners have a right to receive dividends only if declared by the directors

---

Features of preferred shares

- Owners have a higher claim on assets and earnings than do common shareholders
- Owners generally get paid a regular dividend, especially before any dividends are paid to common shareholders
- Preferred shares often have the right to accumulate dividends from previous years. If a dividend on cumulative preferred shares are missed, it will accumulate and will have to be paid off before any dividend payments are made to the common shareholders
- **Dividends in arrears** are the amount of dividends on cumulative preferred shares from past periods that have not been paid. It is not a liability, but should be subtracted from the shareholder's equity.

Par and No Par Value Shares

Both common and preferred shares can be sold with the feature of **"par value"** or **"no-par value"**.

Par value shares are shares that are issued with a stated value. Although some countries may allow shares with a par value to be issued, the *Canada Business Corporations Act* indicates that corporations in Canada are not allowed to issue par value shares. Instead, Canadian corporations must issue no-par value shares.

No-par value means that the shares have no "stated value" so that when they are sold, the equity account is credited for the entire proceeds. If 1,000 shares were sold for $15 per share, the following journal entry would be recorded:

JOURNAL			
Date	Account Title and Explanation	Debit	Credit
	Cash	15,000	
	Common Shares		15,000
	Issued 1,000 shares of no-par common shares for $15 per share		

FIGURE 10.10

Accounting for Cash Dividends

From an investor's standpoint, there are two monetary reasons to buy shares in a company. One reason is the anticipation of a capital gain if the share price rises. The other reason is the anticipation of annual **dividend payments**.

A corporation's share price may not be entirely within management's control as it fluctuates depending on macroeconomic factors, investor confidence and analysts' recommendations. The frequency and level of dividend payments, however, are within management's control (management can set the terms of dividend payments).

Given the amount of control and responsibility that a company has over the payment of dividends, and the predictability usually associated with this responsibility, accountants need to be familiar with the transactions involved.

First, there are three dates to be kept in mind relative to dividends:

- *The date of declaration:* when the directors make the decision (or declaration) that a dividend payment is to be made to shareholders.
- *The date of record:* all those holding shares on this date are eligible to receive the dividend payment that has been declared.
- *The date of payment:* when the company eventually makes the dividend payment to eligible shareholders.

We'll examine what the company's accounting responsibilities are, relative to each of these dates.

On the date of declaration

If a company decides that a dividend payment of $10,000 is in order on December 1st, and sets the terms of the payment, a journal entry like this would be recorded:

JOURNAL			
Date	Account Title and Explanation	Debit	Credit
Dec 1	Retained Earnings	10,000	
	Dividends Payable		10,000
	Dividend payable of $1 per share on 10,000 shares		

Dividends are paid from operating income after taxes have been deducted. Dividends cannot be paid if the resulting balance in retained earnings is negative. This rule can be different in some jurisdictions.

FIGURE 10.11

Although the payment is not made right away, the company must subtract the amount of the payment from retained earnings (debit), while establishing and crediting the dividends payable account under current liabilities. In other words, the dividend payment is accrued until payment is finally made.

You will notice that the item is not expensed, since dividend payments do not constitute a normal operating expense, so the transaction does not involve the income statement portion of the financial statements.

Although the amount of $10,000 was used in this specific example, the amount of a dividend is ultimately determined by a company's board of directors. Of course, the company must have the cash to make the dividend payment. This means that there should be enough cash to pay the dividends which the company owes .

On the date of record

The challenge for a corporation regarding the date of record is not so much one of accounting as it is one of recordkeeping. In other words, the company must determine who its shareholders are on the date of record so that it knows who is eligible for the declared dividend payment.

The person responsible for this is the corporate secretary. This person is in charge of all official company documentation. Among other things, this responsibility involves maintaining and examining the company's share register, which serves much like a subledger, by listing information on a per individual basis. Additionally, some large corporations obtain the services of a transfer agent to record changes in ownership of shares as a result of trading on the shares market.

On the date of payment

Finally, the company's accountant must record the transaction to be made on the date of payment, which is essentially a closing out of the dividend payable liability created on the date of declaration. Assume the date of payment is December 12; here is how this is done:

JOURNAL			
Date	Account Title and Explanation	Debit	Credit
Dec 12	Dividends Payable	10,000	
	Cash		10,000
	Payment of dividend declared (date)		

FIGURE 10.12

Since the payment is finally made, it is the cash account that receives the credit, while the original dividends payable account that was established gets closed out with the debit decrease of $10,000.

Dividends in Arrears

Dividends in arrears occurs when preferred shares are present with a cumulative feature, the corporation must consider or include the amount owing to the preferred shareholders from previous years.

For example: on December 31, 2010, Corporation ABC declared $100,000 dividends, payable on January 10, 2011 to the shareholders. There are 100,000 common shares and 20,000, $2, cumulative preferred shares issued. No dividends have been declared since the end of 2008. This means the corporation owes the preferred shareholders a total of $80,000 ($2 × 20,000 from year 2009 and $2 × 20,000 from year 2010). The journal entry to record the declaration and subsequent payment of the above dividends is shown in figure 10.13 and 10.14:

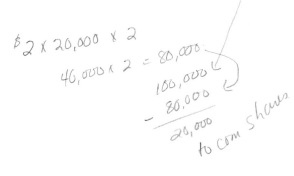

declare

JOURNAL

Date	Account Title and Explanation	Debit	Credit
Dec 31	Retained Earnings	100,000	
	Dividends Payable – Preferred		80,000
	Dividends Payable – Common		20,000
	Dividend payable on 20,000 preferred shares and 100,000 common shares		

FIGURE 10.13

pay

JOURNAL

Date	Account Title and Explanation	Debit	Credit
Jan 10	Dividends Payable – Preferred	80,000	
	Dividends Payable – Common	20,000	
	Cash		100,000
	Payment of dividend declared		

FIGURE 10.14

CURRENT ASSETS

CASH
Jan 10th
-100,000 (CR)

SHORT TERM INVESTMENTS

ACCOUNTS RECEIVABLE

DOUBTFUL ACCOUNTS

INVENTORY

PREPAID EXPENSES

OTHER CURRENT ASSETS

NON-CURRENT ASSETS

PROPERTY, PLANT & EQUIPMENT

ACCUMULATED DEPRECIATION

INTANGIBLE ASSETS

CURRENT LIABILITIES

ACCOUNTS PAYABLE & ACCRUED LIABILITIES
Dec 31st
+100,000 (CR)
Jan 10th
-100,000 (DR)

LOANS PAYABLE (CURRENT)

SHAREHOLDERS' LOANS

NON-CURRENT LIABILITIES

LOANS PAYABLE (NON-CURRENT)

BONDS PAYABLE

SHAREHOLDER'S EQUITY

SHARE CAPITAL

RETAINED EARNINGS
Dec 31st
-100,000 (DR)

Shares Splits and Share Dividends

A **shares split** is a corporate action that increases the number of a corporation's outstanding shares which in turn diminishes the individual price of each share. For example, with a 2-for-1 shares split, each shareholder now owns two shares for every one share they held in the company; however, the value of each share is reduced by half. Because the total value of the shares outstanding is not affected, no journal entry is needed to account for a shares split. A memorandum (note) is usually recorded indicating the decreased per share value and increased number of shares outstanding.

One of the main reasons for splitting shares is to increase their liquidity. If the price of a share is too high, some investors may feel the shares are too expensive or unaffordable. An example demonstrating how expensive shares can be is the case of Berkshire Hathaway, a conglomerate holding company headquartered in Omaha, which has never had a shares split. On December 13, 2007, Berkshire's "Class A" shares closed at an all-time high of $150,000 per share. The refusal to split the shares reflects the management's desire to attract long-term as opposed to short-term investors.

Share dividends may be issued in lieu of cash dividends when the company chooses to retain cash in the company. If a corporation declares a share dividend of its own shares of the same class, each shareholder will own a larger number of shares, but the same percentage of the business as before.

For example, on December 31, 2010, Corporation ABC has 100,000 common shares issued. Current market price is $10 per share. The company decided to declare a 20% shares dividend. The journal entry to record the declaration and distribution of the dividend is shown in figure 10.15.

JOURNAL			
Date	**Account Title and Explanation**	**Debit**	**Credit**
Dec 31	Retained Earnings	200,000	
	Common Share Dividends Distributable		200,000
	Share dividend of 20,000 shares		

JOURNAL			
Date	**Account Title and Explanation**	**Debit**	**Credit**
Jan 10	Common Share Dividends Distributable	200,000	
	Common Shares		200,000
	To record distribution of 20,000 shares		

SHAREHOLDER'S EQUITY

SHARE CAPITAL

Jan 10th
+200,000 (CR)

COMMON SHARE DIVIDEND DISTRIBUTABLE

Dec 31st
+200,000 (CR)

Jan 10th
-200,000 (DR)

RETAINED EARNINGS

Dec 31st
-200,000 (DR)

FIGURE 10.15

The account *Common Share Dividend Distributable* is an equity account, not a liability (like the Dividends Payable account used for cash dividends). The end result of a share dividend is a rearrangement of the makeup of shareholders equity. Some of the value of retained earnings is moved to the common shares account. Since only equity will be impacted by this series of transactions, only equity accounts will be used. Also, since there will be no transfer of assets, there will be no promise to pay any assets (i.e. no liability).

All of the above transactions illustrate how public corporations account for issuing shares and recording dividends. For private corporations, issuing shares would be recorded in the same manner as illustrated. However, the recording and paying of dividends is usually less formal for private corporations because the shares are not publicly traded and the list of shareholders is usually short.

319

An Ethical Approach to Corporations and Insider Trading

One of the most important ethical principles for all businesses, large or small, is the need to maintain the integrity of information released publicly, which is why **insider trading** is considered one of the worst violations at the corporate level.

As some of the discussion in this chapter has already revealed, the shares market can be an unpredictable animal at the best of times. Market trends can fluctuate, speculation can run rampant, and even the most informed investors can have a difficult time making the right decisions.

Nevertheless, one of the basic foundations of the shares market is fair and public access to all company-related information. In other words, if current or potential shareholders have a right to information about a company, then it should be disclosed to the public in a timely fashion.

Insider trading occurs when anyone involved with a company discloses shareholder-relevant information privately, before it is released publicly. For example, a secretary in a company might overhear information on an upcoming announcement of better-than expected company earnings for the year. This secretary may have a close friend who invests in shares, and she passes on this information to him.

Knowing that the announcement will increase the price, the friend buys a large amount of shares and might even tell a few of his friends.

By the time the announcement is finally made, the price of the shares may have increased dramatically, and the friend and his friends may have made a substantial amount of money. This, of course, is highly illegal. Everyone involved should be charged with insider trading. The crime is very serious and comes with some harsh penalties.

The purpose of insider trading laws is to give everyone a fair chance to make profits on the shares market — given the same amount of information. That is why securities regulators go to great lengths to detect the spread of information by way of insider activity. As tempting as it might be to tell a friend what's going on inside the company before anyone else knows, doing so violates the principle of fairness and openness that exists in world markets. Anything less threatens the way that capitalism and free markets should work.

IN THE REAL WORLD

Celebrity homemaking and insider trading are two concepts that do not often come to mind at the same time. However, anything is bound to happen when shares market, money and celebrity ambition clash with one another. That is precisely what happened to Martha Stewart, and her activities in the world of finance.

What most people do not know is that Martha Stewart rose to fame and fortune by way of the shares market. In the late 1990s, she took Martha Stewart Living Omnimedia Inc. public and made a fortune on the subsequent rise of the company's shares. This is not the road to the top that most people associate with celebrity, but it is one that worked miracles for the rising homemaking star.

Stewart's familiarity and success with the shares market, however, was ultimately responsible for her downfall. It all started to unravel in late 2001 with events surrounding shares of a company called ImClone, which is a biopharmaceutical corporation.

During that period, ImClone shares took a tumble as a result of regulatory procedures that were detrimental to the company. Records show that Stewart sold almost 4,000 shares in the company, making her a gain of $229,000, shortly before public disclosure about the regulations.

It appears that Stewart was good friends with Samuel Waksel, the CEO of ImClone. Investigations revealed that Stewart was advised by her sharesbroker, Peter Bacanovic, to sell her shares, based on information he was privy to regarding Waksel. The situation was a clear case of insider trading.

As is often the case with insider trading, however, it is very hard to prove who knew what and when. The investigators therefore focused on the cover-up, and discovered that Stewart had deceived investigators numerous times as they tried to gather information on insider activity in this case. In July of 2004, she was found guilty of obstructing justice and served a five-month sentence.

The IFRS Perspective

As part of the set of financial statements prepare under IFRS is a Statement of Changes in Equity. The equity section of a corporation can have other components besides share capital and retained earnings (such as other comprehensive income, revaluation surplus or transactions of foreign operations). Every component of equity must show a reconciliation between the opening balance and the balance at the end of the period.

In Summary

⇨ The shares of public corporations are traded on a stock market exchange whereas the shares of private corporations are not.

⇨ All public corporations must comply with IFRS. Private corporations have the option to adopt IFRS like public corporations or continue relying on Private Enterprise GAAP.

⇨ Corporations take business ownership to the next level by separating ownership, in the form of shares, from management, in the form of executives. The board of directors serves the interests of ownership by hiring senior executives who together establish the broad objectives of the corporation.

⇨ Corporations essentially divide the shareholders' equity section of the balance sheet into share capital and retained earnings. Share capital is represented by the different classes of shares, common and preferred, and their respective values (dollar amount and number of shares issued and outstanding).

⇨ Retained earnings represent the amount of equity that the company has kept in the business and not distributed to shareholders.

⇨ While dividing corporations into shares allows companies to raise much larger sums of money, it can also create difficulties in terms of control of ownership and uncontrolled changes in the company's share price.

⇨ Although issuing shares in exchange for money is most common, and constitutes the essence of the shares market, a company can also issue shares in exchange for other things of value, such as assets owned or services rendered.

⇨ A company has a choice of issuing common or preferred shares. Common shares constitute ownership in the company, but doesn't come with guaranteed dividend payments. Preferred shares, on the other hand, doesn't come with voting rights, but does come with regular dividend payments and a higher claim to company assets than with common shares.

⇨ There are three important dates that an accountant must keep track of with respect to the payment of dividends: the date of declaration, the date of record, and the date of payment.

⇨ The book value of shares essentially represents that portion of company assets that would belong to shareholders upon liquidation. In an ideal world, book value would equal market value with respect to shares. However, various market forces allow for the two values to deviate from one another — sometimes by a significant amount.

⇨ Insider trading involves one of the greatest violations of information integrity at the corporate level by revealing facts to private individuals that should be disclosed openly and fairly to the public at large.

Review Exercise

Marcel Canpos and Fidel Feisthamel have operated their company as a partnership for several years. Over the years, the company has grown, and the partners believe that it is appropriate to incorporate their company (as Camphamel Limited) and raise more capital to expand to further geographic areas.

Accordingly, Marcel and Fidel engaged a qualified bookkeeper to provide accounting services for their new corporation. The corporate charter authorized the company to issue an unlimited number of common shares and 100,000, $3 preferred shares worth $100 each. On March 3, 2010, the partners transferred assets worth $2,000,000 and liabilities worth $1,250,000 to the company in exchange for 20,000 shares.

Then, Marcel and Fidel proceeded to seek investment capital from private investors. On April 15, 2010, a group of investors agreed to buy a further 20,000 shares for $1,000,000 cash.

Instead of paying the accountant $100,000 of fees in cash, Marcel and Fidel gave the accountant 1,000, $3 preferred shares on April 30, 2010. (These shares have a total value of $100,000.)

For the year ended December 31, 2010, the newly incorporated company made a net income of $200,000. At the directors' meeting held on January 15, 2011, Marcel, Fidel, and a director appointed by the private investors decided to pay out a total of 5% of the net income to preferred and common shareholders of record on January 30, 2011. The dividend is to be paid on February 28, 2011. During the period January 1 – February 28, 2011, the company produced net income of $30,000.

Required:

    a) Record the required journal entries.

    b) Prepare the statement of retained earnings for the year 2010, and for the period January 1 to February 28, 2011.

    c) Prepare the shareholders' equity section of the balance sheet as at December 31, 2010.

Review Exercise – Answer

Part a

Date	Account Title and Explanation	Debit	Credit
Mar 3, 2010	Assets	2,000,000	
	Liabilities		1,250,000
	Common Shares		750,000
	Issue of 20,000 common shares for net assets of partnership		
Apr 15, 2010	Cash	1,000,000	
	Common Shares		1,000,000
	Issue of 20,000 common shares for cash		
Apr 30, 2010	Accounting Fee Expense	100,000	
	Preferred Shares		100,000
	Issue of preferred shares in exchange for accounting services		
Dec 31, 2010	Income Summary	200,000	
	Retained Earnings		200,000
	To close income summary account for the year		
Jan 15, 2011	Retained Earnings	10,000	
	Dividends Payable – Common		$7,000
	Dividends Payable – Preferred		$3,000
	Total Dividends (5% × $200,000 = $10,000). Preferred ($3 × 1,000 = $3,000) Common ($10,000 – $3,000 = $7,000)		
Jan 30, 2011	No journal entry required on date of record		
Feb 28, 2011	Dividends Payable - Common	$7,000	
	Dividends Payable - Preferred	$3,000	
	Cash		10,000
	Recording dividends paid		

Part b

Camphamel Limited Statement of Retained Earnings For the Year Ended December 31, 2010	
Opening balance	$0
Net income for the year	200,000
Balance – December 31, 2010	200,000

Camphamel Limited Statement of Retained Earnings For the Two Months Ended February 28, 2011	
Balance - January 1, 2011	$200,000
Add: net income for the period	30,000
	230,000
Less: dividends paid	10,000
Balance - February 28, 2011	220,000

Part c

Camphamel Limited Statement of Shareholders' Equity As at December 31, 2010	
Share Capital	
Common shares, unlimited shares authorized, 40,000 shares issued and outstanding	$1,750,000
Preferred shares, $3, 100,000 share authorized, 1,000 shares issued and outstanding	100,000
Total Share Capital	1,850,000
Retained Earnings	200,000
Total Shareholders' Equity	$2,050,000

Notes

Chapter 11
CORPORATIONS: THE FINANCIAL STATEMENTS

LEARNING OUTCOMES:

❶ Record income tax expense

❷ Record the closing entries for corporations

❸ Prepare an income statement

❹ Prepare a statement of retained earnings

❺ Record prior period adjustments

❻ Prepare a balance sheet

❼ Calculate financial ratios:

- ✓ Book Value per Common Share
- ✓ Debt-to-Equity Ratio
- ✓ Dividend Payout Ratio
- ✓ Earnings per Share (EPS)
- ✓ Price to Earnings Ratio

Earnings of A Corporation: An Introduction

For investors to make informed decisions about their investments, they need to obtain detailed information about the corporation's assets, liabilities, shareholders' equity and earnings. IFRS provides the rules for reporting these items. The law requires that public corporations provide financial statements that are in accordance with IFRS.

Chapter 10 provided the details of the shareholders' equity accounts and, in particular, the share capital account. Now that we have learned how to record the investments by shareholders, and how the accounts are reported in the shareholders' equity section of the balance sheet, we need to take a look at the earnings of the corporation and how these earnings are reported on the income statement. We will also take a closer look at how net income, dividends and other items affect the balance of the retained earnings account.

Thus far, we have learned how the income statement reports revenues and expenses. As we move from a proprietorship to a partnership and now a corporation, we see how the number of accounts and complexities of operating a business increase. Before discussing these complexities any further, we will demonstrate how to account for income taxes on corporate earnings.

Income Tax Expense

Unlike a proprietorship or partnership, a corporation must file and pay taxes on the income it has earned because it is considered a separate legal entity from its owners. Federal income tax rates and laws are determined by the Government of Canada and set out in the Income Tax Act (ITA). Since this is not an income tax course, we will not be going into the details and intricacies of the ITA. However, we will explain how income tax is accrued for and reported on the books and financial statements of a corporation.

Income tax expense is recorded in the accounting records on the accrual basis. We apply a given percentage (based on average corporate income tax rates) to the accounting income.

For example, Star Company reported a net income before tax of $266,000. Assuming the corporation pays tax at a rate (average) of 30%, the entry to record income tax expense for the year on December 31 would be:

JOURNAL			
Date	**Account Title and Explanation**	**Debit**	**Credit**
Dec 31	Income Tax Expense	79,800	
	Income Tax Payable		79,800
	To record income tax expense at the year end		

The transaction is recorded with a debit (increase) to the income tax expense and a credit (increase) to the income tax payable(liability).

As mentioned, the income tax owing to the government is based on laws and rates as set out in the ITA (Income Tax Act) and not on IFRS or our accrual basis of accounting; therefore, the actual income tax owing to the government may be quite different from that calculated above.

On occasion, the amount of tax a business should pay is different from the amount due in the current fiscal year. Using the above example, let us now assume that Star Company incurred $20,000 of warranty expenses in year 2011. However, the amount would not be paid in the same year. Based on the income tax law, the warranty expense is only allowed as a deduction on the corporation's tax return in the period it is paid. Therefore, the warranty expense decreases the accounting income with no

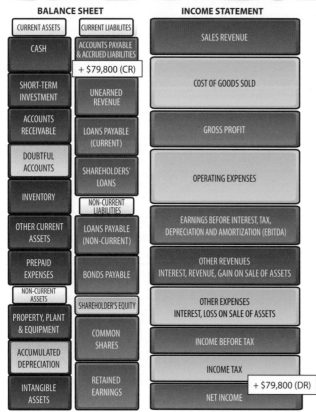

FIGURE 11.1

impact on the taxable income in fiscal 2011. **Accounting income** represents the amount of profit a company makes during a specific period of time (as reported on the income statement). **Taxable income** is the portion of income subject to taxation by law. Income tax payable is calculated from taxable income. The difference between income tax expense and income tax payable is known as *deferred income taxes*. Deferred income taxes can be an asset or liability and are classified as non-current items. As a result, Star Company's taxable income would be $286,000 ($266,000 + $20,000). The journal entry for this transaction is shown in figure 11.2.

In this example, the deferred income tax is an asset. This means that the company has paid more taxes than what was calculated from their accounting income. In a sense, they have prepaid a portion of their taxes. At some point in the future, the company will get a deduction based on this "prepaid" amount. This is known as a temporary or "timing" difference.

In the following year, however, the opposite could be true. There may be an expense that can be deducted for tax purposes but not for accounting purposes. This would result in taxable income being lower than accounting income. In this case, a deferred tax liability would be recorded as a non-current liability. For example, a company may be depreciating an asset quicker for tax purposes (as per the Income Tax Act rules) than through their accounting policies. This will give rise to lower taxable income than accounting income resulting in a future income tax liability.

It may seem reasonable to consolidate the deferred tax asset and liability into one amount when preparing the statement of financial position (balance sheet). Some companies may be able to, however certain criteria must be met before IFRS rules will allow them to. Since the criteria may be difficult to meet, most corporations will simply list them separately as non-current items.

JOURNAL

Date	Account Title and Explanation	Debit	Credit
Dec 31	Income Tax Expense	79,800	
	Deferred Tax Asset	6,000	
	Income Tax Payable		85,800
	Record income tax expense ($266,000 × 30% = $79,800; $286,000 × 30% = $85,800)		

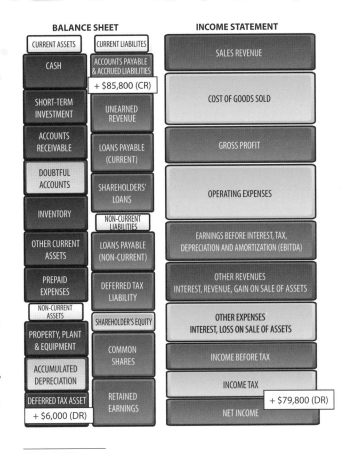

FIGURE 11.2

Closing Entries for Corporations

If you recall from our examination of partnerships in Chapter 9, company earnings are divided at the end of the fiscal year when the income summary account is closed. The balances are transferred to the capital accounts of each individual partner.

With corporations, revenue and expenses (including income tax expense) are also closed in the income summary. However, unlike partnerships, a corporation closes out the income summary account by transferring the balance to the retained earnings account.

> ### WORTH REPEATING...
>
> Recall that the term "closing the books" means updating equity and starting with a new income statement for the next period. There are two methods to accomplish this:
>
> 1. Directly, through owners' capital/retained earnings, or
>
> 2. Through the income summary account

Thus, corporations would transfer the credit balance of revenue accounts to the income summary and transfer the debit balance of expense accounts to the income summary.

JOURNAL			
Date	Account Title and Explanation	Debit	Credit
	Sales Revenue	200,000	
	Income Summary		200,000
	Close revenue accounts		
	Income Summary	150,000	
	Cost of Goods Sold		80,000
	Salary Expense		35,000
	Rent Expense		25,000
	Income Tax Expense		10,000
	Close expense accounts		

FIGURE 11.3

In the example shown in figure 11.3, the income summary account is left with a $50,000 credit balance, which indicates that a net income was generated. To close the income summary account, the journal entry in figure 11.4 must be made.

JOURNAL			
Date	Account Title and Explanation	Debit	Credit
	Income Summary	50,000	
	Retained Earnings		50,000
	To close net income for the year to retained earnings		

FIGURE 11.4

Measuring Income

The presentation of financial statements of a corporation will differ depending on whether the corporation is private or public. Remember, private corporations can continue to follow GAAP, while public corporations must follow IFRS. Most of the components of an income statement are not new at this point in an accounting course.

From previous studies, we have learned that revenue less cost of goods sold tells us the gross profit of the company. From gross profit, operating expenses are subtracted to provide operating income. Operating expenses are incurred to run the day-to-day operations of the company. Other revenue and expenses are then added or subtracted to provide income before tax. Other revenue and expenses are items that not part of the company's regular day-to-day operations. For example, selling property, plant and equipment is not part of the day-to-day operations of a business. Any gain or loss on the sale will therefore be listed as other revenue or expenses.

A large corporation can have many business activities that can be very complex. There are many items that must be presented that impact income in a material way. We will use Darma Corporation as an example to illustrate the reporting difference between a private and public corporation. We will examine the financial statements for this corporation firstly assuming it is a private corporation, then assuming it is a public corporation. Figure 11.5 show the income statement for Darma Corporation, assuming that the business is a private corporation. The new items on the income statement will be discussed in the paragraphs following the figure.

Darma Corporation (Private - GAAP) Income Statement For the Year Ended December 31, 2011		
Sales Revenue		$2,505,750
Less: Sales Discounts	$1,200	
Sales Returns and Allowances	3,800	5,000
Net Sales		2,500,750
Cost of Goods Sold		1,100,000
Gross Profit		1,400,750
Operating Expenses		
Salary Expense	275,000	
Depreciation Expense	44,000	
Administrative Expenses	300,000	619,000
Results from Operating Activities		781,750
Other Revenue and Expenses		
Gain on Sale of Assets	4,500	
Gain on Foreign Currency Translation	5,200	
Gain on value of Available-For-Sale assets	8,700	
Interest Expense	(21,000)	(2,600)
Income before Tax		779,150
Income Tax Expense		233,745
Income from Continuing Operations		545,405
Discontinued Operations		
Operating Income from Discontinued Operations	125,000	
Gain on Sale of Assets from Discontinued Operations	45,000	
Income Tax Expense	(51,000)	119,000
Net Income		$664,405

FIGURE 11.5

In figure 11.5, the term "Income from Continuing Operations" appears where you would normally expect to see "Net Income." The section below "Income from Continuing Operations" includes information for discontinued operations.

A discontinued operation is a segment of a business that is no longer part of regular operating activities. For example, in addition to manufacturing computer parts, Darma Corporation also operates several divisions specializing in the creation of computer software. During the current year, Darma discontinued one of their software divisions in an attempt to become more competitive in the market. This discontinued division reported an operating income of $125,000 and realized a $45,000 gain from selling the capital assets. The income from the division is classified as operating income from discontinued operations.

Some financial statements may take the entire amount earned from the discontinued operations and list it as a single line item. If Darma Corporation were to do this, they would simply list the $119,000 earned from the discontinued operations and label it "Profit from Discontinued Operation (net of income tax)". By listing items as "net of income tax", the corporation simply eliminates the details, including the amount of income tax owed (or recovered), and displays a single value.

Even though companies prepare consolidated financial statements, GAAP and IFRS require separate disclosure of discontinued operations. This is done so that shareholders will have a better understanding of the composition of net income when comparing investment opportunities.

Statement Differences between GAAP and IFRS

If Darma Corporation was a public corporation, they would have to prepare an income statement using IFRS guidelines. Under IFRS, an income statement is called a Statement of Comprehensive Income. Some of the key changes are:

- IFRS has a separate section to report Other Comprehensive Income
- Other Comprehensive Income includes items like foreign currency translation and changes in value of available-for-sale assets
- IFRS allows a corporation to revalue property, plant and equipment as part of their accounting policy, whereas GAAP does not

Other comprehensive income will be briefly discussed after the statement of comprehensive income in figure 11.6. This statement is shown only to provide an awareness of some of the differences between GAAP and IFRS presentation. You will not be required to prepare a statement of comprehensive income for this course.

Darma Corporation (Public - IFRS) Statement of Comprehensive Income For the Year Ended December 31, 2011		
Sales Revenue		$2,505,750
Less: Sales Discounts	$1,200	
Sales Returns and Allowances	3,800	5,000
Net Sales		2,500,750
Cost of Goods Sold		1,100,000
Gross Profit		1,400,750
Operating Expenses		
Salary Expense	275,000	
Depreciation Expense	44,000	
Administrative Expenses	300,000	619,000
Results from Operating Activities		781,750
Other Revenue and Expenses		
Gain on Sale of Assets	4,500	
Interest Expense	(21,000)	(16,500)
Income before Tax		765,250
Income Tax Expense		229,575
Income from Continuing Operations		535,675
Discontinued Operations		
Operating Income from Discontinued Operations	125,000	
Gain on Sale of Assets from Discontinued Operations	45,000	
Income Tax Expense	(51,000)	119,000
Income for the Period		654,675
Other Comprehensive Income		
Foreign Currency Translation Difference	5,200	
Revaluation of Property, Plant & Equipment	12,400	
Net Change in fair value of Available-For-Sale assets	8,700	
Income Tax Expense	(7,890)	18,410
Total Comprehensive Income for the Period		$673,085

FIGURE 11.6

Other comprehensive income includes items that IFRS does not allow to be reported as part of continuing operations. The International Accounting Standards Board has yet to provide a firm definition of what other comprehensive income is, however they have provided multiple examples of what it does include. Other comprehensive income can arise from adjustments in fair value of investments, pension or property, plant and equipment, and also differences in foreign currency translation transactions. The entire section of other comprehensive income is listed below income from continuing operations and is added or subtracting from income from continuing operations to get a total comprehensive income for the company for the period. The details of the items in other comprehensive income are beyond the scope of this text.

Measuring Changes in Equity

As part of the year-end financial statements, a corporation that follows GAAP must report on how their equity changed over the year. This must include changes in retained earnings, the changes in share capital, and any other changes to items that must be reported in equity. These changes can be reported only in the notes of the financial statements, or within an actual statement.

An example of a statement of retained earnings will be used to illustrate how the changes to the retained earnings account will be reported. Retained earnings will increase if the company reported a net income and decrease if the company paid out dividends.

Figure 11.7 shows the statement of retained earnings for Darma Corporation, assuming they are a private corporation and follow GAAP. The opening value of retained earnings and the dividend amount paid are assumed for this example.

Darma Corporation (Private - GAAP) Statement of Retained Earnings For the Year Ended December 31, 2011	
Retained Earnings, January 1, 2011	$1,340,000
Add: Net Income	664,405
Less: Dividends	(400,000)
Retained Earnings, December 31, 2011	$1,604,405

FIGURE 11.7

The statement of retained earnings is very straight forward. The first value shown is the opening value at the beginning of the period, followed by items that will increase or decrease the value of retained earnings. After the additions and subtractions, the last value is the balance at the end of the period. This value will then appear on the balance sheet.

There are two basic calculations when it comes to calculating shareholders' equity.

Shareholders' Equity = Share Capital + Retained Earnings

Retained earnings can be calculated by using the figures provided in the statement of retained earnings. The formula is very similar to how owner's equity is calculated.

Ending Retained Earnings = Beginning Retained Earnings + Net Income - Dividends

Statement Differences between GAAP and IFRS

For a public corporation, following IFRS requires a report called the statement of changes in equity. This replaces the statement of retained earnings and reports more than just the change in retained earnings. The following list indicates the major changes between GAAP and IFRS for reporting the changes in equity.

- IFRS must present a statement of changes in equity
- The statement of changes in equity must show the changes in all components of equity for the period (e.g. share capital and retained earnings)

Once the statement of changes in equity is prepared, it reconciles the opening balances of various equity accounts with the closing balance of these accounts. If Darma Corporation did not have any other comprehensive income reported for the period, the only items that would appear on the statement of changes in equity would be share capital and retained earnings. Figure 11.8 shows this simple version for Darma Corporation. This statement is prepared for comparison purposes only. You will not be required to prepare a statement of changes in equity for this course.

Darma Corporation (Public - IFRS) Statement of Changes in Equity For the Year Ended December 31, 2011			
	Share Capital	Retained Earnings	Total
Balance at January 1, 2011	2,600,000	1,340,000	3,940,000
Total Comprehensive Income for the Period		654,675	654,675
Contributions by and Distributions to Owners			
Issued Common Shares	1,300,000		1,300,000
Dividends to Shareholders		(400,000)	(400,000)
Total Contributions by and Distributions to Owners	1,300,000	(400,000)	900,000
Balance at December 31, 2011	3,900,000	1,594,675	5,494,675

FIGURE 11.8

The balances at January 1, 2011 in figure 11.8 are assumed for our example. The two headings across the top of the table indicate the two equity accounts that are being tracked, share capital and retained earnings. The retained earnings column is showing the same information that was shown in the statement of retained earnings in figure 11.7. The share capital column shows that $1,300,000 worth of shares was issued during the year. We also assume that $400,000 worth of dividends was paid out. The items on the left side of the table list the items that caused changes to equity.

While GAAP will allow the changes in equity to be reported in notes within the financial statements, IFRS requires a proper statement to be prepared. This statement would include retained earnings, share capital, and every "Other Comprehensive Income" item the statement of comprehensive income. These items must have their beginning and ending values reconciled. From figure 11.6, there are several items listed under "Other Comprehensive Income" which must be presented properly in the statement of changes in equity. The following figure expands on what was shown in figure 11.8.

Darma Corporation (Public - IFRS) Statement of Changes in Equity For the Year Ended December 31, 2011						
	Share Capital	Translation Reserve	Revaluation Reserve	Fair Value Reserve	Retained Earnings	Total
Balance at January 1, 2011	2,600,000	0	0	0	1,340,000	3,940,000
Total Comprehensive Income for the Period					654,675	654,675
Other Comprehensive Income						
Foreign Currency Translation Difference, net of tax		3,640				3,640
Revaluation of Property, Plant & Equipment, net of tax			8,680			8,680
Change in fair value of Available-For-Sale assets, net of tax				6,090		6,090
Total Comprehensive Income		3,640	8,680	6,090		18,410
Contributions by and Distributions to Owners						
Issued Common Shares	1,300,000					1,300,000
Dividends to Shareholders					(400,000)	(400,000)
Total Contributions by and Distributions to Owners	1,300,000				(400,000)	900,000
Balance at December 31, 2011	3,900,000	3,640	8,680	6,090	1,594,675	5,513,085

FIGURE 11.9

The items under "Other Comprehensive Income" in figure 11.9 are taken directly from the statement of comprehensive income in figure 11.6. Where applicable, the item is listed net of tax, which means that income tax expense has been deducted from the amount in this statement.

Other comprehensive income contains items that have very detailed rules regarding valuation. These items are covered in intermediate accounting courses.

Prior Period Adjustments

The statement of changes in equity is also the place where adjustments for accounting errors and changes to accounting policies having an effect on prior periods are made.

A CLOSER LOOK

The shareholders' equity section of a corporation's balance sheet is an important one for accountants and analysts to become familiar with. It is an account that in many ways separates corporations from other types of business ownership.

That is, unlike proprietorships and partnerships, corporations divide their owners' equity section into two: share capital, which represents the value of all company shares, and retained earnings, representing company earnings to date not paid out in the form of dividends.

	(in thousands)
Net Income	1,103.6
Retained Earnings, Beginning of Year	1,286.4
Change in Accounting Policy (Note 3)	0.2
Repurchase of Common Shares (Note 17)	–
Dividends	(110.6)
Retained Earnings, End of Year	$2,276.6

Retained earnings is essentially calculated by adding net income to retained earnings at the start of the year and then deducting any dividends that are paid. That is precisely what is done in this sample calculation of retained earnings.

Assume an auditor discovered that the 2010 records included a $25,000 debit entry in the repairs and maintenance account that should have been posted as a debit in the equipment (capital asset) account. The effect of this error is that income for 2010 was understated by $25,000. Should we simply do a reversing entry to correct the error? The answer is no. While a reversing entry would correct the equipment account, it would also understate the repairs and maintenance account for the current year. The following entry is required:

JOURNAL			
Date	Account Title and Explanation	Debit	Credit
	Equipment	25,000	
	Retained Earnings		17,500
	Income tax payable (25,000 × 30%)		7,500
	To correct accounts for error recorded in 2010		

FIGURE 11.10

The error caused net income for 2010 to be understated by a net amount of $17,500 ($25,000 less the tax on this amount at a rate of 30%). By crediting retained earnings for the net effect of the error, we have restated (corrected) this account to reflect the income that would have been recorded had the error not occurred. Income taxes payable are also corrected to reflect the actual amount owing on the income earned.

If Darma was a private corporation that followed GAAP, the statement of retained earnings would look like the figure shown below.

Darma Corporation (Private - GAAP) Statement of Retained Earnings For the Year Ended December 31, 2011	
Retained Earnings, January 1, 2011	$1,340,000
Add: Prior Year Adjustment	17,500
Add: Net Income	664,405
Less: Dividends	(400,000)
Retained Earnings, December 31, 2011	$1,621,905

FIGURE 11.11

The adjustment to retained earnings is listed before any other items are added or subtracted from retained earnings.

As a public corporation, Darma would have to present this adjustment on their statement of changes in equity. To keep things simple, figure 11.12 ignores other comprehensive income and just focuses on share capital and retained earnings.

Darma Corporation (Public - IFRS) Statement of Changes in Equity For the Year Ended December 31, 2011			
	Share Capital	Retained Earnings	Total
Balance at January 1, 2011	2,600,000	1,340,000	3,940,000
Adjustment to Correct Error from 2010		17,500	
Total Comprehensive Income for the Period		654,675	654,675
Contributions by and Distributions to Owners			
Issued Common Shares	1,300,000		1,300,000
Dividends to Shareholders		(400,000)	(400,000)
Total Contributions by and Distributions to Owners	1,300,000	(400,000)	900,000
Balance at December 31, 2011	3,900,000	1,612,175	5,512,175

FIGURE 11.12

Changes in Accounting Policies

A prior period adjustment may also be needed when the corporation is reporting comparative numbers (statements for two or more years) and a change in accounting policy has occurred. For example, assume Darma Corporation decided to change its method of depreciation from straight-line to double-declining balance and reported 2011 and 2010 financial statements. The opening balance of retained earnings for 2010 would have to be adjusted for the cumulative effect of using one method over the other. In this case there would have been a larger depreciation expense (lower net income) for 2010.

Measuring Financial Position

The balance sheet indicates the financial standing of a business. It reports on the value of assets, liabilities and equity. For a corporation that follows GAAP, the balance sheet looks very similar to the balance sheets that you are familiar with during your accounting studies. Assets and liabilities are split into current and non-current items, with the current items listed first. Equity for a corporation is split between shares and retained earnings as was discussed in chapter 10. Figure 11.13 shows the balance sheet for Darma Corporation if they followed GAAP.

Darma Corporation (Private - GAAP) Balance Sheet As at December 31, 2011	
Assets	
Current Assets	
Cash	$87,650
Short-Term Investments	287,580
Accounts Receivable	685,725
Inventory	1,652,840
Prepaid Expenses	16,840
Total Current Assets	2,730,635
Non-Current Assets	
Property, Plant & Equipment (net)	3,206,740
Goodwill	777,185
Total Assets	$6,714,560
Liabilities	
Current Liabilities	
Accrued Liabilities	$145,845
Accounts Payable	426,890
Current Portion of Non-Current Debt	43,870
Total Current Liabilities	616,605
Non-Current Liabilities	
Non-Current Debt	568,750
Deferred Tax Liability	24,800
Total Liabilities	1,210,155
Shareholders' Equity	
Common shares unlimited shares authorized, 200,000 shares issued and outstanding	3,900,000
Retained Earnings	1,604,405
Total Shareholders' Equity	5,504,405
Total Liabilities and Shareholders' Equity	$6,714,560

FIGURE 11.13

Statement Differences between GAAP and IFRS

If Darma Corporation was a public corporation, they would follow IFRS guidelines and their balance sheet would be called a statement of financial standing. The statement of financial standing is prepared with a slightly different layout than a balance sheet. It still includes assets, liabilities and equity, but presents them in a different order.

- Non-current items are listed before current items
- Equity is listed before liabilities

Figure 11.14 shows the statement of financial position for Darma Corporation if they were a public corporation and followed IFRS guidelines. The other comprehensive income item in the shareholders' equity section is a summary of the three reserves shown in figure 11.9. This statement is shown for comparison purposes only. You will not be required to prepare a statement of financial position in this course.

Darma Corporation (Public - IFRS) Statement of Financial Position As at December 31, 2011	
Assets	
Non-Current Assets	
Property, Plant & Equipment (net)	$3,215,420
Goodwill	777,185
Total Non-Current Assets	3,992,605
Current Assets	
Prepaid Expenses	16,840
Inventory	1,652,840
Accounts Receivable	685,725
Available for Sale Investments	287,580
Cash	87,650
Total Current Assets	2,730,635
Total Assets	$6,723,240
Shareholders' Equity	
Common shares unlimited shares authorized 200,000 shares issued and outstanding	$3,900,000
Other Comprehensive Income	18,410
Retained Earnings	1,594,675
Total Shareholders' Equity	5,513,085
Liabilities	
Non-Current Liabilities	
Non-Current Debt	568,750
Deferred Tax Liability	24,800
Total Non-Current Liabilities	593,550
Current Liabilities	
Accrued Liabilities	145,845
Accounts Payable	426,890
Current Portion of Non-Current Debt	43,870
Total Current Liabilities	616,605
Total Liabilities	1,210,155
Total Liabilities and Shareholders' Equity	$6,723,240

FIGURE 11.14

Financial statements prepared by public corporations will show the current year's performance and the previous year's performance. This allows a potential investor to see how the company has performed compared to their last year. For a real world example, the appendix shows an excerpt from Bombardier's annual report from 2011.

IN THE REAL WORLD

Although the IFRS guidelines recommend presenting the statement of financial position as shown in the example, some companies will still use the balance sheet format of displaying current items before non-current items.

Calculation of Financial Ratios

Book Value per Share

When referring to the value of company shares, there are two terms that are generally used; one is market value, which represents the price at which shares are traded on the stock market. The other is book value, which represents the theoretical value of share based on a shareholder's claim to the company's assets.

Theoretically, a share's market value should mirror its book value. In other words, what the company is worth on the financial statements should be reflected in the price at which its shares are trading. However, in the real world shares are often bought and sold for a very different price than reflected on the financial statements. In other words, the book value does not match the market value.

For various reasons, a share's market value can deviate significantly from its book value. Again, theoretically speaking, this should not happen. A share of ownership in a company should represent the stake that the shareholder has in the actual value of the company. Nevertheless, once a company issues shares and sells them on the market, the price at which they trade often takes on a life of its own.

Remember that shares in a company represent a claim on assets if they are liquidated. People buy shares for all sorts of reasons, such as an expectation of a dividend, the existence of a bull market, or the prediction of an increase in price due to speculation. All these factors and more affect the value at which shares trade on the market; therefore it does not always equate to a company's worth on its books.

The calculation of book value per share is relatively simple. Here is the formula that is often used:

$$\text{Book Value per Share} = \frac{\text{Sharesholders' Equity} - \text{Preferred Equity}}{\text{Average Number of Common Shares Outstanding}}$$

Note that preferred equity should include preferred dividends if there are any outstanding.

In other words, the formula calculates the amount of money that each common shareholder would receive if all the company's assets were immediately liquidated.

Let's use some actual figures to demonstrate how this formula really works. To do this, we will use the information from figure 11.15.

WORTH REPEATING...

Common shareholders have voting rights and are awarded dividends at the discretion of management. Preferred shareholders usually do not have voting rights but are privy to regular and fixed dividend payments.

(figures in millions)

Sample Company Statement of Financial Position As at December 31, 2011		
Liabilities	**2011**	**2010**
Current Liabilities		
Short-term debt	$90.0	$157.9
Accounts Payable	911.7	545.2
Current Portion of Non-Current Debt	0.2	400.4
Total Current Liabilities	1,001.9	1,103.5
Non-Current Liabilities		
Non-Current Debt	1,339.4	1,357.1
Deferred Tax Liability	988.1	632.1
Accrued Pension Benefits	244.8	219.6
Accrued Environmental Costs	121.0	110.3
Other Non-Current Liabilities	2.7	14.1
Total Non-Current Liabilities	2,696.0	2,333.2
Total Liabilities	3,697.9	3,436.7
Shareholders' Equity		
Share Capital		
Preferred shares, $2, 10,000 shares authorized none issued and outstanding		
Common shares, unlimited shares authorized 316,411,209 and 314,403,147 shares issued and outstanding at December 31, 2011 and 2010 respectively	1,461.3	1,431.6
Total Share Capital	1,461.3	1,431.6
Retained Earnings	4,557.4	1,348.7
Total Shareholders' Equity	6,018.7	2,780.3
Total Liabilities and Shareholders' Equity	$9,716.6	$6,217.0

FIGURE 11.15

All the numbers we need for our formula are located in the shareholders' equity section of this company's financial statements.

Since the entire section summarizes shareholders' equity, that figure is tallied for us at the bottom of the column for 2011: $6,018,700,000.

The company has no preferred shares outstanding. Therefore, the number we plug into our formula for preferred shares is zero.

The paragraph under share capital gives us the information we need here. There were 314,403,147 common shares outstanding at the 2010 year end and 316,411,209 common shares outstanding at the 2011 year end. The average of these two numbers produces the following to be included in the formula:

$$\frac{314,403,147 + 316,411,209}{2} = 315,407,178$$

It should also be noted that companies may use various methods to calculate the average number of shares outstanding, which is why reproducing the exact number provided in published financial statements might be difficult. For example, companies might use a monthly or daily average number instead of a yearly number.

The complete calculation for book value per share is presented as shown below:

$$\text{Book Value per Share} = \frac{\text{Total Shareholders' Equity} - \text{Preferred Equity}}{\text{Average Number of Common Shares Outstanding}}$$

$$= \frac{\$6,018,700,000}{315,407,178} = \$19.08$$

The book value per common share for this corporation at the 2011 year end is $19.08.

However, anyone looking up the actual share price in the financial statements during 2011 might find a number ranging anywhere from $80 to $100 a share.

So, what accounts for this difference between book value and market value? Again, a number of factors can account for this discrepancy. The market price of a share is ultimately determined by speculation — speculation about how the company will do in the upcoming year, speculation about how the industry will do, as well as market trends in general.

This doesn't mean that a share price reflects a random calculation made by investors. Instead, some consensus is developed about how well the company is performing, which drives demand for the share and ultimately determines the price.

Debt-to-Equity Ratio

The **debt-to-equity ratio** is another tool that investors and analysts have at their disposal to assess a corporation's financial statements. In fact, the name of the ratio speaks for itself, since it simply divides the company's total debt by total equity to produce a figure that the public uses to assess performance.

In other words, to calculate the debt-to-equity ratio, one goes to the balance sheet to find the figure for total liabilities, and the figure for total shareholders' equity.

If we refer back to figure 11.15 and look at the totals (at the bottom of the page), under 'liabilities', we see total amount of debt for 2011 is $3,697,900,000, and under 'shareholders' equity' the total amount of equity for 2011 is $6,018,700,000. These numbers are all we need to produce our debt-to-equity ratio as follows:

$$\text{Debt-to-Equity Ratio} = \frac{\text{Total Liabilities}}{\text{Shareholders' Equity}}$$

$$= \frac{\$3,697,900,000}{\$6,018,700,000} = 0.62$$

What does this number mean? A debt-to-equity ratio of 1:1 would mean that, for every dollar of equity a company has, it has one dollar of debt. If the debt-to-equity ratio is higher than one, it means that the company's lenders have more dollars tied up in the company than the owners — or shareholders. Consequently, if the debt-to-equity ratio is lower than one, then ownership is essentially more responsible for financing the company.

Which situation do you think is preferable for a company: to have the company financed by lenders — or have it financed by ownership? It is usually preferable that owners finance the company, more so than creditors. When that happens, more of the company's assets belong to shareholders.

This is indicative of how families approach home ownership, how small proprietorships and partnerships approach business ownership, and how small corporations ideally approach financing.

The sample corporation's debt-to-equity ratio of 0.62 calculated for the year 2011 represents a preferable way of financing the business. The alternative, which is a ratio greater than 1, would mean that the company is likely vulnerable to lenders and the interest rates they charge over the long term.

Dividend Payout Ratio

Since dividends, or at least the potential for dividends, must form part of an analysis of company shares, the investing community has produced a ratio to assess just how much in dividends a corporation is paying out to shareholders. This is called the ***dividend payout ratio***. In fact, the dividend payout ratio is relatively easy to put together and analyze, because all it does is calculate dividends paid as a percentage of net income. In other words, the ratio answers the following question: How much of the company's earnings does the company pay out in dividends? Here is the basic formula that is used:

$$\text{Dividend Payout Ratio} = \frac{\text{Dividends Paid in a Year}}{\text{Net Income after Tax (NIAT)}}$$

For example, if a company made $1 million, and paid out $100,000 in dividends to its shareholders, the resulting dividend payout ratio would be:

$$\frac{\$100,000}{\$1,000,000} = 10\%$$

In other words, the company is paying out 10% of its earnings in the form of dividends, and the rest of net income, which is 90%, is being kept in the business in the form of retained earnings.

Earnings per Share (EPS)

Another stock market term that one might see frequently used in the financial press is **earnings per share**; this is calculated using a similar method to that used with book value per share. Here is a basic formula for earnings per share that is used to calculate earnings per share:

$$\frac{\text{Net Income} - \text{Preferred Dividends}}{\text{Average \# Common Shares Outstanding}}$$

As you may have noticed, the only difference between this formula and the one used earlier for book value is that net income replaces shareholders' equity in the numerator. That is because the earnings-per-share ratio attempts to assess how profitable a company is. To that end, the company's net income figure is used to make the calculation.

Using the exact same financial reports used to calculate the book value per share, we will also calculate earnings per share. Assume the net income for 2011 is $1,103,600,000. As in our previous example, the average number of common shares outstanding is 315,407,178.

The earnings per share ratio is:

$$\frac{\$1,103,600,000}{315,407,178} = \$3.50$$

In other words, the company is making $3.50 for every outstanding share. The general interpretation is the larger the number, the more profitable the company.

IN THE REAL WORLD

A share's book value essentially represents the value associated with a company's net assets. In an ideal world, this book value would be reflected in the share's price. In other words, a share would represent a portion of value in company assets. In fact, there was a time when share values did in fact match book values. Although that hasn't happened in a while, the financial crisis of 2008 might mean that what was old is now new again. That is, book value might be coming back in style.

After World War II, and before the high-flying days of the 1980s on Wall Street, it was generally expected that a share would trade at a price equal to its book value. Indeed, this reflects a common sense approach to ownership. If you own part of a company, which shareholders do, then you own its assets and are entitled to the value of these assets.

However, this era of prudent investment and modest expectation of share performance started to change. By 2004, share prices were trading at an average of 280% of their book value. That means that shares were being bought and sold at almost three times the worth of the stock's underlying assets, so to speak. People were willing to buy shares at high prices, and even more people seemed willing to snatch them up. This was the state of affairs until recently. Then in the fall of 2008, the financial crisis hit world markets. Prices had skyrocketed, but the underlying fundamentals of investments were not solid enough. So, prices started to tumble at record rates. Pensions were plummeting in value, speculators were selling like mad, and investor confidence hit lows not seen in decades. The good times in the stock market were over as financial players worldwide started reevaluating their options.

One of those options was to start searching for shares of companies whose fundamentals were sound and whose book value actually reflected market prices. In other words, the financial crisis might lead to a new trend: the expectation that shares are sold at something closer to the value of assets owned by the company.

When strong performing companies have share prices that mirror book prices it means, among other things, that the share price won't suffer the stresses of a market downturn, nor is market speculation artificially propping up insane prices.

Instead, it might mean that companies and the economy might be getting back to fundamentals which bodes well for financial markets trying to see the light at the end of the tunnel during otherwise difficult times.

In addition, if our sample company had preferred dividends of $50,000,000 for 2011, this amount should be subtracted from the net income when calculating earnings per share:

$$\frac{(\$1,103,600,000 - \$50,000,000)}{315,407,178} = \$3.34$$

This results in lower earnings per share calculation.

Variations in Presentation of Earnings per Share

Sometimes companies will report EPS calculations for each area reported on the income statement. Using the information provided on the income statement of Darma Corporation, we will calculate the EPS assuming there were no preferred shares and the average number of common shares during the year was 100,000.

Earnings per Share:

Income from continuing operations: $535,675 ÷ 100,000	$5.36
Income from discontinued operations: $119,000 ÷ 100,000	1.19
Income before other comprehensive income: $654,675 ÷ 100,000	6.55
Other comprehensive income: $19,970 ÷ 100,000	0.20
Net income: $674,645 ÷ 100,000	6.75

FIGURE 11.16

Price-Earnings Ratio

Another ratio commonly used by shareholders to evaluate their investment in a corporation is that of the **price-earnings ratio** (P/E ratio), which divides the market price per common share by earnings per share. This provides the investor with a measurement of share price to actual earnings of the corporation. It is sometimes used as an indicator to buy/sell or hold shares.

Assume the following details for Darma Corporation:

	2011	2010
EPS	$6.75	$4.56
Market price per share	43.50	35.80
Calculate the P/E for each year:		
P/E	43.50/6.75	35.80/4.56
	= 6.44	= 7.85

FIGURE 11.17

The ratios indicate the shares are selling for 6.44 and 7.85 times the earnings in 2011 and 2010 respectively.

It should be mentioned that an increasing P/E ratio may not necessarily mean the corporation has improved its attractiveness as an investment because shareholders may suddenly react negatively to the higher share price and sell their shares which will then cause share prices to fall.

The IFRS Perspective

When examining corporate financial statements, it is common to see two earnings per share figures: basic and diluted. The basic EPS is what is shown in this text. It is based on actual shares that have been issued to shareholders. The diluted EPS is based on actual and potential shares that have or could be issued. Potential shares can arise from a few places:

- Management compensation. Some corporations give senior management options to purchase shares of the company at a reduced price.

- Corporations can sell bonds that are convertible into shares in the company.

The diluted EPS is calculated as if management purchased the share and the bonds were converted. This will cause the diluted EPS to be a smaller figure than the basic EPS. The concept of diluted EPS is covered in more advanced accounting courses.

In Summary

↪ The focus of this chapter has been on reporting and analyzing the earnings of corporations.

↪ Corporations are liable for income taxes based on profits earned by the business. While we base income tax expense on accounting income, we also recognize that actual taxes (income taxes payable) are based on government laws and rates. We account for the temporary difference between the two amounts using a deferred income taxes account.

↪ Shareholders demand timely and accurate financial information to make good investment decisions. A complex income statement reports income from continuing operations, discontinued operations and extraordinary items.

↪ Corporations sometimes have certain types of income and expenses that meet the definition of "other comprehensive items". These are presented separately on the income statement.

↪ The statement of retained earnings provides shareholders with a summary of the changes in retained earnings from the beginning to the end of the current accounting period. It takes into consideration: prior period adjustments, earnings in the current year and dividend payments.

↪ Earnings per share and price to earnings ratios are two measures shareholders use to evaluate their investment in a corporation.

Review Exercise

The following information was taken from the accounting records of Shah Inc. at December 31, 2010. Assume the tax rate is 35%.

FINANCIAL STATEMENT ITEMS	AMOUNT
Prior-year error – debit to Retained Earnings	7,500
Income tax expense on operating income from discontinued operations	12,250
Total dividends	25,000
Common shares, 40,000 issued	155,000
Sales revenue	710,000
Interest expense	30,000
Operating income, discontinued operations	35,000
Loss due to lawsuit	11,000
Sales Discounts	15,000
Income tax savings on sale of discontinued operations (sold at a loss)	14,000
General expenses	62,000
Income tax expense on continuing operations	74,200
Preferred shares, $5.00, 1,000 issued	50,000
Retained Earnings, January 1, 2010 (prior to adjustment)	110,000
Loss on sale of discontinued operations	40,000
Cost of goods sold	380,000

Required:

1. Prepare a statement of comprehensive income for the year ended December 31, 2010.

2. Prepare a statement of change in equity, just showing changes in retained earnings for Shah Inc. for the year ended December 31, 2010.

3. Calculate the EPS ratio.

Review Exercise – Answer

Part 1

Shah Inc.
Statement of Comprehensive Income
For the Year Ended December 31, 2010

Sales Revenue		$710,000
Less: Sales Discounts		(15,000)
Net Sales		695,000
Cost of Goods Sold		(380,000)
Gross Profit		315,000
Less: Operating Expenses		
General Expenses	62,000	
Operating Income		253,000
Less: Other Expenses		
Interest Expense	30,000	
Loss Due to Lawsuit	11,000	
Income Tax Expense	74,200	177,200
Income from Continuing Operations		137,800
Discontinued Operations		
Operating Income	35,000	
Less: Income Tax	12,250	22,750
Loss on Sale of Discontinued Operations	(40,000)	
Less: Income Tax Saving	14,000	(26,000)
Net Income		$134,550

Part 2

Shah Inc.
Statement of Changes in Equity
For the Year Ended December 31, 2010

Retained earnings, January 1, 2010 (as originally reported)	$110,000
Correction to prior-year error - debit	(7,500)
Retained earnings, January 1, 2010, as adjusted	102,500
Net Income for current year	134,550
	237,050
Dividends for 2010	(25,000)
Retained earnings, December 31, 2010	$212,050

Part 3

$$EPS = \frac{\text{Net Income} - \text{Preferred Dividends}}{\text{Average \# Common Shares Outstanding}}$$

Since Preferred Dividends = $5.00 x 1000 = $5,000 and assuming the same number of shares has been outstanding throughout the year:

EPS = (134,550 – 5,000) ÷ 40,000 = $3.24

Chapter 12
THE STATEMENT OF CASH FLOW

LEARNING OUTCOMES:

❶ Understand the importance of cash flow within a business

❷ Classify operating, investing and financing activities

❸ Prepare a cash flow statement using the indirect method

❹ Prepare a cash flow statement using the direct method

Beyond the Balance Sheet and Income Statement

Most of our discussion of accounting procedures and principles so far has focused on two types of financial statements: the balance sheet and the income statement. Indeed, these financial statements have become synonymous with the accounting profession. When people think about business finance, they usually think about balance sheets and income statements.

However, there are two reasons why analyzing the state of a business requires more than just the balance sheet and income statement.

First, balance sheets and income statements are prepared on an accrual basis. In other words, the matching principle dictates that revenues and expenses be recorded for the period in which they are earned or incurred. However, these types of transactions do not always involve an actual exchange of cash. Conversely, other transactions such as borrowing or repaying loans do not affect net income.

Second, well-publicized accounting scandals have exposed some of the flaws of balance sheets and income statements. In other words, some businesses have become adept at manipulating them for their advantage. The financial statements are not necessarily flawed, but analysts have, to a certain extent, less confidence in them.

Cash flow statements (or statement of cash flows) essentially follow the cash within a business. They ignore accruals and other book transactions, while revealing and analyzing actual changes to a company's cash account. Cash flow statements involve a different way of looking at financial numbers. For this reason, preparing a cash flow statement can take some time to get used to. In other words, it takes practice. This chapter provides the basis for enhancing your understanding of, and proficiency with, cash flow statements.

Cash Flow Statements: Follow the Money

Accountants are required to prepare balance sheets and income statements for the business. These important documents represent the state of company finances and adhere to the matching principle, accruals and so on. Balance sheets and income statements are filled with promises of an exchange of money that must be recorded in one period, but may take place in another period. Company bills may not get paid for several months. Prepaid expenses can be left unadjusted for a number of periods. A borrower may default on a loan. Depreciation is recorded in the books, but there is no exchange of cash.

Because of the way these transactions are accounted for in balance sheets and income statements, it can be difficult to know where the cash is actually going within the business. As a result, the accounting profession has devised another financial statement whose purpose is to specifically indicate both the *sources* of cash and the *uses* of cash within an organization. This document is known as the **cash flow statement** or the **statement of cash flow**. Both terms will be used throughout this chapter.

The cash flow statement shows how net income is converted to cash. Remember, net income does not necessarily translate into cash in the bank. The way a business is structured – in terms of financing, dividend schedules, debt collection, etc. – can have a significant impact on the way net income is turned into cash. It is this aspect of a business that the cash flow statement reveals to readers, who may include management, accountants, potential lenders and investment analysts.

Though cash flow statements can be of significant help to these financial players, they also constitute a requirement under GAAP and IFRS. In other words, cash flow statements are not only useful but necessary. Knowing what they are, understanding what they can do and becoming familiar with preparing them are essential tasks for an accountant. In this chapter, we explain how to perform these tasks.

Three Ways of Generating Cash Flow

A business generates and consumes cash in one of the following three ways:

- Operations
- Investments
- Financing

In fact, all cash flow statements are structured in this manner.

Cash flow from operations

This component of the cash flow statement tracks the movement of cash within a business on the basis of day-to-day activities. All items listed in this section affect the value of shareholders' equity. It is the most important section of the cash flow statement because the future of a business largely depends on the activities reported in this section.

Cash flow from investments

This component of the cash flow statement tracks the movement of cash in a business on the basis of the purchases and sales of non-current assets. For example, if a truck was sold during the year, cash flow would have increased. Alternatively, if the business purchased land, cash flow would have decreased, since the business had to use cash to buy the land.

Cash flow from financing

This component of the cash flow statement tracks the movement of cash within a business on the basis of the way a company receives money from those providing financing and pays it back. These sources of financing could be banks or bondholders. These financiers could also be shareholders, who are paid with dividend payments. All these exchanges of cash, whether considered current or non-current, need to be accounted for in this section of the cash flow statement.

The following table will help summarize the events that are recorded in each of the three sections of the cash flow statement.

Operations	Cash sales and collecting cash from customers Cash received from investments Payments made to suppliers for assets or expenses Paying employee salaries Paying interest
Investments	Buying or selling non-current assets
Financing	Issuing shares Borrowing money Paying dividends Payments made to reduce financing loans

FIGURE 12.1

Preparing a Cash Flow Statement

Two methods are used to prepare a cash flow statement: the **indirect method**, which is the most commonly used method, and the **direct method**.

The term indirect refers to tracking the changes to cash without direct reference to cash receipts or payments. In other words, the **indirect method** analyzes cash flow from operations indirectly by starting with accrual-based net income and adding or subtracting certain items from the income statement and changes on the balance sheet.

The direct method is another way of tracing the changes to cash from one period to the next. Like the indirect method, the **direct method** breaks down the three ways of generating and using cash into operating, investing and financing activities. However, unlike the indirect method, the direct method calculates cash flow from operations directly (from scratch). The direct method is often deemed as too burdensome to execute. Therefore, in this chapter we will only focus on the indirect method.

IN THE REAL WORLD

Academic studies have shown that if two versions of the cash flow statement are shown (i.e. direct and indirect method), investors can make better decisions. By disclosing both the direct and indirect method, a company would be improving its accounting transparency. Furthermore, through statistical studies, it has been shown that the indirect method is more useful than the direct method. However, a reason for this discrepancy was not revealed by the studies. Furthermore, the direct method is, on average, more easily understood by users than the indirect method.

Prior to executing the indirect method of preparing the cash flow statement, the balance sheet and income statement should be examined. The cash flow statement presents the change in cash over a period of time and is presented with a date format covering a specified time period similar to the income statement and statement of owner's equity.

Examine the Balance Sheet and the Income Statement

The first document we need is the balance sheet – or a comparative balance sheet for two periods – that tells us how much is in the cash account. Consider Soho Supplies, a manufacturer of office supplies with a year-end of December 31. Soho's financial statements will be used for cash flow analysis in this chapter. We will use this specific balance sheet for Soho Supplies for the remainder of the chapter, and keep referring to it as we move along.

When you examine the balance sheet, you will see that the last column calculates the difference between 2009 and 2010 amounts. This difference will be used when preparing the cash flow statement. As you can see from the first line of the balance sheet, the cash account decreased from $72,642 in 2009 to $13,265 in 2010. This represents a decrease of $59,377.

Soho Supplies
Balance Sheet
As at December 31

	2010	2009	Changes
ASSETS			
Current Assets			*Start with*
Cash	$13,265	$72,642	($59,377)
Accounts receivable	1,286,138	1,065,812	220,326
Inventory	1,683,560	840,091	843,469
Prepaid expenses	48,612	42,625	5,987
Total Current Assets	3,031,575	2,021,170	1,010,405
Property, plant & equipment[(1)]	322,518	170,000	152,518
Less: Accumulated depreciation	(79,262)	(36,000)	(43,262)
TOTAL ASSETS	$3,274,831	$2,155,170	$1,119,661
LIABILITIES AND EQUITY			
Liabilities			
Current Liabilities			
Accounts payable	$783,602	$475,645	$307,957
Current portion of bank loan	380,000	240,000	140,000
Shareholders' loans	170,000	200,000	(30,000)
Total Current Liabilities	1,333,602	915,645	417,957
Non-current portion of bank loan	420,000	356,000	64,000
TOTAL LIABILITIES	1,753,602	1,271,645	481,957
Shareholders' Equity			
Common shares	15,000	5,000	10,000
Retained earnings[(2)]	1,506,229	878,525	627,704
TOTAL SHAREHOLDERS' EQUITY	1,521,229	883,525	637,704
TOTAL LIABILITIES AND EQUITY	$3,274,831	$2,155,170	$1,119,661

Operating *Financing* *Additional Info for inv* *Investments — Non current*

(1) Property, Plant & Equipment:
    a) During 2010, factory equipment was sold for $50,000, which was also the book value of the equipment.
    b) During 2010, Soho made purchases of property, plant & equipment for $202,518.

(2) Retained Earnings:
    Soho declared and paid $10,000 in dividends in 2010.

FIGURE 12.2

We now need to examine Soho's income statement.

Start with cash balance.

Soho Supplies
Income Statement
For the Year Ended December 31, 2010

Sales	$8,685,025
COGS	5,998,612
Gross Profit	2,686,413
Operating Expenses	
Administration charges	8,652
Advertising & marketing	42,645
Depreciation	43,262 *→ Add back.*
Bonuses	65,000
Commission	420,250
Interest	51,875
Insurance	16,000
Sales and administration salaries	610,325
Management salaries	320,560
Occupancy	52,000
Consulting	22,500
Repairs and maintenance	36,860
Professional fees	11,560
Other operating expenses	61,200
Total Operating Expenses	1,762,689
Operating Income Before Tax	923,724
Income Tax	286,020
Net Income	$637,704 *→ Add back*

FIGURE 12.3

The company's net income is $637,704 for 2010. We will be using this income statement for the remainder of the chapter, so keep it handy as we assemble our cash flow statement for 2010.

You may have asked yourself an obvious question after noticing a change in balance of the cash account (which reflects a decrease of $59,377) and a net income of $637,704. What happened to all the cash? This type of question can be answered by the cash flow statement, which ignores accruals and reflects only transactions involving cash. Let us start getting some answers.

Indirect Method

The figure we start with is the balance of cash at the end of 2009 (i.e. the beginning of 2010), which is $72,642.

Cash Flow from Operations

The following illustrations will help you understand the change in cash through day-to-day operations.

As the value of various current assets and liabilities change from one period to another, cash flow is affected. Figures 12.4 to 12.7 illustrate this principle.

If accounts receivable decreases, it means that the cash has been collected, resulting in an increase to cash (as shown in figure 12.4).

If inventory increases, it means that the cash has been used (or will be used) to pay for it, resulting in a decrease in cash (as shown in figure 12.5).

If accounts payable decreases, it means that cash has been used to pay it off, resulting in a decrease in cash (as shown in figure 12.6).

If prepaid expenses increases, this means that cash has been used to pay for it, resulting in a decrease in cash (as shown in figure 12.7).

FIGURE 12.5

FIGURE 12.6

FIGURE 12.7

Now let us start preparing our cash flow from operations. Remember that cash flow from operations under the indirect method starts with net income and then adds or subtracts certain items from the income statement and changes on the balance sheet. In our current example, the company's net income for 2010 is $637,704.

Net income is added to (or net loss is deducted from) our opening cash account balance. Since we are focusing on cash flow instead of accruals, we need to only account for the money that actually changes hands during a period. Therefore, in the cash flow from operations section, we begin with net income and initially add or subtract for non-cash items such as depreciation. Since depreciation is simply the decrease in the value of an asset, without any change to cash, depreciation deductions are taken out of any equations involving cash flow. Then, we add or subtract changes in items related to operations that do not flow through directly to the income statement (i.e. specifically, changes in current assets and current liabilities such as accounts receivable, inventory and accounts payable).

Therefore the next step in assembling the cash flow from operations section is to add back any depreciation that was originally deducted. As shown in the income statement, Soho's depreciation expense for 2010 is $43,262.

Here is how our opening cash balance changes: As you can see in figure 12.8, we take our opening cash balance, add the net income (or deduct the losses if any) and add back depreciation expense. This gives us an updated cash balance of $753,608.

This column is used to calculate the updated cash balance to help you understand the process.

You will not see this theoretical column illustrated in a regular cash flow statement.

Cash Flow Statement for 2010	Amount	Updated Cash Balance
Opening Cash Balance		$72,642
Cash Flow from Operations		
Add: Net income	637,704	710,346
Add: Depreciation	43,262	753,608

FIGURE 12.8

First

Figure 12.8 is only the first part of our cash flow from operations. We start with cash, then add net income or deduct losses and then add depreciation. The second part involves referring back to our comparative balance sheet and going down the list of current assets and liabilities. Loans will be dealt with in the cash flow from financing section, below.

Cash Flow Statement for 2010	Amount	Updated Cash Balance
Opening Cash Balance		$72,642
Opening Cash Balance		
Add: Net income	$637,704	710,346
Add: Depreciation	43,262	753,608
Changes in Current Assets & Current Liabilities:		
Increase in accounts receivable	(220,326)	533,282
Increase in prepaid expenses	(5,987)	527,295
Increase in inventory	(843,469)	(316,174)
Increase in accounts payable	307,957	(8,217)
Change in Cash due to Operations	**(80,859)**	

(handwritten annotations: "Balance Sheet", "Income Statement", "Current Assets Bal. Sh.", "1.", "2.")

FIGURE 12.9

Our first listed current asset in our comparative balance sheet (after cash) is accounts receivable. As indicated in the balance sheet, this account increased by $220,326 from 2009 to 2010. Remember that since accounts receivable increased, it will decrease cash because it is yet to be collected. We therefore deduct this amount from the cash balance of $753,608. As indicated above, the updated cash balance is $533,282.

Prepaid expenses increased by $5,987 resulting in a decrease in cash because the prepaid expenses must have been paid with cash, resulting in an updated cash balance of $527,295.

Inventory increased by $843,469, resulting once again in a decrease in cash because cash must be used to pay for the additional inventory resulting in a negative updated cash balance of $316,174.

Accounts payable increased by $307,957. This will result in more cash in the bank, causing the updated cash balance to increase and ending up with a decrease in cash from operations of $80,859, as indicated in bold in figure 12.9.

Under the indirect method of preparing cash flow statements, the following figure outlines the impact on the cash flow statement an increase or decrease to current assets or current liabilities will have.

Impact on Cash Flow Statement:
Change in Current Assets and Current Liabilities

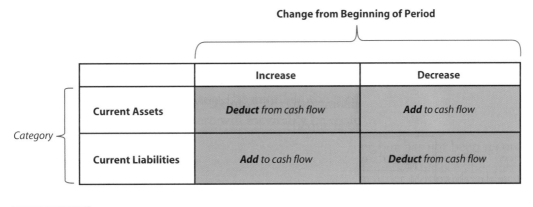

FIGURE 12.10

Cash Flow from Investments

Changes in the value of non-current assets (i.e. property, plant and equipment) affect cash flow. However, measuring the affect is not as straightforward as observing the change in the property, plant and equipment balance from one year to the next.

This section of the cash flow statement deals with the way cash flow changes through the investment in or sale of capital assets. In our current example with Soho Supplies, the information required to complete the cash flow from investments section is provided in the 'Additional Information' portion below Soho's balance sheet (figure 12.2).

The proceeds from the sale of the factory equipment in the amount of $50,000 is added to the updated cash balance since the transaction represents a cash inflow. The $202,518 in purchases of property, plant & equipment is deducted from the updated cash balance because it represents a cash outflow. In figure 12.11, the cash flow from investment section is the new addition to our illustrative cash flow statement.

Cash Flow Statement for 2010	Amount	Updated Cash Balance
Opening Cash Balance		$72,642
Cash Flow from Operations		
Add: Net income	$637,704	710,346
Add: Depreciation	43,262	753,608
Changes in Current Assets & Current Liabilities:		
Increase in accounts receivable	(220,326)	533,282
Increase in prepaid expenses	(5,987)	527,295
Increase in inventory	(843,469)	(316,174)
Increase in accounts payable	307,957	(8,217)
Change in Cash due to Operations	**(80,859)**	
Cash Flow from Investments		
Sale of equipment	50,000	41,783
Purchase of property, plant & equipment	(202,518)	(160,735)
Change in Cash due to Investments	**(152,518)**	

Additional Info

FIGURE 12.11

This is our change in cash due to investments, and essentially constitutes that entire section of the cash flow statement.

Cash Flow from Financing

Cash flow from financing is the last section of the cash flow statement that we need to prepare. As loans or contributed capital (i.e. in our example, common shares) increase or decrease, cash flow is correspondingly affected.

If loans or common shares increases, this means that cash has been received, resulting in an increase in cash. If, on the other hand, loans or common shares decreases, this would lead to a decrease in cash.

Remember that this section accounts for cash resulting from any financing activities during the year. It includes borrowing money or receiving cash as a result of a stock issue. In addition, this section also includes any payments involved with financing, such as dividend payments or loan repayments.

The cash flow from financing section is somewhat different from the other cash flow sections in that it involves changes to more than one section of the statement. For example, in the operations section of the cash flow statement, accounts receivable is one account, inventory is another, and so on.

Cash flow from financing is divided into two areas in our balance sheet: non-current and current. In addition, payments in the form of dividends also affect the cash position directly from year to year. That is why it is especially important to keep track of money as it changes hands while the cash flow statement, particularly the financing section, is being assembled.

First, we need to take a look at our balance sheet again and check all aspects pertaining to financing. The three parts that are affected are shareholder loans, bank loans and dividends.

Let us look at shareholder loans in the current liabilities section of the balance sheet. This is relatively simple since there is only one account here. The decrease in shareholder loans of $30,000 implies that cash also decreased by $30,000 from 2009 to 2010.   Shareholder Loans ↓
Cash ↓

Now look at bank loans. An extra step is involved because bank loans are divided into two areas on our balance sheet: current and non-current. We must extract from the balance sheet the changes from period to period that occurred for both combined.

As shown in figure 12.12 (the liabilities portion of the balance sheet), the current portion of the bank loan increased by $140,000 from 2009 to 2010. The non-current portion of the bank loan increased by $64,000. Therefore, the total increase in the bank loan balance is $204,000 ($140,000 + $64,000). This amount is an increase to cash since Soho is taking additional money out as a loan. Therefore, it represents a cash inflow.

Bank Loan ↑
Cash ↑

	2010	2009	Changes
Liabilities			
Current Liabilities			
Accounts payable	$783,602	$475,645	$307,957
Current portion of bank loan	380,000	240,000	140,000
Shareholders' loans	170,000	200,000	(30,000)
Total Current Liabilities	1,333,602	915,645	417,957
Non-current portion of bank loan	420,000	356,000	64,000
TOTAL LIABILITIES	1,753,602	1,271,645	481,957

❶ Sum = $204,000

FIGURE 12.12

Next, we need to look at dividends. In the 'Additional Information' section under Soho's balance sheet (figure 12.2), it is mentioned that Soho declared and paid $10,000 in dividends during 2010. This represents a decrease to cash because it is a cash outflow.

Pay Div / *Cash ↓* (handwritten margin note)

A CLOSER LOOK

In most problems that ask you to prepare a cash flow statement, total dividends paid is provided to you. However, there are a few cases where this number is not explicitly stated. An alternate way to determine total dividends paid is by referring to the calculation of retained earnings. Recall the following formula for calculating closing retained earnings for a given period:

Closing Retained Earnings = Beginning Retained Earnings + Net Income - Dividends

Rearranging for dividends, the formula is expressed as:

Dividends = Beginning Retained Earnings + Net Income - Closing Retained Earnings

Now, dividends can be calculated provided that beginning retained earnings, net income and closing retained earnings all are provided in the question.

Lastly, the balance of common shares increased by $10,000 from 2009 to 2010. This means that new shares were issued for $10,000 in cash. Therefore, the cash balance is increased by $10,000.

Shares / *Cash ↑* (handwritten margin note)

As should now be clear, changes in cash due to financing account for an increase to our cash account of $174,000 (-$30,000 + $204,000 - $10,000 + $10,000). The cash flow from financing section is added on in figure 12.13 below.

Cash Flow Statement for 2010	Amount	Updated Cash Balance
Opening Cash Balance		$72,642
Cash Flow from Operations		
Add: Net income	$637,704	710,346
Add: Depreciation	43,262	753,608
Changes in Current Assets & Current Liabilities:		
Increase in accounts receivable	(220,326)	533,282
Increase in prepaid expenses	(5,987)	527,295
Increase in inventory	(843,469)	(316,174)
Increase in accounts payable	307,957	(8,217)
Change in Cash due to Operations	**(80,859)**	
Cash Flow from Investments		
Sale of equipment	50,000	41,783
Purchase of property, plant & equipment	(202,518)	(160,735)
Change in Cash due to Investments	**(152,518)**	
Cash Flow from Financing		
Payment towards shareholders' loans	(30,000)	(190,735)
Proceeds from bank loan	204,000 ❶	13,265
Payment of cash dividend	(10,000)	3,265
Issuance of common shares	10,000	13,265
Change in Cash due to Financing	**174,000**	

*Note that the $204,000 proceeds from the bank loan is from the calculation in figure 12.12.

FIGURE 12.13

Summary of the Indirect Method

We have now completed the three sections of our cash flow statement: cash flow from operations, investments and financing. It is now just a matter of putting them all together to form one complete cash flow statement in proper format for 2010 as shown in figure 12.14 below.

Soho Supplies
Cash Flow Statement
For the Year Ended December 31, 2010

Cash Flow from Operations		
Add: Net income	$637,704	
Add: Depreciation	43,262	
Changes in Current Assets & Current Liabilities:		
Increase in accounts receivable	(220,326)	
Increase in prepaid expenses	(5,987)	
Increase in inventory	(843,469)	
Increase in accounts payable	307,957	
Change in Cash due to Operations		($80,859)
Cash Flow from Investments		
Sale of equipment	50,000	
Purchase of property, plant & equipment	(202,518)	
Change in Cash due to Investments		(152,518)
Cash Flow from Financing		
Payment towards shareholders' loans	(30,000)	
Proceeds from bank loan	204,000	
Payment of cash dividend	(10,000)	
Issuance of common shares	10,000	
Change in Cash due to Financing		174,000
Net increase (decrease) in cash		(59,377)
Cash at the beginning of the year		72,642
Cash at the end of the year		$13,265

FIGURE 12.14

Sale of Property, Plant & Equipment

In the sample balance sheet and income statement used to prepare the cash flow statement above, the equipment was sold for the book value. Remember that selling assets for the book value does not affect equity (since there is no gain on the sale) and therefore does not appear on the income statement. *No change in cash.*

Suppose the equipment was sold for $60,000 instead of the $50,000 book value. This would mean that the company made a profit (or gain) of $10,000 on the sale. Anytime non-current assets are sold for more than their book value, a gain is recorded. If the sale price is less than the book value, a loss is recorded. *GAIN   CASH ↑*
LOSS   CASH ↓

By selling the equipment for a gain of $10,000, the financial statements will have to change. On the balance sheet, the extra $10,000 will increase cash and also increase equity (specifically, retained earnings). Because equity increased, the $10,000 gain will also have to be reported on the income statement.

The updated balance sheet is shown in figure 12.15. The items that are different from the balance sheet in figure 12.2 are outlined in green.

Soho Supplies
Balance Sheet
As at December 31

	2010	2009	Changes
ASSETS			
Current Assets			
Cash *(changed)*	$23,265	$72,642	($49,377)
Accounts receivable	1,286,138	1,065,812	220,326
Inventory	1,683,560	840,091	843,469
Prepaid expenses	48,612	42,625	5,987
Total Current Assets	3,041,575	2,021,170	1,020,405
Property, plant & equipment[1]	322,518	170,000	152,518
Less: Accumulated depreciation	(79,262)	(36,000)	(43,262)
TOTAL ASSETS	$3,284,831	$2,155,170	$1,129,661
LIABILITIES AND EQUITY			
Liabilities			
Current Liabilities			
Accounts payable	$783,602	$475,645	$307,957
Current portion of bank loan	380,000	240,000	140,000
Shareholders' loans	170,000	200,000	(30,000)
Total Current Liabilities	1,333,602	915,645	417,957
Non-current portion of bank loan	420,000	356,000	64,000
TOTAL LIABILITIES	1,753,602	1,271,645	481,957
Shareholders' Equity			
Common shares	15,000	5,000	10,000
Retained earnings[2] *(changed)*	1,516,229	878,525	637,704
TOTAL SHAREHOLDERS' EQUITY	1,531,229	883,525	647,704
TOTAL LIABILITIES AND EQUITY	$3,284,831	$2,155,170	$1,129,661

Additional Information:

(1) Property, Plant & Equipment:
    a) During 2010, factory equipment was sold for a gain of $10,000. The cash proceeds from the sale totaled $60,000.

    b) During 2010, Soho made purchases of property, plant & equipment for $202,518.

(2) Retained Earnings:
    Soho declared and paid $10,000 in dividends in 2010.

FIGURE 12.15

The income statement must now show a gain on the sale of the assets as a separate line item. The new income statement is shown below. The items outlined in green represent the differences from the income statement shown in figure 12.3.

Soho Supplies
Income Statement
For the Year Ended December 31, 2010

Sales	$8,685,025
COGS	5,998,612
Gross Profit	2,686,413
Operating Expenses	
Administration charges	8,652
Advertising & marketing	42,645
Depreciation	43,262
Bonuses	65,000
Commission	420,250
Interest	51,875
Insurance	16,000
Sales and administration salaries	610,325
Management salaries	320,560
Occupancy	52,000
Consulting	22,500
Repairs and maintenance	36,860
Professional fees	11,560
Other operating expenses	61,200
Total Operating Expenses	1,762,689
Operating Income	923,724
Other Income	
Gain on Sale of Factory Equipment	10,000
Net Income Before Tax	933,724
Income Tax	286,020
Net Income	$647,704

added.

changed.

FIGURE 12.16

The gain or loss that occurs when property is sold for a value that is different from the book value is not part of day-to-day operations. Therefore, gains and losses must be reported separately from sales and operating expenses. They will appear in a section called "Other Income" or "Other Expenses".

On the cash flow statement, the gain of $10,000 from the sale of factory equipment is deducted from net income in the cash flow from operations section. The net income includes the gain; however the gain is not part of day-to-day operating activities and must be removed from this section. Although the gain will be removed from the operations section, it will be included in the proceeds that Soho received from this sale. The proceeds will be reported in the cash flow from investments section.

Therefore, the $10,000 gain is deducted from net income in the cash flow from operations section to avoid double counting. If, instead, Soho incurred a *loss* from the sale of equipment, the amount would be added back to net income in the cash flow from operations section.

The cash proceeds of $60,000 from the sale of factory equipment are added in the cash flow from investments section since it represents a cash inflow. The new cash flow statement is shown below. The sections in green outline how the gain and the proceeds from the sales are reported on the cash flow statement.

Soho Supplies
Cash Flow Statement
For the Year Ended December 31, 2010

Cash Flow from Operations		
Add: Net income	$647,704	
Add: Depreciation	43,262	
Deduct: Gain on sale of equipment	(10,000)	
Changes in Current Assets & Current Liabilities:		
Increase in accounts receivable	(220,326)	
Increase in prepaid expenses	(5,987)	
Increase in inventory	(843,469)	
Increase in accounts payable	307,957	
Change in Cash due to Operations		($80,859)
Cash Flow from Investments		
Sale of equipment	60,000	
Purchase of property, plant & equipment	(202,518)	
Change in Cash due to Investments		(142,518)
Cash Flow from Financing		
Payment towards shareholders' loans	(30,000)	
Proceeds from bank loan	204,000	
Payment of cash dividend	(10,000)	
Issuance of common shares	10,000	
Change in Cash due to Financing		174,000
Net increase (decrease) in cash		(49,377)
Cash at the beginning of the year		72,642
Cash at the end of the year		$23,265

(handwritten margin notes: "deduct gain" and "Add sale")

FIGURE 12.17

Direct Method

We have assembled a cash flow statement using the *indirect method*. The term indirect refers to tracking the changes to cash without direct reference to cash receipts or payments. In other words, this method analyzes cash flow indirectly by starting with accrual-based net income and making related adjustments for changes on the balance sheet and income statement.

We will now turn our attention to the **direct method**, which is another way of tracing the changes to cash from one period to the next. Like the indirect method, the **direct method** breaks down the three ways of generating and using cash into: operating, investing and financing activities. In this section, we will illustrate how the direct method accomplishes this by looking at, specifically, *cash receipts* and *payments*. The direct method is not often used because it can be burdensome to execute.

Here is a simple example to illustrate the fundamental difference between the indirect method and the direct method presented in this chapter. Jane is a student who currently pays her tuition in cash and gets paid in cash for her part-time job. In an attempt to control her spending, she has opted to use her debit card for all purchases and never pay by credit card. Suppose that, at the end of the year, Jane wants to determine by how much her cash situation changed in the year. There are two ways she can go about doing this:

1. She can review her bank statements and calculate the difference between the December (end of year) bank balance and January (beginning of year) bank balance. Since all her transactions are made with cash, she can simply subtract the beginning of year balance from the end of year balance and determine how her cash situation changed during the year. Or,

2. Jane can calculate her cash flow for the year by adding together all the individual purchase receipts and pay stubs she received throughout the year.

Both methods will add to the same value, assuming all receipts and stubs are accounted for and there are no errors.

Method 1 is, essentially, the indirect method. This is because Jane indirectly determined her cash flow situation by reading off the balances on her bank statements. Method 2, on the other hand, demonstrates the direct cash flow method because Jane directly summed up all her collections and disbursements for the year using source documents. Notice that the direct method can be a lot more time-consuming and prone to error since Jane would have to search for all her documents (e.g. she may have accidentally thrown out some receipts). Similarly to Jane, most companies opt to use the indirect method for simplicity purposes.

In the following example, we will examine how to determine the cash flow of a company using the direct method.

Suppose ArmorVilla Corporation had the following transactions at year end July 31, 2011.

a)	Depreciation expense of	$22,000
b)	Cash sales of	284,000
c)	Loan to another company of	75,000
d)	Credit sales of	966,000
e)	Cash received from issuing current debt of	26,000
f)	Dividends received in cash on investments in shares of	9,000
g)	Payments of salaries amounting to	180,000
h)	Accrued salary expense of	105,000
i)	Collection of interest on notes receivable of	32,000
j)	Cash received from issuing common shares of	81,000
k)	Purchase of inventory on credit of	605,000
l)	Declaration and payment of cash dividends of	144,000
m)	Collections from credit customers of	638,000
n)	Payments to suppliers of	313,000
o)	Payment of non-current debt of	175,000
p)	Cash received from selling equipment (includes gain of $5,000)	30,000
q)	Interest expenses and payments of	21,000
r)	Cash payments to acquire capital assets	204,000
s)	Cash balance: August 1, 2010	$178,000
	July 31, 2011	$166,000

FIGURE 12.18

Since we are using the direct method, we are interested primarily in *cash receipts* and *payments*. Therefore, let's identify only those items that affect cash flow:

b)	Cash sales of	$284,000
c)	Loan to another company of	75,000
e)	Cash received from issuing current debt of	26,000
f)	Dividends received in cash on investments in shares of	9,000
g)	Payments of salaries amounting to	180,000
i)	Collection of interest on notes receivable of	32,000
j)	Cash received from issuing common shares of	81,000
l)	Declaration and payment of cash dividends of	144,000
m)	Collections from credit customers of	638,000
n)	Payments to suppliers of	313,000
o)	Payment of non-current debt of	175,000
p)	Cash received from selling equipment (includes gain of $5,000)	30,000
q)	Interest expenses and payments of	21,000
r)	Cash payments to acquire capital assets	204,000

FIGURE 12.19

Now let's categorize each cash item into the appropriate category to create our statement of cash flow. First, we will consider cash receipts/disbursements that relate to regular business operations.

Cash Flow from Operations		
Cash Sales	$284,000	
Collections from Credit Customers	638,000	
Dividends Received on Investments in Shares	9,000	
Collection of Interest on Notes Receivable	32,000	
Total Cash Receipts		$963,000
Payment of Salaries	180,000	
Payments to suppliers	313,000	
Interest Expenses and Payments	$21,000	
Total Cash Payments		514,000
Change in Cash due to Operations		449,000

FIGURE 12.20

Notice that to perform a cash flow calculation using the direct method, a company has to be able to track information regarding cash inflows and outflows. This makes it more difficult to use the direct method.

Note that the cash flow calculations for investing and financing activities using the direct method are very similar to the indirect method.

The gain that is realized on the sale of the equipment is already included in the sales price of $30,000. There is no need to list the gain anywhere when using the direct method.

Also, the current debt that is issued is considered part of financing activities. The reason for this is that the debt is incurred specifically to help finance the company. This makes it different from other current debt such as accounts payable, which is simply a supplier allowing the company some time to pay their bills.

Cash Flow from Investments		
Loan to Another Company	(75,000)	
Sale of Equipment	30,000	
Capital Asset Acquisition	(204,000)	
Change in Cash due to Investments		(249,000)
Cash Flow from Financing		
Issuance of Current Debt	26,000	
Issuance of Common Shares	81,000	
Declaration And Payment of Dividends (Cash)	(144,000)	
Payment of Non-Current Debt	(175,000)	
Change in Cash due to Financing		(212,000)

FIGURE 12.21

Summary of the direct method

In summary, the cash flow statement of ArmorVilla Corporation prepared by using the direct method is shown in figure 12.22.

Although the direct and indirect method use different approaches to determine the cash flow, both approaches still provide the same end result and allow for an assessment of a company's cash management effectiveness.

ArmorVilla Corporation Cash Flow Statement July 31, 2011		
Cash Flow from Operations		
Cash Sales	$284,000	
Collections from Credit Customers	638,000	
Dividends Received on Investments in Shares	9,000	
Collection of Interest on Notes Receivable	32,000	
Total Cash Receipts		$963,000
Payment of Salaries	180,000	
Payments to suppliers	313,000	
Interest Expenses and Payments	$21,000	
Total Cash Payments		514,000
Change in Cash due to Operations		449,000
Cash Flow from Investments		
Loan to Another Company	(75,000)	
Sale of Equipment	30,000	
Capital Asset Acquisition	(204,000)	
Change in Cash due to Investments		(249,000)
Cash Flow from Financing		
Issuance of Current Debt	$26,000	
Issuance of Common Shares	81,000	
Declaration And Payment of Dividends (Cash)	(144,000)	
Payment of Non-Current Debt	(175,000)	
Change in Cash due to Financing		(212,000)
Net increase (decrease) in cash		(12,000)
Opening Cash Balance, August 1, 2010		178,000
Ending Cash Balance, July 31, 2011		$166,000

FIGURE 12.22

Ethics and Controls

The accounting scandals that began in 2001 with Enron served as a warning to much of the financial community that income statements and balance sheets can be manipulated to present a false financial picture of a business. As a result, an increasing number of people started using the cash flow statement as a more revealing snapshot of a company's financial well-being.

Indeed, the motivation behind relying more on cash flow statements to analyze company performance is understandable. Cash flow statements are supposed to show where the money is coming from and where it is going. However, no financial statement is immune from flaws, and this is certainly also the case with cash flow statements.

The following three situations should be viewed with caution when analyzing the cash flow statement of a business:

- *Some companies may stretch out their payables.* One way of artificially enhancing a company's cash position from operations is to deliberately delay paying bills. In fact, some companies will even go so far as to institute such a policy and label it as a form of shrewd cash flow decision making. Of course, the company has not improved its underlying cash flow, but has simply manipulated it.
- *Some companies may finance their payables.* Some companies try to manipulate their cash flow statements by having a third party pay their payables for them – although regulators have tried to crack down on this practice. This means that the company itself shows no payments in its cash flow and, instead, pays a fee to the third party at a later date. Picking and choosing the periods in which this is done artificially manipulates the cash flow statement — almost at will.
- *Cash flow categories can be artificial.* Although businesses may handle their finances differently, including receiving and paying out cash, cash flow statements should exhibit the same categories listed under the same headings for every business. In essence, information can be lost in translation, and analysts can become too dependent on numbers that are made to fit into the cash flow statement.

The IFRS Perspective

The statement of cash flow is very similar between GAAP and IFRS. IFRS allows corporations to make choices to accounting policy that impacts how interest and dividends are reported. Interest and dividends received because of an investment can be classified as either operating or investing activities. GAAP requires these items to be classified only as operating activities. Also, IFRS will allow dividends paid to be classified as an operating or a financing activity. Under GAAP, dividends paid must be classified as a financing activity only.

Whichever method is decided upon to classify these events, the company must ensure that this classification is consistent from year to year.

In Summary

- Balance sheets and income statements are prepared on an accrual basis, which involves recording transactions that do not necessarily involve any exchange of money. Cash flow statements differ in that they reveal both the sources and uses of cash within a business.

- The three ways of generating cash flow, which form the basis of the way cash flow statements are structured, are operations, investments and financing.

- Two generally accepted methods of preparing a cash flow statement exist for a business: the direct method and the indirect method.

- The indirect method of preparing cash flow statements starts with net income and then tracks changes in balances (within the cash flow from operations section).

- The cash flow statement contains three sections: cash flow from operations, cash flow from investments and cash flow from financing.

- The cash flow from operations section tracks the movement of cash related to day-to-day activities of the business.

- The cash flow from investments section tracks the movement of cash on the basis of the purchases and sales of non-current assets.

- The cash flow from financing section tracks the movement of cash related to the way a company receives money for financing purposes and pays it back.

- The indirect method tends to be universally used in preparing cash flow statements, since the direct method takes a more burdensome approach to tracking cash receipts and payments.

- The direct method of preparing the cash flow statement breaks down cash flows based on actual receipts and payments associated with sales and expenses.

Chapter 12

Review Exercise

Shown below is the balance sheet for MLF. Net income for 2010 was $207,144. N Inc.

Required: Prepare the cash flow statement for 2010. Use the indirect method.

MLF Balance Sheet As at December 31, 2010		
	2010	**2009**
Assets		
Current Assets		
Cash	$28,222	$64,494
Other Current Assets	605,379	902,417
Total Current Assets	633,601	966,911
Non-Current Assets		
Property, Plant and Equipment	3,490,970	3,389,108
Less: Accumulated Depreciation	(1,126,727)	(1,080,293)
Total Non-Current Assets	2,364,243	2,308,815
Total Assets	$2,997,844	$3,275,726
Liabilities		
Current Liabilities	$591,199	$778,299
Non-Current Liabilities	1,245,218	1,502,985
Total Liabilities	1,836,417	2,281,284
Shareholders' Equity		
Contributed Capital	790,027	790,027 [a]
Opening Retained Earnings	204,415	231,907
Net Income for the Year	207,144	4,525
Dividends Paid	(40,159)	(32,017)
Closing Retained Earnings	371,400	204,415 [b]
Total Shareholders' Equity	1,161,427	994,442 [a + b]
Total Liabilities and Shareholders' Equity	$2,997,844	$3,275,726

Handwritten annotations: Op, Op., In, Op., Op, FIN, FIN; Opening Cash (297 038); 101,862; 46 434; (187,100); (257 767)

Assume current liabilities include only items from operations (e.g. accounts payable, tax payable). Non-current liabilities include items from financing (e.g. bonds and other non-current liabilities)

MLF Cash Flow Statement For the Year Ended December 31, 2010		
	Change	**New Cash Balance**
Opening Cash		$64,494
Cash Flows from Operations		
Net Income	$207,144 ✓	271,638
Add: Depreciation	46,434 ✓	318,072
Decrease in Other Current Assets	297,038 ✓	615,110
Decrease in Current Liabilities	(187,100) ✓	428,010
Total Increase in Cash from Operations	363,516	
Cash Flows from Investments		
Purchase of Property, Plant and Equipment	(101,862) ✓	326,148
Total Decrease in Cash from Investing	(101,862)	
Cash Flows from Financing		
Paid Non-Current Liabilities	(257,767) ✓	68,381
Dividends Paid	(40,159) ✓	28,222
Total Decrease in Cash from Financing	(297,926)	
Total Decrease in Cash from All Sources	(36,272)	
Closing Cash		$28,222

Chapter 13
FINANCIAL STATEMENT ANALYSIS

LEARNING OUTCOMES:

❶ Understand the importance of analyzing a combination of financial ratios to determine financial performance

❷ Calculate and comprehend ratios that pertain to profitability

❸ Calculate and comprehend ratios that pertain to cash flow

❹ Calculate and comprehend ratios that pertain to management performance

❺ Perform horizontal and vertical analysis of financial statements

The Importance of Financial Statement Analysis

It might be tempting to believe that once the financial statements are prepared and read, the job of the accountant, or anyone interested in analyzing the health of the business, is over. However (with perhaps the exception of some added notes), these financial statements do not provide all the answers needed to form conclusions on where the business is heading. These answers are, however, needed by the organization's accountants, its management team, potential lenders and investors, or others with an interest in the state of the business.

In order to start getting answers, and to draw conclusions on the financial state of the business, accountants and other interested parties perform what is known as a **financial analysis** of the financial statements. **Financial ratios** are used to perform this kind of analysis.

We have learned about different financial ratios in previous chapters, each providing a snapshot of a particular area of the business. Some financial ratios provide answers relative to profitability, while others address inventory, and so on. No financial ratio, on its own, can form the basis of the financial analysis of a business. Instead, a combination of ratios must be used to draw a complete picture of the state of an organization's finances. In a sense, financial analysis is much like peeling an orange. An orange with its peel on can give you a sense of how ripe it is. Peel away the skin, and you get a closer picture. Does it have bruises? Is it firm or soft? To truly know how good the orange is, it is then necessary to take a bite. Finally, more bites are taken and a conclusion is formed as to the taste and quality of the orange.

Our approach to financial analysis follows a similar logic. Here is the progression that we take:

Revenues are Vanity

Much like an orange with its peel on, glancing at business revenues does not necessarily give us an accurate picture. In other words, sales do not guarantee profits.

Profits are Sanity

Some serious weaknesses can exist within a business if profits are not quickly transformed into cash. In other words, a business should have a good degree of liquidity. Just as taking off the orange peel provides a better look at the fruit, but not necessarily an accurate judgment as to its quality, a company's profit figures may not provide all the information we need.

Cash Flow is Reality

Getting more information about the well-being of a business comes from looking at its cash flow. It gives us the most accurate picture of the true state of the financial affairs of a business. Accountants and analysts can only give a business a clean bill of health if they are satisfied that profits result in enough cash flow for the business.

Management Ensures Stability

You will not get a sense of what the orange tastes like unless you put it in your mouth and start savoring its flavour. Similarly, you will not get a sense of how the company's cash flow is managed unless you take a look at some management ratios.

The rest of this chapter is dedicated to performing a financial analysis based on this precise sequence. Soho Supplies is a manufacturer of office supplies and was introduced in the previous chapter. Soho's financial statements will be used for analysis in this chapter. The income statement is presented below.

Soho Supplies
Income Statement
For the Year Ended December 31

	2010	2009
Sales	$8,685,025	$6,482,000
Cost of goods sold	5,998,612	4,397,200
Gross Profit	2,686,413	2,084,800
Operating Expenses		
Administration charges	8,652	6,861
Advertising & marketing	42,645	32,975
Depreciation	43,262	15,862
Bonuses	65,000	62,432
Commission	420,250	325,210
Interest	51,875	31,253
Insurance	16,000	12,000
Sales and administration salaries	610,325	435,951
Management salaries	320,560	226,548
Occupancy	52,000	48,000
Consulting	22,500	21,356
Repairs and maintenance	36,860	26,845
Professional fees	11,560	8,642
Other operating expenses	61,200	48,672
Total Operating Expenses	1,762,689	1,302,607
Operating Income Before Tax	923,724	782,193
Income Tax	286,020	223,652
Net Income	$637,704	$558,541

FIGURE 13.1

Revenues are Vanity

The first part of our analysis is to consider changes in revenue. Presented below is a portion of Soho's income statement, illustrating the change in revenue.

Soho Supplies
Income Statement
For the Year Ended December 31

	2010	2009	
Sales	$8,685,025	$6,482,000	↑ $2,203,025 (or 34%)
Cost of goods sold	5,998,612	4,397,200	
Gross Profit	2,686,413	2,084,800	
Operating Expenses			
Administration charges	8,652	6,861	

FIGURE 13.2

As shown in figure 13.2, revenue jumped from $6,482,000 in 2009 to $8,685,025 in 2010. This constitutes an increase of $2,203,025 (or 34%).

Revenues only form the first superficial glance at the numbers for the business. In this case, growing revenues, numbering in the millions of dollars, might look great. However, we need more analysis and ratios to determine if they are in fact great figures, or merely superficial indicators of business health. For example, if revenues increased by $2.2 million but costs increased by $4 million then just looking at changes in revenues, alone, will not give us a true understanding of how the company has performed in the past year.

Profits are Sanity

The next step in our approach to financial analysis is to look at profits. Remember, profits are sanity. In other words, profits can serve as a deeper indicator of financial stability, beyond revenues. For Soho Supplies, gross profit (revenues minus cost of goods sold) has increased by $601,613 (from $2,084,800 in 2009 to $2,686,413 in 2010).

However, just as with revenues, gross profit figures can only tell us so much. In this case, they indicate the business is turning revenues into profit. But we need more information — which means that we need to introduce some ratios into the mix. We will start with the gross profit margin.

Gross Profit Margin

We use the gross profit margin to demonstrate the impact of cost of goods sold on the financial statements. In other words, the gross profit margin subtracts cost of goods sold from sales revenue, the result of which is divided by sales revenue. Here is the formula:

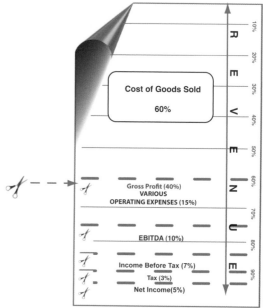

Our approach to analyzing the entire income statement is rather simple, and is depicted in this diagram of a piece of paper. The entire paper represents business revenues. As our analysis proceeds, a certain chunk - or percentage - is taken from revenues, which leaves something behind for us to analyze. By the end of the income statement, we are left with the smallest chunk, which is net income. By then it will be time to move on to the balance sheet.

FIGURE 13.3

$$\text{Gross Profit Margin} \quad = \quad \frac{\text{Gross Profit*}}{\text{Sales Revenue}}$$

* Gross Profit = Sales Revenue − Cost of Goods Sold

Gross profit margin tells us how much money is left to pay expenses, other than those directly involved in producing the goods or services of the business. That is, how much profitability remains after deducting the cost of goods sold.

The following chart calculates the gross profit margin using figures from the income statement:

	2010	2009
Sales	$8,685,025	$6,482,000
COGS	5,998,612	4,397,200
Gross Profit	2,686,413	2,084,800
Gross Profit Margin	30.93%	32.16%

FIGURE 13.4

As you can see, gross profit margin has decreased by more than one percentage point over the course of the period. There are various reasons why this might occur, ranging from discount prices and changes in product mix, to inventory shrinkage and under-valuation.

EBITDA

It might be tempting to believe that the next step in our analysis is to start peeling away all costs after gross profit has been calculated. As enticing as it might be to jump from gross profit to net income, there is a step in between that many accountants and analysts take to get an even clearer picture of business performance. Specifically, certain costs (that are considered largely under the control of management) are added back after net income is calculated. These costs generally include interest, tax, depreciation and amortization. Note that amortization is an alternate term for depreciation. Together, they are referred to as EBITDA or earnings before interest, tax, depreciation and amortization.

Adding these costs back after net income is calculated essentially levels the playing field when analyzing the performance of one business compared to another. In other words, items such as depreciation and taxes are not the result of day-to-day managerial decision-making. Instead, these types of costs can vary from jurisdiction to jurisdiction or from one business to another. Net income, therefore, does not reflect the direct performance that the business controls.

The expenses that are added back to net income to calculate EBITDA are highlighted below. Thus, EBITDA for 2010 is $1,018,861 and EBITDA for 2009 is $829,308.

Soho Supplies
Income Statement
For the Year Ended December 31

	2010	2009	
Sales	$8,685,025	$6,482,000	
Cost of goods sold	5,998,612	4,397,200	
Gross Profit	2,686,413	2,084,800	
Operating Expenses			
Administration charges	8,652	6,861	
Advertising & marketing	42,645	32,975	
Depreciation	43,262	15,862	**Add back**
Bonuses	65,000	62,432	
Commission	420,250	325,210	
Interest	51,875	31,253	**Add back**
Insurance	16,000	12,000	
Sales and administration salaries	610,325	435,951	
Management salaries	320,560	226,548	
Occupancy	52,000	48,000	
Consulting	22,500	21,356	
Repairs and maintenance	36,860	26,845	
Professional fees	11,560	8,642	
Other operating expenses	61,200	48,672	
Total Operating Expenses	1,762,689	1,302,607	
Operating Income Before Tax	923,724	782,193	
Income Tax	286,020	223,652	**Add back**
Net Income	$637,704	$558,541	**Start with Net Income**

FIGURE 13.5

EBITDA Percentage to Sales

Given that we now have a better understanding of what EBITDA is, and why associated expenses are added back to net income; it is time to start formulating some ratios as a result. You may have noticed a trend in the ratios we have used so far. Specifically, we have taken that part of the pie remaining after certain expenses are deducted — such as COGS, operating expenses, and so on — and divided it by revenues. In other words, we have been deducting slices of expenses from revenue and then dividing the remainder by revenue itself. This gives us a corresponding percentage relative to revenue, which, in essence, tells us how much money we are working with on a percentage basis. The exact same thing is done with EBITDA.

In other words, we want to take our EBITDA number and divide it by revenue, to obtain yet another percentage figure to work with in our analysis.

$$\text{EBITDA Percentage to Sales} = \frac{\text{EBITDA}}{\text{Sales Revenue}}$$

This ratio has been calculated for us in the following chart:

	2010	2009
Sales	$8,685,025	$6,482,000
EBITDA:		
Net Income	637,704	558,541
Add back:		
Depreciation Expense	+ 43,262	15,862
Interest Expense	+ 51,875	31,253
Income Tax	+ 286,020	223,652
EBITDA	$1,018,861	$829,308
EBITDA Percentage to Sales	11.73%	12.79%

FIGURE 13.6

As you can see, although EBITDA has increased in absolute dollars from 2009 to 2010, the percentage has, in fact, decreased. This probably means that the business has become less efficient during the period and further analysis needs to be done to find out which expenses are contributing to the decline.

Interest Coverage Ratio

You may have noticed that financial ratios are often nothing more than a comparison of numbers involving one figure divided by another. In fact, most of the ratios analyzed so far in this chapter involve dividing a number by revenues, which provides us with a percentage relative to revenues.

The second ratio we will look at with respect to EBITDA is the **interest coverage ratio** which is very similar to the EBITDA to sales ratio. The only difference is that instead of dividing EBITDA by revenues, it is interest that serves as the denominator in the ratio. In other words, the interest coverage ratio measures the extent to which earnings before interest, taxes, depreciation and amortization covers the interest payments that are to be made by the business. That is, to what extent does EBITDA cover the ability to pay lenders cash in the form of regular interest payments that are due within the period?

For example, an interest coverage ratio of only 1 time would mean that the business has just enough earnings (before EBITDA expenses are deducted) to cover the amount of interest paid during the year.

Here is how the interest coverage ratio is calculated:

$$\text{Interest Coverage Ratio} = \frac{\text{EBITDA}}{\text{Interest Expense}}$$

The corresponding numbers related to interest coverage are provided in the following chart:

	2010	2009
EBITDA	$1,018,861	$829,308
Interest Expense	$51,875	$31,253
Interest Coverage Ratio	**19.64 times**	**26.54 times**

FIGURE 13.7

As you can see, total interest has increased at a rate greater than that for EBITDA. Although the interest coverage ratios for both periods are well above 2 times (which is desirable), if this downward trend continues, it may mean that the business will have an increasingly difficult time covering its interest payments with EBITDA.

There is one last thing about EBITDA. As useful a tool as it can be when analyzing financial statements, it is not sanctioned by GAAP or IFRS. This means that businesses may exercise some flexibility when it comes to what is included in EBITDA calculations. This should be kept in mind when reading published financial reports released by an organization.

Net Profit Margin

Now that we have taken EBITDA into account, we can finally move on to net income. Specifically, we can use **net profit margin** to assess profitability after all expenses have been deducted.

$$\text{Net Profit Margin} = \frac{\text{Net Income}}{\text{Sales Revenue}}$$

Here are the net profit (i.e. net income) numbers from the income statement we have been using:

	2010	2009
Net Income	$637,704	$558,541
Revenue	$8,685,025	$6,482,000
Net Profit Margin	**7.34%**	**8.62%**

FIGURE 13.8

Although the absolute revenue and net income dollar figures have risen over the course of the period, the net profit margin has decreased. In order to perform a complete analysis of net profit margins, comparisons should be made on a monthly and yearly basis to historical company performance, industry averages and direct competitors. Only then will these net income figures be placed in context so that assessments can be made and conclusions drawn.

As was alluded to earlier in this chapter, you should notice another trend in the ratios we have been calculating so far, especially those done with respect to revenues — where revenues serve as the denominator in the corresponding ratio.

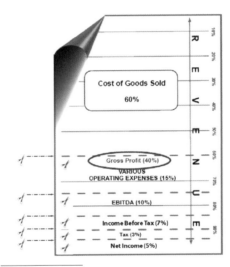

FIGURE 13.9

Specifically, these percentages, or margins, are getting smaller as we go along. That is because as expenses get deducted from revenues, the remaining figure gets increasingly smaller. Therefore, gross profit margin will be larger than EBITDA percentage to sales, which will be larger than net profit margin. In other words, the more we break down the income statement, the less we have left to analyze.

Linking the Income Statement to the Balance Sheet

The next part of our approach to analyzing financial statements takes us from the income statement to the balance sheet. We will analyze Soho Supplies' balance sheet.

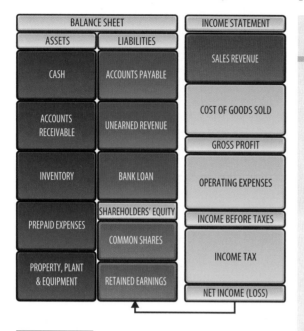

FIGURE 13.10

As the diagram shows, the next step in our analysis of Soho Supplies' financial statements is to essentially link the income statement to the balance sheet. We do this by moving from net income on the income statement to shareholders' equity on the balance sheet.

Soho Supplies Balance Sheet As at December 31	2010	2009
ASSETS		
Current Assets		
Cash	$13,265	$72,642
Accounts receivable	1,286,138	1,065,812
Inventory	1,683,560	840,091
Prepaid expenses	48,612	42,625
Total Current Assets	3,031,575	2,021,170
Property, plant & equipment	243,256	134,000
TOTAL ASSETS	$3,274,831	$2,155,170
LIABILITIES AND EQUITY		
Liabilities		
Current Liabilities		
Accounts payable	$783,602	$475,645
Current portion of bank loan	380,000	240,000
Shareholders' loans	170,000	200,000
Total Current Liabilities	1,333,602	915,645
Non-current portion of bank loan	420,000	356,000
TOTAL LIABILITIES	1,753,602	1,271,645
Shareholders' Equity		
Common shares	15,000	5,000
Retained earnings	1,506,229	878,525
TOTAL SHAREHOLDERS' EQUITY	1,521,229	883,525
TOTAL LIABILITIES AND EQUITY	$3,274,831	$2,155,170

FIGURE 13.11

Return on Equity (ROE)

We went from gross profit margin, to EBITDA, to net profit margin. Each step of the way told us something more about how well the company was using the revenues it earned. It is now time to move onto the balance sheet of the business, which essentially tells us how strong a position the organization is in with respect to what it owns versus what it owes. We proceed with our analysis of financial statements by assessing owners' equity, shareholders' equity, capital accounts, or other accounts that describe the net worth of the business.

IN THE REAL WORLD

One of the most important assessments that owners of a business can make is to know if they are getting a decent return on their investment. How is this done and how do they know if they are getting their money's worth out of the business?

Any determination of return on investment revolves around shareholders' equity. In other words, how much cash would the owners have left if they sold all the assets of the business and paid off all their debt? Given that this is a hypothetical question, and that the owners do not have to sell everything to assess the return on investment, there are other ways of assessing the value of the investment in the business.

For example, the owners could ask themselves another theoretical question: Should we keep our money in the business, or put it elsewhere? Safe investments such as fixed deposit accounts come with relatively lower returns on investment. Investing in a friend's new business comes with a potentially much larger return on investment — but also with greater risk.

In fact, a general rule of thumb can be applied to assessing return on investment associated with certain levels of risk. Generally speaking, investments in publicly traded companies come with the expectation of a return ranging from 15%- 25%. Alternatively, the rate of return associated with private companies is expected to be much higher. In fact, it is not unusual to expect a rate of return of 100% or more for an investment in a small private company.

As with most things in life, everything comes at a price. With return on investment, the price can be a matter of risk. If owners want a better return, they must have a greater tolerance for risk.

The first basic analysis to be performed on the balance sheet involves assessing **return on equity (ROE)**. ROE is a measure of what the owners are getting out of the business relative to the amount they invested.

Although there are various ways to calculate ROE, we will examine the most common method:

$$\text{Return on Equity} = \frac{\text{Net Income}}{\text{Average Shareholders' Equity}}$$

First, we calculate average shareholders' equity by adding opening shareholders' equity and closing shareholders' equity and then dividing the result by two. Second, net income is the numerator for the ratio, which means that the last figure on the income statement serves as the basis from which we start measuring balance sheet performance. That is, net income serves as our link to the balance sheet at this stage of our financial analysis.

A CLOSER LOOK

The return on equity formula assumes that there is no preferred share equity included in shareholders' equity. If preferred equity exists, the formula would be as follows:

Return on Equity = (Net Income - Preferred Dividends) ÷ Average Common Shareholders' Equity

Preferred shares are beyond the scope of this course.

The following chart provides a breakdown of the ROE calculation for our ongoing example. Two assumptions are made. One, assume that the beginning shareholders' equity balance for 2009 is $716,475. Two, assume that the sample company has no outstanding preferred shares.

	2010	2009
Net Income	$637,704	$558,541
Average Shareholders' Equity[1]	$1,202,377	$800,000
Return on Equity	**53.04%**	**69.82%**

(1) Average Shareholders' Equity for 2009: (716,475 + 883,525) ÷ 2 = 800,000
    Average Shareholders' Equity for 2010: (883,525 + 1,521,229) ÷ 2 = 1,202,377

FIGURE 13.12

Although net income and average shareholders' equity values have increased, the return on equity has decreased fairly significantly from 2009 to 2010.

Return on Assets (ROA)

During the income statement portion of our financial analysis, we peeled away certain layers by starting with revenues and then working our way down to net income. We do much of the same thing during the balance sheet portion of our financial analysis. Specifically, we start with net income from the income statement, jump over to the shareholders' equity account on the balance sheet, and are now ready for the next step. That is, we are ready to take liabilities out of the equation and focus specifically on assets. We do this by using the **return on assets (ROA)** ratio, which is calculated as follows:

$$\text{Return on Assets} = \frac{\text{Net Income}}{\text{Average Total Assets}}$$

ROA essentially provides an assessment of what the company does with what it has; it measures every dollar earned against each dollar's worth of assets. A business invests in assets for the purpose of generating sales and making a profit. This is what ROA tries to measure. Although assessing ROA depends on the type of business being analyzed, a higher ROA number is generally considered better than a lower one. A higher ratio means that the business is earning more money on its investment in assets.

Let us now calculate ROA using our sample company. We have already used the net income numbers needed from the income statement. The total asset figures are to be found on the balance sheet. Assume that the balance of total assets as at December 31, 2008 was $1,844,830.

The following chart provides the necessary ROA calculations:

		2010	2009
Net Income	*2010*	$637,704	$558,541
Average Total Assets[1]	*2009 + 2010 ÷ 2*	$2,715,001	$2,000,000
Return on Assets		**23.49%**	**27.93%**

(1) Average Total Assets for 2009: (1,844,830 + 2,155,170) ÷ 2 = 2,000,000
Average Total Assets for 2010: (2,155,170 + 3,274,831) ÷ 2 = 2,715,001
2009 + 2010

FIGURE 13.13

As you can see, although both net income and asset values have increased, the rate of return has decreased. This discrepancy between absolute figures and percentages is precisely why we use the latter. It also reveals a trend in the business. Specifically, although revenue, income and asset values keep increasing, they can also go down in relative terms.

Regarding our ROA calculations, the ratio for 2010 is 23.49%. This essentially means that the business earned more than 23¢ for each dollar invested in assets. This is a decrease from 28¢ in the 2009. Various factors might explain the decrease ranging from an increase in the cost of fixed assets, to an increase in production costs that affect the cost of goods sold directly.

In fact, the list of factors contributing to a change in ROA can be almost endless. Some of the most important business decisions by managers pertain to how well resources are allocated. Efficient use of assets should increase ROA. A less productive use of assets can ultimately lead to a decrease in ROA. In essence, ROA measures how efficiently business assets are used relative to profits generated.

As a general rule, an ROA of below 5% is considered capital-intensive or asset-heavy. This means that the business is investing a considerable amount in assets relative to profits. Industries that tend to display low ROA figures include manufacturers and large transportation companies such as railroads. Alternatively, an ROA of over 20% is considered much less capital-intensive or asset-heavy. In other words, such businesses tend to get more 'bang for the buck' when it comes to investing in assets. Examples include professional practices, software companies and retailers.

Asset Turnover

Another way to assess how well business assets are being utilized is to test how much revenue is generated for every dollar of assets. This is calculated by dividing revenue by average total assets.

Asset turnover measures the ability of a company to generate sales revenue from asset investments—the higher the number the better.

$$\text{Asset Turnover} = \frac{\text{Sales Revenue}}{\text{Average Total Assets}}$$

Using our sample statements, let us compare the results for 2009 and 2010.

	2010	2009
Sales Revenue	$8,685,025	$6,482,000
Average Total Assets[1] 2009 + 2000 ÷ 2	$2,715,001	$2,000,000
Asset Turnover	**3.20 times**	**3.24 times**

(1) See Figure 13.13 for calculation of average total assets.

FIGURE 13.14

In 2009, the business generated $3.24 of revenue for every dollar tied up in assets. In 2010, however, the return dropped to $3.20 in revenue for every dollar tied up in assets. What does this tell us? If the business invested less cash in assets but generated more revenue this would mean that the business is "selling more with less". The higher the revenue per dollar tied up in assets the more efficiently the assets are being utilized.

Cash Flow Is Reality

Our analysis of the balance sheet so far has been related to net income. It is now time to leave the income statement altogether. We will focus on the balance sheet exclusively to look at cash flow and related financial ratios.

An analysis of business cash flow determines the extent to which profits are transformed into actual cash in the bank. In other words, cash flow analysis is an attempt to assess the liquidity of the business. Will the business have enough cash on hand when needed? Does it have the ability to get cash when necessary? Can this cash cover debts and more? We will provide the answers to these questions as we look at liquidity ratios. Liquidity ratios are used to evaluate a company's ability to meet debt obligations (primarily short-term debt).

Current Ratio

The **current ratio** assesses the ability of the business to pay its current debt. The formula for the ratio is:

$$\text{Current Ratio} = \frac{\text{Current Assets}}{\text{Current Liabilities}}$$

The "current" label on the balance sheet is almost always associated with a period of 12 months or less. Therefore, current assets and current liabilities both have terms of less than a year.

Soho Supplies Balance Sheet As at December 31	2010	2009
ASSETS		
Current Assets		
Cash	$13,265	$72,642
Accounts receivable	1,286,138	1,065,812
Inventory	1,683,560	840,091
Prepaid expenses	48,612	42,625
Total Current Assets	3,031,575	2,021,170
Property, plant & equipment	243,256	134,000
TOTAL ASSETS	$3,274,831	$2,155,170
LIABILITIES AND EQUITY		
Liabilities		
Current Liabilities		
Accounts payable	$783,602	$475,645
Current portion of bank loan	380,000	240,000
Shareholders' loans	170,000	200,000
Total Current Liabilities	1,333,602	915,645
Non-current portion of bank loan	420,000	356,000
TOTAL LIABILITIES	1,753,602	1,271,645

FIGURE 13.15

2.27   2.21

above 2   Good.

+ increased

The current ratio assesses business liquidity by determining the extent to which current assets can cover current debts. No business wants to find itself in a position of having to sell fixed assets to pay current bills. A current ratio of at least 1 indicates that the business has just enough current assets to pay for its current liabilities. If the current ratio is less than 1, the business will have to pay close attention to its cash balance to ensure it can pay the current liabilities as they come due.

Depending on the industry in question, the higher the current ratio, the more assurance that the business has enough of a cushion that it can afford to have some cash tied up in current assets, such as inventory and accounts receivable. Once these assets are cashed, so to speak, they can be used to pay for current liabilities such as current portions of bank loans or bills to suppliers.

It may seem counterintuitive to say that a business that is too liquid is using its capital inefficiently. For example, if the current ratio of a business is 5, it has $5.00 in current assets for every dollar that it owes in the next 12 months. This would indicate that the business does not need so much cash. Money in a bank account earning 3% is not an efficient use of assets, especially if the business is earning a return on investment of 20%. Cash should either be invested in new fixed assets or perhaps invested in the short-term until a better use for the cash can be established.

The following chart calculates the current ratio using the numbers provided in Soho Supplies' financial statements:

	2010	2009
Current Assets	$3,031,575	$2,021,170
Current Liabilities	$1,333,602	$915,645
Current Ratio	2.27	2.21

FIGURE 13.16

In this case, our ratio indicates a healthy state of affairs. Not only is the ratio above 2 for both years, but it has increased from one year to the next.

Investing too much money in fixed assets that are not liquid enough could compromise a healthy current ratio. Property, plant and equipment should be financed with non-current liabilities such as term loans. Current liabilities should not be used for this purpose.

Quick Ratio

The other liquidity ratio that is relevant to our current analysis of business cash flow is the **quick ratio** (also known as the acid test).

Here is the calculation for this ratio:

$$\text{Quick Ratio} = \frac{\text{Cash} + \text{Short Term Investments} + \text{Accounts Receivable}}{\text{Current Liabilities}}$$

The quick ratio is much like the current ratio; the only difference is that the quick ratio excludes some current assets which cannot be quickly converted to cash (such as inventory and prepaid expenses). Short term investments occur when a company has excess cash and wishes to invest it. This cash can be invested in shares of other companies. The details of short term investments are beyond the scope of this course.

In essence, the quick ratio assesses the ability of the business to meet its most immediate debt obligations without relying on the liquidation of inventory (which may take some time to sell). A quick ratio of at least 1 indicates that the business has just enough liquid assets to pay for its current liabilities. Anything below 1 might mean the business has too much of its money tied up in inventory and may be unable to pay its short-term bills.

Quick ratios have been calculated using the numbers in our sample financial statements. Note that Soho Supplies does not have any short-term investments.

	2010	2009
Cash + Accounts Receivable	$1,299,403	$1,138,454
Current Liabilities	$1,333,602	$915,645
Quick Ratio	0.97	1.24

FIGURE 13.17

With a quick glance, you will notice that the quick ratio has decreased from 2009 (1.24) to 2010 (0.97). This means that the business has gone from a sound short-term liquidity position to a potentially dangerous one.

To address any potential problems here, and since the balance sheet provides only a snapshot of business finances, further analyses should be performed over the course of the next few months on the specific assets and liabilities of the business. This is to ensure that bills can in fact be paid on time.

The situation could have developed due to too much money being invested in inventory or fixed assets. A review should be performed to address the situation and rectify any problems found.

Debt-to-Equity Ratio

The **debt-to-equity ratio** is used to assess how much of a company is being financed by lenders, and how much is being financed by the owners or shareholders. In other words, this ratio assesses the extent to which a business is indebted to lenders and whether it can afford to borrow more cash if necessary.

Here is the how the debt-to-equity ratio is calculated:

$$\text{Debt-to-Equity Ratio} = \frac{\text{Total Liabilities}}{\text{Total Shareholders' Equity}}$$

It is simply not healthy for a business to borrow too much relative to what it is worth. The industry the business is in will usually have a bearing on how much will have to be borrowed. If a business has a debt-to-equity ratio of 0.50, this means that for every $0.50 of debt it has, it has $1.00 in shareholders' equity.

WORTH REPEATING...
Acquiring loans or paying back loan principals has no effect on equity.

Look at the debt-to-equity numbers from Soho's balance sheet:

Liabilities		
Current Liabilities		
Accounts payable	$783,602	$475,645
Current portion of bank loan	380,000	240,000
Shareholders' loans	170,000	200,000
Total Current Liabilities	1,333,602	915,645
Non-current portion of bank loan	420,000	356,000
TOTAL LIABILITIES	1,753,602	1,271,645
Shareholders' Equity		
Common shares	15,000	5,000
Retained earnings	1,506,229	878,525
TOTAL SHAREHOLDERS' EQUITY	1,521,229	883,525
TOTAL LIABILITIES AND EQUITY	$3,274,831	$2,155,170

FIGURE 13.18

Entering these numbers into the debt-to-equity formula, we get the following:

	2010	2009
Total Liabilities	$1,753,602	$1,271,645
Shareholders' Equity	$1,521,229	$883,525
Debt-to-Equity	**1.15**	**1.44**

Should be < 1.00

FIGURE 13.19

As you can see, although the debt-to-equity ratio has improved from 2009 to 2010, it is still above 1.

There are a few ways a business can improve the debt-to-equity ratio. First, making more profit might do the trick (although it is easier said than done), since it directly results in an increase to shareholders' equity. Second, the business might think about issuing equity (possibly in the form of shares), in exchange for cash.

A CLOSER LOOK

The debt to equity ratio above is calculated as total liabilities divided by total shareholders' equity (as at a given date). This form of the calculation of the debt to equity ratio will be used throughout the book, unless otherwise stated. There exist slight variations of the debt to equity ratio such as non-current debt divided by shareholders' equity or average liabilities divided by average shareholders' equity. Any one of these forms of the calculation is acceptable as long as the company uses the same form from year to year and discloses how the ratio is calculated.

Management Ensures Stability

We have reached the last part of our approach to analyzing the financial statements of a business. We started with revenues on the income statement, worked our way down to net income, jumped over to shareholders' equity on the balance sheet, and looked at various relationships between assets and liabilities on that balance sheet. Now it is time to assess some of the decision-making aspects of running a business. We need to take a look at what management is doing.

Using financial ratios, we can assess managerial performance by looking at two components of the business: accounts receivable and inventory. Ratios related to each of these components provide us with some sense of what people are doing with the business. It is not just about the bottom line. The further we get into our analysis, the more we try to go beyond the bottom line. That is why we look at managerial performance indicators.

Accounts Receivable Ratios

One key to business success is the ability to collect on its bills. In other words, sales have to result in cash. If customers are buying a product or service on credit, they have to pay within a reasonable amount of time to ensure cash flow and financial health. That is what the **days-sales-outstanding** (DSO) and **accounts receivable turnover** are all about.

Days-Sales-Outstanding (DSO):

The formula for days-sales-outstanding is as follows:

$$\text{Days-Sales-Outstanding} = \left(\frac{\text{Average Accounts Receivable}}{\text{Net Credit Sales}} \right) \times 365$$

From here on in, we will assume that all sales revenues are credit sales for the DSO calculation. The DSO provides an indication of how many days it takes for customers to pay their bills. This number is important because late payments can cost a business lost interest from cash, or additional administration costs required to collect payments from customers.

We will take a look at DSO as they relate to our ongoing example for Soho Supplies. Assume that the accounts receivable balance for Soho as at December 31, 2008 was $934,188.

	2010	2009
Average Accounts Receivable[1]	$1,175,975	$1,000,000
Revenue (all credit sales)	$8,685,025	$6,482,000
	× 365	× 365
Days-Sales-Outstanding	**49.42 days**	**56.31 days**

(1) Average Accounts Receivable for 2009: (934,188 + 1,065,812) ÷ 2 = 1,000,000
Average Accounts Receivable for 2010: (1,065,812 + 1,286,138) ÷ 2 = 1,175,975

FIGURE 13.20

As you can see, the business is improving its ability to collect from customers. The DSO decreased from over 56 days in 2009, to below 50 days in 2010. That is the kind of performance that owners, investors, and analysts want to see from an organization.

However, there are some cautionary notes to keep in mind related to the DSO. First, the revenue figure used in the ratio should exclude all cash sales, since it is only sales on account (credit sales) that are of concern, relative to collecting customer payments. Second, sales to a major customer should be kept out of the total revenue figure used to calculate DSO, because they can skew the ratio.

Accounts Receivable Turnover

The accounts receivable turnover ratio (ART) is similar to DSO. It involves dividing a company's net credit sales by the average amount of accounts receivable.

$$\text{Accounts Receivable Turnover} = \frac{\text{Net Credit Sales}}{\text{Average Accounts Receivable}}$$

A higher ratio indicates a greater ability to convert accounts receivable into cash. If a business turns its receivables over 12 times per year, it would mean that it is collecting the average balance of receivables every month.

Inventory Ratios

The second component of a business that we look at to assess managerial performance is inventory. We can use two ratios to measure how successful a business is at moving inventory out the door: **inventory days on hand** (also known as day-sales-on-hand) and **inventory turnover**. Let us take a look at these ratios.

Inventory Days on Hand

There are various ways of calculating some of these ratios. For our purpose, we will calculate inventory days on hand this way:

$$\text{Inventory Days on Hand} = \left(\frac{\text{Average Inventory}}{\text{Cost of Goods Sold}} \right) \times 365$$

In other words, the inventory days on hand ratio calculates approximately how many days inventory stays on the company's premises before being moved out.

Inventory Turnover

The inventory turnover ratio is calculated as follows:

$$\text{Inventory Turnover} = \frac{\text{Cost of Goods Sold}}{\text{Average Inventory}}$$

In other words, inventory turnover takes the basic fraction used for the inventory days on hand calculation, flips it, and leaves out the factor of 365 days. The result essentially tells us how many times inventory is "turned over" within a year. If the value of the inventory on hand is equivalent to 100% of how much was used (cost of goods sold) for one year, then it was turned only once. If, however, the value of the inventory on hand is equivalent to 50% of how much was used then it was turned twice. Here is an example: If the cost of goods sold for the year is $120,000 and the value of inventory at the end of the year was $40,000 then the inventory was turned over three times ($120,000 ÷ 40,000).

Now, we will calculate these two inventory ratios for Soho Supplies.

Soho Supplies Balance Sheet As at December 31		
	2010	2009
ASSETS		
Current Assets		
Cash	$13,265	$72,642
Accounts receivable	1,286,138	1,065,812
Inventory	1,683,560	840,091
Prepaid expenses	48,612	42,625
Total Current Assets	3,031,575	2,021,170
Property, plant & equipment	243,256	134,000
TOTAL ASSETS	$3,274,831	$2,155,170

Soho Supplies Income Statement For the Year Ended December 31		
	2010	2009
Sales	$8,685,025	$6,482,000
Cost of goods sold	5,998,612	4,397,200
Gross Profit	2,686,413	2,084,800
Operating Expenses		
Administration charges	8,652	6,861
Advertising & marketing	42,645	32,975
Depreciation	43,262	15,862
Bonuses	65,000	62,432

FIGURE 13.21

Assume that Soho's inventory balance as at December 31, 2008 was $359,909. Applying our inventory days on hand formula to these numbers gives us the following:

	2010	2009
Average Inventory[1]	$1,261,826	$600,000
Cost of Goods Sold	$5,998,612	$4,397,200
	× 365	× 365
Inventory Days on Hand	76.8 days	49.8 days

(1) Average Inventory for 2009: (359,909 + 840,091) ÷ 2 = 600,000
Average Inventory for 2010: (1,683,560 + 840,091) ÷ 2 = 1,261,826

FIGURE 13.22

As you can see, the average number of days that inventory was on the premises rose dramatically, from 50 to 77 days in one year. Unless something unusual occurred during the year that can account for such an increase, the business might be in jeopardy of having too much inventory on hand. This freezes capital that could be used in other parts of the organization.

Now let us apply the inventory turnover ratio to the same inventory and cost of goods sold figures:

	2010	2009
Cost of Goods Sold	$5,998,612	$4,397,200
Average Inventory[(1)]	$1,261,826	$600,000
Inventory Turnover	**4.75 times**	**7.33 times**

(1) See Figure 13.22 for calculation of average inventory.

FIGURE 13.23

In essence, inventory turnover tells us the same thing, but in a different way. It tells us that in 2010, inventory was turned over only slightly more than 4.7 times. This is a sharp decrease from 7.3 times in the previous year and indicates that inventory is staying too long in the organization's warehouse.

On a broader scale, inventory performance should be assessed relative to the industry involved. For example, winter skis will be turned over less frequently (and on a seasonal basis), as compared to loaves of bread in a bakery. It might take months for a sporting goods store to sell a pair of skis it has stored in the back room, and probably much longer in the summer. Conversely, a loaf of bread normally stays on the shelf no longer than a couple of days — regardless of the time of year.

Market Value

In addition to calculating financial ratios for internal measurements, some ratios are used by investors to determine whether a public corporation has desirable shares to purchase. The ratios that measure the share performance of a public corporation were covered in chapter 11, so this is a review of them.

Shares that are publically traded on the stock markets can have their price change daily, hourly, or even by the minute. The changes in market value will affect investors as they buy and sell shares, but the corporation does not record any of these changes in their books.

According to the balance sheet shown in figure 13.11, Soho Supplies does not have preferred shares, only common shares. Assume that the number of common shares outstanding at the end of 2009 was 1,250 and the number of common shares outstanding at the end of 2010 was 3,250. Dividends paid out during 2010 amounted to $10,000 and the market value on December 31, 2010 was $650 per share.

Book Value per Share

Book value represents the theoretical value of shares based on a shareholder's claim to the company's assets. It will not necessarily match the market value of the shares.

The calculation of book value per share is relatively simple. Here is the formula that is often used:

$$\text{Book Value per Share} = \frac{\text{Shareholders' Equity} - \text{Preferred Equity}}{\text{Average Number of Common Shares Outstanding}}$$

Note that preferred equity should include preferred dividends if there are any outstanding. The formula calculates the amount of money that each common shareholder would receive if all the company's assets were immediately liquidated.

For Soho Supplies the book value per share at the end of 2010 can be calculated as:

$$\text{Book Value per Share} = \frac{\$1,506,229}{(1,250 + 3,250) \div 2}$$
$$= \$669.47$$

As noted in chapter 11, companies may use various methods to calculate the average number of shares outstanding, which is why reproducing the exact number provided in published financial statements might be difficult. For example, companies might use a monthly average number instead of a yearly number.

The company has a very high dollar amount for the book value per share. This would indicate that the company has a large amount of equity in comparison to the quantity of shares. For Soho Supplies, it appears that the company has been generating a large amount of income based on a relatively small equity investment.

Dividend Payout Ratio

Since dividends, or at least the potential for dividends, must form part of an analysis of company shares, the investing community has produced a ratio to assess just how much in dividends a corporation is paying out to shareholders. This is called the *dividend payout ratio* and calculates dividends paid as a percentage of net income. Here is the basic formula that is used:

$$\text{Dividend Payout Ratio} = \frac{\text{Dividends Paid in a Year}}{\text{Net Income after Tax}}$$

For Soho Supplies, they paid out $10,000 in dividends and had a net income of $637,704. Their dividend payout ratio is:

$$\text{Dividend Payout Ratio} = \frac{\$10,000}{\$637,704}$$

$$= 1.6\%$$

Soho is only paying out a small portion of their after tax income, deciding to keep most of the profits within the company.

Earnings per Share (EPS)

Another stock market term that one might see frequently used in the financial press is **earnings per share**. This measures how much profit is made for each share that is outstanding. Here is the basic formula for earnings per share:

$$\text{Earnings Per Share} = \frac{\text{Net Income} - \text{Preferred Dividends}}{\text{Average Number of Common Shares Outstanding}}$$

Since Soho Supplies does not have any preferred shares, there are no preferred dividends to subtract. Therefore, Soho's earnings per share ratio is:

$$\text{Earnings per Share} = \frac{\$637,704}{(1{,}250 + 3{,}250) \div 2}$$

$$= \$283.42$$

In other words, the company is making $283.24 for every outstanding share. The general interpretation is the larger the number, the more profitable the company.

Price-Earnings Ratio

Another ratio commonly used by shareholders to evaluate their investment in a corporation is that of the **price-earnings ratio** (P/E ratio), which provides the investor with a measurement of share price to actual earnings of the corporation. It is sometimes used as an indicator to buy/sell or hold shares. The formula is shown below:

$$\text{P/E Ratio} = \frac{\text{Market Price}}{\text{Earnings Per Share}}$$

Soho's EPS was $283.42 and the market price on December 31, 2010 was $650 per share. Therefore, the P/E ratio is:

$$P/E\ Ratio\ =\ \frac{\$650}{\$283.42}$$

$$=\ 2.29$$

The ratios indicate the shares are selling for 2.29 times the earnings in 2010. The P/E ratio can be used when comparing stocks between companies, although the comparison should be done with companies in the same industry. This will allow for a more even and fair comparison.

Horizontal and Vertical Financial Statement Analysis

Now that we have a better understanding of the various ratios at our disposal, we need to look at a few methods of comparing the results from the above calculations.

Management and other readers of financial statements use **horizontal analysis** to quickly compare the changes, both in dollars and percentages, in a given financial statement from one period to the next. Using the balance sheet accounts from the above examples, we can now calculate the dollar and percentage changes.

 # div by

Balance Sheet	2011	2010	$ Change	% Change
Assets				
Current Assets				
Cash	$13,265	$72,642	($59,377)	-81.74%
Accounts Receivable	1,286,138	1,065,812	220,326	20.67%
Prepaid Expenses	48,612	42,625	5,987	14.05%
Inventory	1,683,560	840,091	843,469	100.40%
Total Current Assets	3,031,575	2,021,170	1,010,405	49.99%
Non-Current Assets				
Plant & Equipment	322,518	170,000	152,518	89.72%
Less: Accumulated Depreciation	-89,262	-46,000	(43,262)	94.05%
Total Non-Current Assets	233,256	124,000	109,256	88.11%
Total Assets	$3,264,831	$2,145,170	1,119,661	52.19%
Liabilities				
Current Liabilities				
Accounts Payable & Accrued Liabilities	$783,602	$475,645	$307,957	64.75%
Current Portion of Bank Loan	380,000	240,000	140,000	58.33%
Shareholders' Loans	170,000	200,000	(30,000)	-15.00%
Total Current Liabilities	1,333,602	915,645	417,957	45.65%
Non-Current Debt	420,000	356,000	64,000	17.98%
Total Liabilities	1,753,602	1,271,645	481,957	37.90%
Shareholders' Equity	1,511,229	873,525	637,704	73.00%
Liabilities & Equity	$3,264,831	$2,145,170	1,119,661	52.19%

FIGURE 13.24

To calculate the dollar increase (or decrease), we simply take the current year amount for one line and deduct the amount reported for the previous year. For example, we see that cash decreased by $59,377, a decrease of 81.74%, calculated as follows:

$$(\$59,377) \div \$72,642 = (81.74\%)$$

Change ÷ previous yr = %

This appears to be a significant decrease and may prompt readers to inquire about the reason for such a large decrease in cash.

Horizontal analysis is most effective when comparing a number of years, say, three to five. Comparative statements for these years are presented and, using horizontal analysis techniques, we can determine possible trends in the results.

Let us look at some key elements of a published income statement for American Eagle Outfitters, a U.S. retail chain.

American Eagle Outfitters In Millions of USD				
	2009	**2008**	**2007**	**2006**
Revenue	$2,988.87	$3,055.42	$2,794.41	$2,321.96
Operating Income	279.25	598.75	586.79	458.69
Net income	179.06	400.02	387.36	294.15

base yr
base.

FIGURE 13.25

We must first select a base year. In this case we will pick 2006 as the year against which we will compare all other years.

Here are the results:

2009   *base yr.*

	2009	**2008**	**2007**	**2006**
Revenue	$2,988.87 ÷ $2,321.96	$3,055.42 ÷ $2321.96	$2,794.41 ÷ $2,321.96	$2,321.96 ÷ $2,321.96
% of Base Year	128.72%	131.59%	120.35%	100.00%

FIGURE 13.26

The horizontal analysis reveals that sales in all three years were higher than in the base year, and 2008 was the highest of the four years.

However, when we do a horizontal analysis of net income, we get a different picture of the company. Using the data from the above table, we calculate the following:

	2009	**2008**	**2007**	**2006**
Net Income	$179.06 ÷ $294.15	$400.02 ÷ $294.15	$387.36 ÷ $294.15	$294.15 ÷ $294.15
% of Base Year	60.87%	135.99%	131.69%	100%

FIGURE 13.27

What happened during 2009 to cause net income to be so much less than in the other years, even the base year? The answer to this question will require further financial analysis, perhaps using some of the ratios discussed above.

Vertical analysis is another common type of financial statement analysis. This method expresses individual accounts in the same period as a percentage of another account. For example, vertical analysis of the balance sheet indicates each account as a percentage of total assets. Vertical analysis of the income statement indicates each account as a percentage of net sales. Once again, we will use the financial statement data provided earlier in the chapter. Using the income statement data, the following table reports each line of this statement as a percentage of net sales:

Income Statement	2011	% of Net Sales	2010	% of Net Sales
Revenue (Net Sales)	$8,685,025	100.00%	$6,482,000	100.00%
Cost of Goods Sold	5,998,612	69.07%	4,397,200	67.84%
Gross Profit	2,686,413	30.93%	2,084,800	32.16%
Operating Expenses				
Administration Charges	8,652	0.10%	6,861	0.11%
Advertising & Marketing	42,645	0.49%	32,975	0.51%
Depreciation	43,262	0.50%	15,862	0.24%
Bonuses	65,000	0.75%	62,432	0.96%
Commission	420,250	4.84%	325,210	5.02%
Interest	51,875	0.60%	31,253	0.48%
Insurance	16,000	0.18%	12,000	0.19%
Sales and Admin Salaries and Benefits	610,325	7.03%	435,951	6.73%
Management Salaries	320,560	3.69%	226,548	3.50%
Occupancy (Rent, Cleaning, etc.)	52,000	0.60%	48,000	0.74%
Other Operating Expenses	61,200	0.70%	48,672	0.75%
Consulting	22,500	0.26%	21,356	0.33%
Repairs and Maintenance	36,860	0.42%	26,845	0.41%
Professional Fees	11,560	0.13%	8,642	0.13%
Total Expenses	1,762,689	20.30%	1,302,607	20.10%
Operating Income Before Tax	923,724	10.64%	782,193	12.07%
Tax	286,020	3.29%	223,652	3.45%
Net Income (Loss) Added to Retained Earnings	$637,704	7.34%	$558,541	8.62%

FIGURE 13.28

For example, COGS is calculated as 69.07% by dividing $5,998,612 by net sales of $8,685,025. Finding out each item's percentage of net sales, using the vertical analysis, helps management and other company stakeholders to compare the financial results of the current and other years presented. For example, the income statement above clearly shows that gross profit as a percentage of net sales has decreased by more than 1% from 2010 to 2011. This could indicate a serious problem such as theft of inventory or errors in recording transactions, and should be investigated.

Other methods of analyzing the financial statements exist, such as preparing **common-size statements** and benchmarking. Preparing common-size statements simply involves stating all dollar amounts on the statements as percentages. All items on the balance sheet are reported as a percentage of total assets and all items on the income statement are reported as a percentage of net sales. The above data have been used to prepare the common-size income statement below.

Common-size Income Statement	2011	2010
Revenue (Net Sales)	100.00%	100.00%
Cost of Goods Sold	69.07%	67.84%
Gross Profit	30.93%	32.16%
Operating Expenses		
Administration Charges	0.10%	0.11%
Advertising & Marketing	0.49%	0.51%
Depreciation	0.50%	0.24%
Bonuses	0.75%	0.96%
Commission	4.84%	5.02%
Interest	0.60%	0.48%
Insurance	0.18%	0.19%
Sales and Admin Salaries and Benefits	7.03%	6.73%
Management Salaries	3.69%	3.50%
Occupancy (Rent, Cleaning, etc.)	0.60%	0.74%
Other Operating Expenses	0.70%	0.75%
Consulting	0.26%	0.33%
Repairs and Maintenance	0.42%	0.41%
Professional Fees	0.13%	0.13%
Total Expenses	20.30%	20.10%
Operating Income Before Tax	10.64%	12.07%
Tax	3.29%	3.45%
Net Income (Loss) Added to Retained Earnings	7.34%	8.62%

FIGURE 13.29

The purpose of preparing common-size statements is to make the statements as easy to read as possible without overwhelming the reader with details and large numbers. Because dollar amounts are not used, these statements are quite often used to compare and analyze the results of different companies within the same industry. For example, suppose Company A had a net income of $100,000 and Company B had a net income of $200,000. If the statements were only reported in dollars, we might conclude that Company B had a more profitable year than Company A; however, after converting the dollar amounts into percentages, we see that Company A's net income represented 20% of net sales whereas Company B's represented only 5%. A common-size statement would have revealed this difference immediately.

Another term often used in conjunction with common-size statements is **benchmarking**, whereby the financial statements are compared against averages in the relevant industry, not just with the financial statements of another company. Using the data for the above company, we will now benchmark the company's performance against the following industry averages:

Common-Size Income Statement for Comparison with Industry Average		
2011	Company	Industry
Revenue (Net sales)	100.00%	100.00%
Cost of Goods Sold	69.07%	68.50%
Gross Profit	30.93%	31.00%
Operating Expenses	20.30%	25.00%
Income Taxes	3.29%	3.00%
Net Income	7.34%	3.00%

FIGURE 13.30

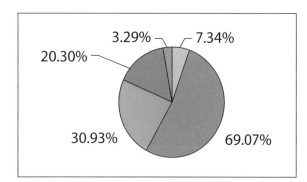

FIGURE 13.31

Pie charts and other graphics are often used to report differences between the company and others in the industry when benchmarking tools are applied. The above reveals that our company is more effective at generating net income from its sales (7.34% vs. 3.0%) than players in the same industry.

Ethics and Controls

When a company borrows a loan from a bank, the bank often imposes debt covenants in the contractual agreement. A **debt covenant** is a limitation on the behaviors or financial performance measures of a company. If a company violates a debt covenant while the bank loan is outstanding, the loan is said to be in default. Thereafter, the bank may penalize the debtholder by reducing the term of the loan or by negotiating a more unfavourable loan agreement (from the perspective of the debtholder).

Some of the covenants that banks impose are in the form of ratios. For instance, the bank may require the debtholder to stay below a specific debt to equity ratio throughout the term of the loan. Assuming that the company is close to the maximum debt to equity ratio, management may unethically take measures to manipulate the numerator or denominator in order to satisfy the bank covenant. For instance, overstating net income will reduce the debt to equity ratio (since equity increases). Understating liabilities will also reduce the ratio. It is up to the bank to decide which covenants will be used and define exactly how they will be calculated. The bank should always request audited financial statements to be reasonably assured of the debtholder's reported financial information and covenant calculations.

In Summary

⇨ Performing a comprehensive financial analysis on a business is important because it gleans important information from the financial statements.

⇨ The financial ratio is the primary tool used to analyze financial statements. The well-being of a business can be assessed by using a combination of these financial ratios.

⇨ Our approach to analyzing financial statements can be summarized in four phrases: "revenues are vanity", "profits are sanity", "cash flow is reality", and "management ensures stability".

⇨ The income statement is broken down by expense category. This produces a percentage relative to revenue along the way. We start with gross profit, and then consider EBITDA (earnings before interest, taxes, depreciation and amortization). Finally, we move on to net income.

⇨ The jump over to the balance sheet portion of our analysis is made through net income and stops first at shareholders' equity. The analysis then breaks down the balance sheet just as it did the income statement.

⇨ Cash flow analysis tends to focus almost exclusively on the balance sheet and assesses the extent to which the company has satisfactory liquidity.

⇨ The performance of management can be assessed by using financial ratios that measure accounts receivable and inventory. It is these components of a business that are a result of decisions made by real people in the business.

⇨ Other methods and tools used in financial statement analysis include horizontal and vertical analysis of the balance sheet and income statements as well as preparation of common-sized statements used in benchmarking.

Review Exercise

Use the financial statements for Basil's Bakery to calculate the following for 2010:

- gross profit margin
- net profit margin
- EBITDA
- EBITDA percentage to sales
- interest coverage ratio
- return on equity
- current ratio
- quick ratio
- debt-to-equity ratio
- days-sales-outstanding
- inventory days on hand

Prepare a common-size income statement for Basil's Bakery for 2010.

Basil's Bakery
Balance Sheet
As at December 31

	2010	2009
ASSETS		
Current Assets		
Cash	$1,605	$987
Accounts receivable	1,175	573
Inventory	396	256
Other current assets	301	103
Total Current Assets	3,477	1,919
Property, plant & equipment	2,034	1,170
TOTAL ASSETS	$5,511	$3,089
LIABILITIES AND EQUITY		
Liabilities		
Current liabilities	$1,474	$547
Non-Current liabilities	104	58
TOTAL LIABILITIES	1,578	605
Shareholders' Equity	3,933	2,484
TOTAL LIABILITIES AND EQUITY	$5,511	$3,089

Basil's Bakery
Income Statement
For the Year Ended December 31, 2010

Sales Revenue	$6,009
Cost of goods sold	2,928
Gross Profit	3,081
Operating Expenses	
Depreciation	108
Interest	518
Other operating expenses	723
Total Operating Expenses	1,349
Income from Operations	1,732
Investment income	79
Operating Income Before Tax	1,811
Income tax	516
Net Income	$1,295

Review Exercise – Answer

Name	Calculation	Result
Gross Profit Margin	$\dfrac{3{,}081}{6{,}009}$	51.3%
Net Profit Margin	$\dfrac{1{,}295}{6{,}009}$	21.6%
EBITDA	$1{,}295 + 518 + 516 + 108$	$2,437
EBITDA Percentage to Sales	$\dfrac{2{,}437}{6{,}009}$	40.6%
Interest Coverage Ratio	$\dfrac{2{,}437}{518}$	4.7 times
Return on Equity	$1{,}295 \div \left(\dfrac{(3{,}933 + 2{,}484)}{2} \right)$	40.4%
Current Ratio	$\dfrac{3{,}477}{1{,}474}$	2.36
Quick Ratio	$\dfrac{(1{,}605 + 1{,}175)}{1{,}474}$	1.89
Debt-to-Equity Ratio	$\dfrac{1{,}578}{3{,}933}$	0.4
Days Sales Outstanding	$\dfrac{(1{,}175 + 573) \div 2}{6{,}009} \times 365$	53.09 days
Inventory Days on Hand	$\dfrac{(396 + 256) \div 2}{2{,}928} \times 365$	40.64 days

Basil's Bakery
Common-Size Income Statement
For the Year Ended December 31, 2010

Sales Revenue	$6,009	100.00%
Cost of goods sold	2,928	48.73%
Gross Profit	3,081	51.27%
Operating Expenses		
Depreciation	108	1.80%
Interest	518	8.62%
Other operating expenses	723	12.03%
Total Operating Expenses	1,349	22.45%
Income from Operations	1,732	28.82%
Investment income	79	1.31%
Operating Income Before Tax	1,811	30.14%
Income tax	516	8.59%
Net Income	$1,295	21.55%

Appendix I
SUMMARY OF FINANCIAL RATIOS

The following is a guide to some common ratios used to measure the financial performance of a business. Different industries have different benchmarks for each ratio. It is important to understand the trends in a company's performance from period-to-period and the relative performance of a company within its industry for each ratio.

Revenue Growth

$$\frac{\text{Year 2 Sales} - \text{Year 1 Sales}}{\text{Year 1 Sales}} \times 100\%$$

Measures the percentage growth of revenues from one year to the next.

Gross Profit Margin

$$\frac{\text{Gross Profit}}{\text{Revenue}} \times 100\%$$

Measures the percentage of revenue remaining to contribute towards operating expenses, after deducting product costs per dollar of revenue. The higher the percentage, the higher the contribution per dollar of revenue.

Overhead Margin

$$\frac{\text{Overhead Expenses}}{\text{Revenue}} \times 100\%$$

Measures the relative cost of operating the business. Can be measured for each individual expense (e.g. rent, wages, etc.) as a percentage of revenue. The lower the percentage, the lower the expenses relative to revenue.

EBITDA Percentage of Sales

$$\frac{\text{EBITDA}}{\text{Revenue}} \times 100\%$$

EBITDA measures the **E**arnings **B**efore **I**nterest, **T**ax, **D**epreciation and **A**mortization. EBITDA margin measures the operating costs of a business relative to sales.

Net Profit Margin

$$\frac{\text{Net Profit}}{\text{Revenue}} \times 100\%$$

Represents the profitability and efficiency of the business. Generally, the higher the percentage, the better because it indicates efficient management and expense control.

Interest Coverage Ratio

$$\frac{\text{EBITDA}}{\text{Interest Expense}}$$

Measures an organization's ability to pay interest owing. Generally, the higher the number the better – 2 times interest coverage is a common benchmark in many industries.

Return on Equity (ROE)

$$\frac{\text{Net Income}}{\text{Average Owner's Equity}} \times 100\%$$

Tests the financial return the owners of a business are earning, relative to their investment. Generally, the higher the percentage, the better. Use this ratio to assess risk and reward.

Current Ratio

$$\frac{\text{Current Assets}}{\text{Current Liabilities}}$$

Measures the ability of the company to pay current debt over the next 12 months (specifically, the number of times current assets can cover current debts). Generally, the higher the number the better (2:1 is a common benchmark in many industries). If the ratio is too high (e.g. 4:1), it indicates inefficient use of capital as current assets generally have the lowest returns.

Quick Ratio (or Acid Test)

$$\frac{\text{Cash} + \text{Short-Term Investments} + \text{Net Accounts Receivable}}{\text{Current Liabilities}}$$

The number of times the most liquid assets (e.g. cash, short-term investments, and accounts receivable) can cover immediate debts (usually 90 days). Generally, the higher the number the better (1:1 is a common benchmark in many industries). If the ratio is too high, it indicates inefficient use of capital (see current ratio).

Debt to Equity Ratio

$$\frac{\text{Total Liabilities (Debt)}}{\text{Total Owners' Equity}}$$

Used by lenders to examine their risk relative to the owners' risk. Some debt is good, but too much can cause financial distress. $1 of debt for every $2 of equity is a common benchmark in many industries (1:2).

Debt to Total Assets

$$\frac{\text{Total Liabilities (Debt)}}{\text{Total Assets}}$$

Measures how much a company's assets are financed through debt. The higher the ratio, the greater the difficulty a company will have in repaying its creditors.

Days Sales Outstanding (DSO)

$$\frac{\text{Average Accounts Receivable}}{\text{Credit Sales}} \times 365$$

Calculates the average number of days the A/R is outstanding, and indicates how well it is being managed. Generally, the less days outstanding, the less risk. This ratio is crucial in the service industry. DSO should be compared to similar periods in a cyclical business.

Inventory Days on Hand

$$\frac{\text{Average Inventory}}{\text{Cost of Goods Sold}} \times 365$$

Calculates the average number of days the current inventory will last, and how well the inventory is being managed. Generally, the lower the inventory days on hand, the less the holding costs (e.g. shrinkage, interest, etc.). Inventory days on hand should be compared to similar periods in a cyclical business.

Inventory Turnover

$$\frac{\text{Cost of Goods Sold}}{\text{Average Inventory}}$$

Calculates the number of times inventory is replenished within one year. Generally, the lower the inventory turnover, the less times per year inventory is being replenished which results in elevated holding costs. Inventory turnover should be compared to similar periods in a cyclical business.

Return on Assets (ROA)

$$\frac{\text{Net Income}}{\text{Average Total Assets}} \times 100\%$$

Compares the net income earned in a period to the amount of assets used to generate that income. Generally, the higher the percentage, the better.

Assets Turnover

$$\frac{\text{Revenue}}{\text{Average Total Assets}}$$

Tests how efficiently a business utilizes its assets to generate sales.

Accounts Receivable Turnover (ART)

$$\frac{\text{Net Credit Sales}}{\text{Average Net Accounts Receivable}}$$

Calculates how many times a business collects its accounts receivable throughout the year. The higher the ratio, the more times per year accounts receivable is being collected.

Earnings per Share (EPS)

$$\frac{\text{(Net Income – Preferred Dividends)}}{\text{Average Number of Common Shares Outstanding}}$$

Tests the amount of dollar return a company is making for every outstanding common share. This ratio assesses the profitability of a company.

Book Value per Common Share

$$\frac{\text{(Shareholder's Equity – Preferred Equity)}}{\text{Average Number of Common Shares Outstanding}}$$

Determines the value associated with each common share after all debts are paid.

Dividend Payout Ratio

$$\frac{\text{Dividends Paid in a Year}}{\text{Net Income after Tax}}$$

Calculates dividends paid as a percentage of net income.

Price to Earnings Ratio

$$\frac{\text{Market Price per Share}}{\text{Earnings per Share}}$$

Provides the investor with a measurement of share price to actual earnings of the corporation. It is sometimes used as an indicator to buy or sell shares.

Note:

The purpose of ratio analysis is to help the reader of financial statements ask the appropriate questions and understand which issues need to be addressed. Keep in mind that no single ratio will be able to provide the complete story. Much like a puzzle, you need all the pieces to see the whole picture.

Appendix II

BOMBARDIER'S FINANCIAL STATEMENTS

(for the year ended January 31, 2011)

CONSOLIDATED BALANCE SHEETS

(in millions of U.S. dollars)

As at January 31	Notes	2011	2010
Assets			
Cash and cash equivalents	11	$ 4,195	$ 3,372
Invested collateral	11	676	682
Receivables	4	2,022	1,897
Aircraft financing	5	668	473
Inventories	6	5,155	5,268
PP&E	7	1,767	1,643
Intangible assets	8	2,304	1,696
Fractional ownership deferred costs		176	271
Deferred income taxes	19	1,172	1,166
Accrued benefit assets	24	1,209	1,070
Derivative financial instruments	3	535	482
Goodwill	9	2,358	2,247
Other assets	10	1,193	1,006
		$23,430	$21,273
Liabilities			
Accounts payable and accrued liabilities	12	$ 8,027	$ 7,427
Advances and progress billings in excess of related long-term contract costs		2,421	1,899
Advances on aerospace programs		1,937	2,092
Fractional ownership deferred revenues		218	346
Deferred income taxes	19	53	65
Long-term debt	13	4,635	4,162
Accrued benefit liabilities	24	1,132	1,084
Derivative financial instruments	3	655	429
		19,078	17,504
Equity			
Equity attributable to shareholders of Bombardier Inc.		4,274	3,701
Equity attributable to non-controlling interests		78	68
		4,352	3,769
		$23,430	$21,273
Commitments and contingencies	25		

The accompanying notes are an integral part of these Consolidated Financial Statements.

On behalf of the Board of Directors,

Laurent Beaudoin, C.C., FCA
Director

L. Denis Desautels, O.C., FCA
Director

CONSOLIDATED STATEMENTS OF CHANGES IN EQUITY

(in millions of U.S. dollars, except number of shares)

For the fiscal years ended January 31	Notes	2011		2010	
		Number (in thousands)	Amount	Number (in thousands)	Amount
EQUITY ATTRIBUTABLE TO SHAREHOLDERS OF BOMBARDIER INC.	14				
Preferred shares					
Series 2		9,465	$ 159	9,465	$ 159
Series 3		2,535	40	2,535	40
Series 4		9,400	148	9,400	148
		21,400	347	21,400	347
Common shares					
Class A Shares (Multiple Voting)					
Balance at beginning of year		316,232	29	316,583	29
Converted to Class B		(122)	–	(351)	–
Balance at end of year		316,110	29	316,232	29
Class B Shares (Subordinate Voting)					
Balance at beginning of year		1,438,518	1,430	1,437,520	1,428
Issuance of shares		1,358	6	647	2
Repurchase of shares	14	(3,000)	(3)	–	–
Converted from Class A		122	–	351	–
		1,436,998	1,433	1,438,518	1,430
Held in trust under the PSU plan	14				
Balance at beginning of year		(25,099)	(135)	(23,654)	(130)
Purchased	14	(10,539)	(50)	(7,068)	(21)
Distributed		8,178	47	5,623	16
Balance at end of year		(27,460)	(138)	(25,099)	(135)
Balance at end of year		1,409,538	1,295	1,413,419	1,295
Balance at end of year–common shares		1,725,648	1,324	1,729,651	1,324
Total–share capital			$1,671		$1,671
Contributed surplus					
Balance at beginning of year			$ 132		$ 104
Stock-based compensation	15		47		46
Options exercised and shares distributed under the PSU plan			(48)		(18)
Balance at end of year			131		132
Retained earnings					
Balance at beginning of year			2,087		1,567
Net income attributable to shareholders of Bombardier Inc.			755		698
Excess of price paid over carrying value of repurchased Class B Shares	14		(13)		–
Dividends:					
Common shares			(173)		(157)
Preferred shares, net of tax			(24)		(21)
Balance at end of year			2,632		2,087
AOCI	16				
Balance at beginning of year			(189)		(801)
OCI attributable to shareholders of Bombardier Inc.			29		612
Balance at end of year			(160)		(189)
			4,274		3,701
EQUITY ATTRIBUTABLE TO NON-CONTROLLING INTERESTS					
Balance at beginning of year			68		66
Foreign exchange re-evaluation			–		5
Net income attributable to non-controlling interests			14		9
OCI attributable to non-controlling interests			1		–
Capital distribution			(8)		(12)
Capital injection			3		–
Balance at end of year			78		68
EQUITY			$4,352		$3,769

The accompanying notes are an integral part of these Consolidated Financial Statements.

CONSOLIDATED STATEMENTS OF INCOME

(in millions of U.S. dollars, except per share amounts)

For the fiscal years ended January 31	Notes	2011	2010
Revenues			
Manufacturing		$12,903	$14,739
Services		2,872	2,767
Other		1,937	1,860
		17,712	19,366
Cost of sales	6	14,668	16,202
SG&A		1,369	1,453
R&D		193	141
Other expense (income)	17	22	(26)
Amortization		410	498
		16,662	18,268
EBIT		1,050	1,098
Financing income	18	(137)	(96)
Financing expense	18	256	279
EBT		931	915
Income taxes	19	162	208
Net income		$ 769	$ 707
Attributable to:			
Shareholders of Bombardier Inc.		$ 755	$ 698
Non-controlling interests		$ 14	$ 9
EPS (in dollars)			
Basic and diluted	20	$ 0.42	$ 0.39

The accompanying notes are an integral part of these Consolidated Financial Statements.

CONSOLIDATED STATEMENTS OF COMPREHENSIVE INCOME

(in millions of U.S. dollars)

For the fiscal years ended January 31	Notes	2011	2010
Net income		$ 769	$ 707
OCI	16		
Net unrealized gain on financial assets AFS, net of tax		7	20
Net change in cash flow hedges:			
Foreign exchange re-evaluation		(6)	8
Net gain (loss) on derivative financial instruments designated as cash flow hedges		(27)	451
Reclassification to income or to the related non-financial asset		(78)	125
Income tax recovery (expense)		5	(204)
		(106)	380
CTA			
Net investments in self-sustaining foreign operations[1]		128	356
Net gain (loss) on related hedging items		1	(144)
		129	212
Total OCI		30	612
Total Comprehensive income		$ 799	$ 1,319
Attributable to:			
Shareholders of Bombardier Inc.		$ 784	$ 1,310
Non-controlling interests		$ 15	$ 9

1   Includes a gain of $1 million attributable to non-controlling interests in fiscal year 2011 (nil in fiscal year 2010).

The accompanying notes are an integral part of these Consolidated Financial Statements.

CONSOLIDATED STATEMENTS OF CASH FLOWS

(in millions of U.S. dollars)

For the fiscal years ended January 31	Notes	2011	2010
Operating activities			
Net income		$ 769	$ 707
Non-cash items:			
Amortization		410	498
Deferred income taxes	19	7	(9)
Stock-based compensation	15	47	46
Gain on repurchase of long-term debt	18	(47)	–
Gain on disposals of PP&E	17	(11)	(19)
Impairment of PP&E	17	8	–
Net change in non-cash balances related to operations	21	495	(671)
Cash flows from operating activities		1,678	552
Investing activities			
Additions to PP&E and intangible assets		(1,094)	(805)
Disposals of PP&E and intangible assets		21	38
Invested collateral		–	145
Other		(100)	(82)
Cash flows from investing activities		(1,173)	(704)
Financing activities			
Proceeds from issuance of long-term debt	13	2,625	4
Repayments of long-term debt	13	(2,125)	(11)
Dividends paid		(197)	(178)
Purchase of Class B shares–held in trust under the PSU plan	14	(50)	(21)
Repurchase of Class B Shares	14	(16)	–
Other		(21)	(10)
Cash flows from financing activities		216	(216)
Effect of exchange rate changes on cash and cash equivalents		102	270
Net increase (decrease) in cash and cash equivalents		823	(98)
Cash and cash equivalents at beginning of year		3,372	3,470
Cash and cash equivalents at end of year		$ 4,195	$3,372
Supplemental information			
Cash paid for:			
Interest		$ 343	$ 254
Income taxes		$ 132	$ 115

The accompanying notes are an integral part of these Consolidated Financial Statements.

GLOSSARY

A

Accountant — A professional, who develops and maintains the accounting system, interprets the data, prepares various management reports and supervises the clerks to ensure that the information is correct.

Accounting — Accounting accurately measures all the financial activities of an individual or a business.

Accounting Cycle — The steps repeated each reporting period for the purpose of preparing financial statements for users.

Accounting Equation — The logic of the double entry is based on this equation, which is: Assets = Liabilities + Net Worth.

Accounting Ethics — The standards of reporting, practice, professionalism and behavior an accountant must meet in discharging this responsibility.

Accounts Payable — The amount the business has been billed but has yet to pay. This is the money the business owes to its business suppliers from whom it has purchased goods or services.

Accounts Payable Subsidiary Ledger — A subsidiary ledger listing individual credit supplier accounts.

Accounting Period — The length of time covered by financial statements and other reports; also called reporting periods.

Accounts Receivable — The amount that is billed to customers and owing from them but has not yet been collected.

Accounts Receivable Subsidiary Ledger — A subsidiary ledger listing individual credit customer accounts.

Accounts Receivable Turnover Ratio — The ratio calculated by dividing a company's net credit sales by the average amount of net accounts receivable.

Accrual Accounting — The approach to preparing financial statements that uses the adjusting process to recognize revenues when earned and expenses when incurred, not when cash is paid or received; the basis for Generally Accepted Accounting Principles.

Accrued Expenses — Costs incurred in a period that are unpaid and/or unrecorded; adjusting entries for recording accrued expenses involve increasing (debiting) expenses and increasing (crediting) liabilities.

Accrued Revenue — Revenues earned in a period that are unrecorded and/or not yet received in cash (or other assets); adjusting entries for recording accrued revenues involve increasing (debiting) assets and increasing (crediting) revenues.

Acid-Test Ratio — A ratio used to assess a company's ability to cover its current debts with existing assets calculated as quick assets (cash, short-term investments and receivables) divided by current liabilities; also called quick ratio.

Adjusting Entry — A journal entry at the end of an accounting period to bring an asset or liability account balance to its proper amount while also updating the related expense or revenue account.

Adjusted Trial Balance — A trial balance that is prepared once adjusting entries have been made and posted to the general ledger.

Allowance for Doubtful Accounts (AFDA) — A contra account used to record debts that may not be collected.

Allowance Method — The method uses the bad debt expense account and the allowance for doubtful accounts (AFDA) account to record bad debts in the same period as when the revenue is actually generated, which adheres to the matching principle.

Amortization — The decline of an intangible asset such as a patent (which is only good for 20 years) or a copyright.

Assets — All the items that are owned such as cash, inventory, land, machinery, accounts receivable, etc.

Asset Turnover — A general measure of a firm's ability to generate sales in relation to total assets.

Auditing — An examination and verification of the records and systems of a company, and an assessment of the fairness of a company's financial statements.

B

Bad Debts — Money owed to the company (accounts receivable) that has been proven as non-collectable. This non-collectable money is regarded as an expense.

Balance Sheet — A permanent document that shows what a company owns (assets) and what it owes (liabilities). The difference between assets and liabilities represents the net worth at a specific point in time.

Bank Reconciliation — An analysis that explains the difference between the balance of a chequing account shown in the depositor's records and the balance reported on the bank statement.

Bookkeepers — (also known as accounting clerks) People who enter all the daily accounting transactions, accounts payable and receivable, payroll and employer-filed taxes; or they may work with an accounts receivable clerk, an accounts payable clerk and a payroll clerk.

Bank Statement — The document provided by the bank, which summarizes deposits, cheques, withdrawals, interest received, and other debits and credits to a bank account.

Bonds — An "IOU" issued by a company. The corporation pays interest on the bond and pays the entire amount (called principal) when due. Corporate bonds are usually traded publicly and they will rise and fall in value on the bond market. These are included in long-term debt on the Balance Sheet.

Book Value — The cost of the asset less its accumulated depreciation.

C

Capital (Owner's Capital) — The difference between total assets and total liabilities (same as net worth, owner's equity).

Capital Assets — Includes long-term tangible assets such as plant and equipment and intangible assets such as patents. Capital assets are expected to provide benefits for more than one period.

Cash — Either cash in the bank, petty cash, or cash equivalents.

Cash-Based Accounting — Revenues are recognized when cash is received and expenses are recorded when cash is paid.

Cash Disbursement — Cash spent during the reporting (or accounting) period.

Cash Discount — A reduction in the price of merchandise that is granted by a seller to a purchaser in exchange for the purchaser paying within a specified period of time.

Cash Flow Statement — A financial report that shows the inflows and outflows of actual cash during a specific period of time; where the company's cash came from and where it was spent.

Cash Short and Over — The difference between cash receipts and cash disbursed from petty cash.

Certified Public Accountant (CPA) — An accountant in the United States who is licensed by a state to practice public accounting in a professionally competent manner.

Chart of Accounts — A list of all accounts used by a company; includes the identification number assigned to each account.

Classified Balance Sheet — The type of balance sheet where assets and liabilities are subdivided into current and long-term categories to further define a company's financial position.

Closing Entries — Journal entries recorded at the end of each accounting period that transfer the end of-period balances in revenues, expenses, and withdrawals accounts to the permanent owner's capital account in order to prepare for the upcoming period and update the owner's capital account for the events of the period just finished.

Common Shares — The name for a class of shares in a company that has a claim on the assets of the company after preferred shareholders.

Controls — Measures, procedures, performance indicators and other methods used to systematically check and regulate business operations.

Conservatism — A principle that states that accounting for a business be fair and reasonable; when in doubt understate assets and income and overstate liabilities.

Consistency Principle — The accounting requirement that a company use the same accounting methods period after period so that the financial statements of succeeding periods will be comparable.

Contra Account — An account linked with another account and having an opposite normal debit or credit balance; reported as a subtraction from the other account's balance so that more complete information than simply the net amount is provided.

Consulting — Some professionals use their knowledge and expertise to advise the actions of other businesses. Their services could include providing advice on information technology (IT), financial matters and investments.

Contingent Liabilities — A financial obligation that will happen only if a certain event occurs. Companies establish a contingent liability account to try and cover the costs involved with the possible occurrence of an event; also known as an estimated liability account.

Copyright — An intangible asset that is similar to a patent in that it gives exclusive rights of ownership to a person or group that has created something.

Corporation — A business that is a separate legal entity under provincial, state or federal laws with owners that are called shareholders.

Cost of Goods Sold — The cost to directly produce the product or deliver the service. In the case of retail the "cost of goods" is the cost that the store paid for the goods. In manufacturing the "cost of goods" is the material cost, labour overheads, supervision or any other cost attributing to produce the product.

Credit Note — The form issued by a vendor to reverse charges made on a regular sales invoice.

Credit Period — The time period that can pass before a customer's payment is due.

Credit Terms — The description of the amounts and timing of payments that a buyer agrees to make in the future.

Current Assets — Cash and those assets, which in the normal course of business can be turned into cash typically within one year.

Current Liabilities — All liabilities that are due within the next 12 months.

Current Ratio — Current assets divided by current liabilities. This is used to measure the company's ability to pay its current debts in the short term.

D

Database — An electronic information storage space that allows information to be input and reports to be output in a variety of ways, depending upon the information required.

Days of Inventory on Hand — An estimate of how many days it will take to convert the inventory on hand at the end of the period into accounts receivable or cash; calculated by dividing the ending inventory by the cost of goods sold and multiplying the result by 365.

Days Sales Outstanding (DSO) — A management ratio that measures the average amount of days it takes the business to collect outstanding accounts receivable.

Debit — An entry that increases asset, expense and owner's withdrawals accounts or decreases liability, owner's capital and revenue accounts; recorded on the left side of a T-account.

Debt-to-Equity Ratio — Total liabilities divided by total shareholders' equity. This ratio indicates how much has been borrowed versus how much has been invested by the shareholders. This ratio is helpful in determining whether or not the company has too much debt.

Deferred Taxes — The amount of tax that must eventually be paid.

Deficit — A business loss; an owner's capital account with a debit balance.

Depletion — The decline in value of natural resources due to its use over time.

Depreciation — The decline in the useful value of an asset due to its use over time.

Discount Period — The time period in which a cash discount is available and a reduced payment can be made by the buyer.

Determinable Liabilities — Debts taken on by the company for which the terms are readily known.

Dividends — The amount paid to the shareholders from the profits of the company.

Dividends in Arrears — Dividends on current shares that are not paid currently but will be paid to the holder at a future date.

Dividend Payout Ratio — Assess how much in dividends a corporation is paying out to shareholders.

Double Entry Accounting — An accounting system where every transaction affects and is recorded in at least two accounts; the sum of the debits for all entries must equal the sum of the credits for all entries.

E

Earnings per Share — Net income divided by the total number of shares of the company owned by the shareholders. This gives a good indication of the earning ability of the company relative to the number of people who may at some point share in the benefit of those earnings.

EBITDA — Calculates earnings before interest, tax, depreciation and amortization because generally these expenses cannot be controlled by most business operators.

EBITDA Percentage to Sales — Calculated by taking our EBITDA number and dividing it by revenue, to obtain yet another percentage figure to work with in our analysis.

Electronic Data Interchange (EDI) — A computerized system that allows companies to transfer electronic information to one another.

Electronic Fund Transfers (EFTs) — Automatic cash payments to other accounts or automatic cash receipts from others.

Estimated Liabilities — A financial obligation that will happen only if a certain event occurs. Companies establish an estimated liability account to try and cover the costs involved with the possible occurrence.

Expense — A decrease in equity as a result of the costs of the product or services used to produce revenue.

F

FOB Shipping Point — Means that the buyer pays the shipping costs and accepts ownership of the goods at the seller's place of business.

FOB Destination — Means that the seller pays the shipping costs and the ownership of the goods transfers to the buyer at the buyer's place of business.

Financial Statements — Written records of the financial status of an individual, association or business organization. It usually includes balance sheet, income statement, statement of owner's equity and cash flow statement.

First In First Out (FIFO) — The pricing of an inventory under the assumption that inventory items are sold in the order acquired; the first items received were the first items sold.

Fiscal Year — Defined as a period consisting of 12 consecutive months. A fiscal year does not necessarily start and end in a calendar year.

Fixed Assets — Long-term assets used in producing goods or services.

Freight — The cost of shipping goods.

Full Disclosure Principle — Requires financial statements (including footnotes) to report all relevant information about the operations and financial position of the entity.

G

GAAP — Generally Accepted Accounting Principles are the rules that indicate acceptable accounting practice.

General and Administrative Expenses — Costs that support the overall operations of a business and include the expenses of such activities as providing accounting services, human resource management and financial management.

General Ledger — A book or file used to record all the accounts of the business (other than those in the subsidiary ledgers); these accounts represent the complete financial position of the business.

General Partnership — A type of business in which the owners are jointly liable for business operations and as such share the unlimited liability.

Goods and Services Tax (GST) — A federal sales imposed by the federal government on most transactions between businesses and between businesses and consumers.

Goodwill — An intangible asset of a business that has value in excess of the sum of its net assets.

Gross Profit — Net sales less the cost of goods or the cost of sales. It is called "gross" because it does not take into account other types of expenses, which must still be deducted from sales before the net income (or profit) is calculated, (e.g. operating expenses).

Gross Profit Margin — Gross profit (the difference between revenues and COGS) divided by revenues; also called gross margin ratio.

Gross Profit (Inventory) Method — A method for estimating ending inventory using a company's historical gross profit figure.

H

Harmonized Sales Tax (HST) — A sales tax that combines the provincial and federal taxes into one sales tax amount.

I

IFRS — International Financial Reporting Standards; the uniform international accounting standard that many countries have adopted; a transition from GAAP that is the accounting profession's response and contribution to globalization.

Income Statement — The temporary record (financial statement) used to record revenue and expenses thereby calculating a profit or loss for the accounting period.

Income Summary — A temporary account used only in the closing process to which the balances of revenue and expense accounts are transferred; its balance equals net income or net loss and is transferred to the owner's capital account.

Income Tax — The amount of money the government charges the company for making money. The more the profit, the more the tax.

Income Taxes Payable — Money owed to various tax agencies but not yet paid. This is a liability to the company.

Intangible Assets — Long-lived (capital) assets that have no physical substance but convey a right to use a product or process, e.g. patents, copyrights and goodwill.

Interest — A charge related to monies borrowed; imposed on the borrower by the lender.

Interest Coverage Ratio — Is a ratio which indicates the ability of a company to cover net interest expenses with EBITDA.

Internal Controls — Procedures set up to protect assets, ensure reliable accounting reports, promote efficiency and encourage adherence to company policies.

Inventory — Composed of three classes of material: raw material used in making goods; work in progress, which is goods in the process of being manufactured; and finished goods ready to be shipped to customers. In a retail store or distribution business the value of the inventory would generally be what the company was charged for it plus the shipping costs.

Inventory Days on Hand — Tells us how many days inventory is held before being sold.

Inventory Turnover Ratio — Estimates how many times a year a company replenishes the full value of inventory.

Invoice — An itemized statement of goods prepared by the vendor that lists the customer's name, the items sold, the sales prices and the terms of sale.

J

Journal — A record where transactions are recorded before they are recorded in accounts; amounts are posted from the journal to the ledger; also called the book of original entry.

Journalizing — The process of recording transactions in a journal.

L

Ledger — A record containing all accounts used by a business.

Liabilities — All the debts and legal obligations that the business owes and must pay.

Limited Liability Partnership — Restricts partners' liabilities to their own acts and the acts of individuals under their control.

Limited Partnership — Includes both general partner(s) with unlimited liability and limited partner(s) with liability restricted to the amount invested.

Liquid Assets — Can be easily converted to cash or used to pay for services or obligations; cash is the most liquid asset, (e.g. accounts receivable and inventory).

Liquidity — The ability to pay day-to-day obligations (current liabilities) with existing liquid assets.

Liquidation — The sale of the assets of the company. This is done when the business goes broke. The assets are sold and the proceeds are used to pay the creditors.

Lower of Cost or Market (LCM) — The required method of reporting merchandise inventory on the balance sheet, where market value is reported, when market is lower than cost; the market value may be defined as net realizable value or current replacement cost on the date of the balance sheet.

M

Market Value — The value of an asset that buyers are willing to pay for in the market; market value is not tied to the book value of an asset.

Matching Principle — The broad principle that requires expenses to be reported in the same period as the revenues that were earned as a result of the expenses.

Materiality — This GAAP states that an amount may be ignored if its affect on the financial statements is not important to their users; also called cost-to benefit constraint.

Merchandise — Products, also called goods, which a company acquires for the purpose of reselling them to customers.

Miscellaneous Assets — Assets that do not fit into another specific asset class or account

Multistep Income Statement — An income statement divides revenue and expenses further to show subtotals such as COGS, gross profit, operating expenses and operating income. This format highlights significant relationships because gross profit and operating income are two different but important measures for a merchandising business.

N

Net Accounts Receivable — Total accounts receivable less allowance for doubtful accounts.

Net Income — The excess that is left after all expenses have been paid; also called net profit.

Net Profit Margin — A profitability ratio, which measures how much profit, a company generates relative to their revenue.

Net Realizable Value — The expected sales price of an item minus the cost of making the sale.

Net Sales — The amount of sales billed, less any refunds, returns or bad debts.

Net Worth — If you were to sell all your assets and pay all your debts, the remaining cash represents how much you are worth.

No-par Value Shares — Shares that have no "stated value" so that when they are sold, the equity account is credited for the entire proceeds.

Non-Current Assets — Used to operate a business and are not expected to turn into cash within the next 12 months unless they are sold for reasons other than the day-to-day operations of the business.

Non-Current Liabilities — All debts that are due by the company that are payable after 12 months.

Not-for-Profit Organizations — Profits made by not-for-profit organizations may be paid out (redistributed) to the community by providing services. Not-for-profit organizations include religious organizations, community care centers, charitable organizations, hospitals and the Red Cross.

Notes Payable — Money owed to the bank, an individual, corporation or other lender.

Note Receivable — An unconditional written promise to pay a definite sum of money on demand or on a defined future date(s); also called a promissory note.

NSF Cheque — Nonsufficient funds cheque, returned due to a lack of funds.

O

Operating Expenses — Total expenses incurred in promoting and selling the product or service and running the operation that makes and sells the product or service; they are different from direct expenses such as material and labor; they are usually divided into selling expenses and general administration expenses.

Operating Income — Calculated by subtracting operating expenses from gross profit. This figure shows what a company is making or losing when it produces and sells the product or service.

Other Assets — See miscellaneous assets definition.

Other Income/Expenses — Money earned or expenses incurred not directly involved in making and selling the product or service. For example, interest earned on bank deposits or paid for bank loans.

Outstanding Cheques — An outstanding cheque is one that has been recorded in the general ledger, but has not been recorded on the bank statement. This is so because after the company records the cheque, it is mailed to the supplier. The supplier then records it in the books, prepares the deposit and takes it to the bank.

Outstanding Deposits — An outstanding deposit is one that has been recorded in the company's general ledger but not shown on the bank statement. This can occur when the company makes a deposit in the bank (perhaps using the night deposit box) on the last day of the month, but the bank does not record the deposit until the following business day.

Overhead Margin — A management ratio which measures the relative cost of operating the business as a percentage of sales; the lower the percentage the better.

Owner's Equity — Everything that the company owns, less what it owes.

P

Partnership — A business owned by two or more people. Each partner's share of profits is reported and taxed on that partner's tax return.

Par Value (bonds) — When a bond is issued at the value printed on the bond, also known as face value.

Par Value Shares — Shares that are issued with a stated value. Corporations in Canada are not permitted to issue par value shares.

Patent — Is a legal form of protection that provides a person or legal entity with exclusive rights to exclude others from making, using, or selling a concept or invention for the duration of the patent.

Periodic Inventory System — A method of accounting that records the cost of inventory purchased but does not track the quantity on hand or sold to customers; the records are updated at the end of each period to reflect the results of physical counts of the items on hand.

Perpetual Inventory System — A method of accounting that maintains continuous records of the cost of inventory on hand and the cost of goods sold.

Petty Cash — Small amounts of cash set up as a petty cash fund to be used by companies for small (petty) expenses such as stamps, courier fees, and parking.

Post-Closing Trial Balance — Once the income statement is cleared, it is necessary to ensure that the balance sheet still balances. This is done by completing another trial balance called the post-closing trial balance

Posting Reference (PR) Column — A column in journals where individual account numbers are entered when entries are posted to the ledger; a column in ledgers where journal page numbers are entered when entries are posted.

Prepaid Expenses — Payments for items that will not immediately be used and are therefore not charged immediately as an expense. For example, six months worth of office supplies are purchased, and at the end of the reporting period only two months worth of supplies have been used. The additional four months that are unused are considered prepaid expenses.

Preferred Shares — Shares of a company that have preference with respect to dividends and distribution of assets in case of liquidation.

Present Value — Determines the amount invested today to produce a certain amount in the future.

Price-Earnings Ratio — A ratio commonly used by shareholders to evaluate their investment in a corporation is that of the price-earnings ratio (P/E ratio) which divides the market price per share by earnings per share.

Principal — The amount of a loan or note payable on which interest is calculated.

Proprietorship — A business owned by one person also known as a sole proprietorship. The financial affairs of the business must be separate from the owner. However, from a legal perspective, a sole proprietor is personally liable for the business.

Promissory Note — An unconditional written promise to pay a definite sum of money on demand or on a defined future date(s); also called a note receivable.

Provincial Sales Tax (PST) — A provincial tax on goods or services paid by the final consumer of a product.

Purchase Allowances — Occur when the buyer agrees to keep the undesirable goods at a reduced cost.

Purchase Discount — A term used by a purchaser to describe a cash discount granted to them for paying within the discount period.

Purchases Journal — A journal that is used to record all purchases on credit.

Purchase Returns — Goods often need to be returned for reasons such as incorrect product, over-shipments, or inferior quality product.

Q

Quick Ratio — The total of cash, short-term investments and accounts receivable divided by the total of current liabilities. In other words, those items that can be rapidly converted into cash with which the current liabilities can be paid. Another way of calculating the quick ratio is simply to add cash plus accounts receivable divided by current liabilities; also known as the Acid Test.

R

Residual Value — The amount remaining after all depreciation has been deducted from the original cost of a depreciable asset, also known as Salvage Value.

Return on Assets (ROA) — Shows the after tax earnings of assets. Return on assets is an indicator of how profitable a company is.

Retained Earnings — Retained earnings accumulate as the company earns profits and reinvests, or retains, the profits in the company rather than paying out the profits to the shareholders in the form of dividends.

Return on Equity — Net income divided by average shareholders' equity. This is an indicator of how well the company is making use of its equity to bring a return to its investors.

Return on Investment — Annual revenue less annual costs, both associated with a specific project, divided by the total investment required for that project.

Revenue — Income received by a business, usually for product or services provided by the business (also referred to as sales).

Revenue Recognition — The principle stating that revenue is earned (recognized) when services have been provided.

Residual Value — The amount remaining after all depreciation has been deducted from the original cost of a depreciable asset, also known as Salvage Value

S

Sales Discount — A term used by a seller to describe a cash discount granted to the purchaser for paying within the discount period.

Sales Journal — A journal used to record sales of merchandise on credit.

Sales Returns — A business may have to deal with numerous returns from customers, and these returns must be tracked over a period of time. High return levels may indicate serious problems. Therefore, instead of reversing the revenue account with a debit when recording returns, a contra-revenue account called sales returns and allowances is used to track the amount of returns.

Sales Tax — A tax that is applied by the government to goods or services that are sold. Sales taxes can be applied by both the federal and provincial government.

Salvage Value — The amount remaining after all depreciation has been deducted from the original cost of a depreciable asset, also known as a residual value.

Share Dividend — Companies can choose to give a dividend payment in the form of additional shares rather than cash.

Shareholders' Equity — In a corporation, if all assets were sold and all liabilities paid, the remaining cash would belong to the shareholders in proportion to the shares they own.

Share Split — A 2 for 1 stock split means companies decide to give each shareholder an additional share for each share held; however, the value of each share is reduced by half.

Short-Term Investments — Instead of investing surplus cash in a bank account (with minimal returns), forward-looking business managers invest in short-term opportunities which mature within one year and provide a higher rate of return.

Shrinkage — The cost of goods "not sold", which is typically caused by theft, goods signed for and not received, spoilage, reject production, etc.

Single-Step Income Statement — An income statement format that includes cost of goods sold as an operating expense and shows only one subtotal for total expenses.

Special Journal — A journal that is used for recording and posting transactions of a similar type.

Specific Identification — A method of valuing inventory when a business wants to value specific items individually. High value or unique items such as cars and diamonds are often valued this way.

Sole Proprietorship — A business owned by one person also known as a proprietorship. The financial affairs of the business must be separate from the owner. However, from a legal perspective, a sole proprietor is personally liable for the business.

Source Documents — Source of information recorded with accounting entries; can be in either paper or electronic form.

Statement of Cash Flow — A financial report that shows the inflows and outflows of actual cash during a specific period of time; where the company's cash came from and where it was spent.

Straight-line Depreciation Method — Allocates equal amounts of an asset's cost to depreciation expenses during its useful life.

Subsidiary Ledger — is a group of subsidiary accounts where the sum of the balances is equal to the balance of the related control account in the general ledger.

Sundry Assets — See miscellaneous assets definition.

T

T-Account — A simple characterization of an account form used as a helpful tool in showing the effects of transactions and events on specific accounts.

Temporary Accounts — The type of accounts that are used to describe revenues, expenses, and owner's withdrawals for one accounting period; they are closed at the end of the reporting period; also called nominal accounts.

Trademark — A formally registered symbol identifying the manufacturer or distributor of a product.

Trial Balance — A list of accounts and their balances at a point in time; the total debit balances should equal the total credit balances.

U

Unearned Revenue — Liabilities created when customers pay in advance for products or services; created when cash is received before revenues are earned; satisfied by delivering the products or services in the future.

Units of Production (Method) — Amortization Method of amortizing an asset based on its usage.

V

Voluntary Deductions — The type of deductions agreed upon between employer and employee.

W

Weighted Average Cost (Method) — A method of valuing inventory where a business applies an average cost to its entire inventory.

Wholesaler — A middleman that buys products from manufacturers or other wholesalers and sells them to retailers or other wholesalers.

Workers' Compensation — An insurance program paid for by the employer that represents a statutory deduction to be tracked by accountants and/or the payroll department.

Working Capital — Current assets less current liabilities; called "working capital" or "operating capital" because it is capital that has been put to work in the business and has taken the form of inventory, accounts receivable, cash etc.

Notes

INDEX

A

B

F

G

total dividends paid, 362
Total Quality Management (TQM), 145
trade discounts, 114
trade investments, 65
trade names, 218
trademarks, 218
traditional loans, 63

U

unearned revenue, 243–245
units-of-production depreciation method, 201–202
unlimited liability, 288
unrealized gain or loss, 75
unrecorded charges from bank statement, 42–44
unrecorded deposits from bank statement, 40–42
unsecured bonds, 262

V

valuation methods for inventory, 124–129
variations in presentation of earnings per share ratio, 345–346
vertical analysis, 402–406

W

Waksel, Samuel, 321
warranties, product, 250–253
watchdogs, 182
weighted average cost inventory valuation method, 124, 128, 169
withdrawal of partners, 294–295
WorldCom fraud scandal, 223
Wright, Wilbur and Orville (partnership), 299

X

XBRL (Extensible Business Reporting Language), 30

Notes